# THE BIBLE AND HEALING

## A Medical and Theological Commentary

## JOHN WILKINSON

B.D., M.D., F.R.C.P.

THE HANDSEL PRESS LTD
*Edinburgh*

WM. B. EERDMANS
PUBLISHING CO.
*Grand Rapids, Michigan*

British Library Cataloguing in Publication Data:
A catalogue record for this publication
is available from the British Library
ISBN 1 871828 80 5


Library of Congress Cataloging-in-Publication Data
Wilkinson, John
[The Bible and Healing: a Medical and Theological Commentary]

ISBN 0 8028 4876 1
1. Healing   2. Theology - Healing   3. Bible


Typeset in 10.5 pt. Garamond
at the Stables, Carberry

Printed by the British Printing Company
at Exeter


Thanks are expressed to the Drummond Trust of 3 Pitt Terrace, Stirling,
and to others who supported the publication of this book

# CONTENTS

# PREFACE

Health and Healing have been topics of personal and abiding interest to everyone over the years, and they have inspired the writing of many books and articles which still show no sign of decreasing in number. There are few books, however, which have considered these subjects systematically in a Biblical context and in a comprehensive way which includes both their medical and theological aspects. This was the purpose of the first edition of the present volume and we are grateful for the appreciative reception which that edition enjoyed.

Now that the original edition is out of print, we have been encouraged to revise it and to include additional material in the revision. This has been done. Additional material, both medical and Biblical, and both theological and historical, has been included to make the book virtually a medical commentary on the Bible. This is particularly true of the Old Testament whose concept and description of health, disease and healing are now dealt with in four chapters instead of the original single chapter. This increased coverage is also true of the New Testament whose understanding and presentation of the subjects of health, disease and healing are now covered in eighteen chapters as compared with the original twelve.

The title which was given to the first edition of the book was *Health and Healing: Studies in New Testament Principles and Practice*. However, this title is obviously no longer appropriate and so in order to indicate the increased scope of the book, the title has now been changed to that of *The Bible and Healing: A Medical and Theological Commentary*.

The original edition has been thoroughly revised and in part completely rewritten. Major changes and additions have been made to the book. A new Part Two on disease and healing in the Old Testament has been added with a detailed discussion of the possible identity of the various diseases described there. In Part Three, a new Chapter Seven deals in more detail than before with the vocabulary of healing in the gospels, and a new case study on the healing of the man born blind has been included as Chapter Twelve. This latter addition has allowed a discussion of healing in the gospel of John. The preceding two case histories came from the other strands of the gospel tradition. The case of the epileptic boy came from the triple synoptic tradition based on Mark and the case of the bent woman from the special Lukan source.

There are also several major changes and additions to Part Four of the book which deals with healing in the apostolic Church. The examination of the record and practice of healing in the Acts of the Apostles now extends to two chapters instead of the previous single chapter. A more adequate discussion is provided of the nature of the *charismata* which are mentioned in the New Testament epistles. These *charismata* are the gifts given by the Holy Spirit to individuals in the Church, included amongst which is the gift of healing. There is also a more detailed examination of the teaching of the passage about healing in James 5.13-18, which now takes up two chapters and is one of the more comprehensive discussions of the subject now available. However, the greatest change in this Part is in the expanded discussion of Paul's thorn in the flesh, which now occupies a total of four chapters instead of the single chapter of the original edition. This makes it the most detailed discussion of the nature of this incident in Paul's life which is at present available.

The final section of the book is Part Five where the principles and practice of health and healing as described in the Bible, are briefly traced in their historical development through the Christian centuries, and then related to the healing ministry of the Church today. More historical detail has been included in the revision of this Part of the book than was provided in the original edition, in order to produce a better understanding of the progress of the ministry of healing of the Church in recent times.

The number of notes and references provided for each chapter has been increased in order to make the book more useful as a source book. The bibliography has also been expanded and up-dated.

JOHN WILKINSON
Edinburgh, January 1998

# LIST OF BIBLE VERSIONS

The version of the Bible which was used as the main basis of the studies which form the contents of the present volume was the Revised Standard Version (RSV). On some occasions throughout the book, other versions are used and these may be identified from the following list of abbreviations.

| | |
|---|---|
| AV | Authorised Version (King James' Version). |
| Barclay | William Barclay, The New Testament: A New Translation (London: Collins, 1968-1969). |
| GNB | Good News Bible (New York: American Bible Society, 1976). British edition published in 1979 in London by British & Foreign Bible Society. |
| LXX | The Septuagint or the Old Testament in Greek (third century BC). |
| Moffatt | James Moffatt, A New Translation of the Bible (London: Hodder & Stoughton, 1935). |
| NEB | The New English Bible (Oxford: Oxford Uni. Press, 1976). |
| NIV | The New International Version (New York: New York International Bible Society, 1978). British edition published in 1979 in London by Hodder & Stoughton. |
| NRSV | The New Revised Standard Version (Oxford: Oxford University Press, 1989). |
| Phillips | J.B. Phillips, The New Testament in Modern English (London: Collins, 1972). |
| REB | The Revised English Bible (Oxford & Cambridge University Presses, 1989). |
| RV | The Revised Version (Oxford & New York: Oxford University Press, 1881-1884). |
| TCNT | The Twentieth Century New Testament (London: Sunday School Union/New York: Fleming H. Revell, 1904). |
| TNT | The Translator's New Testament (London: The British & Foreign Bible Society, 1973). |
| Vulgate | The Latin Version of the Bible (*Editio Vulgata*) by Jerome (completed AD 404). |

*TO JEAN*

# Introduction
# HEALING IN MEDICINE AND THEOLOGY

There was a time when the three words which taken together describe the subject of this book, namely the Bible, medicine and healing, were more closely related than they are today. The Bible is not the first book that people currently consult when they are concerned about health, unless it be spiritual health. Medicine has become a body of scientific knowledge combined with an accumulation of skills in the diagnosis and treatment of disease which exists as an independent discipline not necessarily related to any other. While 'healing' has become a weasel word, often emptied of specific meaning and used in various contexts, some of which are less honourable than others.

The usage of the word **healing** is often like that described in the scornful reply of Humpty Dumpty to Alice: 'When I use a word, it means just what I choose it to mean - neither more nor less'.[1]

This may be illustrated by the following quotations, selected almost at random:

Healing is 'a synonym for quackery'.[2]

Healing is 'the use of a human being to alleviate and cure disease'.[3]

Healing is 'to restore to health by non-physical means, often involving "the laying on of hands"'.[4]

The fact is that 'healing' is a word which is virtually disowned by both medicine and theology. Its use in medical textbooks is confined to the description of the repair of ulcers of the skin or of the digestive tract, or of the reunion of the broken surfaces of bones when they have been fractured.

Apart from these two specifically technical applications of the term healing, doctors prefer to speak of their work as curing or treating, rather than as healing. They commonly use this latter word to describe non-medical methods of treatment. Other descriptions which they use are 'alternative medicine', 'complementary medicine', 'fringe medicine' or 'non-conventional therapy'. It is important to notice that in each case, these methods are distinguished from orthodox or official medical methods of diagnosis and treatment. There is also a distinction between them. 'Alternative medicine' describes those methods which replace those of current orthodox medicine, while 'complementary medicine' consists of those methods which are applied alongside, and in conjunction with, orthodox medical treatment.

Thus the term 'healing' is used to describe therapies which may either replace or supplement orthodox methods.

However, the word 'healing' has still some way to go to achieve medical acceptability. Lavoisier in the eighteenth century said that when medicine came into the world it was one of twins, the other being charlatanism. This attitude still persists and all that is not accepted as orthodox medicine is often dismissed as charlatanism. As the American public health physician, Eric J. Cassels, has said: 'Today in our society the word "healing" has become identified with charlatanism and quackery, and doctors no longer think of themselves as healers'.[5] However, there are signs that the situation is changing.

So far as theology is concerned, the word **healing** did not occur in the text or index of any standard theological textbook until recent times. Karl Barth was the first modern theologian to discuss health and healing in his *Church Dogmatics*.[6] In this he has been followed by Paul Tillich[7] and Jürgen Moltmann.[8] However, non-medical healing has still to achieve theological respectability. Barth has a long discussion on this type of healing and mentions in particular the work of the German Lutheran pastor J. C. Blumhardt in the nineteenth century, saying that we have much to learn from him.[9] By contrast, Bultmann dismisses his work with the comment that 'the stories of Blumhardt are an abomination'.[10] Earlier theological authors assumed that by 'healing' was meant physical healing and specifically excluded healing of this type from theological consideration by such comments as the following:

> As to the body of man, theology is not concerned with it, except to note how truly, both in material and structure, it is part of the physical universe.[11]

If we are to understand the relation of the concept of healing to both medicine and theology, it is obvious that we must try to define more exactly what we mean by healing.

In this book we shall use the word healing in accordance with the observation that 'as ordinarily used this word means the restoration to normality of deranged physical functions but in the wider meaning which a Christian view of man requires, healing is the enabling of a man to function as a whole in accordance with God's will for him'.[12] This means that healing is neither medical charlatanism nor theological limboism, but includes both the practice of orthodox medicine and the making of people whole in a theological sense.

Healing extends to all areas of human life and being. It cannot be confined to the body and the purely physical phenomena of the repair of wounds and the union of fractures. If human beings are indivisible entities, as we believe them to be, any disturbance of their health affects them as a whole and if it is to be effective, healing must also extend to the whole of their life and being.

Healing embraces all effective methods of treatment. As we shall discover as we proceed with our study of healing, in the Bible these methods are divided into two main groups. There is **natural healing** or healing on the basis of creation. This occurs as the result of the healing processes of repair of the body and mind which God included in his creation of human beings, and the discovery and use of healing agents which he placed in nature. This is the basis of what we commonly describe as 'folk-medicine', but it is also the basis of professional medical healing. All health care professionals are trained in the principles of natural healing. The function of these professionals is to encourage the natural healing processes of the body through the application of methods based on their knowledge and experience of these processes, and of external healing agents derived from the natural creation which assist these processes.

The methods of natural healing are those which are based on the self-healing properties of the human body and mind. In theological terms, as we have already indicated, they are based on the Biblical doctrine of creation for they arise out of the way that God created the body and the mind. When God created human beings he included in their being and structure a number of self-healing processes and properties. He gave them a defence system against infection and a repair system to come into operation when tissues were damaged or broken down. He even provided extra tissue in some organs such as the liver and the kidney to act as a reserve when other similar functioning cells in these organs died.

As we have mentioned, these natural methods are expressed in two types of healing practice. There is first of all what we have called 'folk-medicine', a term which describes the methods of healing used in personal, domestic or social situations by people who have no scientific training but have some knowledge and experience of how the natural processes of healing work. A Biblical example of this would be the application of a fig poultice to King Hezekiah's boil by Isaiah in 2 Kings 20.7.

The second type of natural healing is that which is practised by doctors and other professionally-trained health care people. The older physicians used to speak of the *vis medicatrix naturae* (the healing power of nature) and to see their function as using and assisting this power in their methods of treatment of sick people. This is reflected in the remark of Ambrose Paré (1510-1590), the French Huguenot military surgeon and the father of modern traumatic surgery, 'I dressed the wound, but God healed it'; a remark which occurs many times in Paré's writings.[13]

There is no clear description of the practice of professional natural healing in the Bible. As we shall see, physicians are mentioned only rarely in the Old Testament and we have no details of their training and status. The existence and practice of physicians is recognised by Jesus in the New Testament (Mark 2.17) but we know little about them. Paul calls Luke a physician in Colossians 4.14 but we do not know whether he practised professionally, although Harnack has suggested that he acted as Paul's personal physician.[14]

The other main group of healing methods we find in the Bible is that of **supernatural healing**, of which there are many examples in the gospels. In this kind of healing, recovery is not due to the innate healing properties of the body or mind, or to the use of any healing agent derived from the natural environment. It is due to the intervention of a supernatural power which reverses the disease process and restores health. As we shall see as our study proceeds, supernatural healing is normally the response of God to prayer and has been called 'the prayer-cure'. This name appears in a popular theological lecture given by the Princeton theologian A. A. Hodge in 1887. This lecture appears to be the earliest published academic theological recognition of the existence of the Christian non-medical healing movement which has arisen in the United States in modern times.[15]

There are two extreme attitudes to these methods of healing. The first is the rejection of natural healing on theological grounds. To do this is to deny the obvious effectiveness of healing methods based on the principles and agents found in nature and to reject the relevance of the Christian doctrine of creation. The second is the rejection of supernatural healing on scientific or medical grounds. To do this is to be guilty of a presumption which is not justified in the present state of our knowledge and experience. We need to take a balanced view of the situation and recognise the relevance and validity of both methods in their appropriate spheres. There can be no conflict between them for both forms of healing have their source in God.

Healing in the sense of the restoration of health which has been lost or disturbed is only part of the approach to the problem of health and its maintenance. The ideal situation is one in which healing is not required because health has not broken down and disease has not occurred. We must therefore be concerned with measures which promote the health of body, mind and spirit, and the healthfulness of the environment, and which prevent the development and prevalence of disease. In this way, people will be enabled to function as a whole in accordance with God's will for them. The Bible does not neglect measures such as these and many of them are included in the Mosaic law of the Old Testament which the people of Israel were commanded to obey. As Guthrie has pointed out, 'the Bible is a mine of information on personal and social hygiene, and might even be regarded as the first textbook of public health'.[16]

Healing, then, concerns the whole of the human being and not just one aspect of it whether this be the body, the mind or the spirit. This means that it is not satisfactory to attempt to make the meaning of healing more precise by adding adjectives to it and speak of 'faith healing', 'spiritual healing', 'divine healing', 'miraculous healing' or 'charismatic healing'. Each one of these terms begs its own questions and does not really help us to understand the nature of healing which the terms describe, but only indicates its possible source.[17]

It is sometimes objected that to extend the use of the term healing beyond the sphere of the body is to use it metaphorically and not literally. It is difficult to see the force of this, especially when medicine makes so little use of the term in relation to its care of the body. Healing has no specific application in etymology or semantics which would restrict it to the body and deny its application to the mind or the spirit. Certainly the term may be used metaphorically as its use in 2 Kings 2.21 for the healing of water illustrates, but this is one of the rare metaphorical uses of the word in the Old Testament.

The need to use the word in a more comprehensive sense than is usual in popular speech arises from the fact that we have no single word in English which describes the restoration to normality, well-being or wholeness in every sphere of the life of human beings whether it be body, mind, spirit or community.

If we are accused of extending the meaning of the terms health and healing beyond what is permissible, we may adduce the following facts in our defence. First, that in the New Testament the verb *sozo*, 'to save', is used for the healing of a person's whole being, body. soul and spirit and we need a translation equivalent for it when it is used in this comprehensive way. In spite of its usage in the New Testament for the salvation of the whole human being, this verb has become restricted to the soul in popular and even in theological usage. Second, the modern semantic tendency is to extend the meaning of health and healing in this way, as we can see from the World Health Organisation's definition of health which we shall mention in Chapter One. Finally, there is the plain fact that the Biblical concept of health and healing is much more than the modern concept which tends to confine it to the physical, and we do not have an English term which embraces this wider concept. The alternative to using these terms in this more comprehensive way is to allow them to be emptied of their meaning until they become synonymous with quackery and charlatanism. However they are words of noble ancestry in our linguistic heritage and should not be allowed to be diluted and even deprived of their real meaning in this way.

Another aspect of our use of the word healing in this book is that we include three categories of the restoration to normality within its scope. These are healing of the body, the casting out of demons and the raising of the dead. It is more convenient to have one term to cover all these three categories than to have frequently to distinguish between them each time we refer to them individually. Although they are separate categories, they are all examples of that restoration of human beings to that wholeness of being which we call health.

In this Introduction we have been concerned with the meaning of the term 'healing' which underlies the medical and theological studies in health and healing in the Bible which form the main content of this volume. It is to these studies that we now turn.

# PART ONE

# THE BIBLICAL UNDERSTANDING OF HEALTH

*HEALTH is such a perennial source of interest and concern to people in the modern world that it comes as a great surprise to find that the Bible appears to say little about it. This lack of interest, however, is more apparent than real for in the widest sense of the phrase, 'human wholeness' or health is the main topic of the Bible. What is confined to the body in ordinary thought and conversation, the Bible extends to the whole of the human being and its relationships. It is only when human beings are whole and their relationships right, that they can be described as truly healthy. For the Bible, the basic relationship of all is the relationship to God and when this is disturbed all other human relationships are disturbed too, whether they be of human beings to themselves, their fellows, or to their environment.*

*Part One of this book is concerned with the Biblical concept of health, while subsequent parts will be concerned with disease and sickness and their healing and cure.*

*We begin with the concept of health in the Old Testament. In any study of the teaching of the Bible it is important to begin with the Old Testament for we cannot understand the New Testament unless we read it in the light of the Old. As the German theologian Albrecht Ritschl once put it, 'The Old Testament is the lexicon of the New'.[1] If the Old Testament is the lexicon of the New, then the New is the encyclopaedia of the Old, in which the words of the latter are given fuller significance in concepts which, though already present in the Old, are nevertheless only fully expressed and illustrated in the New, and supremely in the person, teaching and work of Jesus Christ. In the words of Augustine: 'The New Testament is latent in the Old, and the Old Testament is patent in the New'.[2]*

*The Old Testament sets out that perfect pattern and high quality of life which is health, and which was God's intention that human beings should enjoy. They were created in the image of God and, therefore, were healthy as he was healthy. They were intended to continue to live in health, which would be maintained by their constant enjoyment of his presence and their obedience of his will as revealed in his laws and commandments. This is why we are constantly reminded in the Old Testament of God's presence with, and concern for, his people.*

*This means that in general the Old Testament has more to say about health than about healing. However, the people of Israel found that their relationship to*

God was a demanding one if they were to continue enjoy good health. Such a relationship demanded their obedience and this was not always forthcoming. Disobedience produced disease and disturbed their relationship with God and with one another. Means for the healing or restoration of these relationships were provided by institution of sacrifices and the occasional direct healing of disease, but something more generally effective and more permanent was required.

This is why the New Testament was needed and why the New Testament says more about healing than about health. Health had already been described in the Old Testament and was now embodied in the person of Jesus Christ for all to see. He set the standard of health that all should seek to attain and by his gift of the Holy Spirit made such attainment possible. An attainment which would reach its fullness in the resurrection. Any study of the Christian understanding of health must therefore include the teaching of both the Old and the New Testaments.

9

# Chapter 1
# THE CONCEPT OF HEALTH IN THE OLD TESTAMENT

The fact that the word **health** occurs only infrequently in the English versions of the Old Testament may suggest that it has little to say on the subject, and can safely be ignored in any serious study of it.[1]

This conclusion would, however, only be valid if we were to insist on the Old Testament speaking our modern language, using our modern concepts and presenting its teaching in a modern systematic way. It is obviously unreasonable to expect it to do any of these things. It is an ancient book which must be interpreted on its own terms and not ignored because its relevance is not immediately appreciated by the modern mind. In fact, as we begin to study the Old Testament concept of health, we shall soon find that it has a great deal to say on this subject.

## WHOSE HEALTH?

As we begin our study, the first question to arise is, **Whose health?** To answer simply that it is the health of human beings without further analysis is inadequate. This is because when we speak of health and healing in popular speech, the predominant interest is in physical health, the health of the body. We begin then by looking at what the Old Testament has to say about the body as part of the human being which is the subject of health.

### The body in the Old Testament

The modern reader of the Old Testament who is interested in the subject of health will be surprised at the virtual absence of the word **body** from its pages. It is rare enough in the English versions where it is used only thirty-seven times in the AV to translate no fewer than fourteen different Hebrew words. In the original Hebrew text there are names for about eighty different parts of the body, but no word for the body as a whole as we think of it today in western society. The word which comes nearest to meaning the physical body in Hebrew is the word *gevviyah* which occurs thirteen times in the Hebrew Bible. On eight occasions it refers to a dead body, on three to a body seen in a vision or dream, and on only two occasions to living bodies as the potential subjects of starvation (Genesis 47.18) or of slavery (Nehemiah 9.37). It is the only Hebrew anthropological term which does not have a psychical meaning, but only a purely physical one.[2]

However, the Old Testament does have a word for the material of which the body is made. This is the word *basar* which is used to denote the visible part of the physical substance which makes up the body, i.e. 'the flesh'. It is this word which English versions sometimes translate as 'body', but as Wolff points out, it means not so much the body, as human beings in their bodily aspect.[3] It is not used for the body as a separate physical entity although, since there is no word for this, the word *basar* is used in this sense on the rare occasions when such a word is required as, for example, in Leviticus 13 *passim*, Numbers 8.7; 1 Kings 21.27; Job 4.15 and Proverbs 4.22.

The significance of the virtual absence of the word body from the pages of the Old Testament is that health is not presented there primarily in physical terms. This is in contrast to the modern popular concept of health which, as we have already mentioned, is mainly physical in character. In view of this, we need to speak not simply of the health of the body, but of the health of the human being in all its aspects if we are to be true to the insight of the Old Testament.

## The human being in the Old Testament

Old Testament thought is predominantly synthetic in nature and concerned with different aspects of the whole rather than dividing it up into distinct parts.[4] It therefore thinks of the human being as a whole and recognises no divisions or parts within it, only different aspects of such a being, regarded as a whole.

The two main aspects of the human being which are recognised in the Old Testament are illustrated for us by the Psalmist in Psalm 63.1 as he cries out in his weariness from the Wilderness of Judaea:

O God, you are my God, earnestly I seek you;
my soul (*nephesh*) thirsts for you,
my body (*basar*) longs for you,
in a dry and thirsty land where there is no water (NIV).

Eichrodt notes these two aspects when he speaks of the distinction between an inner spiritual aspect and an outer physical aspect of human nature as the constituent elements of the whole Old Testament view of human beings.[5]

Murray describes this distinction in more detail when he writes as follows:

The biblical doctrine is then to the effect that there are two aspects to man. Using the word 'entity' to denote that which has distinctness of being, we can say that there are two entities in man's constitution, diverse in nature and origin, the one derived from the earth, material, corporeal, phenomenal, divisible, the other derived from a distinct action of God, immaterial and ordinarily not phenomenal, indivisible and indestructible. These two entities form one organic unit without disharmony or conflict. In the integral person they are interdependent. They coact and interact. The modes of coaction and interaction are largely hid from us. The union is intimate and intricate and we are not able to define its mode, nor can we discover the relations which they sustain to each other.[6]

We began this section with the question about whose health was the concern of the Old Testament. We have seen now that it is not concerned simply with the health of the body but with the whole human being of which the body is but the physical aspect.

Having decided who is the subject of health, namely, the human being in both the aspects which Murray has described, we turn to the next question which is, What are we to understand by **health**? We begin by looking at the essential characteristics of health as they are presented in the Old Testament.

## THE CHARACTERISTICS OF HEALTH

One of the most striking features of the Old Testament is that it presents its teaching not by definition and argument, but by illustration and example. It lays before its readers not a definition of health systematically expounded, but a picture of the characteristics of healthy people as seen in their life, their character and their actions. One obvious example would be the accounts of the patriarchs in the book of Genesis, but there are many others.

The consequence is that while we cannot find a concise systematic definition of health in the pages of the Old Testament, we can find portrayed there the characteristics of health by which we can recognise healthy people. These characteristics may be listed as follows:

1. Well-being          3. Obedience          5. Fertility

2. Righteousness       4. Strength           6. Longevity

From a consideration of these six characteristics we shall be able to arrive at an understanding of what the Old Testament means by health.

### 1. Well-being

For the writers of the Old Testament the basic characteristic of human beings is life. At its lowest level this is physical and biological existence, and the Old Testament opens with an account of how this began. However, the Old Testament writers are not very interested in the purely biological level of life. They take it for granted rather than describe or investigate it. They refer to different physical organs of the body, but are not interested in their anatomical structure or physiological function, so much as in the moral and spiritual significance which has been given to them.[7] For them life consists not of physical anatomy or physiological function, but of moral activity and spiritual achievement. Its important dimension is its quality rather than its quantity, although it is accepted that its quantity may reflect its quality.

The Hebrew word which expresses the quality of the fullness and well-being of life, and which therefore comes nearest to expressing the Old Testament concept of health is the word *shalom*. This word occurs about two hundred and fifty times in the Hebrew Bible.[8] It is most frequent in the prophetical books of Jeremiah (thirty-one times) and Isaiah (twenty-seven times), and in the Psalms (twenty-seven times).

The meaning of the common Semitic root of the verb *shalem* from which the word *shalom* and all its related words come is that of totality and completeness.[9] The usage of the word in the Old Testament is to denote the presence of wholeness, completeness and well-being in all spheres of life whether physical, mental and spiritual, or individual, social and national. According to Pedersen '*shalom* designates at the same time the entirety, the fact of being whole, and he who is whole (e.g. 2 Samuel 17.3; Micah 5.4 and Job 5.24)'.[10] As von Rad says, this word 'is a general expression of a very comprehensive nature'.[11] It may therefore be understood in an all-inclusive way as comprising 'all that the Israelite understands by "good"'[12] or 'the sum total of all God's good gifts to his people'.[13]

One of the covenant names of God which Gideon used when he built his altar to the Lord at Ophrah was *Yahweh-shalom*, the Lord is *shalom* (Judges 6.24). He it is who offers his people a covenant of *shalom*, that is, a covenant which will secure *shalom* for them (Numbers 25.12; Isaiah 54.10; Jeremiah 32.40; Ezekiel 34.25; 37.2 and Malachi 2.5).

*Shalom* may also be applied to specific situations. This explains why it is commonly translated 'peace' in the English versions, meaning harmony between individuals (Genesis 26.31) or between nations (Judges 4.17 and 1 Samuel 7.14). It may also be translated as 'prosperity' and it is in this sense that the Old Testament can speak of the *shalom* of the wicked, meaning their material prosperity in such verses as Job 15.21; 21.9 and Psalm 73.3. But in its more comprehensive sense there is no *shalom* for the wicked for they do not know God, who is the source of true *shalom* (Isaiah 48.22; 57.21 and 59.8).

The application of the word which is most relevant to our present concern is to the well-being and health of human beings. We find this illustrated in personal greetings and enquiries after the health and welfare of individuals in such verses as Genesis 29.6; 43.27; 2 Samuel 18.29; 20.9 and 2 Kings 4.26. In relation to physical health it is used in Isaiah 1.6 and 38.16; and in Psalm 38.3 the Psalmist complains that he has no *shalom* in his bones.[14] *Shalom* is the result of healing that only God can provide (Isaiah 57.19; Jeremiah 6.14; 8.11, 15 and 14.19).

True *shalom* or well-being comes from God for only in God do we find our true wholeness and complete fulfilment. In God alone can we know the wholeness of our being and the rightness of our relationships which make up what the Old Testament means by health. It formed the climax of the blessing that Aaron and his sons were to use when they blessed the people of Israel, 'The Lord turn his face towards you and give you *shalom*' (Numbers 6.26).

This word *shalom* is not peculiar to Hebrew, for its root is common to all the Semitic languages and was in use long before Israel entered Canaan. However, it was left to Israel to fill it with a new and richer content derived from their experience of God and his provision for them in their individual, domestic, social and national life.

If this presentation of the Old Testament concept of *shalom* is correct, then it explains why it is so difficult to translate this word into the terms which we use to describe our modern ideas of health. This concept is so much more comprehensive than our modern idea of health and is not related primarily to the body but to our whole being. It also explains why *shalom* and its related words 'are among the most important theological words in the Old Testament'.[15] They describe God's gracious gift to his people and the result of that gift in their health and well-being.

The first characteristic of health then is complete well-being, a term which in English means by derivation 'being what you will to be' for the words 'well' and 'will' both come from the same Germanic root. It is significant that this term was the one used for the basic characteristic of health by the founders of the World Health Organisation when in 1948 they adopted their now well-known definition:

Health is a state of complete physical, mental and social well-being and not merely the absence of disease or infirmity.[16]

Reduced to its simplest terms, this definition means that health is well-being.

## 2. Righteousness

The word 'righteousness' is the regular translation-equivalent of the Hebrew word *sedeq* and its feminine form *sedaqah* in the Old Testament. These words are apparently identical in meaning although the feminine form occurs more frequently. Both words come from the root *sadeq* whose original meaning has been lost, but whose usage suggests that it expressed the idea of straightness or conformity to a norm or standard most clearly seen in such verses as Leviticus 19.36; Deuteronomy 25.15; Job 31.6; Psalm 23.3 and Ezekiel 45.10.[17] It describes a relationship which is a right relationship. However, as Davidson pointed out, this idea is incomplete as a description of righteousness in the Old Testament for righteousness there means a right relationship to a norm or standard which is itself right. Davidson's comment was, 'It was not conformity to a standard that made things right, but conformity to a right standard'.[18]

In the case of God's righteousness, the norm or standard is his own nature and character which is expressed in his faithful fulfilment of the terms of the covenant he had made with his people. The effect of the righteousness of God is to produce righteousness in his people by example and command. For them the norm is his holiness and the standard is his will. Their righteousness is part of their grateful response to being in a right relationship to God and God being in a right relationship to them through his grace and covenanted faithfulness. Those people are righteous who fulfil all the demands laid on them by this relationship to God. These demands affect every aspect of their lives, their personal character and responsibility, their ethical behaviour and practice, their social concern and conduct, and their religious commitment and worship.[19]

Von Rad begins the discussion of the subject of righteousness in his book on Old Testament theology by saying,

> There is absolutely no concept in the Old Testament with so central a significance for all the relationships of human life as that of *sedaqah*. It is the standard not only for man's relationship to God, but also for his relationships of his fellows, reaching right down to the most petty wranglings - indeed, it is even the standard for man's relationship to the animals and to his natural environment. *Sedaqah* can be described without more ado as the highest value in life, that upon which all life rests when it is properly ordered.[20]

Expressed in these terms, righteousness is but another word for that human well-being which is *shalom* and health. Indeed, health is defined in similar terms when we speak of it as consisting of a right relationship of a person to God, to themselves, to their fellows and to their environment. In the Old Testament, righteousness involves the recognition and fulfilment of the demands of all these relationships, which is at once the meaning and expression of health.

So righteousness, in the sense of a right relationship to a right standard is basic to the Old Testament concept of health. A right relationship to God produces *shalom* (Isaiah 26.1-3; 32.17; 57.2). Righteousness and *shalom* flourish together (Psalm 35.27-28; 72.7; 85.10; Isaiah 26.2-3; 48.18; 58.8; Malachi 2.6). The pursuit of righteousness is the pursuit of life (Proverbs 11.4, 19, 28, 30). Righteousness is illustrated in the life of Enoch (Genesis 5.22), Noah (Genesis 6.9), and Joseph (Genesis 39.2, 21-23), and supremely in the life of Abraham. In Abraham are linked together faith, obedience and righteousness (Genesis 15.6, 15; 17.23; 18.19; 22.16-18). He was the supreme example of health in the Old Testament understanding of that word. At the end of a long life he was to go to his fathers in *shalom* (Genesis 15.15).

## 3. Obedience

The Old Testament relates health to obedience to God's word and law. Obedience to God's law means freedom from disease, whilst disobedience means liability to disease. This is set out explicitly in such passages as Exodus 15.26; 23.20-26; Leviticus 26.14-16, 23-26; Deuteronomy 5.32; 7.12-15; 28.27-29, 58-62; Psalm 38.3-8; Proverbs 3.7-8. In these passages God tells his people Israel that if they will listen to his voice, do what is right in his eyes and obey his law then he will not bring disease of any kind upon them and will take away sickness from their midst. Conversely, if they disobey his law he will bring upon them and on their descendants 'incurable diseases and horrible epidemics which can never be stopped' (Deuteronomy 28.59 GNB).

What is explicitly stated in these passages about the relationship of obedience and disease is also implied in many other situations described in the Old Testament. In the nature of the case, the commoner situation described is one in which disobedience produces disease. There are examples of this kind of situation in the experience of the Children of Israel during their desert wanderings as well as on later occasions in their history. We shall look at these examples later on, and so meantime we note that they teach us how disobedience results in disease, while health is the product of obedience. Obedience to God's law is the best form of preventive medicine. As Vaux puts it, 'Obedience is our answer to God about what makes for health and salvation'.[21]

Health is far more than the negative state of the absence of disease, and so obedience produces a positive state and condition of well-being, blessing and the consciousness of belonging to God. This is explicitly taught in such verses as Exodus 18.5; Deuteronomy 11.27; 1 Samuel 12.14; Psalm 85.8; 119.165; Isaiah 48.18; Jeremiah 7.23; 42.6; Zechariah 6.15. Obedience to God's law results in the blessing of God on human life which is the basis of that human well-being which constitutes health. 'The blessing is the power by which life is maintained and augmented. The result of the blessing is the condition defined by the word *shalom*.'[22]

In this section we have had in mind more particularly, obedience to God's moral law as this is the predominant emphasis in the Old Testament. However, obedience to God's law includes obedience to his laws of physical health too. To enjoy good health we need to obey the laws of personal and environmental hygiene to ensure the provision of good food, pure water, clean air, adequate exercise, good sanitation and sufficient shelter. If we disobey these laws governing the provision and control of health and hygiene, then ill-health will result. Examples of Old Testament laws covering these aspects are those dealing with unclean and potentially infected food, and meat from animals which have died from disease (Leviticus 11.1-47 and Deuteronomy 14.3-21); with contact with dead bodies (Numbers 19.11-13), and the safe and discreet disposal of human excreta (Deuteronomy 23.12-14).[23]

## 4. Strength

In Psalm 29.11 strength is equated with *shalom*, and in numerous places it is regarded as the gift of God (Exodus 15.2; 2 Samuel 22.33; Psalm 21.1; 28.7-9; 29.11; 46.2; 68.35; 84.5; 86.16; 92.10-14; 138.3; Isaiah 40.29-31; 41.10; 45.24; Daniel 10.10; Zechariah 10.6). It is clear, however, that when the Old Testament speaks of strength it does not mean simply physical strength, but the strength of a person throughout their whole being which of course includes the strength of their body.

Although strength is the gift of God, its maintenance is a human responsibility. We are to wait upon the Lord to renew our strength (Isaiah 40.31, cp. Psalm 105.4). However, there comes a time. as we shall see below, when strength can no longer be renewed and our span of life whether seventy or eighty years comes to an end (Psalm 90.10).

The opposite of strength is weakness and it is therefore not surprising to find that the word *choli*, which is the Hebrew word for weakness, is also used for sickness and disease of which weakness is the main presenting symptom, e.g. in Genesis 48.1; 1 Samuel 19.14 and 1 Kings 14.1.[24]

In recent theology, health has sometimes been defined as strength. Thus Karl Barth speaks of health as 'the strength to be as man',[25] and Jürgen Moltmann as 'the strength to be human'.[26] However, to define health in this way is to confuse health with its expression. We are strong because we are healthy, not healthy because we are strong. Our health is a characteristic and a reflection of our strength and not its essential nature. If we define health as strength then this implies that only strong people are healthy. If we then go on to say that we are only human because we are strong this suggests that only healthy people are fully human. So we cannot define health simply as strength, without considering the further implications of this definition. It may be 'a good pointer' as Atkinson says, but it is only a pointer and not a final definition.[27]

## 5. Fertility

Continued and even exceptional fertility was promised to those of the people of Israel who obeyed the law of the Lord their God (Exodus 13.26; Deuteronomy 7.12-14). There are numerous references in the patriarchal narratives of Genesis to the blessing of fertility which the Lord was to bestow on his people (See Genesis 1.28; 9.1; 12.2; 17.16; 22.17; 26.4; 28.3; 48.3; cp. Deuteronomy 1.10; 10.22; 26.5; 30.9).

In this connection, Brown points out that 'it is impossible to overestimate the importance of fertility in the biblical world'.[28] This finds a vivid illustration in the desperate and despairing cry of Rachel to Jacob, 'Give me children, or I'll die!' (Genesis 30.1). But this fertility was dependent on Israel's obedience, and later the prophet Isaiah was to lament that the descendants of Israel had not become like the numberless grains of the sand as God had previously promised, because of their disobedience (Isaiah 48.19).

## 6. Longevity

Another important characteristic of health from the physical aspect is length of life. Such length of life was promised to Abraham as part of *shalom* (Genesis 15.15) and in due course we are told that he 'died at a good old age, an old man, full of years' (Genesis 25.8). Jacob, Gideon and David also died 'at a good old age' (Genesis 35.29; Judges 8.32; 1 Chronicles 29.28 respectively). Long life is promised to all those who obey God's law (Exodus 20.12; Deuteronomy 5.16; 6.2; 30.20; 32.46-47; 1 Kings 3.14; Psalm 21.4; 34.12-14; 91.16; Proverbs 3.1-2; 9.10-11; 10.27; Isaiah 65.20).

## HEALTH AS WELL-BEING

As we have seen in our consideration of the characteristics of health, the basic definition of health in the Old Testament (and indeed in the human situation generally) is that 'Health is well-being'. This is the concept which underlies all the characteristics which we have just discussed. Our next task is, therefore, to explore the Old Testament concept of human well-being. This does not, of course, exist in a vacuum and so must begin by examining the assumptions which lie behind this concept.

## The context of well-being

The assumptions which form the context of this concept are many and wide-ranging and we can consider them only briefly here.

First, there are assumptions about God. He is the one and only true God. His existence is taken for granted and not argued about. His power is sufficient for him to carry out his will and engage in activities such as the creation and maintenance of the world and humankind. His moral character is that of holiness, righteousness and love, and he desires the well-being of all that he has created.

Second, there are assumptions about humankind. They were created by God in his own image with reason and freewill so that they can make choices about whom and what they are to obey in their lives and conduct. Thus they can choose to be healthy or not, and we learn from the Old Testament how often God's people have disobeyed him and chosen to be unhealthy physically, morally and spiritually.

Third and finally, there are assumptions about the relationship between God and humankind. God created them for fellowship with himself and is interested in all their doings. Humankind find their highest fulfilment and well-being in a close and continuing fellowship with God. They are the object of God's love to whom he has revealed himself and the subject of his redemption when they have rebelled against him.

## The nature of well-being

The nature of well-being is implied in the characteristics we have already discussed and derives its identity from the human constitution and the human relationship with God.

This well-being is holistic for it affects the whole of the human being. If the desire for well-being is confined to the body then the result is likely to be not health, but ill-health resulting from a 'healthism' in which the health of the body is regarded as a desirable end in itself. On the other hand if the desire is confined to the soul or spirit this too will lead to ill-health from neglect of the body. Thus the nature of well-being is that wholeness of being and uprightness of character which are related to what the Old Testament calls 'holiness'.

The etymological and semantic connection between the two words 'wholeness' and 'holiness' which exists in English and the Teutonic languages does not hold for the Hebrew language. Nevertheless there is a real connection in thought between the two concepts in the Old Testament. Health or well-being is the wholeness of human beings and their personality, and the holiness of their character and actions expressed in righteousness and obedience to God's law. Human wholeness derives from divine wholeness and reflects God's wholeness. The supreme call of the Old Testament is expressed in the demand by God of his people: 'Be holy because I the Lord your God, am holy' (Leviticus 11.44-45; 19.2 and 20.26). As Wenham has suggested, this sentence might be termed the motto of Leviticus.[29]

This demand by God of his people, set as it is in the midst of his commandments, has a twofold significance. On the one hand it is a reminder that all his commandments arise from his character as a God of holiness. On the other hand it defines the standard which he expected of his people and which they will only attain by obedience to his commands.

It is important to understand what the Old Testament means by holiness, for our modern usage of the word is not related to health or well-being as we usually understand it. The word tends to conjure up pictures of saints with haloes in the stained glass windows of churches and cathedrals. It is often associated with an unworldly piety and a world-denying asceticism, but this is not the Old Testament understanding of holiness.

Wholeness and holiness are terms of relationship and the relationship they express in this context is that of human beings to God. Both words imply a standard and that standard is the wholeness and perfection of the character of God. This same idea of relationship to a standard or norm also belongs to the other words which describe the different aspects of health such as obedience, righteousness, strength and length of life. As John Robinson points out, the question of the relation of the whole human being to God is the basic interest of the Old Testament.[30] The Hebrew mind was not interested in the body for its own sake or simply as part of the constitution of the human being. This means that it would find modern physiology and modern psychology equally irrelevant to its concept of health.

The important question so far as the historians, poets and prophets of the Old Testament were concerned was this relation of human beings to God. It was this question which determined their view of human health. For them health consisted in the wholeness of being and the holiness of character which found their origin in the human relationship to God and reached full flower as that relationship developed and deepened. This relationship and therefore the health which sprang from it, was not static but dynamic as human beings walked with God and reflected his nature in their being and expressed his character in their actions. It governed their personal behaviour in everyday life whether towards themselves, their family or their community and even determined what they could and could not eat at each meal (Leviticus 11.1-47). For the purposes of daily life, holiness was translated into terms of what was clean and what was unclean, physically, socially, morally and spiritually.[31]

However, the Bible is a realistic book. Although the ideal is a combination of wholeness of personal being and life with holiness of character and behaviour, it recognises that 'in this life, there can be holiness without wholeness, and "wholeness" in some aspects of life, without holiness. Both are important tasks in the journey of faith, but holiness takes priority in the biblical mind'.[32]

This recognition is even more marked in the New Testament where the end of the journey of faith is seen to be in the wholeness and holiness which Jesus Christ came to secure for his people.

## The source of well-being

The source of the well-being of humankind is the love and the will of God combined with their response to his love and their obedience to his will. They cannot become holy simply by their own unaided effort for as God reminds them on several occasions, 'I am the Lord who makes you holy' (Leviticus 20.8; 21.8, 15, 23 and 22.9, 16, 32). His people are to consecrate themselves and be holy, and they do this by their obedience to God's law, so allowing him to make them holy by his grace.

## The scope of well-being

Well-being includes in its scope the whole being of humankind and all their relationships. The World Health Organisation definition which we quoted above speaks of 'physical, mental and social well-being'. This definition is very much in line with the Old Testament concept of health, but it excludes two important aspects of human well-being, namely, the spiritual and the environmental. By the year 1984 WHO realised that it had omitted the spiritual aspect of well-being and at the World Health Assembly of that year agreed that members of the Organisation should be invited to include in their planning for the health of their people 'a spiritual dimension, defined in accordance with their social and cultural patterns'.[33]

The other aspect of well-being which needs to be included is the environmental. Physically, human beings were created from their environment. The Genesis account calls it 'the dust of the earth' (Genesis 2.7). The care and control of their environment was put into their hands by God when he made them his stewards with authority to rule in his name over his creation (Genesis 1.26-28). This is reflected in our modern world in the interest in ecology for it has been realised that the care of the environment plays an important part in human well-being.

## HEALTH AS RIGHT RELATIONSHIPS

As we have already suggested, the basic element in the concept of the health of human beings in the Old Testament and in the Bible as a whole is that of relationship. That is why the words which we used to describe the characteristics of health or well-being are all words of relationships. Righteousness and obedience describe our relationship to God. Righteousness also along with strength, fertility and longevity describes our relationship to other people. In the Old Testament, health is regarded as a matter of right relationships with that which is right, for which the keyword is righteousness. In other words, well-being consists of right relationships.[34]

First of all and most important of all, health consists in a right relationship to God expressed in our obedience to his will and our worship of his name. These result in holiness for righteousness is the content and expression of holiness which is spiritual wholeness.

Second, health is a right relationship to ourselves expressed as an unselfish humility and an acceptance of personal responsibility for the state of our body, mind and spirit. These result in the harmonious functioning of all parts of our being, and so physical and mental wholeness and happiness.

Third, health is a right relationship to our neighbours both domestic, social and national, which is expressed as love and service. These result in mutual fellowship and trust and a stable society.

Fourth and finally, health is a right relationship to our environment expressed as concern to preserve its well-being and steward its resources responsibly. This results in harmony between us and the rest of creation.

However, the Old Testament recognised that these original ideal relationships were broken by humankind's wilful disobedience and rebellion against God, and that many of his people no longer enjoyed the health and wholeness that was his will for them. This means that we must consider also the result of that disobedience in the experience and prevalence of disease amongst God's people, when they failed to display the characteristics of health which we have discussed in this chapter. This we shall do in subsequent chapters.

Nevertheless all is not lost, for the Old Testament historians, poets and prophets all look forward to a time when these relationships will be restored and all creation will enjoy the health and well-being which is God's will for his creatures. In some measure this is possible already and we shall discuss this when we look at healing in the Old Testament in Chapter Five.

## HEALTH, ANCIENT AND MODERN

It may have occasioned some surprise that we have spoken of the concept of health in the Old Testament in such terms as righteousness, holiness and obedience. Nevertheless, these are the terms in which the Old Testament defines health. It certainly includes such physical characteristics as strength, fertility and longevity but these characteristics are rather expressions of health than part of health itself. As we have already suggested, it is because we are healthy that we are strong, fertile and long-lived, and not because of these characteristics that we are healthy.

Today we tend to define health in terms of the normality of anatomical structure, physiological function and mental attributes. We stress the importance of the absence of abnormalities and disease and may often define health simply in terms of the absence of these. While it is true that the Old Testament may take these conditions into account when setting out the disqualifications for the levitical priesthood in Leviticus 21.16-21, the Old Testament lays its stress on the spiritual state of humankind and regards holiness as the supreme description of human health which is expressed daily life as righteousness and obedience. In other words, it includes human character and behaviour in its definition of health and this must also be true of any modern understanding and definition of health if it is to be fully adequate and truly comprehensive.

# Chapter 2
# THE CONCEPT OF HEALTH IN THE NEW TESTAMENT

In our consideration of the concept of health in the New Testament we look first of all at the words in which health is described in its pages, and then at the terms in which it is defined.

## THE DESCRIPTION OF HEALTH

Once it is realised that the New Testament understanding of health is a much more comprehensive concept than the one current in modern popular thought, it will occasion no surprise that the terms which are used to describe the whole or a part of this understanding are relatively numerous. The absence of the usual Classical Greek word for health *hugieia* from the pages of the New Testament is reflected in the rare use of the word 'health' in the English versions of that volume.

The word 'health' occurs in the standard English versions on only seven occasions. These are as follows:

Matthew 15.28 translating *iaomai* (NEB/REB).

Luke 7.10 translating *hugiaino* (NEB/REB/NRSV).

John 7.23 translating *hugies* (NEB).

Acts 3.16 translating *holokleria* (RSV/NRSV).

Acts 27.34 translating *soteria* (AV).

1 Peter 2.2 translating *soteria* (NEB).

3 John 2 translating *hugiaino* (AV/RV/RSV/NRSV/NEB/REB/NIV).

This list illustrates the many-sided nature of the New Testament understanding of health, for only in the case of 3 John 2 do all the versions agree to use the same word in translation. The synonyms used in the different versions show how similar it is to the Old Testament concept. Health is thought of in terms of wholeness and soundness, well-being and life, strength and salvation. All of these concepts are facets of the New Testament understanding of health and express the ideas which we have already found in the Old Testament. The comprehensive nature of health is also to be seen in the words which are used to describe it in the New Testament which we now proceed to examine in more detail.

## Hugies

The first word we consider is the word *hugies* which means having the quality of soundness derived from a proper balance of the whole being. It represents a group of words of which both the adjective and the verb occur in the New Testament. The noun *hugieia* is the Classical Greek word for health but it had become the name of the Greek goddess of health, one of the daughters of Asklepios (Aesculapius in Latin), and this pagan association may explain its absence from the pages of the New Testament. The verb is used mainly in the Pastoral Epistles in a metaphorical sense for the soundness or wholesomeness of teaching which gives spiritual health to those who accept it, but it does occur in its literal sense three times in Luke's gospel where it is used, for instance, by Jesus to describe those who are whole and do not need a physician (Luke 5.31), to describe the healed condition of the centurion's servant (Luke 7.10), and the safe and sound condition of the returned prodigal son (Luke 15.27). It is used also in 3 John 2 where it means good physical health as opposed to spiritual well-being.

It is, however, the adjective *hugies* which is the most frequently used word of this group in its literal sense especially in the fifth chapter of John's gospel where it is used six times. It almost always describes the state of soundness which has resulted from the healing of the sick person by Jesus. In most cases the emphasis is on the physical aspect of soundness as when we are told that the withered hand of the man in the synagogue was restored *hugies* or sound like the other one (Matthew 12.13; Mark 3.5; Luke 6.10), or when we are told that the paralysed man's limbs were made sound enough for him to get up and walk, and take up and carry his mattress (John 5.9). In Matthew 15.31 and Acts 4.10, the limbs of the crippled (*kulloi*) were made sound (*hugies*). On ten occasions, words of this group are used by the LXX to translate the Hebrew word *shalom* in the Old Testament. In most of these cases, the word occurs in an enquiry about a person's personal welfare, e.g. Genesis 29.6; 37.14; 43.27 and 2 Samuel 20.9. Here the emphasis is not so much on the physical well-being as on the general state of the person about whom the enquiry was made. The significant point is that both *shalom* and *hugies* coincide in expressing the idea of the soundness or wholeness of a person's being which is of the essence of health.

## Eirene

The second word is the word *eirene* which originally described a state of peace or tranquillity as opposed to one of war or disturbance.[1] It is the commonest term used in the LXX to translate *shalom*, and this usage is probably the origin of the common Vulgate translation of *shalom* by *pax*, which explains the preference of the English versions for the translation of the word *shalom* by 'peace'. Because of its association with *shalom* as its equivalent in Biblical Greek and because it is now used in the context of Christian faith and experience, the word *eirene* in the New Testament has a much fuller and more positive content than the purely negative sense of the absence of war, which is its primary meaning in Classical Greek.

The Biblical concept of peace is primarily expressed as one of wholeness and harmony, and in the New Testament usage of *eirene* this meaning is applied to people's relationships. There is first of all a person's restored relationship to God (Romans 5.1; Ephesians 2.14-18; Colossians 1.20), then their loving personal relationship with one another (Mark 9.50; Romans 12.18; 14.19; 1 Corinthians 7.15; 2 Corinthians 13.11; 1 Thessalonians 5.13) and finally their relationship to themselves which should be one of internal peace and serenity. This latter relationship is a distinctively Christian meaning of *eirene* (John 14.27; 16.33; Romans 8.5; 15.13; Philippians 4.7; Colossians 3.15).[2] The wholeness and harmony which is *eirene* results from faith in the atoning work of Jesus Christ which restored human relationships to what God intended them to be (Romans 8.6; 2 Corinthians 5.18-20; Philippians 4.7; Colossians 1.20-23).

## Zoe

The third word which describes the New Testament concept of health is *zoe*, life. There are three words for life in Greek, but *bios* and *psuche* generally refer to our common human life lived under the conditions of time and sense, which begins with birth and ends with death. This kind of life is taken for granted in the New Testament which is interested in life in its highest and fullest sense, and for this it uses the word *zoe*. Indeed it may be truly said that the principal theme of the New Testament is the meaning and content of the word *zoe*.[3]

John and Paul are the writers of the New Testament who have the most to say about the concept which this word describes. John uses the word thirty-six times and Paul thirty-seven times. *Zoe* was what Jesus came to bring as the gift of God to the world (John 3.16; 10.10). The reason why John wrote his gospel was that people might have *zoe* by believing that Jesus was the Christ, the Son of God (John 20.31). For John, life consists of knowledge of the Father through the Son and this implies a conscious relationship of human beings with God (John 17.3). For Paul the basis of true life is righteousness which is a right relationship to God (Romans 1.17; Galatians 3.11), and is the gift of God through his Son (Romans 6.23) by whom we have peace with God (Romans 5.1) and new life in Christ (2 Corinthians 5.17). To make it quite clear what kind of life is in view, both John and Paul frequently speak not simply of life, but of *zoe aionios* or 'eternal life'. This is life not with the quantity of time of which the Old Testament spoke, but with the quality of eternity unlimited by time and untouched by decay. It begins with faith now in time but it does not belong to time, for it continues into eternity when time will be no more. It is a concept of life which is not primarily temporal but eternal, and not primarily physical but spiritual. It is the life of God which begins for us when we come to know God and his Son Jesus

Christ (John 17.3) and continues as we share that life through faith in his Son Jesus Christ. The New Testament concept of health expresses the quality and character of this eternal life, for health is the fullness and completeness of life.

In his popular commentary on John's gospel, William Barclay describes eternal life in terms of peace and so combines in a helpful way the meaning of the two words we have been discussing. He defines eternal life as the very life of God which we come to know and share when we trust in God and his Son Jesus Christ (John 17.3). But he asks, What is it like to have eternal life? His answer is, 'To have eternal life envelops every relationship in life with peace'. He then goes on to spell out the effect of eternal life on these relationships:

1. Eternal life gives us peace with God because we are at home with our Father and not arraigned before a king or judge.

2. It gives us peace with our fellows. As we have been forgiven, so we forgive them. We see them as God sees them.

3. It gives us peace with life because our Father is the creator and the universe in which we live is friendly not hostile.

4. It gives us peace with ourselves. We no longer live dependent on ourselves, but on Christ who lives in us (Galatians 2.20).

5. It gives us the assurance of a future beyond death in which we shall know deep and permanent peace in all our relationships, above all with God himself.[4]

What more could we ask for in a definition of health?

## Teleios

We come now to the fourth word which describes another aspect of the New Testament concept of health. This is *teleios* which is usually translated as 'perfect' in the English versions. It describes that which is perfect, mature and complete, having attained the end or goal (*telos*) for which it was created. We are *teleios* when we fulfil the purpose for which we were created, namely, to be like God in whose image we were created. To put it in terms of our present interest, we were created to be healthy as God is healthy for we were created in his image.

As with the adjective *aionios*, we have in *teleios* the two aspects of the future and the present. When we think of the *telos* as the end of the process with the stage of complete perfection and maturity finally achieved, then *teleios* refers to the future. But we are to be *teleios* in the present. This means that we are to be perfect and mature, complete and whole here and now. It is a wholeness which is given to us now and also promised to us at the end, so that we are to be now and shall be hereafter *teleios* in the same manner as God is (Matthew 5.48).

## Soteria

The final word which expresses the concept of health in the New Testament is *soteria*. The adjective *sos* from which this word is derived means 'safe and sound', and so the noun *soteria* means the condition of being safe and sound. In the papyri which came from the rubbish heaps of Hellenistic Egypt at the end of last century, the commonest meaning for this word is 'health or well-being', and this would be the usual meaning of the word in the Hellenistic world in which the New Testament was written.[5]

However, the word had been used by the translators of the Old Testament into Greek in the third century BC to denote God's deliverance of the Israelites at the Red Sea (Exodus 14.13; 15.2), and at other times in their national history (Judges 15.18; 1 Samuel 11.13), as well as his deliverance of the individual believer who trusted in God to deliver him from his enemies (Psalm 18.46; 38.22; 51.14; 88.1). Consequently, the word came to have a rich religious content and application, and came to mean the act of deliverance by which the condition of being safe and sound was attained. In the New Testament it is this meaning of deliverance to a safe and sound condition which prevails.

In the gospels, the noun *soteria* occurs only five times; four times in Luke (1.69, 71, 77; 19.9) and once in John 4.22. In each case it is used in the Old Testament sense of deliverance. The verb *sozo*, on the other hand, is used for both healing and salvation in the gospels, but still with the basic idea of deliverance from a dangerous and threatening situation to a safe and sound condition. In the gospels we find that *sozo* is used for deliverance from danger (Matthew 8.25; John 12.27), from disease (Matthew 9.21; John 12.27), from the condemnation of God (Matthew 10.22; 24.13), and from sin (Matthew 1.21).[6]

When we come to the epistles, however, we find that Paul deliberately limits the application of both the noun and the verb to the relationship of human beings to God as the main area in which *soteria* is required because of human sinfulness, and it was this usage which came to predominate in theological writing.[7] This is not say that the body and its health are excluded from Paul's thought about salvation, for he clearly looks forward to the redemption of the body as part of the salvation and renewal of the whole man as we see from Romans 8.23. Salvation in the New Testament sense is total and affects the whole human being producing that condition of safety and soundness in this life and in the life to come, which forms part of the New Testament concept of health.

The five words which we have now briefly discussed all express some aspect of the New Testament understanding of health. It is significant that all of them except *zoe* had already been used by the Greek translators of the Old Testament to translate the Hebrew word *shalom*. They had each brought their own contribution to the understanding of that comprehensive word, and in turn they had absorbed some of the other facets of its meaning. These then passed over into the New Testament to express and enrich its concept of what belonged to the true health and well-being of humans.

## THE DEFINITION OF HEALTH

The Bible is a plain book so far as 'those things necessary to be known, believed and observed for salvation' are concerned.[8] It is not, however, a book which provides neat definitions of all the ideas and matters with which it deals. If it were, theology would be a less demanding study and Church history a path less strewn with heresy and schism. Nevertheless, it is possible to derive some definitions from it for our own guidance and this we shall now attempt to do in relation to the New Testament understanding of health. As we have already seen, the predominant interest of the New Testament is in healing and it assumes the concept of health previously set forth in the Old Testament. If there is any difference, it does not lie in the substance of the concept, but in the place where the emphasis is laid and in the fuller light shed on the concept by the New Testament revelation.

Several definitions relating to health are to be found in the pages of the New Testament, but all are partial and even fragmentary and all overlap since the words they each use can only be fully understood in the light of those used in the other definitions. In other words, the understanding of health in the New Testament is as many-sided as we found it was in the Old Testament. This is because any adequate definition of human health and wholeness can only be in terms of the life and perfection of God who created human beings for fellowship with himself and whose will it is that they should share and enjoy the same life and perfection as his own.

### Health as life

The first definition we consider is that of health as life. In the tenth chapter of John's gospel, Jesus is speaking about sheep and shepherds in what is the nearest approach to a parable which this gospel affords. In verse ten he contrasts the motive of the sheep-stealer with his own motive as the good shepherd. The thief came to steal and to kill and to destroy, but he came that the sheep 'may have life, and have it abundantly'.

This statement by Jesus of the purpose of his coming has often been regarded as a definition of health. Health is the abundance of the life of which he speaks. The word Jesus uses for life is *zoe*, the meaning of which we have already considered. It emphasises the quality of life as opposed to *bios* which emphasises its quantity or duration. It was not only life which Jesus came to bring, but life with a special quality and even a special quantity of that quality for the adjective *perissos* which the RSV and NRSV translate as 'abundantly' means 'more than sufficient' or 'with a surplus'. The GNB and the REB speak of life 'in all its fullness'; the TNT as life 'in overflowing measure'. The life which Jesus has in mind is eternal life, which is life with no horizon and of which time is not a measure. It is life with the quality of eternity in which God himself dwells. It is the life of God himself.[9]

Nothing could be healthier than the life of God producing in human beings that wholeness, soundness and righteousness which constitute true health and holiness. This relationship of divine and human life is a vital and basic element in the New Testament concept of health. Life apart from God is mere existence and duration. Health forms no necessary part of it and people who live apart from God may therefore lack health all the days of their life. But where human life is infused with the life of God and lived in a close and constant relationship with him, there is life indeed. Here life means health and health is life itself.

## Health as blessedness

In the Sermon on the Mount we have a second definition of health. In its opening verses Jesus gives an analysis of what he regards as complete spiritual well-being. These verses have been called the Beatitudes ever since Ambrose of Milan first gave them this name in his commentary on Luke's gospel written in the fourth century.[10] In the fuller version given in Matthew 5.3-12 it is commonly accepted that there are eight of these Beatitudes and that they set out eight different elements which may be combined in one individual.

The common Classical Greek word for blessedness was *eudaimonia* which literally means 'to possess a good *daimon*', but Jesus did not use this word, nor is it used in the New Testament, probably because of its obvious pagan background. The term which Jesus used was *makarios*, a term which Aristotle ranked lower than *eudaimonia*,[11] but which in the New Testament was given a new dignity and filled with a new content when Jesus used it here of what he regarded as true well-being, and Paul used it of God himself (1 Timothy 1.11; 6.15).

If it is true that we have in the Beatitudes a definition of health in terms of blessedness, then the qualities of a healthy person are very different from what we might expect. The Beatitudes represent a complete reversal of our earthly values and standards, and today the person whose blessedness they portray would be regarded as down-trodden, persecuted, under-privileged and even psychologically abnormal. The meaning of the Beatitudes is that blessedness and health come from within and not from without. The important thing is not the human environment but the human heart. As someone has truly said, 'The heart of the human problem is the problem of the human heart'.

Here the term 'heart' is not used in its physical sense but in the sense of the seat of the whole of human life, physical, intellectual and spiritual. The only mention of the environment in the Beatitudes is in terms of persecution and slander which are at once the product and the occasion of blessedness.

When we speak of health as life and of health as blessedness we are really saying the same thing. for the blessedness of the Beatitudes is but another expression for eternal life. Both blessedness and eternal life belong to God and through Jesus Christ his Son they are offered to us that we might share in the blessedness and life of God which is the purpose for which we were created.

## Health as holiness

The nearest approach to a definition of health in the New Testament epistles is in the prayer with which Paul closes his first letter to the Thessalonian Church (1 Thessalonians 5.23-24). In the REB this prayer is translated as follows:

> May God himself, the God of peace (*eirene*), make you holy through and through (*holotelos*), and keep you sound (*holokleros*) in spirit, soul and body, free of any fault when our Lord Jesus Christ comes. He who calls you keeps faith; he will do it.

The title 'the God of Peace' is a title for God which Paul uses at the close of some of his letters (Romans 15.33; 16.20; 2 Corinthians 13.11; Philippians 4.9) by which he reminds his readers of the one who is the author and giver of peace. It contains more than an echo of the *shalom* of the Old Testament.

This verse in First Thessalonians is the only verse in the New Testament where the three terms for body, soul and spirit are brought together, but as Wheeler Robinson comments, 'This is not a systematic dissection of the distinct elements of personality'.[12] Paul is emphasising the total nature of the preservation and holiness which he requests from God for his readers. His use of the three terms simply underlines the all-inclusiveness of his concept of the wholeness of the human being.

The most significant aspect of this verse is the association of four qualities or attributes which by implication are to be found in God and which through the work of Jesus Christ can also now be found in human beings. These are peace, holiness, soundness and blamelessness. They are to be found in every part or aspect of the Christian believer, body, soul and spirit. This is true wholeness and real health, and of its comprehensive nature there can be no doubt.

In his first letter to the Corinthian Church we find Paul dealing with the problem of sexual immorality in the Church and several times referring to the holiness of the body. He reminds his readers that their bodies are temples in which the Holy Spirit lives (1 Corinthians 3.16; 6.19; cp. Romans 8.9-11), and therefore they are holy and not to be used for any unholy purpose. Using another metaphor, he also reminds them that their bodies are limbs or members of Christ himself (6.15) and it is their duty to use them to bring glory and honour to God. It is their duty because in fact their bodies are not their own but have been bought by God at the price of the death of his Son Jesus Christ (6.20).

## Health as maturity

The word which more than any other summarises Paul's view of health in his epistles is the word *teleiosis* or maturity.[13] The noun itself does not appear in his writings, but he uses the adjective *teleios* and less often the verb *teleioo* to describe the state of maturity and perfection which it should be the aim of every Christian believer to attain. It is Paul's desire that his preaching of the gospel might produce people who are *teleios* or mature in Christ Jesus (Colossians 1.28, cp. 4.12). In Ephesians 4.13 he tells his readers that the aim of office-bearers in the Church should be to produce mature individuals. The phrase he uses is a very significant one. He speaks of *aner teleios* which means a man of adult maturity and of complete development. The standard by which this maturity is to be measured is the fullness of Christ. Paul does not regard himself as having reached this standard of maturity but in Philippians 3.12 he states that this is what he is aiming at. It is clear from the previous verse that this state will only be fully attained after the resurrection of the dead. Even so, a relative *teleiosis* is possible in this present life as we see from verse fifteen where the adjective *teleios* describes a maturity which is related to the stage which Paul and the Philippian Christians have reached in their Christian experience.

An indication of how this maturity might be sought and attained is provided by Paul in Romans 12.1-2. At this point in his epistle Paul passes from the doctrinal part to the practical part of his epistle. In the first eleven chapters he has set forth the mercies of God bestowed on both Jew and Gentile by their common redemption in Christ, and now on the basis of this demonstration he appeals to the Roman Christians to dedicate themselves to God. He exhorts them to present their bodies as a sacrifice to God which is their logical response in terms of worship to what God has done for them. He describes this sacrifice as living, holy and acceptable to God, a description which applied also to the state of the body which was offered in Old Testament sacrificial worship. He then speaks of the mind or *nous* by which he means their moral consciousness, whose content and activity have been governed by the fashions of the present world (*aion*) which are opposed to the things of God and result only in disobedience to his will. Paul entreats his readers to be radically transformed by the renewal of their minds by the Holy Spirit so that they are governed, not by the changing fashions of the world, but by the will of God which they will now be able to discern and obey. It is in these terms which involve both the body and the mind that Paul exhorts the Roman Christians to respond to the mercies of God and so press on to attain the maturity of their whole being as measured by the standard of the fullness of Christ; a maturity which implies not only full growth and perfect development, but also the wholeness, health and well-being of what is mature.

The New Testament presupposes the Old Testament concept of health and accepts its expression in terms of wholeness, obedience, righteousness and life. However, the use and content of these terms were transformed by the fuller revelation of God's will and purpose given in Jesus Christ. Each of them was personified and filled out for us by him. It was he who provided in his person a new standard of wholeness, obedience, righteousness and life. It was he who showed in his death how these might be achieved and in his resurrection demonstrated the source of the power by which they might be attained. In particular he changed the concept of life. In Old Testament terms this had meant life measured by the quantity of time and the quality of this world, but Jesus came to bring eternal life, life measured by the quality of eternity where quantity and duration have no relevance.

# PART TWO

# DISEASE AND HEALING IN THE OLD TESTAMENT

*IN PART ONE we saw how health in the Old Testament is intimately connected with obedience to God's law. Its teaching is a reminder that human beings cannot live as they please. Their life is regulated by physical, mental and social laws and principles which they must observe if they are to be healthy. If they do not observe these, then ill-health results.*

*In Part Two we examine those instances in the Old Testament in which physical diseases have resulted from the collective or individual disobedience of the people of Israel to the law of God. These diseases are the expression of the disturbed relationships of the people of Israel as a group or as individuals. As we shall see, the events of which these diseases form a part are mainly concentrated in two periods of the history of the people of Israel. These are during the ministry of Moses in nomadic period of Israel's history and during the ministry of the prophets Elijah and Elisha during the period of the monarchy.*

*Although most of the episodes we consider are of physical disease it is important to remember that for the Old Testament, the most vital relationship of human beings is not to their bodies but to God. This means that much of the teaching of the Old Testament, especially that of the prophets, is concerned with those human relationships and their disturbances which are not expressed physically or medically. We need, therefore, to remember that what is contained in this section of this book is only part of the Old Testament teaching on health, disease and healing. It has to be seen in the context of the Old Testament concept of health.*

# Chapter 3
# EPIDEMIC DISEASE IN THE OLD TESTAMENT

While the Old Testament is quite clear that all healing comes from God, it is equally clear that God may send disease or inflict injury on his people for their disobedience (Leviticus 26.25; Deuteronomy 7.15; 28.21, 27-28; 32.39; 2 Kings 15.5; 2 Chronicles 7.13; 21.18; 26.20; Psalm 39.11; Jeremiah 8.14; Ezekiel 14.19; 28.23; Hosea 6.1). This explains why references to disease are not infrequent in its pages.

## THE WORDS FOR DISEASE

The usual words for sickness and disease in the Old Testament are derivatives of the Hebrew verb *chalah* which means 'to be or become weak', a condition which is usually the result of sickness or disease. The noun from this root is *choli* meaning 'a state of bodily weakness', a description of the effect of sickness or disease.[1] By contrast, therefore, health is regarded as strength as we have already seen in our first chapter.

Other words which describe the outbreaks of epidemic disease include *maggephah*, *nega* and *negeph* which are usually translated 'plague'. These all come from the root *naga* which expresses the idea of being touched, smitten or struck, and so means disease in much the same way as when in English today we speak of a person having 'a stroke' meaning that they have had a cerebral haemorrhage, with the implication that they have been struck down by God. These words describe occasions when people or individuals were struck or smitten by some disease which may or may not be fatal in outcome. In the Old Testament according to Seybold and Mueller, 'There is not one unambiguous example suggesting that sickness or disease were associated with one of the organs, or even with internal parts of the body. Sickness was viewed as blows or attacks by a higher power in analogy to bodily wounds. There simply are no other etiologies in the Old Testament'.[2]

Another word which is used for outbreaks of epidemic disease is *deber* which is usually translated 'pestilence' in English. The word is related to a Semitic root meaning 'departure' or 'death' and commonly refers to one of the three severe punishments of sword, famine or pestilence which God might send upon his people for their disobedience. It is commonest in Jeremiah where it occurs seventeen times and in Ezekiel, twelve times (See 2 Samuel 24.13; 2 Chronicles 20.9; Jeremiah 24.10; 32.24; Ezekiel 14.21).[3]

This word is also used in Psalm 91.6 where the Psalmist speaks of 'the pestilence which stalks in darkness'. Blakely has suggested that this description may be that of malaria because this infection is transmitted to human beings by mosquitoes which usually bite at night.[4] This suggestion cannot be entirely excluded, but it appears to be very unlikely in view of the scanty evidence the description provides.

## 'THE LORD WILL PLAGUE YOU WITH DISEASES'

It is in the context of the possible physical, social and political consequences of disobedience of the law of God that we find lists of diseases with which he may afflict the people of Israel. These lists occur in Leviticus 26.14-16 and Deuteronomy 28.21-23, 27-29, 34-35. The Jewish name for these passages is the *Tokecha*, the Rebuke or Warning chapters.[5]

In the Leviticus passage, the diseases which may afflict the Israelites are described as 'sudden terror, wasting diseases and fever that will destroy your sight and drain away your life' Leviticus 26.14 (NIV). To these the passage in Deuteronomy 28 adds 'the boils of Egypt, tumours, festering sores and the itch from which you cannot be cured... madness, blindness and confusion of mind' (vv.22 and 28 NIV). The incurable boils which may afflict disobedient people will affect their knees and legs and spread to involve their whole bodies from the soles of their feet to the crowns of their heads (v.35).

At the end of the passage from Deuteronomy, the physical consequences of disobedience are summarised as follows:

> If you do not carefully follow all the words of this law, which are written in this book, and do not revere this glorious and awesome name - the Lord your God - the Lord will send fearful plagues on you and your descendants, harsh and prolonged disasters, and severe and lingering illnesses. He will bring upon you all the diseases of Egypt that you dreaded, and they will cling to you. The Lord will also bring on you every kind of sickness and disaster not recorded in this Book of the Law, until you are destroyed. You who were as numerous as the stars in the sky will be left but few in number, because you did not obey the Lord your God (Deuteronomy 28.56-62 NIV).

The diseases described in this passage resemble one another in that they are all sudden in onset, severe in degree, epidemic in occurrence and fatal in outcome.

The terms used in these two passages to describe the diseases are all too general to allow of their precise identification. However, a few attempts to identify them have been made.

It has been suggested, for instance, that the fever which destroyed sight (Leviticus 26.16) was gonorrhoeal conjunctivitis whose incidence could assume epidemic proportions.[6] However, this infection remains localised to the eyes; it does not produce fever and cannot be described as draining away life. It is therefore unlikely to be the diagnosis here. The LXX translators apparently understood that jaundice characterised this disease and used the word *ikteros* instead of *puretos* for 'fever' in their translation. In the similar list of diseases in Deuteronomy 28.22 the term *yeraqon* appears which means pallor or yellowness and this is translated by the LXX as *ochra* (yellow). If we may add these features together, we have a debilitating disease characterised by fever, anaemia and jaundice (or pallor) which may be accompanied by severe dehydration producing a sunken appearance of the eyes in their sockets in which they appear to be 'consumed', as Sussman suggests.[7] Possible diagnoses for this condition include malaria, chlorosis and chronic kidney disease but its precise nature must remain uncertain.

The wasting disease (*shachepheth*) of Leviticus 26.16 and Deuteronomy 28.22 may have been tuberculosis ('consumption' in AV and RSV) or a chronic febrile disease such as brucellosis (Malta fever), or any chronic disease which produced extreme emaciation.

The 'fiery heat' (*chachur*) of the Deuteronomy 28.22 (RV and RSV) is translated by Moffatt as 'erysipelas', which is an acute febrile inflammation of the skin. However, this disease does not occur in epidemics and was said to be uncommon in Palestine last century.[8] The word *chachur* is one of the three different terms used for fever in this verse, the others being *daleqet* from the verb *dalaq* (to burn) and *qadachat* from the verb *qadach* (to kindle). This may indicate that these terms refer to different types of fever and even different febrile diseases. If they refer to different types of fever then they could suggest the occurrence of the different clinical forms of malaria, but this cannot be regarded as at all certain.

The boil (*shechin*) of Egypt (Deuteronomy 28.27) will be discussed in some detail in our next chapter where it is identified as cutaneous anthrax or 'malignant pustule'. The *ophalim* of the same verse are the buboes or plague boils (RVm) of bubonic plague, and neither emerods (AV) nor scurvy (RSV).[9] The ulcers (*qarab*) may have been tropical sores of infectious or nutritional origin. The itch (*chores*) may have been scabies.

In addition to the physical diseases which are given in these two passages as possible consequences of disobedience we find mental conditions referred to in Deuteronomy 28.28. There we read that 'The LORD will afflict you with madness, blindness and confusion of mind' (NIV and NRSV). These three terms represent Hebrew words which are very rarely used in the Old Testament and only occur together again in Zechariah 12.4 where the prophet describes what the Lord will do to the cavalry of the armies which will besiege Jerusalem. He will strike the cavalrymen with madness and their horses with blindness and panic. These three conditions could be temporary ones which would disappear when the situation had been saved. In other words it may be that the mental conditions referred to in Deuteronomy were not mental diseases, but temporary changes in mental states as reactions to situations of confusion and terror. Attempts have been made to identify these conditions with the advanced stages of syphilis.[10] Such an identification seems improbable since, as we shall mention in the our next chapter, syphilis is not believed to have been prevalent in Palestine in Old Testament times.

Among the rules for the priesthood given in Leviticus 21.18-20 are references to physical conditions which disqualify priests from offering sacrifice. The general term used to refer to these conditions is the word *mum* which means a blemish (AV) or a defect (NIV). These defects are described in terms of physical symptoms but without any indication of the underlying cause whether it was maldevelopment or disease. No one who is blind or lame, disfigured or deformed may offer sacrifice. Neither may one with a crippled hand or foot, one who is hunchbacked or dwarfed, one who has a defective eye, or has a chronic ulcer or has been castrated. Amongst the conditions covered by this list may be those of harelip (*harum* which is translated 'flat nose' in v. 18 in the AV and RV), tuberculosis of the spine causing hunchback (v.20), a corneal opacity or a film over the eye (v.20 REB), polydactyly or superfluous fingers or toes (v.18, cp. 2 Samuel 21.20) and varicose ulcers (v.20).

Old age is not a disease strictly so-called, but it is recognised in the Old Testament as the cause of deterioration in physical and mental powers. Thus we read of the failing eyesight of Isaac (Genesis 27.1), Jacob (Genesis 48.10), Eli (1 Samuel 3.2 and 4.15) and Ahijah (1 Kings 14.4), presumably due to senile cataract, and the effect of the menopause on Sarah's ability to conceive (Genesis 18.11). Psalm 71 is clearly the prayer of an old man and speaks of his increasing weakness (v.9) and his grey hair (v.18, cp. 1 Samuel 12.2). Old people lose the strength of their limbs and sit about in the streets, needing the aid of walking-sticks to move about (Zechariah 8.4). We read too of the increasing loss of the special sensory functions of the body which occurs in the aged as described by the eighty-year old Barzillai in 2 Samuel 19.34-36. Finally, a vivid and comprehensive picture of the diminishing powers of old age is given by the Preacher in Ecclesiastes 12.1-7. These include muscular weakness, loss of the teeth, defective vision and hearing, insomnia and loss of balance and awareness of surroundings. In youth, these symptoms would constitute ill-health but not in age and so our definition of health will vary according to the age and stage of the person whose health we are describing.

By way of contrast to these descriptions of the effects of old age we are told that although Moses was a hundred and twenty years old when he died, 'yet his eyes were not weak nor his strength gone' (Deuteronomy 34.7 NIV). An interesting variation in this verse is found in the Vulgate which refers to Moses' teeth and says *nec dentes illius moti sunt*, which Knox in his English version translates as 'and his teeth stood firm', i.e., in spite of his advanced age, Moses had not lost any of his teeth.

# EPIDEMIC DISEASES

The best known occasion on which a people were struck by plagues (*negaim*) was when God inflicted the ten plagues on the Egyptians to induce the Pharoah to release the Children of Israel (Exodus 7.20-12.30, cp. 1 Samuel 4.8). Only five of these were actually called plagues and although most of them affected the personal or social hygiene of normal life in Egypt, few were concerned with the infliction of disease. Their significance was that each of them was inflicted by God and none of them was 'healed' in the sense that their consequences were immediately removed when they ceased. This is most obvious in the case of the tenth plague when the firstborn of all the families and the livestock died. They were not brought back to life again.

A number of epidemic outbreaks of infectious or communicable disease are described in the Old Testament. They mostly occurred when the people of Israel disobeyed God or incurred his displeasure by their complaints or behaviour. Most of them are of diseases which cannot now be identified because few or no details are given, but in some cases there are one or two clues to their identity.

## Outbreaks which cannot be identified

1. On the return of Moses from Mount Sinai he found the people worshipping the golden calf which Aaron had made. We are told that 'the Lord struck the people with a plague (*nega*) because of what they did with the calf Aaron had made' (Exodus 32.35). There is no indication of the nature of the plague but only that it was sent by God as punishment for their sin of idolatry (v.34).

2. After the return of the spies from Canaan those people who refused to accept their report 'were struck down and died before the Lord' (Numbers 14.37). Again there is no indication of the disease from which these people died.

## Outbreaks of which some details are given

1. The tenth plague of Egypt may be regarded as an epidemic disease in so far as it affected a great number of people and animals over a wide area of the land of Egypt (Exodus 11.4-5; 12.29). However, the unique feature of this plague was its selective nature. It affected only the firstborn males of the Egyptians and their cattle. Other special features were the simultaneous involvement of every Egyptian household (Exodus 11.30), no apparent contact between the victims and no definite incubation period. Death was inevitable and immediate. These features are those of no known naturally-occurring epidemic disease and so we are left with the explanation which is given in the narrative, namely, that this was a supernatural event and not an outbreak of a natural epidemic disease.

2. On two occasions we are told that the Lord provided 'quails' to satisfy the craving of the Israelites for meat on their desert journey. The first occasion was in the Wilderness of Sin as they approached Mount Sinai (Exodus 16.12-13) when there is no mention of any pathological effect following their

consumption of the quails. Soon after they left Mount Sinai they were again provided with a supply of quails and this time we are told that the Lord struck the people with 'a very great plague' (Numbers 11.31-33).

The common quail (*Coturnix coturnix*) is a small game bird of the partridge family which migrates in large numbers between Africa and Europe by a route which includes the Sinai peninsula. Its flesh and its eggs provide delicious food and no bad effects usually follow their consumption. This however was not true of the second occasion on which the Israelites used the birds for food.

In the standard translations we are told that this plague struck them before the meat from the quails had been chewed (AV/RV/RSV/NIV) or even before it had been bitten off the birds (NEB/REB), but the alternative translation is preferable which says that this plague struck them 'while there was still plenty of meat to eat' (GNB).[11] In this case the nature of the plague may have been some form of food poisoning, perhaps because although they gathered the quails over two days, the supply was to last for a month during which period the birds would have become unfit to eat in their hot desert conditions (vv.19, 32). This diagnosis is also suggested by the reference to the flesh of the birds coming out of the nostrils of the people after they had been eating it for a whole month (v.20), which Preuss takes to mean that they experienced much vomiting.[12] This would suggest that the epidemic was one of toxic food poisoning rather than the bacterial variety.

Three other suggestions for the nature of this plague have been made. Creighton thought that the symptoms were those of cardiovascular or wet beriberi due to a dietetic deficiency of thiamine or vitamin B1. [13] This diagnosis may safely be dismissed on the grounds that no relevant symptoms are actually described in the narrative, that the condition would take weeks or months to develop, and that it is not rapidly fatal.

Quails feed chiefly on seeds and berries and from his experience in Algeria, Sergent suggested that the quails had been feeding on hemlock seeds and when their meat was eaten by the Israelites it produced the symptoms of hemlock poisoning.[14] These are due to the alkaloid *coniine* which is an intensely poisonous substance contained in this plant and its seeds. It is unlikely that this was the cause of this outbreak of disease.

The third possible explanation was suggested by Ouzounellis who, during an outbreak of quail poisoning on the island of Lesbos in the Aegean Sea, observed that some people showed an allergic reaction to quail meat and might even die. In these cases the protein of their muscles was broken down and excreted in the urine (acute myoglobinuria). Again this suggestion is unlikely for it was based on the experience of only twenty-eight cases only one of whom died.[15]

The most likely cause of this epidemic was the ingestion of putrified quail meat which produced an acute toxic food poisoning.

3. Following the rebellion led by Korah, the son of Levi. God sent a plague which killed fourteen thousand, seven hundred people (Numbers 16.47-50). The massive mortality from this plague suggested to Bennett that it may have been an epidemic of bubonic plague or of cholera.[16] The description of Aaron's hurried arrival in the midst of the crowd (v.47) where he stood between the living and the dead (v.48) may suggest the rapid spread of the disease, which caused the sudden death of those who were affected.

4. After Israel began to worship the Baal of Peor, the god of the Moabite mountains, twenty-four thousand people died in the plague sent by God. The plague was only stopped when the apostate Israelites were put to death on God's orders (Numbers 25.1-9, cp. Deuteronomy 4.3; Psalm 106.29 and Hosea 9.10). Although this plague was associated with sexual immorality between the Israelite men and the Moabite women it is unlikely to have been an epidemic of sexually transmitted disease. No disease of this type spreads so quickly or is so rapidly fatal as this one was. However, because of the close contact between the two peoples, it is possible that the plague originated from a Moabite source. The massive numbers of the people who died may again suggest that the disease was either bubonic plague or cholera.[17]

In Joshua 22.17 there is a reference to 'the sin of Peor' and its effect as still present among the people. This has been taken to mean that the disease visited on them on the plains of Moab was a chronic one with persistent physical effects, which might support the suggestion that the disease could have been syphilis. However, the reference is to the 'sin' of Peor and not to the disease. The sin was apostasy, and the western tribes obviously thought that the eastern tribes were about to commit this sin again. This reference is therefore not relevant to the diagnosis of the disease which the people of Israel suffered at Peor.

5. After David had conducted a census of the people, which was done at the instigation of Satan according to 1 Chronicles 21.1, God sent a plague by the agency of an angel which lasted three days and killed seven thousand men (2 Samuel 24.15). The plague ceased when God told the angel to withdraw his hand (v.16). Bennett suggests that a short-term fever with a high mortality such as this may have been influenza which would become rapidly fatal when complicated by acute bronchopneumonia.[18]

6. God sent a great plague (*maggephah*) on King Jehoram's family and the people of Judah because of the king's apostasy (2 Chronicles 21.14-17). It is not clear whether this plague was an infective disease or a military disaster which led to a great slaughter.[19] In verse seventeen we read of a military invasion of Judah by the Philistines and the Arabs in which the sons, wives and possessions of Jehoram were all carried off. It is possible that this was 'the great plague' (NRSV) or 'the heavy blow' (NIV) prophesied by Elijah in verse fourteen rather than an epidemic of some infective disease. If it was an

infective disease then it may have been an acute bacillary dysentery due to one of the *Shigella* group of organisms. However, it is more likely that the blow or plague was the military disaster, for the Hebrew word may mean either a disaster or a disease.

7. When Nebuchadnezzar of Babylon was besieging Jerusalem in 587 BC King Zedekiah of Judah sent to Jeremiah to know if the siege would be successful. The prophet replied that it would and that all who remained in the city would die by sword, famine or plague. In his great anger against them, God would strike down all people and animals who stayed in the city with a terrible plague and all who survive the plague will die by the sword of the Babylonians (Jeremiah 21.1-7). No indication of the nature of the plague is given but outbreaks of diseases such as typhus fever, typhoid fever and bubonic plague are common in besieged cities.

## Outbreaks suggestive of bubonic plague

1. Whilst the Ark of the Covenant was in the possession of the Philistines we are told that 'the Lord's hand was heavy' against the people of the three cities of Ashdod, Gath and Ekron which successively harboured it, and he sent an epidemic of bubonic plague amongst them. The first city to be affected was Ashdod which is a seaport on the Mediterranean coast and this may be significant from an epidemiological point of view. The plague could have been introduced by infected rats which came ashore from ships which had come to Ashdod from Egypt or Libya which were well-known centres of plague infection.

The epidemic only came to an end when the Ark was returned to Israel (1 Samuel 5.1-6.21). With the Ark the Philistines sent a guilt offering to Israel's God of five gold tumours and five golden rats (6.4-5). These confirm the diagnosis of bubonic plague for the tumours represent the groin swellings (or buboes) which characterise the disease, and the rats are the carriers of the rat fleas which convey the infection. Unfortunately when the Ark was returned to Israel it must still have contained some infected fleas, for we read that seventy Israelites opened the Ark at Beth Shemesh and looked into it, with the result that they died from the disease (6.19 NIV).[20]

The first person to identify the Philistine epidemic as one of bubonic plague was J. J. Scheuchzer who was professor of medicine, mathematics and physics at the Lyceum of Zurich. In 1725 he made the suggestion in his massive work *Physica Sacra*, which was first published in German and then later in Latin in six volumes (1731-1735). The AV of 1611 had originally used the term 'emerods' for the lesions of the plague, which is the old spelling of 'haemorrhoids', a term which is quite inappropriate here for there is no known epidemic disease of high mortality which has for its principal clinical feature the sudden appearance of haemorrhoids or anything resembling them. When the RV came to be published in 1884, the term 'emerods' was replaced by 'tumours' in the text and 'plague boils' in the margin, thus taking note of Scheuchzer's suggestion that the epidemic was one of bubonic plague.[21]

2. When the army of Sennacherib king of Assyria besieged Jerusalem in 701 BC, 'the angel of the Lord went out and put to death a hundred and eighty-five thousand men in the Assyrian camp' (2 Kings 19.35 and Isaiah 37.36), with the result that the king 'broke camp and withdrew' (2 Kings 19.36).[22] The cause of these deaths may have been acute bacillary dysentery (shigellosis) or cholera both of which may have an incubation period of less than twenty-four hours and are common results of poor camp hygiene. Alternatively, they may have been due to bubonic plague carried by rats, which also has a correspondingly short incubation period.

This latter suggestion receives some support from the Greek historian Herodotus who records an Egyptian tradition that one night during Sennacherib's campaign against Egypt, his camp was invaded by a multitude of rats or field-mice which gnawed through the strings of the soldiers' bows and the leather thongs of their quivers and shields so rendering them quite unusable for fighting.[23] Herodotus states that the Egyptians erected a stone statue of Sethos, the reigning Pharoah, in the temple of Hephaestus at Memphis holding a mouse in his hand to commemorate their victory over the Assyrian army.

## The epidemic of snakes

When the people spoke against God and Moses on their way from Mount Hor complaining about the absence of food and water in the desert, God sent amongst them a plague of venomous snakes (Numbers 21.4-6 NIV and REB). The AV and RSV call them 'fiery serpents'.[24] Moses prayed to God on behalf of the people and God told him that the people would be healed if he made a model of a snake in copper or bronze and mounted it on a standard-bearing pole in the midst of the camp.[25] Then anyone who was bitten by a snake could look at the metal snake on the pole and be healed of their snakebite and its effects (Numbers 21.8-9, cp. John 3.14-15).[26]

Bennett devotes the appendix to his book The Diseases of the Bible to this incident and suggests that these snakes were actually guinea worms of the species Dracunculus medinensis.[27] The larvae of these parasites enter the body in drinking water which contains infected water-fleas of the genus Cyclops which harbour the larvae in their body cavity. Once in the human body, the larvae escape and penetrate the wall of the stomach or duodenum and the adult female worm eventually settles under the skin of the lower part of the leg of the infected person, where it discharges its larvae into water through a small ulcer in the skin. The usual treatment for this condition is the slow extraction of the worm through the ulcer by winding it round a small stick over a period of days. It is the fancied similarity of this form of treatment to a snake being mounted on a pole which has suggested the diagnosis in this case, it being suggested that the snake and the pole were intended as a demonstration to those infected by the worm, of the method of removing the worm from the body.

This diagnosis is unlikely. For one thing, the people complained of the absence of water in the desert where they were (v.5). For another, the worm does not bite the skin but enters the body by the mouth in the larval form in drinking water and cannot exist in the adult form outside the body. Also the infection is not usually an epidemic one as it would need to be in this case, but is usually described as 'endemic', being always present in the area where the people were affected. Finally, people do not die of this infection as they died after being bitten by venomous snakes (v.6).

There seems to be no real reason why we should not accept the record of the invasion of the camp by poisonous snakes as fact. The variety of snake most likely to have been involved is one of the desert vipers, among which the most probable is the Carpet or Saw-scaled Viper (*Echis carinatus*). This species is notorious for striking unprovoked, a feature which is rare among snakes. Its venom is largely haemolytic and is the most toxic of all the desert viperine venoms, causing death after several days. It is rapid in its movements, more active by day than the other desert vipers and is well known to occur in large numbers in limited desert areas.[28]

Plagues of poisonous snakes still occur in the Sinaitic peninsula, as Lawrence of Arabia and his raiding parties found to their cost during their campaign against the Turkish forces there during the First World War.[29]

# Chapter 4
# SYSTEMIC DISEASE IN THE OLD TESTAMENT

The systemic diseases which affected individuals in the Old Testament are described in more detail than the epidemic diseases which affected groups or whole populations. Even so, it is rarely possible to be certain of the identity of the disease in any particular case. This means that the identification of the disease in the following cases can be no more than tentative.

## Cardiovascular disease

The following cases of systemic disease in the Old Testament appear to involve the heart or the blood vessels.

1. Nabal the Calebite and the husband of Abigail is the first example (1 Samuel 25.2-38). Nabal was a wealthy sheep-farmer who fed well and overindulged in alcohol. His name means 'fool' and he lived up to his name by his churlish treatment of David whose men had protected his herds and property. He held a great feast whilst meanly refusing food and help to David and his men. However, his wife Abigail surreptitiously took food to them and when he was sober in the morning she told him what she had done and 'his heart failed him and he became like a stone' (v.37 NIV). This suggests that he went into a state of cardiogenic shock and became as cold as a stone. The result was that 'about ten days later, the Lord struck Nabal and he died' (v.38). This sounds like a classic heart attack (myocardial infarction). The alternative diagnosis is a cerebral haemorrhage although there is no mention of any paralysis.[1] We may add with Preuss: 'It is not necessary to assume that his wife poisoned him, a thought which is certainly plausible'.[2]

2. The second case is that of Uzzah the son of Abinadab in 2 Samuel 6.7. The Ark of God was being taken from its temporary resting place at the house of Abinadab on a cart drawn by oxen. At one point the oxen stumbled and Uzzah took hold of the Ark to steady it. We are told that 'the Lord's anger burned against Uzzah because of his act of irreverence; therefore God struck him down and he died there beside the ark of God' (NIV). As in the case of Nabal, the cause of Uzzah's sudden death may equally well have been due to a heart attack or a cerebral haemorrhage. We have chosen the former as the cause of death because sudden death from heart disease is commoner in younger persons than it is from cerebral haemorrhage. His irreverent act was to have touched the Ark of God (cp. Numbers 4.15 and 1 Samuel 6.19).

3.  The third case was one of vascular disease. Asa, king of Judah, became 'diseased in his feet' in his old age (1 Kings 15.23; 2 Chronicles 16.12). His disease was diagnosed in the Babylonian Talmud as gout, but gout was uncommon in Palestine.³ As Wiseman comments, 'It is more likely, in view of Asa's age, the severity of the disease and death within two years, to have been a peripheral obstructive vascular disease with ensuing gangrene of his feet'.⁴ This is also suggested by the fact that when he was buried, his people used specially prepared spices and perfumes, presumably to disguise the smell of his gangrenous feet (2 Chronicles 16.14). This verse speaks too of a very great fire being lit in his honour, and although this was customary at the funeral of kings (cp. 2 Chronicles 21.19; Jeremiah 34.5), the use of specially prepared spices and perfumes is not mentioned in the case of other kings.

4.  A fourth case may have been that of Jeroboam, the son of Nebat, who was the first king of the northern breakaway kingdom of Israel. When he was sacrificing at the altar at Bethel 'a man of God' from Judah, whose name is not given, objected and the king ordered his arrest (1 Kings 13.4). As he pointed with his hand to the man he lost the use of his hand. The word used is *yabesh* which means 'to dry up (AV), wither or shrivel (so NIV) from lack of water'. A sudden loss of use of this kind may be due to a psychological cause, but it may also be due to a physical cause such as an embolus or blood-clot blocking the brachial artery at its bifurcation in front of the elbow. It could also be due to loss of nervous control of the muscles of the hand perhaps by a localised cerebral haemorrhage or vasospasm.⁵ Whatever the cause may have been, it was removed when the man of God prayed for Jeroboam's recovery (v.6).

5. Finally, amongst the signs which God gave Moses to validate his commission to lead the Israelites out of Egypt was one which may have been vascular in origin. Moses was told to put his hand inside his cloak and when he took it out, it was 'leprous, white as snow' (Exodus 4.6). When he put it back and took it out again, the hand was normal 'like the rest of his flesh' (v.7). Davies suggests that this was a case of Raynaud's syndrome, in which the small blood vessels of the fingers go into temporary spasm and the skin becomes white and cold. This suggestive is attractive but the evidence for it is not very adequate or convincing.⁶

## Gastrointestinal disease

In the reign of Jehoram, king of Judah, the Lord sent a great plague upon the people because of his apostasy (2 Chronicles 21.14-17). When we discussed the identity of this plague in our previous chapter we suggested that this was probably a military disaster rather than an epidemic of infectious disease. Verse eighteen of this chapter tells us that it was after this event, but still part of the dire consequence of Jehoram's apostasy, that the king was afflicted by a chronic painful disease of the bowels. No treatment had any effect and at the end we are told that 'his bowels came out because of the disease, and he died in great agony' (v.19).

The older commentators suggested the diagnosis of chronic amoebic or bacillary dysentery for the chronic disease from which Jehoram suffered, but these diseases would not produce the main feature of the acute final and painful stage of his disease for severe pain is not a feature of either of these diseases. Preuss suggests that Jehoram suffered from rectal cancer from which pieces broke off from time to time giving the impression that his bowels were coming out.[7]

While the exact nature of the chronic disease remains unclear, it is possible that his terminal fatal condition was a separate, though not necessarily unrelated condition, and was much more acute, lasting only two days. There are translation difficulties in verse nineteen, and Curtis and Madsen have suggested that this verse may be translated along the lines followed by the LXX: 'And it came to pass after a prolonged time of illness, when the end of his life came, his bowels came out for two days and he died'.[8]

The acute fatal condition which supervened at the end of two years of this chronic disease may thus have been a large intestinal obstruction due to an intussusception in which one part of the intestine slips into the part below. If this is not corrected, the rounded apex of the intussuscepted part of the intestine may move down inside the intestine and eventually protrude from the anus to give the appearance of the bowels coming out. The presence of great pain and the fatal outcome precipitated by his already greatly weakened condition would favour this diagnosis of intussusception rather than the alternative one of prolapse of the rectum which, although alarming in appearance, does not cause great pain and is not usually fatal as was the case with Jehoram (2 Chronicles 21.19). However he may have died, King Jehoram was not honoured after his death. He had lost the confidence of his people who lit no fire in his honour as they had done for his ancestors, and did not bury him in the tombs of the kings, but in the City of David overlooking the Kedron Valley to the east (2 Chronicles 21.19-20).

## Nervous disease

1. A disease of the peripheral nervous system which appears to have been present in the ancient Near East is acute paralytic poliomyelitis. An Egyptian stela of the Eighteenth Dynasty (1580-1350 BC) portrays a priest of Ruma who lived in Memphis, in the act of offering sacrifice to his god. His left leg shows the typical post-poliomyelitis shortening and atrophy with the limb held in the equinus position which results from flaccid paralysis such as that caused by an attack of paralytic poliomyelitis.[9]

In his book *The Bible and Modern Medicine*, Short proposed this diagnosis for the cause of the crippled condition of the feet of Mephibosheth, the son of Jonathan.[10] However, the account given in 2 Samuel 4.4 states that his lameness was due to an accident in which he fell when he was five years old and damaged both ankles. An attempt has been made to combine these proposals by suggesting that the bones of both his ankle regions were abnormally brittle following recovery from a previous attack of poliomyelitis.[11] When the news came of the death in battle of both his father and grandfather, his nurse took him up and fled in panic. However, he fell and damaged his ankles. It is probable that he sustained fractures of both ankles which healed with marked deformity and displacement which left him permanently crippled. To suggest more than this, is to go beyond the evidence provided in the account.

2. The most probable diagnosis in the case of the young son of the Shunammite woman (2 Kings 4.18-20) is that of subarachnoid haemorrhage which is more sudden in onset, more severe in the intensity of the headache it produces and is more likely to be rapidly fatal than the sunstroke or heat stroke which is usually suggested for the diagnosis in this boy's case.[12] Other suggestions include acute meningococcal meningitis but this is seldom fatal in so short a time, and cerebral malaria which would not be so sudden in onset.[13] A Rabbinic suggestion was that the boy may have been bitten by a poisonous snake hidden amongst the crops which were being harvested at the time.[14] Whatever was the cause, the child died and was restored to life by Elisha's application of a form of artificial cardio-pulmonary resuscitation after he had prayed to the Lord (vv. 33-34).

3. There is little real evidence of the occurrence of a case of epilepsy in the Old Testament. Balaam, a Midianite diviner, was called upon by Balak, the king of Moab, to curse the children of Israel. In the course of his oracles Balaam describes himself as 'one who hears the words of God and sees a vision of the Almighty, who falls prostrate and whose eyes are opened' (Numbers 24.4, 16). Preuss regarded this as the description of an epileptic fit.[15] However it is not really specific enough for such a diagnosis to be made and is more likely to be the prophet's account of his experience when he comes into the presence of his god to receive an oracle.

Preuss also suggested that the reference to Saul's behaviour before Samuel at Naioth when he was said to lie down before Samuel all day and night (1 Samuel 19.24) was an example of the epileptic state.[16] This condition consists of a continuous seizure in which the unconsciousness may persist for hours and even days, and which may be fatal. This diagnosis is most unlikely and there is no other mention of Saul ever having any other possible epileptic symptoms.

### Disease of the eyes

According to the literature of ancient societies as illustrated by the *De Medicina* of Celsus, diseases of the eye were very common in the ancient world. The ancient Egyptians made no attempt to preserve the eyeballs of their mummies. During embalming the bony orbits were packed with linen pads or filled with a round stone, or even a small onion as in the case of Pharoah Rameses IV (1166-1160 BC), to preserve the normal contour of the eyelids.[17]

It is interesting to note that although the eye is mentioned in the Old Testament almost six hundred times there is only one possible mention of active disease affecting it. This is in Genesis 29.17 where we are told that Leah, the elder daughter of Laban, had eyes which were described as weak or delicate (*rak*, LXX *astheneis*). The most probable diagnosis of the cause of this weakness is trachoma, still a common infectious eye disease of Near Eastern countries.

On two occasions we read of groups of people being struck with sudden blindness. The first group was of those residents of Sodom who wished to assault Lot and his family. They were struck blind by the two angelic visitors who were with Lot (Genesis 19.11). The second group was composed of soldiers of the Syrian army who had surrounded Dothan intent on capturing the prophet Elisha. God struck the soldiers with sudden temporary blindness at the request of Elisha and he escaped (2 Kings 6.18). Sudden blindness is usually vascular in origin due to bleeding from or blocking of a retinal artery and it is unlikely that these would occur simultaneously throughout a group of people. We must conclude that we do not know the cause of the sudden blindness in these cases; not even hysteria would be a satisfactory explanation.

## Disease of the skin

Most of the infectious diseases leave no traces of their presence in the body after death unless they affect the bones as in the case of leprosy, syphilis or tuberculosis. Some diseases affecting the skin do however leave traces, and Egyptian mummies of the Eighteenth and Twentieth Dynasties (1550-1050 BC) have been discovered, whose skin showed a vesicular rash resembling that of smallpox. One of these mummies was that of Rameses V, a Pharoah of the Twentieth Dynasty whose dates are usually given as 1160-1156 BC which would fall within the period of the Judges in Old Testament history. Elliot Smith, who described the mummy of Rameses V in his book on *The Royal Mummies*, found the rash resembling that of smallpox on the face, the lower abdominal wall and the sexual organs of the mummy.[18] Short suggested that the description given of Job's disease 'fits smallpox well' and that this was the disease from which Job suffered.[19] However, the multiplicity of symptoms and signs which Job's disease presents make this diagnosis unlikely.[20]

Diseases of the skin are not commonly mentioned in the Old Testament and the most problematical of those which are is the condition called *sara'at*, a word which is commonly translated 'leprosy' in the English versions.

A detailed description of the human disease (*nega*) called *sara'at* is given in Leviticus 13.1-46. The name has been derived from the Hebrew root *sara'* which means 'prostration'. Driver has suggested that the meaning of the name for the disease may be understood as 'a stroke inflicted by God for a transgression of the Law' and including the experience of prostration produced by the onset of the disease and also the visible consequences in the skin which characterised it.[21] A more recent suggestion by Sawyer is that the name is related to the Hebrew term for a wasp or hornet (sir'ah) on the basis that the skin lesions may resemble those which follow an individual or a multiple wasp sting.[22] However, Driver dismisses this suggestion as philologically unjustified'.[23]

As we have just mentioned, the term sara'at has commonly been translated 'leprosy', but in more recent translations other terms have been used such as 'a leprous disease', (RSV & NRSV), 'a malignant skin disease' (NEB), 'an infectious skin disease' (NIV), 'a virulent skin disease' (REB) and 'a dreaded skin-disease' (GNB).[24] A recent suggestion is that we should use the term 'scale disease' to translate the word sara'at.[25] The number of these names reveals the uncertainty which exists about the nature of the disease.

We may summarise the clinical features of the disease as follows. It is an infectious or contagious disease of human skin. It produces various changes in the skin such as colour changes which may also affect the hair, infiltration or thickening of the skin, and the appearance of scales, spots, pustules or ulcers on the skin surface. The disease may spread in the skin, but may also heal spontaneously. It does not appear to have been fatal, but it could be life-long in duration. This description would cover some features of such diseases as psoriasis, pityriasis versicolor, leucoderma (vitiligo), scleroderma and some forms of ringworm.

There are five individuals in the Old Testament who are described as suffering from sara'at. The first is Moses (Exodus 4.6-7) and the second is Moses' sister Miriam (Numbers 12.10-15). In both cases the lesions are described as white as snow and in both cases they lasted only a short time and then disappeared. We have already noted the suggestion that in the case of Moses the cause was Raynaud's syndrome, but it was described as sara'at. In both these cases the appearance of the condition was a sign to the individuals concerned, the one of God's presence with Moses and the other of his displeasure with Miriam's critical remarks about Moses, her brother. Driver suggests that Miriam may have had some form of dermatitis, but nevertheless he regards these appearances as miraculous (i.e., supernatural) and this seems to be the best solution.[26]

The other cases of sara'at described in the Old Testament are those of Naaman, the commander of the army of Syria, who was cured by bathing seven times in the river Jordan (2 Kings 5.1-14); Gehazi who obtained money and clothing from Naaman under false pretences and was punished by being stricken with Naaman's disease for the rest of his life (2 Kings 5.27); and finally King Azariah (Uzziah) of Judah who was smitten with sara'at for life because of his presumption in burning incense on the altar of incense in the Temple at Jerusalem which was the prerogative of the priests (2 Kings 15.5 and 2 Chronicles 26.16-21).

The most probable conclusion we can draw about the meaning and usage of the Hebrew word sara'at is that it is not a specific term for one disease, such as leprosy, but a generic term covering a whole group of skin diseases which share some common abnormal features.[27] When the term is applied to any of these features or diseases, it is not applied in a medical sense for the purpose of pathological diagnosis but in a ritual sense to decide about the sufferers' ceremonial cleanness or uncleanness which will determine their ability to share in the life and worship of the community.

The important practical point about the disease sara'at is that it was always regarded in the Old Testament as infectious (or contagious). Once the priest had diagnosed the presence of the disease, the levitical legislation required that the affected person must live alone, isolated from other people until pronounced free from the disease (Leviticus 13.46). This regulation applied even to kings, for we find that after King Azariah (Uzziah) was afflicted with sara'at he lived in a separate house from his palace and took no part in the government of the kingdom of Judah, which was taken over by his Jotham as regent (2 Kings 15.5).[28]

Job's disease has sometimes been regarded as leprosy and his condition seen as an example of a prolonged lepra reaction which occurs not infrequently in both of the main forms of leprosy. However, the term sara'at is not used at all in its description and, as we have already mentioned, there are so many and varied symptoms and signs described for the condition from which Job suffered, that it is impossible to identify any one disease which could cause them all.[29] His disease certainly affected the skin for he was covered with painful sores and ulcers from the soles of his feet to the top of his head (Job 2.7). The most recent suggestion for the diagnosis of Job's disease is that it was a case of insulin-independent diabetes mellitus.[30]

The only skin lesions which remain to be mentioned are the boils, for which the word shechin is used as we have already seen earlier in this chapter. One type of this condition is specifically called 'the boil of Egypt' in Deuteronomy 28.27 which presumably is the same as that which formed the sixth plague that God sent on the Egyptians according to Exodus 9.8-11. The condition is described in this passage in Exodus as 'boils that break into blisters upon man and animals' (v.9 Moffatt). The word translated 'blisters' is abauoth which does not occur elsewhere in the Hebrew Old Testament. There have been five suggestions for the identity of the boil of Egypt, namely, smallpox, pemphigus, prickly heat ('Nile blisters'), cutaneous leishmaniasis ('oriental sore') and cutaneous anthrax ('malignant pustule').[31] Of these five possibilities, cutaneous anthrax is the most probable diagnosis. In the sequence of the ten plagues of Egypt it was preceded by the fifth plague which was an outbreak of a fatal infection amongst the domestic livestock of the Egyptians which was probably septicaemic anthrax. It is from contact with infected domestic livestock that human beings are infected. Within a few hours or days of the infection a reddish-brown spot appears at the point of contact and quickly develops a swollen boil-like appearance. As it develops it becomes surrounded by a ring of secondary blisters. After two or three days the centre of the lesion is covered by a thick black scab, the colour of which probably explains its association with the black soot from a furnace used to herald the infection (v.8). The English name for the disease, anthrax, is the Greek word for coal or charcoal.

The other example of a boil is that which affected King Hezekiah of Judah (2 Kings 20.7). Hezekiah's boil was not a simple boil or furuncle for it brought him to the point of death (v.1). It may have been a carbuncle complicated by a staphylococcal septicaemia. Another suggestion is that it was the bubo of bubonic plague and that the infection may have come from the Assyrian army of Sennacherib which had just withdrawn from besieging Jerusalem. On the basis that Hezekiah's boil may have affected his throat and his speech according to Isaiah 38.14, Bartholin in the seventeenth century and more recently Castiglioni have suggested that it was a pharyngeal abscess which ruptured spontaneously on the third day (2 Kings 20.5).[32] This seems unlikely from the evidence provided by this verse. The most probable diagnosis in Hezekiah's case is that it was a carbuncle, which is essentially composed of a cluster of simple boils most commonly occurring on the nape of the neck. The name itself means 'a small coal' in Latin referring to the dark colour and the increased temperature over the area of skin covering the carbuncle before it breaks down and discharges its purulent contents.

The account of Hezekiah's boil includes one of the rare references to medical treatment that we have in the Old Testament. After Hezekiah's fervent prayer for his recovery, his attendants were told by the prophet Isaiah to prepare a poultice of figs and apply it to the boil with the result that the king recovered (2 Kings 20.7).[33]

## Sexually transmitted disease

The sexually transmitted disease gonorrhoea appears to be referred to in Leviticus 15.1-15. It speaks of a 'discharge' ('issue' in AV) from the *basar* of a man (v.2). As we saw in the Chapter One this word usually means 'flesh', but on occasion it can mean the male sexual organ or penis (See Genesis 17.14; Exodus 28.42; Leviticus 6.10; 16.4; Ezekiel 23.20 and 44.7).[34] The LXX translated the word 'discharge' by *gonorrhues* which is the origin of the English term gonorrhoea and means a discharge of *gonos*, a word which means 'seed' or 'sperm'. This Greek phrase would more accurately describe the normal male nocturnal emission of semen or its ejaculation during sexual intercourse when the discharge or ejaculate does consist of sperm. However, these are described separately later in the chapter (vv. 16-18) and give rise to a lesser degree of ritual uncleanness than gonorrhoea does. Therefore the reference in the earlier part of the chapter is most probably to the purulent discharge of gonorrhoea in the male.[35]

The occurrence of gonorrhoea in the female is briefly recognised by the use of the phrase 'a woman with a discharge' (v.33). This discharge is distinguished from the blood of normal menstruation (v.19) and from abnormal bleeding either beyond the normal menstrual period as in menorrhagia or in between normal periods which is called metrorrhagia (v.25). The menstrual blood is described as coming from the *basar* which in this case must mean the female vagina (v.19).

As we mentioned in the previous chapter, there is no evidence from the Bible or from archaeology for the existence of syphilis in Palestine in Biblical times. The widely-accepted view is that syphilis only arrived in the Old World with the sailors of Columbus when they returned from the New World in 1493.[36] At first the type of the disease was non-venereal and spread by skin contact. Soon it changed its character and became a virulent infection spread by sexual contact. However when it arrived in the Near East it reverted to its original non-venereal type which became known as *bejel* an endemic disease amongst the Arab population of Palestine until recent years. Both types of the disease produce characteristic changes in the bones of those afflicted with them and no skeletons have been found with these changes which date from before the Turkish period in the history of Palestine (1516-1917 AD).[37]

## Mental disease

The Old Testament has little to say explicitly about mental disease. We have already commented on the reference to mental disorders in Deuteronomy 28.28 where these are included amongst the possible consequences of the disobedience of God's commands and decrees. However, people appear to have been familiar with the manifestations of mental disease so that David knew how to feign madness in order to escape from Achish, the king of Gath. Four such manifestations in David's behaviour are described in 1 Samuel 21.13. A display of a lack of understanding of his situation shown by abnormal social behaviour and inappropriate responses meant to suggest that he was out of his mind; a violent reaction to being manhandled in order to control his outbursts of violence; making marks (Hebrew) or drumming with his fists (LXX) on the palace doors; finally, drooling or letting his saliva run out of his mouth and down his beard.[38] Achish knew that these manifestations were those of madness (v.14) and so we may conclude that mental disease was not unknown in the Old Testament world.

Kinnier-Wilson, a Cambridge orientalist, suggested that there were references in the Psalms which might indicate that their authors suffered from mental disease. For instance, he attributed Psalm 35 to an author who was a schizophrenic and Psalm 38 to one who suffered from a depressive psychosis.[39] He also thought that the disease which afflicted Job was schizophrenia.[40] These suggestions are quite speculative and without foundation in the texts they claim to elucidate.

There are, however, two examples of mental illness to be found in the Old Testament. The first is that of Saul, the first king of Israel, who appears to have suffered from a manic-depressive psychosis, now called a bipolar affective disorder. He had periods of intense depression which are attributed to possession by an evil spirit (1 Samuel 16.14-15). These periods alternated with occasional outbreaks of mania characterised by paranoia and homicidal violence. He showed intense hatred and jealousy of David (1 Samuel 18.12) and believed that David was bent on harming him (1 Samuel 24.9). Saul attempted to kill him personally twice (1 Samuel 18.10-11 and 19.9-10) and tried to arrange his death on two other occasions (1 Samuel 18.25 and 19.11). On a later occasion, Saul tried to kill his own son Jonathan because of the latter's loyalty to David. He even murdered Ahimelech the high priest of Israel and eighty-five priests for the same reason (1 Samuel 22.11-19).

In the case of Saul, we have the only reference to any form of treatment of mental disease in the Old Testament. The servants of Saul recommended that when a fit of depression came upon him, he should call for someone to play the harp (or lyre) to him and this would make him feel better (1 Samuel 16.16). One of his servants recommended David, the son of Jesse of Bethlehem, as a harpist and Saul took him on to his staff as harpist and one of his armour-bearers. The result was that whenever a fit of depression came upon Saul, David would take his harp and play with the result that relief would come to Saul and he would feel better (v.23). This must be one of the earliest references to music therapy in ancient literature. However, David's involvement in this music therapy for Saul, did not have very pleasant consequences for the therapist, as we have seen in the previous paragraph.

Another interesting feature in this case is that Saul's periodic mental disorder is attributed to 'an evil spirit from God' (1 Samuel 16.14-16). This is the only example in the Old Testament of a disease being attributed to an evil spiritual agency, with the exception of the case of Job where his disease is attributed to the action of Satan the Adversary (Job 2.7). In the case of Job it was physical while in the case of Saul it was mental disease. This rare mention of an evil spirit in relation to disease is in marked contrast to the numerous references to disease and its treatment in the ancient literature of the lands surrounding Israel, where most diseases were attributed to the activity of evil demons and were often treated by 'ritualistic incantations or exorcism-related manipulations'.[41]

The second case of mental illness recorded in the Old Testament is that of Nebuchadnezzar, the king of Babylon. His pride in his achievement in building the city of Babylon went to his head and brought upon him the judgement of God. For a period of seven years he suffered from a severe mental illness (Daniel 4.29-32). This illness was characterised by rapid onset, mental depression, neglect of personal hygiene and abnormal social behaviour. These features were combined with the rare delusional state known as boanthropy in which persons believe themselves to be an ox (*bous* in Greek) and actually live and eat like one. The result was that the king was relieved of his royal duties and driven away from human society to live with wild animals in the open countryside where he ate grass like the cattle (Daniel 4.33). After seven years ('seven times' in v.32) he recovered spontaneously and his kingdom was restored to him (v.36). After his recovery, he appears to have had complete insight into what had happened (vv.34-37). This apparently complete recovery excludes the presence of organic brain disease and so we must seek a psychiatric diagnosis for his disease. The various suggestions which have been proposed for this include a depressive psychosis, paranoid schizophrenia or hysterical dissociation. However, whatever the diagnosis may have been, the account in Daniel makes it clear that there was a large spiritual contribution to the causation of the king's condition in addition to any psychological element which may have been present.[42]

## THE HOW AND THE WHY

In our discussion of the epidemic and systemic diseases which are described in the Old Testament, we have endeavoured as far as possible to identify their nature in terms of modern medical knowledge and experience. This procedure is sometimes accused of being naturalistic or rationalistic, of explaining events or phenomena which are supernatural in causation, character or purpose, in purely natural terms.

However, such an accusation is based on a misunderstanding of the function and competence of science in general and medicine in particular. The role of science is to describe 'how' phenomena may occur, not 'why' they occur. It describes their mechanism and behaviour, but not their meaning or purpose. To explain these, we have to invoke a discipline other than science which, although it may not be able to describe how the phenomena in question may occur as science may be able to do, is able nevertheless to explain why they occur, and more specifically why they occur at a particular time, in a particular place and to a particular person or people.

This is why when the Old Testament describes the occurrence of disease in individuals or in the general population of Israel, it is not satisfied simply with giving a description of what occurred, but goes on to explain the meaning and purpose behind the occurrence. The experience of Job is a good example of this in the case of an individual, while the appearance of epidemic diseases amongst the people of Israel during their desert journey provides numerous examples from their experience.

In its explanation of the meaning and purpose which lie behind the human experience of disease, the Old Testament is concerned to make two essential points. The first is that God is in control of all natural phenomena whatever their character may be. The second is that he can use the occurrence and effect of those natural phenomena in the training and discipline of his people.

# Chapter 5
# HEALING IN THE OLD TESTAMENT

In previous chapters we have considered the concept of health as we found it in the Old Testament and then sought to identify some of the diseases recorded there. We now turn to the concept of healing or the restoration of health where this has been lost or impaired.

## THE WORDS USED FOR HEALING

A number of different words are translated 'healing' in the Hebrew Old Testament. Most of them contain the idea of the restoration of something to its previously normal state, or the removal of something which is causing ill-health or an abnormal condition.

When we considered the concept of health in the Old Testament in our first chapter we found that there was one word which more than any other enshrined that concept, and that was the word *shalom*. When we come to examine the concept of healing we find that there is one word root which acts in a similar way, and that is the root *rapha* which Brown describes as 'central to the Old Testament language of healing'.[1] The various noun and verb derivatives of this root occur eighty-six times in the Hebrew text. However, while there is no doubt that this root means 'to heal', there is some doubt about its basic meaning.

The older view is that this basic meaning was 'to stitch together', and that the application of the root to healing came from the action of stitching the edges of wounds together to restore skin continuity and so promote healing. The term *rophe* comes from this root to denote a physician (Genesis 50.2; Exodus 15.26; 2 Chronicles 16.12; Job 13.4; Jeremiah 8.22) and so meant 'one who stitches together', which today would describe a surgeon. However, there is no evidence that a separate specialty of surgery existed in Israel in ancient times. Even in Rabbinic times every physician was a general practitioner.[2]

The newer view is that the primary meaning of the root is 'to restore, make whole', and 'to heal' is to be regarded as an important secondary meaning which is nevertheless prominent in Old Testament usage.[3] This view makes it easier to understand why, although people are usually the subject of the healing as in Genesis 20.17; Exodus 21.19 and 2 Chronicles 30.20, the word may also be used of the repair of broken objects (1 Kings

18.30; Jeremiah 19.11), the purification of water (2 Kings 2.22; Ezekiel 47.8-9) and the rehabilitation of a devastated and plague-stricken land (2 Chronicles 7.13-14). The meaning common to all these descriptions is that of restoration, of which one application is to the healing of sickness which restores the state of a person to that of health.

Most of the other words used for healing in the Old Testament are used only infrequently, and do not add much to the concept of healing found there. However, there are one or two interesting words which should mentioned. The first is *aruka* whose root *arak* means 'to be long', almost always referring to time.[4] It is used of healing in Isaiah 58.8; Jeremiah 8.22; 30.17; 33.6). The connection with healing may be because *aruka* also denotes the 'proud flesh' or granulation tissue which covers the surface of an open wound during the process of healing.[5] The appearance of this tissue means that the wound will take a much longer time to heal than a narrow incised wound, and this fact may explain the application of this word to healing. The second word which is worth noting is *chabash* which means 'to bind or to bandage' and refers to the healing which is promoted by the covering and bandaging of wounds (See Isaiah 1.6; 30.26; Ezekiel 39.21; Hosea 6.1).

All these words presuppose a state of ill-health and may also be used figuratively for the restoration of Israel to God's favour after a period of declension. Whilst these words are usually used to describe healing, they are also used occasionally for the health which is the result of healing.

## 'I AM THE LORD YOUR HEALER'

The verse which is the foundation of the Old Testament theology of healing is Exodus 15.26 which Karl Barth called 'the divine Magna Carta in all matters of health and all related questions'.[6] This verse records what the Lord said to the people of Israel in the Desert of Shur:

> If you listen carefully to the voice of the Lord your God and do what is right in his eyes, if you pay attention to his commands and keep all his decrees, I will not bring on you any of the diseases I brought on the Egyptians, for I am the Lord who heals you (NIV).

This last clause translates one of the covenant names of the God of Israel, *Yahweh-Rephucha*, 'The Lord your Healer'.

The people of Israel had just been delivered from Egypt and were about to begin their desert wanderings. They had left the shores of the Red Sea and marched for three days into the Desert of Shur or Etham (Numbers 23.8). They had failed to find water until they arrived at Marah where they found water, only to discover it was brackish and undrinkable. This fact gave the place its Hebrew name, for the name Marah means 'bitter'. The Lord showed Moses a certain kind of tree which when cut down and thrown into the water made it drinkable.

Following this experience at Marah, the Lord took the opportunity to issue his first decree to the Israelites now that they had left Egypt and to remind them of their obligation to obey his commands and keep his decrees. To this he added the promise that if they did this, he would not inflict on them any of the diseases he had inflicted on the Egyptians during their captivity in Egypt. As they heard this, the people would remember that at least one of the ten plagues of Egypt had rendered the water of the Nile undrinkable, namely, when it was turned into blood (Exodus 7.18). Also they had just seen how the Lord had 'healed' the brackish water and made it sweet so that they could drink it (cp. 2 Kings 2.21-22). He had already become their healer.

There are five points to be noted about this promise to keep the people of Israel healthy which the Lord made at Marah. First of all, it was conditional upon their obedience to his commands and statutes and not an absolute promise to keep them healthy at all times and in all situations. As we suggested in Chapter One, obedience is part of health and disobedience produces ill-health. Secondly, the promise is of the prevention of disease and not of its healing. If the people are obedient then they will not be afflicted with certain diseases, with the corollary that if they are not obedient they will suffer from these diseases. Thirdly, these diseases are specified as those which were suffered by the Egyptians before they let the Israelites leave Egypt. Fourthly, this promise implies that the Lord can and does afflict people with disease. Finally, the people are assured that if they do suffer disease, the Lord is able to heal them.

These points raise the question of the meaning and modern relevance of the promise that the Lord would be the healer of his people. It is important to notice that this promise was given after the purification of the water at Marah and before the test of obedience had been laid down (Exodus 15.25b). This suggests that not all the Lord's healing was related to obedience. In fact, the healing of the water at Marah was the result of the grumbling of the Israelites that the water there was undrinkable (Exodus 15.24) and no question of obedience was involved. It was, nevertheless, the first example of healing that the Lord had given to his people.

However, there is no doubt that the primary intention of this promise is the prevention of ill-health. This is made even more explicit in the later promise in Deuteronomy 7.15 where Moses says to the people of Israel that if they will follow the commands, decrees and laws of the Lord their God, 'the Lord will keep you free from every disease' (NIV). The best way for them to keep healthy is to obey the commands and statutes of the Lord and we know that many of these statutes are designed to promote and maintain health (Proverbs 3.7-8; 4.22).

The Jewish physician Sussman Muntner estimated that 'of the 613 biblical commands and prohibitions, no less than 213 are health rules imposed in the form of rigorously observed ceremonial rites'.[7] Nevertheless we know also that when his people became ill whether through disobedience or not, the Lord did heal them (Psalm 30.2; 103.3; 107.19-20; 147.3; 2 Kings 20.5). However, although he might heal all their diseases, he did not necessarily remove their consequences for we read of the presence of those who were blind, deaf and lame amongst the people of Israel (Leviticus 19.14; 21.18); conditions which were presumably the result of disease or injury. There are no examples of the healing of any of these conditions in the Old Testament (cp. John 9.32); nor are there any instances in which the effects of growing old were reversed.

Martin Luther in his translation of the Bible into German rendered the clause which we have used at the heading of this section as *'Ich bin der Herr, dein Artz'* ('I am the Lord, your physician'). Similarly in her translation of the Old Testament into English, Miss Helen Spurrell rendered it 'I am Jehovah, thy physician'.[8] Meek who translated the book of Exodus in the American Translation of Smith and Goodspeed made God say 'I, the LORD, make you immune to them' (i.e. to the diseases which I inflicted on the Egyptians).[9]

In view of what we have seen above as the primary meaning of *rapha* as restoration and the Old Testament usage of the word and its derivatives, it is better not to restrict its meaning only to that of the healing of sickness, but to take references to the Lord as Israel's *rophe* or healer 'in the broadest possible sense' covering the restoration to normality of the conditions and situations which the Israelites were to meet.[10] Nevertheless, an important area in which they would experience God's restoration to normality was that of health and disease.

The claim of the Lord to be the healer of his people is sometimes taken today to mean that they would have no need of human physicians and their treatment of disease and sickness. However, it is more appropriate to understand the contrast to be, not between Israel's own divine healer and human physicians, but between Israel's God and the healing deities of other nations such as Egypt and Canaan. It is in opposition to the claims for these foreign deities that the Lord asserts that he is the real healer of his people.[11] In contrast to these other deities, the Lord was never sick himself as they could be. The gods of Egypt, like men, could suffer from disease. When an eclipse of the sun occurred in Egypt it was attributed to an eye disease of the god Ra. This same god nearly died after being stung in his heel by a scorpion.[12] These things could never happen to the God of Israel. He was always healthy and was the healer of his people.

## AGENTS OF HEALING IN THE OLD TESTAMENT

While the Old Testament has no doubt that all healing comes from God as the primary source there are very few cases described there in which we are told that God healed directly. These cases include those of infertility recorded in the book of Genesis where the women have been unable to conceive. These concern Sarah (Genesis 18.11-14; 21.1-2), the women of Abimelech's household (Genesis 20.17-18), Rebekah (Genesis 25.21) and Rachel (Genesis 30.22-23). Dickinson notes that three out of these four cases were rendered fertile in response to prayer.[13] Infertility, of course, is a symptom and not a disease. It may have many causes, but in none of these cases are we told the actual physical cause.

In general, then, healing in the Old Testament is provided or mediated by secondary sources. It is interesting to note that these sources do not include priests, although in Egypt priests were often practising physicians able to examine and treat sick people. By contrast, in Israel the priests were 'the custodians of public health'.[14] They were diagnosticians of ritually unclean conditions and situations, but were not expected to treat or remove them.

Much of the healing which occurred in Israel must have come about by the operation of the natural healing and defensive processes of the body and mind, and the practices of 'folk-medicine' based on these processes. In addition, however, there are references in the Old Testament to healing mediated through two classes of people; these are the physicians and the prophets.

## Healing by physicians

Physicians are not prominent in the Old Testament. Their existence is acknowledged or implied, and their activity and worth are not denied. This is in marked contrast to what we know of physicians and their status and practice in Egypt and Mesopotamia. In Israel, physicians are much more prominent in post-Biblical times and what we know of them then may reflect something of their place in the society of the later Old Testament times. In Talmudic times there was a physician in every town and scholars were advised by the Talmud not to live in a place where there was no physician.[15] The staff of the Temple at Jerusalem included an officer named Ben Ahijah who was responsible for the treatment of the bowel sickness of the priests to which they were said to be susceptible because of their going about barefoot, their frequent bathing and their abundant diet of meat.[16]

As we have already mentioned, the Hebrew name for a physician is *rophe* which comes from the root *rapha*, 'to restore', and this name occurs nine times in the Old Testament. Physicians appear first as the embalmers of the body of Jacob in preparation for its eventual transfer to Canaan and burial there (Genesis 50.2, where the LXX translates the name as 'grave-diggers'). Their final mention is when the prophet Jeremiah enquires about their presence in Gilead (Jeremiah 8.22).

There are several references in the prophetic literature of the Old Testament which appear to describe the practice of physicians. In Isaiah 1.6

the medical treatment of wounds and ulcers is given as cleansing, dressing and soothing with oil, and bandaging (cp. Isaiah 30.26; Jeremiah 6.14; Hosea 6.1). A special healing balm is used for healing wounds and soothing their pain, of which that prepared in Gilead from an aromatic resin is specially mentioned along with the presence of physicians there (Jeremiah 8.22; 46.11; 51.8). Fractures of bones were bound up with bandages and where necessary splinted. In the case of fractures of the upper limb the clinical criterion of their sound union was the ability to hold and use a sword (Ezekiel 30.21). The duties of the physician are summarised in Ezekiel 34.4 as the strengthening of the weak, the healing of the sick and the bandaging of wounds.

The Rabbis found the specific mandate for the practice of healing by physicians in the interpretation of two verses of the Law (Torah). These were Exodus 21.19 and Leviticus 19.16. The former verse refers to a person who has been wounded in a quarrel with another and has to take to his bed until he is thoroughly healed and is able to return to work. His assailant must then pay compensation for the loss of his time from work and the physician's fee for his services. This verse is therefore taken to imply the obligation of a person suffering from a wound or a disease to seek treatment, and the divine authority for the physician to provide treatment.[17] The second part of the latter verse from Leviticus, according to the Talmud, consists of the command, 'Thou shalt not stand idly by the blood of thy neighbour'. This is interpreted as meaning that anyone who is able to save a life is obliged to do so and since saving life is pre-eminently the work of physicians this verse too is taken to be a divine mandate for their work of healing.[18]

It is sometimes suggested that physicians were not held in high regard in Israel. Job certainly called his friends 'worthless physicians' (Job 13.4), but this need not mean that all physicians were worthless and incompetent, only that his friends were like some physicians trying to treat a condition of which they had no knowledge or experience. The other reference to physicians in the Old Testament which is said to portray them in an unfavourable light is 2 Chronicles 16.12. Here we are told that Asa, the king of Judah, suffered from advanced senile gangrene of his feet and 'did not seek help from the Lord, but only from the physicians' (NIV). This need not be a condemnation of the physicians, but only of Asa. He was acting medically as he had acted before militarily, when he had relied on the help of Ben-Hadad, king of Aram (Syria), rather than on that of the Lord in his campaign against Israel (vv.2-3). On that occasion Hanani the seer had denounced him for his reliance on human rather than divine help (vv.7-9). When at the end of his life he became severely ill, Asa was acting true to form by relying on human help rather than divine. It was no condemnation of the physicians that the king preferred their help to that of the Lord his God.[19]

An indication of the status of the physician in later Jewish society is given in the apocryphal book of Ecclesiasticus which dates from the second century BC. Its author was Jesus ben Sirach, a professional scholar and scribe who lived in Jerusalem (50.27). In the course of his book he describes what the Jewish attitude towards the physician should be in the following terms:

Give doctors the honour they deserve,
for the Lord gave them their work to do.
Their skill came from the Most High,
and kings reward them for it.
Their knowledge gives them a position of importance,
and powerful people hold them in high regard.

(Ecclesiasticus 38.1-3 GNB)

This passage summarises the Biblical view of the place and activity of the physician, namely that he was only the agent of healing for he derived his knowledge and skill from God, the true healer of his people.

## Healing by prophets

There are some references to the involvement of prophets in healing either by way of giving advice or by carrying out healing procedures. As Macalister suggests, these references appear to indicate that the sick who required medical aid usually applied to the prophets rather than the physicians.[20] However, the references are so few and incidental that it is difficult to be certain that they describe a common custom.

Examples of healing which follows prophetic advice include Elisha's advice to Naaman the Syrian army commander to wash in the River Jordan which led to the cure of his *sara'at* (2 Kings 5.1-14). Naaman was disappointed and angry at this mundane advice for he had expected the prophet to perform a dramatic ritual in which he called on the name of his God and waved his hand over the spot so that his disease disappeared. At first he refused to co-operate (vv.11-12). However, once his servants had persuaded him to accept the prophet's advice about treatment, he was cured of his *sara'at*. When he reported back to Elisha to pay his fee, the prophet refused to accept any payment and simply told Naaman, 'Go in *shalom*' (v.19).

Another example of healing which followed a prophet's advice is the application of a fig poultice to Hezekiah's boil by his attendants on the advice of Isaiah which we have already mentioned in Chapter Four (2 Kings 20.7; Isaiah 38.21). As we noted then, this was combined with earnest prayer by the patient that he might recover.

Sometimes this advice included the giving of a prognosis in particular diseases or situations. The prophet Nathan told King David that the child born to him and Bathsheba would fall ill and die (2 Samuel 12.14-23). The prophet Ahijah told the wife of King Jeroboam I of Israel that their young son Abijah would die as soon as she returned home and that he would be the only male of Jeroboam's family who would not meet a violent end (1 Kings 14.12-13). After King Ahaziah's fall from an upstairs window of his palace in Samaria, he sent messengers to the god of Ekron to know if he would recover, but Elijah met them and turned them back saying that the king would not recover but would die in his bed (2 Kings 1.1-4, 16-17). All these prognoses were given verbally, but on one occasion a prognosis was sent by letter when the prophet Elijah wrote a letter to King Jehoram of Judah foretelling the occurrence of the plague or slaughter which would come upon his people and the bowel illness which would afflict the king himself (2 Chronicles 21.12-15).

The knowledge that the prophets of Israel were skilled in the prognosis and treatment of disease appears to have spread beyond the borders of that land. We have already seen how Naaman came from Syria seeking the cure of his skin disease. We read later of how when Ben-Hadad I, king of Syria, was ill he sent Hazael, one of his royal officials, to the prophet Elisha who was visiting his capital Damascus, to know if he would recover. The prophet replied that he would not die from his illness, but by the hand of an assassin. That assassin was to be Hazael himself who on the day after he had reported part of Elisha's prognosis to the king, laid a thick cloth soaked in water over his face and smothered him. He then became king in his stead (2 Kings 8.7-15).

The cases where actual treatment was carried out by prophets include the artificial cardio-respiratory resuscitation carried out by Elijah on the widow's son (1 Kings 17.21) and Elisha on the Shunammite boy (2 Kings 4.34-35). In the latter case, Wiseman points out that there was a significantly long interval between the boy's death and his return to life, so that this may be a case of answered prayer and resurrection rather than a successful resuscitation.[21]

The prophets may also have had special knowledge of poisonous plants and their antidotes. An example of this is Elisha in 2 Kings 4.38-41. After he had restored the Shunammite boy to life Elisha returned to Gilgal and told his servant to prepare a stew to feed the students of the prophetic school there. One of the students went out and gathered the little yellow bitter apples of the wild vine *Citrullus colocyntis* which he sliced into the stew. These apples contain the alkaloid *colocynth* which has a drastic purgative action and may be fatal if taken in quantity. The bitter taste of the stew alerted the students to its poisonous content and they reported this to Elisha who put some flour into the pot of stew to neutralise its poisonous effect.[22]

Elisha was also able to purify the perennial spring at Jericho whose water was unwholesome causing death and the land to be unproductive by adding salt to it (2 Kings 2.19-22). As the record says, the Lord healed the water, but it was Elisha who put the salt into the spring. Various causes have been suggested for the unwholesomeness of the water such as radioactivity and the presence of the snails which convey schistosomiasis but these are only guesses.[23] It seems unlikely that schistosomiasis was the cause for the snails require sluggish or slow-moving water to live in and the disease does not affect the soil.

In all their healing activity, the prophets insist that all healing comes from God and that they are only his agents. They look forward to a future time of restoration when none in Zion shall be able to say, 'I am sick' and there will be none whose sins have not been forgiven (Isaiah 33.24).

## THOSE WHO WERE NOT HEALED

Four individuals are named in the Old Testament as being in need of healing and yet were not healed. In addition, there must have been many who are not named and who suffered from disease and injury and even died from their effects without finding healing. This is a problem we shall meet again in the New Testament where, for example, one man was healed at the Pool of Bethesda and many more were left unhealed (John 5.1-9).

We have already mentioned Abijah, the son of Jereboam I, the first king of the northern kingdom of Israel, as the subject of a prognosis by the prophet Ahijah. He is also an example of one who was not healed of his sickness. We are given no details of this sickness, but his father appears to have thought it might be fatal, and so it proved to be. Ahijah made no attempt to heal him and he died as soon as his mother returned home from consulting the prophet (1 Kings 14.17). He had told her that the boy would die from his sickness so that he might escape the violent fate which would overtake the rest of his family at the hands of the usurper Baasha (1 Kings 15.29).

Ahaziah was the eighth king of Israel and he fell through an upper floor window of his palace in Samaria and was bedridden from his injuries (2 Kings 1.2). He sent messengers to consult the Canaanite god of Ekron, but Elijah turned them back and told them to tell the king that he would certainly die because he worshipped the god of Ekron and had sought help from that god and not from the God of Israel (v.16).

Gehazi was the personal servant of the prophet Elisha who was present when Naaman the Syrian general returned to thank Elisha after he had been healed by bathing in the River Jordan. When his master refused to accept any gift from Naaman for his healing, Gehazi went after him and by false pretences obtained money and clothes from him. As a punishment for his greed and deceit Elisha said that Naaman's disease of *sara'at* would never depart from him or his descendants for ever (2 Kings 5.27). He would never be healed.

The fourth person who was not healed was Azariah (or Uzziah), the tenth king of Judah. After a long and prosperous reign he became very powerful and proud and on one occasion tried to usurp the function of a priest by offering incense on the altar of incense in the Temple. His namesake Azariah the chief priest and eighty priests remonstrated with him and he became very angry until the signs of *sara'at* appeared on his forehead which made the priests rush him out of the Temple into isolation (2 Chronicles 26.19-29). Azariah was afflicted with *sara'at* and isolated until the day of his death without any attempt being made to heal him.

The reason why none of these four cases was healed was sin. In the first two cases it was the sin of their family or dynasty which had caused the people to sin by leading them away from the true worship of the God of Israel. In the second two it was personal sin either of covetousness or pride. In each case their sickness was part of their punishment and could not be healed.

There is a final episode where an attempt at healing failed at first, but was successful later. It was the case of the Shunammite boy in 2 Kings 4.29-35. The long-desired and precious son had died and his mother in her distress sought Elisha's help. As Wiseman puts it, 'she had lost her child but not her faith'.[24] Gehazi tried to push her away from the prophet but she would not be deterred. Elisha gave Gehazi his staff and told him to go ahead quickly and lay it on the boy's face to revive him. Gehazi failed to revive him with the staff and so Elisha found the boy dead on the bed when he arrived. Elisha prayed and where Gehazi had failed, he was successful in reviving the boy.

# PART THREE

## HEALING IN THE GOSPELS

*THE STUDIES which form Part Three of this volume are concerned with healing in the four gospels. In Part One of the book we considered the Biblical concepts and principles of health. In the gospels we have these concepts and principles expressed in practice as we have described for us the healing activity of Jesus.*

In his book The Mission and Expansion of Christianity, *Adolf Harnack declared that 'Jesus appeared amongst his people as a physician'. Harnack quoted the saying of Jesus that those who are well have no need of a physician, but those who are sick, as recorded in Mark 2.17 and Luke 5.31, to support his statement. He then went on to say that 'the first three gospels depict him as the physician of soul and body'.[1] Whilst this is true, it is interesting to note that he is never called a physician (iatros) in the New Testament, although the verb iaomai from which this Greek word for physician is derived is frequently used of his healing activity.*

*The first author to call Jesus a physician was Ignatius of Antioch (AD 35-107). He wrote a letter to the Church at Ephesus before he was martyred in which he said there was only one physician, namely Jesus Christ our Lord.[2] It is to be noted, however, that the reference here is metaphorical for those who were to be cured (therapeuo) were afflicted with heresy and not with disease of the body or mind. Clement of Alexandria (AD 150-215) in the opening Book of his* Paedagogus *(The Teacher) has several references to Jesus as the physician who heals suffering and here the reference is to the healing of the body and the soul.[3] Clement calls him 'the all-sufficient (panakes) physician of humanity'.[4] There are other occasional references to Jesus as a physician in early Christian literature, but it was Origen (AD 185-254) who more frequently and more fully than anyone else spoke of Jesus as the physician, and in his work* Contra Celsum *called him 'the good physician'.[5] In his enthusiasm, Origen in another place went so far as to say that Jesus was called a physician in the Holy Scriptures,[6] which as we have already seen is not strictly correct. Finally, Eusebius of Caesarea (AD 260-340) spoke of Jesus as 'like some excellent physician' in his panegyric addressed to Paulinus, the bishop of Tyre.[7]*

*Although Jesus may not have been given the name of physician in the New Testament, there is no doubt that he is described there as carrying out the work of a physician and healing men and women of disease. It is to a consideration of this work in the four gospels that we now turn.*

# Chapter 6
# THE RECORDS OF HEALING

Even a cursory examination of the four gospels will reveal how frequently the healing activity of Jesus is described there. So we begin our study of the records of his healing activity by examining the amount of space the authors of the gospels give to describing it. Then we seek to classify the accounts in these records according to the diseases which Jesus healed.

## THE SPACE DEVOTED TO HEALING

We can measure the space the gospels devote to the healing activity of Jesus by the number of verses they each use to describe it. By its very nature this measure cannot be exact, for the verses vary in length and sometimes we are not sure how many of the verses in a particular passage should be included. However, it is sufficiently approximate for our present purpose.

If we take the text of the gospels in the AV and count first the total number of verses in each, and then the total number of verses devoted to healing, we obtain the following results:

| Gospel | Matthew | Mark | Luke | John |
|---|---|---|---|---|
| Total verses | 1058 | 678 | 1149 | 879 |
| Verses on healing | 99 | 139 | 134 | 112 |
| Percentage | 9% | 20% | 12% | 13% |

This comparison is a very crude one and takes no account of the nature of the contents of the four gospels. An obvious and relevant division of these contents is into narrative and discourse which describe events and record oral teaching respectively. If we now examine the relative proportion of space given to these in each gospel we obtain the following results:

| Gospel | Matthew | Mark | Luke | John |
|---|---|---|---|---|
| *Narrative:* | | | | |
| Total verses | 267 | 339 | 339 | 312 |
| Percentage | 25% | 50% | 34% | 36% |
| *Discourse:* | | | | |
| Total verses | 801 | 339 | 810 | 567 |
| Percentage | 75% | 50% | 66% | 64% |

The description of the healing miracles of Jesus belongs to the narrative portion of the content of the gospels, and so we shall obtain a truer picture of the amount of space given by each gospel to healing if we now compare the amount of the narrative portion they each contain with the amount taken up by the accounts of the healing activities of Jesus.

| Gospel | Matthew | Mark | Luke | John |
|---|---|---|---|---|
| Total narrative | 267 | 339 | 339 | 312 |
| Healing narrative | 99 | 139 | 134 | 112 |
| Percentage | 40% | 40% | 35% | 33% |

These statistics are by no means exact and can only be rough indicators of significance, but they are nevertheless of great interest for they show how relatively constant is the amount of narrative space which is devoted to healing in each gospel. This means that all four of the gospel writers regard the healing activity of Jesus as an important part of his ministry and give it a significant amount of space in their narrative.

When we review modern New Testament studies in the light of these statistics, we find that such a review does not usually reveal a corresponding degree of recognition of the importance of the healing activity of Jesus as is found in the New Testament. The emphasis in almost all these studies is on Jesus the Teacher and his teaching, and very rarely on Jesus the Healer and his miracles of healing. Where his healing activity is referred to, it is in terms of teaching rather than healing. His healing miracles are regarded solely as illustrations of his teaching about the power and coming of the kingdom of God and not as examples of that kingdom actually breaking into history in all its healing power.[1] The result is an unbalanced picture of the ministry of Jesus which compares unfavourably with that which is presented in the gospels. Much of this lack of balance arises from a reluctance to recognise the undoubted presence of an important supernatural element in the gospel accounts of Jesus. Even where the historicity of the healing miracles is accepted, there is still a tendency to try to explain them in naturalistic terms rather than admit their supernatural character.[2]

## THE NARRATIVES OF HEALING

The narratives of healing in the gospels can be divided into two main categories. There are those which describe the healing of an individual sick person, or more rarely of two or more, in a variable amount of detail, and there are those which refer usually only briefly to the healing by Jesus of a group of people suffering from some disease or demon possession.

## The Accounts of the Healing of Individuals

The accounts of the healing of the sick or possessed individuals in which some clinical detail of the disease and its healing is given may be further classified into three distinct groups according to the clinical condition and the nature of its healing. These groups include examples of physical healing, the exorcism of demons, and the raising of the dead. The groups may be classified as follows in accordance with their occurrence in the four gospels.

| I. Accounts of physical healing | Matthew | Mark | Luke | John |
|---|---|---|---|---|
| A. *In one gospel only* | | | | |
| 1. The two blind men | 9.27-31 | | | |
| 2. The deaf mute | | 7.31-37 | | |
| 3. The blind man of Bethsaida | | 8.22-26 | | |
| 4. The woman with a spirit of weakness | | | 13.11-17 | |
| 5. The man with dropsy | | | 14.1-6 | |
| 6. The ten leprosy patients | | | 17.11-19 | |
| 7. The ear of Malchus | | | 22.50-51 | |
| 8. The nobleman's son | | | | 4.46-54 |
| 9. The Bethesda paralytic | | | | 5.1-16 |
| 10. The man born blind | | | | 9.1-41 |
| B. *In two gospels only* | 8.5-13 | | | |
| 11. The centurion's servant | | | 7.1-10 | |
| C. *In three gospels* (listed in the Markan order) | | | | |
| 12. Peter's mother-in-law | 8.14-15 | 1.30-31 | 4.38-39 | |
| 13. The man full of leprosy | 8.1-4 | 1.40-45 | 5.12-15 | |
| 14. The paralysed man | 9.1-8 | 2.1-12 | 5.18-26 | |
| 15. The man with the withered hand | 12.10-13 | 3.1-6 | 6.6-11 | |
| 16. The woman with the flow of blood | 9.20-22 | 5.25-34 | 8.43-48 | |
| 17. Blind Bartimaeus | 20.29-34 | 10.46-52 | 18.35-43 | |

| II. Accounts of the exorcism of demons | Matthew | Mark | Luke | John |
|---|---|---|---|---|
| **A.** *In one gospel only* | | | | |
| 1.The dumb demoniac | 9.32-34 | | | |
| **B.** *In two gospels only* | | | | |
| 2.The blind and dumb demoniac | 12.22-24 | | 11.14-16 | |
| 3.The synagogue demoniac | | 1.21-28 | 4.31-37 | |
| 4.The Syrophoenician girl | 15.22-28 | 7.24-30 | | |
| **C.** *In three gospels* | | | | |
| 5.The Gadarene demoniac | 8.28-34 | 5.1-20 | 8.26-39 | |
| 6.The epileptic boy | 17.14-21 | 9.14-29 | 9.37-43 | |
| **III. Accounts of raising the dead** | | | | |
| **A.** *In one gospel only* | | | | |
| 1.The widow's son at Nain | | | 7.11-18 | |
| 2.Lazarus | | | | 11.1-46 |
| **B.** *In three gospels* | | | | |
| 3.Jairus' daughter | 9.18-19, 23-26 | 5.22-24, 35-43 | 8.41-42, 49-56 | |

According to this list there are twenty-six accounts of the healing of individuals in the four gospels. If we count the number recorded in each gospel and add them together we obtain a total of forty-eight accounts, but a careful reading of the gospels will reveal that there are four duplicate accounts and nine triplicate accounts of the same incidents and this can be seen from the list above. When we subtract these from the total of forty-eight we arrive at the figure of twenty-six.

There is doubt about only two of the triplicate accounts. The first is the case of the Gadarene demoniac and the second is the healing of Bartimaeus. In both cases it is reasonable to suppose that two men were healed as Matthew records, but Mark and Luke concentrated on one of them because they had more details about him or knew him personally so that in the case of the blind man, Mark could even name him as Bartimaeus. There are differences between two of the duplicate accounts which should be noted, but they are not significant enough to require us to conclude that they refer to different incidents. In one case Matthew speaks of a blind and dumb demoniac (Matthew 12.22), while Luke speaks only of a demon that was dumb (Luke 11.14). In the other case, Matthew speaks of a centurion approaching Jesus personally (Matthew 8.5) where Luke says he sent Jewish elders to Jesus (Luke 7.3).

No fewer than nine of the other accounts of have been regarded by various authors as doublets or duplicate accounts, and it is true that some accounts do show points of resemblance to others which are not usually regarded as their duplicates. However, we remain unconvinced of the probability of these other suggested identifications. There are similarities of language in the descriptions which are understandable when it is realised that the accounts come from a common linguistic tradition and milieu. But it seems unlikely that a withered hand (Luke 6.6) could be confused with the swollen ankles of dropsy (Luke 14.2) as Beare suggests,[3] or that Mark should record the healing of the same man on two separate occasions, first as a deaf mute (Mark 7.31-37) and then as a blind man (Mark 8.22-26) as Bultmann proposes.[4]

We are, of course, assuming that these accounts of healing by Jesus are historical and that the events are not invented. If they had been invented, it is more probable that their authors would have taken care to remove any apparent inconsistencies than that they would allow them to remain.

## The References to the Healing of Groups

In addition to the twenty-six accounts of the healing of sick individuals which occur in the gospels, there are twelve references to occasions when Jesus healed sick people in groups. In these we are given few details and simply told that he healed an unspecified number of sick people in a group.

|  | Matthew | Mark | Luke |
|---|---|---|---|
| *I. References in one gospel only* |  |  |  |
| 1. In a Galilean town |  |  | 5.15 |
| 2. In the Temple | 21.14 |  |  |
| *II. References in two gospels* |  |  |  |
| 3. On a tour in Galilee | 9.35 | 6.5 |  |
| 4. In answer to the Baptist | 11.1-6 |  | 7.18-23* |
| 5. At Gennesaret | 14.35-36 | 6.54-56 |  |
| 6. In the hills of Galilee | 15.3-31 | 7.31-37 |  |
| 7. In Judaea | 19.2 | (10.1) |  |
| *III. References in three gospels* |  |  |  |
| 8. At Capernaum | 8.16-17* | 1.32-34* | 4.40-41* |
| 9. On another tour in Galilee | 4.23-25* | 1.39* | (4.44) |
| 10. By the seaside | 12.15-16 | 3.10-12* | 6.17-19* |
| 11. At Nazareth | 13.58 | 6.5 | (4.24) |
| 12. Across the sea of Galilee | 14.14 | (6.34) | 9.11 |

Some of the above references mention both physical healing and exorcism as occurring in the same collective incident, and these are indicated by an asterisk. Where there is no asterisk, the reference is to physical healing alone. In some of the parallel references no mention of healing may occur although we are told in the other accounts of the same incident that healing did occur. These references which speak only of preaching or healing are those included within brackets in the above list. It is noteworthy that Matthew never omits a reference to healing in all the eleven incidents he records, while both Mark and Luke omit such a reference on two occasions (Mark 6.34; 10.1 and Luke 4.24, 44). On the other hand, Matthew omits a reference to exorcism on two occasions on which it is said to have occurred in the parallel reference in Luke (Matthew 11.1-6; 12.15, cp. Luke 7.21 and 6.17-18 respectively).

Amongst the references to occasions on which Jesus healed groups or crowds of sick people there is no mention of any incident in which he raised the dead. In his answer to the question of John the Baptist, Jesus mentioned the fact that the dead were raised up by him as an indication that he was indeed the Messiah, 'the one who was to come (*ho erchomenos*)' as John had called him in Matthew 11.3 and Luke 7.20. This absence of any such reference in the accounts of group healings may mean that cases in which Jesus raised people from the dead were always reported in full since they were so important. If this is so, then it means that Jesus raised only three people from the dead during his ministry on earth, and the reference to raising the dead in his answer to the Baptist was to the raising of the widow's son at Nain, an incident which immediately precedes the Baptist's question in Luke (cp.7.11-17). However, this may not be so and Jesus may have raised others from the dead of whom we are not told. Certainly it is very probable that he healed far more people than we are told about in the gospels. John tells us at the end of his gospel that Jesus did many other things including many other *semeia* or signs, which as we shall see later is John's word for miracles, over and above those that he had recorded in order that people might believe that Jesus was the Christ, the Son of God (John 20.30; 21.25).

We have, therefore, a total of thirty-eight accounts of healing by Jesus recorded in the gospels. Twenty-six of these are concerned with individual sick people about whose healing some details are usually provided, and twelve with the healing of groups of sick people of whom no specific detail is given. These accounts form the basis of our study of the healing practice of Jesus in the gospels.

## THE DISEASES HEALED

### In the Healing of Individuals

Now that we have identified these twenty-six accounts of the healing of individuals by Jesus in which details are given of the sick and their sickness, it is possible to classify them according to the nature of the disease from which they suffered. In most cases the diagnosis cannot be more than a general or symptomatic one, but in a few cases sufficient significant detail is given to allow a more specific diagnosis to be made. In the following classification of the diseases healed by Jesus, the verses quoted are those which contain the relevant information on which the suggested diagnosis is based.

## Physical diseases

### I. Acute diseases

1. Fever: The nobleman's son (John 4.52)
      Peter's mother-in-law (Matthew 8.4; Mark 1.30; Luke 4.38)
2. Acute anterior poliomyelitis:
      The centurion's servant (Matthew 8.6; Luke 7.2 )
3. Incised wound:
      Malchus's ear (Luke 22.50)
4. Unknown fatal disease:
      Widow's only son at Nain (Luke 7.12).
      Jairus' daughter: meningitis? (Matthew 9.18; Mark 5.23: Luke 8.42)
      Lazarus (John 11.3, 13)

### II. Chronic diseases

1. Nervous diseases:
   a. Paraplegia or paralysis of the lower limbs:
      The paralysed man (Matthew 9.2; Mark 2.3; Luke 5.18)
      The Bethesda paralytic (John 5.5-7)
   b. Paralysis of the hand:
      The man with the withered right hand (Matthew 12.10; Mark 3.1; Luke 6.6)
   c. Blindness:
      The two blind men (Matthew 9.27)
      The blind man of Bethsaida (Mark 8.22)
      Blind Bartimaeus (Matthew 20.30; Mark 10.46; Luke 8.35-43)
   d. Deafness and defective speech:
      The deaf mute (Mark 7.32)
2. Rheumatic disease of the spine (spondylitis ankylopoietica):
      The bent woman with a spirit of weakness (Luke 13.11)
3. Chronic heart disease:
      The man with dropsy (Luke 14.2)
4. Gynaecological disease (uterine fibroid tumours):
      The woman with the flow of blood (Matthew 9.20; Mark 5.25; Luke 8.43)
5. Infectious skin disease:
      The ten leprosy patients (Luke 17.12)
      The man full of leprosy (Matthew 8.2; Mark 1.40; Luke 5.12)

A close examination of these references will show how often it is Luke who records the significant detail. It is he who tells us that Peter's mother-in-law had a 'high' fever (*huperpuretos*, Luke 4.38); that the leprosy patient was 'full' of leprosy (*aner pleres lepras*, Luke 5.12 RSV); that the withered hand was the man's 'right' hand (Luke 6.7); that the young man of Nain was the 'only' son of his mother who was a 'widow' (Luke 7.12) and that the epileptic boy was the 'only' child of his father (Luke 9.38).

## Demon possession

### I. With specific physical manifestations described.[5]

1. Major epilepsy:
   The synagogue demoniac (Mark 1.26; Luke 4.35)
   The epileptic boy (Matthew 17.15; Mark 9.17-26; Luke 9.39)

2. Acute mania:
   The Gadarene demoniac (Matthew 8.28; Mark 5.2-7; Luke 8.29)

3. Mutism or an inability to speak:
   The dumb demoniac (Matthew 9.32-33)

4. Mutism accompanied by blindness:
   The blind and dumb demoniac (Matthew 12.22; Luke 11.14)

### II. With no specific physical manifestation described.

5. The Syrophoenician girl (Matthew 15.22; Mark 7.25)

It is important to notice that there are only six cases of demon possession amongst the twenty-six cases in which it is recorded that Jesus healed individuals of their diseases. Also, as we shall see below, demon possession was mentioned on only four of the twelve occasions on which he healed groups of sick people. This means that it is not true to say that 'the Medicine of the New Testament is mainly that of possession by evil spirits'.[6]

The evidence that the demoniac who was healed in the synagogue at Nazareth suffered from major epilepsy is found in the words used to describe what happened to him when Jesus healed him. Mark tells us that the demon cried out with a loud voice and produced a convulsion in the man (Mark 1.26). He uses the verb *sparasso*, 'to tear or to rend', to describe the convulsion. Luke describes how the demon threw him to the ground and uses the verb *ripto* which the Greek physician Hippocrates frequently uses of convulsions (Luke 4.35).[7] This evidence convinced Alexander that this man had major epilepsy,[8] but Micklem was not so sure.[9] All that we can say is that although the evidence is not strong, it is suggestive of the diagnosis of major epilepsy in this case. It is worth noting how Luke once again adds the significant detail that although the man fell to the ground in his convulsion, he suffered no injury (Luke 4.35b). It is also worth noting that this was the first healing miracle of Jesus' ministry and took place in his own locality. On this occasion the people were amazed at his teaching and his ability to cast out the demon in contrast to their later attitude to him described in Mark 6.1-6.

In the case of the Syrophoenician girl, Alexander suggested that she too suffered from major epilepsy as the result of demon possession. He calls her condition one of 'epileptic idiocy'.[10] The basis of this diagnosis is Mark's description of the state of the girl when her mother returned home. Mark 7.30 describes the girl as *beblemenos epi ten klinen* which the AV and the RV render as 'laid upon the bed' and the RSV and the REB as 'lying in bed'. The perfect participle *beblemenos* comes from the verb *ballo*, 'to throw', and Alexander understands it to mean that the girl had been thrown on her bed by an epileptic convulsion before she was healed. However, the verb *ballo* may be used without any suggestion of violence about it. For instance, the same participle is used to describe Peter's mother-in-law lying in bed with a fever in Matthew 8.14, and of the paralytic lying on his bed in Matthew 9.2. Mark's description need not therefore mean that the girl had had a convulsion before she was healed, and it is also unnecessary to regard her as suffering from epilepsy. It is equally unnecessary to suggest that she suffered from idiocy in any form for there is no evidence in the text to support this suggestion.

Demon possession is often regarded as a concept which has been rendered unnecessary by modern psychiatry. What the ancient writers called demon possession is said to be mental disorder of the various types which are familiar to psychiatrists today. It is then argued that since modern psychiatry can now explain the phenomena formerly attributed to demon possession, we no longer need to believe in existence or activity of demons. This is the thesis maintained by McCasland in his book, *By the Finger of God*.[11] However, the matter is not as simple as this view would suggest, for the introduction of psychiatry by no means excludes the possibility of demon possession.

Psychiatry is rarely able to 'explain' mental disorder, but only to 'describe' it. We can see this from its terminology which is almost entirely symptomatic or descriptive in character. It deals with descriptions more than causes, although in a few cases it is able to identify specific causes of mental disorder. The term 'demon possession' defines a cause of mental disorder and is in a different category from the descriptive terminology which modern psychiatry uses.

In psychiatric terms we may diagnose the Gadarene demoniac of Mark 5.2-7 as suffering from a manic-depressive psychosis. At the time he met Jesus this man was in a state of acute mania and from his local reputation he appears to have been in such a state frequently. By calling his disease 'manic-depressive psychosis' or 'bipolar affective disorder' we have simply described his condition as a disorder of his personality (psychosis) which manifests itself by the occurrence of attacks of either mania or depression, or of both states at different times in the same person. The diagnosis therefore is purely descriptive and tells us nothing about the cause.

Psychiatry can tell us little about the cause of this disorder although it can describe various concomitant features of the condition such as its occurrence in other members of the patient's family, its association with a particular type of personality, and a possible correlation with biochemical changes at the base of the patient's brain. It can also describe certain factors or states which are observed to precede the attacks of the psychosis and may therefore be held to precipitate their onset. However, nothing that psychiatry can tell us about manic-depressive psychosis can exclude demon possession as a possible cause of the condition. This is not to say that every case of this condition or of any type of mental disorder is always due to demon possession. We shall see this illustrated when we come to discuss the case of the epileptic boy in Chapter Ten. In epilepsy we may be able to demonstrate the presence of specific causes such as a brain tumour or head injury in some cases, but in the majority of cases no physical cause is demonstrable and there is no reason why demon possession could not be the underlying cause in these cases. It is not true, therefore, that modern psychiatry excludes the possibility that demon possession may be a cause of mental disorder.[12]

The diagnosis may not always be clear in these individual cases of disease which Jesus healed, but it is evident that they were almost all cases which the medical profession of his day had failed to cure. In the case of the woman with the flow of blood, this failure is explicitly stated in Mark 5.26 and admitted in Luke 8.43, and it must have been true for most of the others cases too. It is relevant to add that they are mostly examples of conditions which medical knowledge and skill are still not able to cure today.

## In the Healing of Groups

The description of the diseases healed on the twelve occasions on which it is recorded that Jesus dealt with a group or a crowd of sick people is much more general than in the case of the healings of individual sick persons. Physical conditions predominate in these group healings and only a third of the accounts mention demon possession. The terms used to describe the different conditions which were brought to Jesus for healing are set out in the list overleaf.

| Occasion | Reference | English | Greek |
|---|---|---|---|
| 1. In Galilee | Luke 5.15 | infirmity | *astheneia* |
| 2. In the Temple | Matt 21.14 | blindness | *tuphlos* |
| 3. In Galilee | Matt 9.35 | disease | *nosos* |
| | | illness | *malakia* |
| 4. The Baptist's question | Luke 7.21 | disease | *nosos* |
| | | plague | *mastix* |
| | | evil spirits | *pneumata ponera* |
| 5. At Gennesaret | Matt 14.35 | sickness | *kakos echo* |
| 6. In the hills | Matt 15.30 | lameness | *cholos kullos* |
| | | blindness | *tuphlos* |
| | | mutism | *kophos* |
| 7. In Judaea | Matt 19.2 | no description | no description |
| 8. At Capernaum | Matt 8.16 | demonised | *daimonizomai* |
| | | sickness | *kakos echo* |
| | Luke 4.40 | various diseases | *astheneo nosois* |
| 9. In Galilee | Matt 4.23-24 | disease | *nosos* |
| | | illness | *malakia* |
| | | sickness | *kakos echo* |
| | | pains | *basanois echo* |
| | | demonised | *daimonizomai* |
| | | epileptic | *seleniazomai* |
| | | paralysis | *paralutikos* |
| 10. By the sea | Mark 3.10 | plague | *mastix* |
| | | unclean spirits | *pneumata akatharta* |
| | Luke 6.17 | disease | *nosos* |
| 11. At Nazareth | Mark 6.5 | sickness | *arrostos* |
| 12. Across the sea | Matt 14.14 | sickness | *arrostos* |

## Terms used for sickness

The terms used in this list of the occasions when group healings were performed by Jesus may be divided into two main categories. The first consists of those which describe symptoms which are referable to a specific organ or system of the body. Examples of the terms which belong to this group are blindness, mutism, lameness, and paralysis. They give no indication of the cause of the condition they describe, but the disability produced by these conditions is severe enough to make those afflicted by them come to Jesus for healing.

The other category consists of terms which are much more general in meaning and give little assistance in the recognition of the condition they describe. In most languages the words used to denote illness are general in meaning like the terms in this category. In English terms the effect of sickness is to produce dis-ease or discomfort; an illness makes a person feel bad or ill (i.e. evil, of which the word 'ill' is a contraction); and an ailment causes the person to feel pain or distress. These English words describe the effects of sickness rather than the nature of the sickness itself. A brief survey of the Greek terms used for sickness in the gospels and set out in the above list will show that this is true of them also.

1. *Astheneia* and its related verb *astheneo* are the commonest words used to denote sickness in the gospels. They denote weakness or a lack of strength (*sthenos*) which results from disease of all types, and are commonly translated as 'infirmity' in the English versions. Of the four gospels it is Luke and John who use these words most frequently with Luke showing some preference for the noun and John for the verb.

2. *Kakos echo* or some variant of it is the commonest idiomatic phrase used for sickness in the gospels. It means literally 'being in a bad way' and is used in the Hellenistic Greek papyri for sickness in both man and cattle. It is chiefly a Markan phrase and is used only once by Matthew (4.24) and Luke (7.2) except where they have derived it from Mark.[13] John does not use it at all.

3. *Nosos* is cognate with the Latin verb *noceo*, 'to harm or injure'. It is the commonest word for disease in Hellenistic Greek, but is rare in the New Testament where it is used only eleven times. Mark uses it once (Mark 1.34), while Matthew and Luke each use it four times.

4. *Arrostos* means literally 'powerless, without strength (*rhosis*)' with the implication that this weakness is due to some chronic, lingering physical disease. It is used of sickness three times by Mark (6.5, 13 and 16.18) and once by Matthew (14.14). The noun *arrostia* is the term used for disease in Modern Greek where *nosos* has dropped out of use except in compound words such as *nosokomeion*, 'hospital'.[14]

5. *Mastix* originally meant a horse-whip and then a scourge for punishing soldiers. It is used metaphorically to denote disease on four occasions when it is usually translated as 'plague' (Mark 3.10; 5.29; 5.34; Luke 7.21).

6. *Malakia* is used only by Matthew and always in combination with *nosos* (Matthew 4.23; 9.35; 10.1). It literally means 'softness' and refers to the debility and weakness produced by disease.

7. *Basanos* is used of disease only in Matthew 4.24. It is a word with an interesting history for it originally meant the Lydian touchstone which was used to test the purity of a sample of gold. It then came to mean the torture applied in the interrogation of slaves and prisoners and finally it was applied to disease as that which tortured and tormented people and so tested them and their resistance to pain and suffering.

None of these terms appears to have a specific application to any disease. They all refer to physical disease and are distinguished from demon possession. It is difficult to distinguish between them in usage with any precision but it does appear to be possible to recognise a distinction between acute and chronic disease. The term *hoi kakos echontes* means simply that those who are described in this way are ill. Acute illness appears to be indicated by the use of the terms *nosos*, *mastix* and *basanos*, whilst chronic disease is described as *astheneia* (with its verb *astheneo*) and *malakia*. These distinctions are not hard and fast for we find the term *mastix* being used for the chronic debilitated condition of the woman with the flow of blood in Mark 5.29,34 in spite of the fact that its derivation would suggest an acute condition.

# Chapter 7
# THE WORDS FOR HEALING

The words for healing in the gospels of the New Testament reflect the ideas of health and healing which we have already found in the Old Testament. In fact, all these words had already been used in the Greek translation of the Old Testament, which was made long before the gospels were written.

As we shall see, the number of these words is not great and the frequency of their usage is not marked. Nevertheless, it may be claimed that in the gospels they acquire a fuller and deeper meaning, especially when used by Jesus himself, as they were on a number of occasions.

## THE VERBS OF HEALING

The word **health** does not occur in the gospels in the English AV, RV, RSV or NIV and only once in the NRSV (at Luke 7.10). By contrast the verb **to heal** and its derivatives occur fifty-five times in the AV, fifty-eight times in the RSV, forty times in the NIV and twenty-seven times in the NRSV. This fact illustrates how the gospels are more interested in describing healing than in defining health. The main verbs used for healing in the gospels may be listed as follows in the order of their frequency of usage.

| Verb | Matthew | Mark | Luke | John | Total |
|------|---------|------|------|------|-------|
| *Therapeuo* | 16 | 6 | 14 | 1 | 37 |
| *Iaomai* | 4 | 1 | 12 | 3 | 20 |
| *Sozo* | 3 | 6 | 4 | 0 | 13 |
| *Apokathistemi* | 1 | 2 | 1 | 0 | 4 |
| *Diasozo* | 1 | 0 | 1 | 0 | 2 |

This table takes no account of the occurrence of the words in the parallel narratives of the gospels. When we exclude these parallel usages we obtain the following figures for the absolute usage of the words:

*Therapeuo* is used twenty-six times and is commonest in Matthew and Luke.

*Iaomai* occurs nineteen times and is most frequent in Luke.

*Sozo* is used eleven times and most frequently by Mark.

*Apokathistemi* and *diasozo* are both used twice.

With the exception of *diasozo* all these verbs are much more frequently used in the gospels with the sense of healing than elsewhere in the New Testament. In other words, it is in the gospels that attention is focused on the healing activity of Jesus.

## Therapeuo

We see from the above table that the commonest verb used for healing in the gospels is the verb *therapeuo*. In Classical Greek this word has the root meaning of 'service', or often of 'worship' of a god, as in Acts 17.25.[1] It described the work of a *therapon* who was someone who gave willing personal service or attention to another. Socrates speaks of such service as directed to the good and welfare of the one to whom it is given and illustrates its function in different areas of life. One such area is in healing the sick, the object of which is to produce health (*hugieia*).[2] It is in this sense that the verb *therapeuo* is used in the gospels where it is never used in the general sense of rendering service but always in the sense of healing. The word *therapon* is never used in the gospels and never used of Jesus in the New Testament and only once of Moses in Hebrews 3.5. However, it is frequently used in the LXX to translate the Hebrew word *ebed* which means 'a servant'.

Out of the twenty-six times this verb occurs in the gospels, twice it refers to the work of physicians, i.e., to medical healing. The first reference is in the proverb quoted by Jesus in Luke 4.23, 'Physician, heal yourself'.[3] The second is in the reference to the failure of the physicians to heal the woman with the flow of blood in Luke 8.43. Thus the implication of its use in these two cases is that the medical healing was not successful. On every other occasion the verb refers to non-medical healing, or healing carried out by those who were not physicians. On one occasion, even this type of healing was unsuccessful when it was attempted on the epileptic boy in the absence of Jesus in Matthew 17.16.

With these three exceptions the verb is always used of miraculous or supernatural healing. In the majority of cases it refers to the healing of physical disease, but it may also be used of exorcism as in Matthew 4.24; 12.22; 17.16; Luke 6.18; 7.21 and 8.2. It is most frequently used by the writers of the gospels to describe the healing activity of Jesus, but the verb is also used by Jesus himself to describe his own healing activity in Matthew 8.7 and Luke 14.3. It is also used by Jesus to describe the kind of healing he commissioned his disciples to perform when he sent them out on their mission in Matthew 10.8 and Luke 10.9.

In summary, then, *therapeuo* is the most comprehensive of all the verbs used in the gospels for healing. It is used to describe three kinds of healing.
1. Healing of physical disease by physicians (Luke 4.23; 8.43).
2. Healing by Jesus:      (a) of physical disease (Matthew 4.23 *et passim*);
                          (b) of demon possession (Matthew 4.24 *et passim*).
3. Healing by the disciples of Jesus of physical disease (Matthew 10.8; Mark 6.13; Luke 10.8).

*Iaomai*

The verb *iaomai* is the origin of the word *iatros* which is the Greek name for a physician and appears to have been in general use by the time of Homer's *Iliad* (c.800 BC).⁴ This verb is less frequent in the New Testament than *therapeuo*, while the reverse is true in the Greek Old Testament. In the New Testament it is more commonly used by Luke than by the other writers, perhaps because he himself was a *iatros* or physician, as we know from Colossians 4.14 where Paul calls him 'the beloved physician (*iatros*)'. The derivation of the verb is uncertain, but from its earliest appearance in Homer it is used in the medical sense of curing or healing. It is used by the ancient Greek medical writers more frequently in this sense than any other word.⁵ Nevertheless, it does not refer to the medical kind of healing practised by physicians as we have just seen that *therapeuo* may do.

*Iaomai* is used almost exclusively of physical healing in the gospels, the only exceptions being in Luke 9.42 where it is used of the casting out of the demon from the epileptic boy and in Matthew 13.15; Luke 4.18 and John 12.40 where it is used metaphorically in quotations from the prophet Isaiah. Luke 9.42 is an example of how Luke sometimes replaces the verb *therapeuo* by *iaomai* (cp. Matthew 17.16). Another example is the group healing described in Matthew 14.14 where *therapeuo* is used, but Luke replaces it with *iaomai* in his account in Luke 9.11. On several occasions Luke uses the two verbs synonymously in the same context. In Luke 9.1-2 he says that Jesus gave the Twelve authority to heal (*therapeuo*), and then sent them out to heal (*iaomai*). Matthew had used *therapeuo* in both cases. Shortly after that, Luke speaks of Jesus healing (*iaomai*) those who had need of healing (*therapeuo*) using both verbs in the same clause (Luke 9.11).

In Luke 14.3-4 we find Jesus using *therapeuo* when speaking about healing, and Luke using *iaomai* to describe the healing which Jesus had just carried out on the man with dropsy. Similarly in the fourth gospel, John appears to regard the two verbs as synonymous for he uses both of them to describe the healed state of the paralysed man at the pool of Bethesda (John 5.10,13). It appears therefore that in their usage in the gospels these two verbs are to be regarded as synonymous.

As in the case of *therapeuo*, we find Jesus describing his work of healing using a participle from this verb (Luke 13.32), and also we find this work ascribed to a power (*dunamis*) which resided in him (Mark 5.29-30; Luke 8.46-47).

The verb *iaomai* is also used synonymously with *sozo* and *diasozo* to mean heal as we see if we compare Luke 6.19 with Matthew 14.36 and Mark 6.56, and Mark 5.29-30 with Matthew 9.21 and Luke 8.48. Amongst the four gospels, Luke used the verb *iaomai* most frequently and even on occasions preferred it to *therapeuo* which may be evidence of his medical training.

## Sozo

The occurrence of the verb *sozo* amongst the words used for healing in the gospels is of great interest, and potentially of great significance for the understanding of the New Testament concept of health and healing. We have already considered the use of the noun *soteria* as meaning health and now we come to consider the use of the verb *sozo* as meaning 'to heal'. Both words are derived from the adjective *sos* which means 'safe'. The verb originally meant 'to make safe' and was used of deliverance from natural dangers or afflictions by an acute divine or human intervention. It came to have a wide range of use in daily life and in religion and this broad spectrum of usage is reflected in the gospels, where it may mean deliverance from danger, disease and death, both physical and spiritual.

*Sozo* and its intensive form *diasozo* occur fifty-eight times in the gospels, but when we exclude its use in parallel passages, this figure is reduced to a total of thirty-eight. In eleven of these thirty-eight occurrences, the verb refers to physical healing or exorcism, and in most of these cases the verb is translated as 'made well' or 'made whole'. These occasions are as follows, given in the order of the gospels.

| Reference | Incident |
|---|---|
| 1. Matthew 9.21 = Mark 5.28. | } |
| 2. Matthew 9.22a = Mark 5.34 = Luke 8.48. | }The woman with the flow of blood. |
| 3. Matthew 9.22b. | } |
| 4. Matthew 14.36 = Mark 6.56. | The healings at Gennesaret. |
| 5. Mark 5.23. | The request of Jairus to Jesus. |
| 6. Luke 8.50. | The reassurance of Jairus by Jesus. |
| 7. Mark 10.52 = Luke 18.42. | Blind Bartimaeus. |
| 8. Luke 7.3 (*diasozo*). | The centurion's servant. |
| 9. Luke 8.36. | The Gadarene demoniac. |
| 10. Luke 17.19. | The Samaritan leper. |
| 11. John 11.12. | The raising of Lazarus. |

In addition to these eleven examples of the use of *sozo* or *diasozo* to describe the healing of physical disease or exorcism, there are nine more occurrences of the verb *sozo* (or eighteen, if we include the parallel references) in which the word refers to deliverance from physical danger or death.

These additional nine occurrences are as follows:

*I. Deliverance from drowning.*

    1. Matthew 8.25: *'Lord, save us'*. The stilling of the storm.

    2. Matthew 14.30: *'Lord, save me'*. Peter walking on the water.

*II. Deliverance from death.*

    3. Mark 3.4 = Luke 6.9: *'To save life or to kill'*. The man with the withered hand.

    4. Matthew 16.25 = Mark 8.35 = Luke 9.24: *'Whoever would save his life'*. Teaching on discipleship.

    5. Matthew 27.40 = Mark 15.30 = Luke 23.37: *'Save yourself'*.

    6. Matthew 27.42a = Mark 15.31a = Luke 23.35a: *'He saved others'*.

    7. Matthew 27.42b = Mark 15.31b = Luke 23.35b: *'He cannot save himself'*.

    8. Matthew 27.49: *'Let us see if Elijah will come to save him'*.

    9. Luke 23.39: *'Save yourself and us'*.

          *(References 5 to 9 are from the accounts of the Crucifixion)*

The most significant of these nine occurrences of the verb *sozo* is the double use of the word in Matthew 27.42 where the taunt of the Jewish religious leaders is quoted as, 'He saved others; he cannot save himself'. McNeile explains this as a sarcastic reference to Jesus' claim to be king, implying that as Messiah he had not brought salvation to anyone.[6] However, this does not do justice to the past tense of *sozo* in this verse. It is more probable that the Jewish leaders are throwing in his teeth the fact that he had saved others from sickness, demons and death as Filson suggests, and yet was now apparently unable to deliver himself from death on the Cross.[7] In this remark they are admitting that Jesus did heal disease and did raise people from the dead, for they have little to lose by admitting this now that he is dying himself.

These twenty cases in which *sozo* means deliverance from disease, demons or death make up over half of the occurrences of the verb in the gospels. It is probable that in these twenty cases the reference is not only to physical deliverance, but includes the physical as part of the deliverance of the one healed or delivered. Foerster goes so far as to say, 'In the healings of Jesus *sozo* never refers to a single member of the body but always to the whole man'.[8] He supports this statement by drawing attention to the fact that Jesus addressed the phrase, 'Your faith has saved (*sesoken*) you', equally to the woman with the flow of blood (Mark 5.34) and to the woman who was a great sinner but did not need physical healing (Luke 7.50). In the remaining eighteen occurrences of *sozo* in the gospels it is mostly used in an unqualified sense. In these cases the physical part of the human being is not specifically in view, but that is not to say that it is excluded, for it is the whole of the human being in all its aspects which is the object of salvation. Green speaks of *sozo* being used 'ambiguously' in the gospels to refer to both physical and spiritual healing,[9] but its use is comprehensive rather than ambiguous for it includes both the physical and the spiritual together with all aspects of the human being in its scope.

As a final example of the different usages and applications of the verb *sozo*, we should notice its occurrence in the eighth chapter of the gospel of Luke. The verb occurs four times in the space of thirty-eight verses of this chapter and in each case its application is distinct from the other three.

In verse twelve it refers to the spiritual salvation obtained by faith which follows hearing and receiving the word of God.

In verse thirty-six it describes the deliverance from demons of the demon-possessed man of Gadara.

In verse forty-eight it denotes the cure of the disease of the woman with the flow of blood.

Finally, in verse fifty it is used for the raising from the dead of the daughter of Jairus.

In each case the basic idea is that of rescue, deliverance from an undesirable state and transference to a desirable one. In these verses the undesirable state is portrayed as spiritual death or demonisation, or as physical disease or death. Also, in each case it is the work of Jesus which effects the deliverance no matter what the situation may be.

With a word of such comprehensive meaning and application as *sozo* enjoys, it is not always easy to define its meaning in any particular context. However it is clear that its wide application in the gospels indicates that the Christian concept of healing and the Christian concept of salvation overlap to a degree which varies in different situations, but are never completely separable. Healing of the body is never purely physical, and the salvation of the soul is never purely spiritual for both are combined in the total deliverance of the whole human being, a deliverance which is foreshadowed and illustrated in the healing miracles of Jesus in the gospels.

## *Apokathistemi*

The fourth verb used in the gospels for healing is *apokathistemi*, which means 'to restore to a former condition', e.g. of health or soundness. It is used of the restoration to its previous condition of soundness (*hugies*) of the withered hand of the man Jesus met in the synagogue (Matthew 12.13 and parallels). It was his right hand which was affected (Luke 6.6) and Jerome tells us that according to the apocryphal Gospel of the Nazaraeans, the man was a stone-mason to trade and therefore worked with his hands.[10] The atrophy of his right hand presumably from damage to its nerve supply sustained at work was therefore an economic tragedy for him and his family.

The other medical use of the verb is in Mark 8.25 where its use of the restoration of his sight to the blind man of Bethsaida implies that he had formerly been able to see and then had gone blind. This explains how he was able to describe people as trees walking when Jesus restored his near vision. He could remember what trees looked like when he had been able to see previously, and people carrying loads on their heads or on their backs looked very much the same as he remembered trees had done. This miracle is one of the two miracles in the gospels in which the physical healing of the man took place in two stages.[11] In the first stage no verb of healing is used but his visual appreciation of the shape and movement of objects returns, but he remains short-sighted. In the second stage his full vision is restored together with his distance vision and it is for this full restoration of sight that the verb *apokathistemi* is used.

## Apoluo

Another verb can which mean to free a person from disease is the verb *apoluo*. This word means literally 'to free a person from some condition or situation' and occurs sixty-nine times in the New Testament. However, it is applied to release from disease on only occasion. This is when Jesus uses the word in Luke 13.12 as he says to the woman with the spirit of weakness, 'Woman, you are freed from your weakness'. There is a similar construction in Mark 5.34 where Jesus says to the woman with the flow of blood, 'Daughter, your faith has healed you. Go in peace and be freed from your suffering' (NIV). Here the words Jesus uses are literally, 'be sound (*hugies*) of your plague (*mastix*)', but he does not use the verb *apoluo*.

## Katharizo

There is one special word we must consider to complete our survey of the verbs used for healing in the gospels. This is the verb *katharizo* which is used to describe the healing of leprosy in the two incidents in which Jesus healed leprosy patients and which means 'to cleanse or make clean'.

The first incident involved the man who had advanced leprosy which is recorded in all three synoptic gospels (Matthew 8.1-4; Mark 1.40-45 and Luke 5.12-15) with Mark giving the fullest account. All three gospels give the man's statement to Jesus in identical words, 'If you will, you can make me clean (*katharisai*)'. In other words, 'If you want to, you can heal me and make me ritually clean'.[12] When Jesus stretched out his hand to touch the man and say 'I will, be clean', we are told that 'immediately the leprosy left him and he was made clean (*ekatharisthai*)'. The result was that his healing and his cleansing occurred together. However, he had still be officially certified clean and so Jesus told him to go to the priest and offer the sacrifice which the law of Moses required for his official ritual cleansing as set out in Leviticus 14.1-32. In this case, the only verb used for healing is the verb *katharizo*.

The second incident was the healing of the ten leprosy patients recorded in Luke 17.11-19. Jesus met them on the southern border of Galilee and when they asked for mercy he healed them. Here too their healing was combined with their cleansing. Their healing is described by the use of the verbs *iaomai* (v.15) and *sozo* (v.19) and their cleansing by *katharizo* (vv.14 & 19). In this case too, Jesus told them to go to the priest and show him that their leprosy had disappeared. This command of Jesus to show themselves to the priest is a reminder that healing has a social element too, and that the men would remain social outcasts and not be accepted back into the community, until a priest had officially confirmed the disappearance and cure of their disease and they had offered the appropriate sacrifices for their cleansing.

The use of the verb *katharizo* thus implies two changes of state in the person suffering from leprosy. First of all, there is the removal of the disease which has caused the person to become ceremonially unclean, and secondly, there is the removal of the ceremonial uncleanness itself so that the person becomes ritually clean again. In levitical terms there was also a third stage in the process to allow the person to return to normal community life. This occurred when a priest certified that the signs of the disease were no longer present and the person had offered the required sacrifices for his cleansing.[13]

## The synonyms of health and healing

The account of the healing of the woman with the flow of blood provides one of the most interesting accounts of a healing miracle from the point of view of the vocabulary used. This healing miracle is recorded in all three synoptic gospels and the relationship of the various words used for healing in these gospels can be seen in the following table:

| Source | Matthew 9 | Mark 5 | Luke 8 |
|---|---|---|---|
| Narrator | -- | 26 *opheleo* | 43 *therapeuo* |
| Woman | 21 *sozo* | 28 *sozo* | -- |
| Narrator | 22b *sozo* | 29 *iaomai* | -- |
| Narrator (indirect speech for woman) | -- | -- | 47 *iaomai* |
| Jesus | 22a *sozo* | 34 *sozo* | 48 *sozo* |
| | -- | *eirene* | *eirene* |
| | -- | *hugies* | -- |

The first thing to notice in this story is Luke's defence of the physicians in Luke 8.43. Mark had accused them of taking all her money from her in fees, of causing her much suffering and pain by their methods of treatment, and in the end of leaving her no better (*opheleo*) but actually increasingly worse (Mark 5.26). According to the most probable reading of Luke 8.43,

Luke says simply that the woman 'could not be healed by anyone' (RSV)[14] and uses the verb *therapeuo* which we take to mean in this context 'heal by normal medical methods'. The next thing to notice is that Matthew uses the verb *sozo* throughout his account, and in one case uses it as the synonym of *iaomai* which Mark had used (Matthew 9.22b, cp. Mark 5.29). Finally, it is noteworthy that when Jesus dismisses the woman, he describes her healed state by three different words according to Mark 5.34. First, he says to her that she is 'healed' (NIV) or 'made well' (RSV) and uses the verb *sozo* to describe this. Then he tells the woman to 'go in peace (*eirene*)' which we must regard as more than the conventional formula of dismissal for she certainly did not come in peace, but in distress and weakness with no peace of body or mind. Behind *eirene* lies the concept of *shalom* and the idea of wholeness which it denotes. In the third place she was now 'sound (*hugies*)' and free from the disease which had troubled her for so long. The story of this woman who was healed of a chronic gynaecological complaint provides a very vivid illustration both in event and vocabulary of the comprehensive concept of healing which characterises the gospel record.

## The usage of Jesus

In the incident of healing we have just considered, the words of Jesus are quoted in which he describes the woman's healing and her resulting state of health. This raises the interesting question of what were the words by which Jesus described his healing activity in so far as they are preserved and recorded for us by the writers of the gospels.

When we examine the gospels we find that Jesus himself is recorded as using the verb *therapeuo* on six occasions. These are as follows in the order of the gospels:

1. Matthew 8.7: *'I will come and heal him'*. (The centurion's servant)

2. Matthew 10.8: *'Heal the sick'*. (The commission to the Twelve)

3. Matthew 12.10: *'Is it lawful to heal on the sabbath?'* (The man with the withered hand)

4. Luke 4.23: *'Physician, heal yourself'*. (Proverb quoted by Jesus in the synagogue at Nazareth)

5. Luke 10.9: *'Heal the sick'*. (The commission to the Seventy)

6. Luke 14.3: *'Is it lawful to heal on the sabbath?'* (The man with dropsy)

It is interesting to notice that although Jesus is recorded as using *therapeuo* in the commission to the Twelve in Matthew 10.8, when Luke records it using indirect speech, he uses the verb *iaomai* (Luke 9.2). This is another indication that Luke appears to regard these two verbs as synonymous.

On only one occasion is Jesus recorded as using the verb *iaomai* to describe his own healing activity. This is in Luke 13.32 where he bids the Pharisees tell Herod Antipas, the tetrarch of Galilee, about the exorcisms and cures (*iaseis*) which he is performing. This statement is one of the most specific claims of Jesus that he is healing people and casting out demons. On one other occasion he uses the verb *iaomai* when he quotes Isaiah 6.9-10 to explain to his disciples why he taught in parables (Matthew 13.15). In this case the quotation includes the verb *iaomai*, but this does not refer specifically to his own healing activity.

Neither of the verbs we have considered is used by Jesus in addressing the sick whom he had healed. When he does this, the verb he uses is *sozo* and, as we have already mentioned, the tense he uses is the perfect *sesoken* meaning that the sick person has been healed and will remain healed. We find this in the case of the woman with the flow of blood (Matthew 9.22; Mark 5.34 and Luke 8.48), the grateful leprosy patient (Luke 17.19) and Blind Bartimaeus (Mark 10.52 and Luke 18.42). But Jesus does not say that he has healed the sick person, for in each case we are told that what he said was, 'Your faith has made you well'. It was, of course, their faith in the power of the healer which was the means of their healing.

There are two passages in which a more direct reference to Jesus himself as the agent of healing appears to be made. The first is that which describes the healing of the woman with the flow of blood which in Mark 5.30 is said to be due to power (*dunamis*) going forth from Jesus to heal the woman, a phenomenon of which Mark says Jesus himself was aware. It is, however, significant that Jesus then attributes her healing to her faith (v.34). The second is in the case of the healing of the bent woman, where Jesus tells the woman she has been loosed from her weakness (using the verb *apoluo*) and then immediately lays hands on her and she is able to stand up straight (Luke 13.12-13). Here there is no reference to faith.

In this chapter we are concerned with the words used for healing and what they reveal of the healing activity of Jesus. There is, of course, much more to say about this and in Chapter Nine we shall discuss the methods of healing used by Jesus and these will show more clearly how these indicate that he was the real agent of healing.

## THE NOUNS OF HEALING

Surprisingly enough, the noun *therapeia* which is derived from *therapeuo*, the commonest verb used for healing in the gospels, occurs only three times there, and on only one occasion does it meaning 'healing' (Luke 9.11, cp. Matthew 14.14 where the verb is used instead). The other occurrences are in Matthew 24.45 and Luke 12.42 where it is translated 'household' in the English versions. Although this word was the usual term for medical treatment in the Greek medical authors such as Hippocrates and Aretaeus, it was not adopted by the writers of the gospels.[15]

In the synoptic gospels the commonest term used to describe an incident of healing is *dunamis*, which means the power or 'the potentiality to exert force in performing some function',[16] with the common implication that such force is supernatural in origin and character. While the word originally meant the power behind the act, it then came to mean the act of power itself. Thus *dunamis* is specifically related to healing acts by Jesus in Luke 5.17; 6.19 and 8.46 (cp. Matthew 13.54; 14.2). When *dunamis* is used to describe healing, it is usually translated in the English versions as 'a mighty work'.

By contrast, the usual word for healing incidents in John's gospel is *semeion*, and the word *dunamis* is not used there to describe any 'mighty work'. The word *semeion* means 'a sign or something which is usually seen, but may occasionally be heard, and which points to a meaning beyond itself'.[17] The term is used not only for healing incidents, but also for other incidents such as the turning of water into wine in John 2.11. Its use by Nicodemus in his midnight interview with Jesus illustrates its significance. He said to Jesus, 'No one can do the miracles (*semeia*) which you do if God were not with him' (John 3.2). By using the word *semeia*, Nicodemus indicated that he realised that Jesus' miracles were not simply wonders but they had an underlying meaning, and it was that meaning that Nicodemus came to Jesus to discover.[18]

In the gospel of John, *semeion* describes events which occur in the life and ministry of Jesus on earth. In the synoptic gospels on the other hand the word is used for events which are associated with the end of the world and the return of Jesus to earth as we can see from such verses as Matthew 16.3; 24.30-31; Mark 13.4; Luke 21.7, 11; 25.16. The Jewish religious leaders sought a sign of this kind from Jesus which would show his foreknowledge of future events and thus prove to them that he came from God. However, Jesus consistently refused to give them a sign of this kind (cp. Matthew 12.39; 16.4; Mark 8.12; Luke 11.29).[19] He did, however, refer them to a sign which had already been given, 'the sign of the prophet Jonah'. This sign had led to the repentance of the Ninevites and foretold his own death and resurrection (Matthew 12.38-41; 16.4; Luke 11.29-30). In other words, as Jonah had been God's sign in his generation so Jesus was the sign the present generation demanded, but they did not recognise him as such. He was the one to which all the signs (in the Johannine sense of the word) pointed, and in whom all the signs (in the synoptic sense) would be revealed and fulfilled.

John also records how Jesus frequently spoke of his *erga* or 'works' and even promised that his disciples would be able to do greater works than he had done (John 14.12). Although this term is not specifically applied to any healing incident by John, such incidents must be included amongst the works Jesus did whilst he was on earth (See John 5.19-21). They were works which no other man had done (John 15.24, cp. Matthew 9.33). These works, Jesus insisted were not only his works but the works of God his Father (John 5.17). In this way he was associating his work with that of the creation and God's saving acts for his people in the past. They bore witness to him as the

Son of God sent by his Father (John 5.36; 10.25, 32, 38; 14.11). It is of interest to notice that the word *erga* is used by Matthew of the miracles of Jesus when John the Baptist when sent to Jesus for reassurance that he was indeed the Christ who should come (Matthew 11.2).

Each of these words expresses a different aspect of the healing miracles of Jesus. *Dunamis* describes the source and cause of the healing in the supernatural power by which the act of healing was performed. *Semeion* reminds us of the significance of the miracles indicating the divine origin of the healer and his power. The word *erga* expresses the fact that they represent the activity of God in the world.

Other words are also used which draw attention to the wonderful character of the healing miracles but they each occur only once in the gospels. These words are *thaumasia* ('wonderful things', Matthew 21.15), *paradoxa* ('strange things' not previously seen, Luke 5.26), *endoxa* ('glorious things' or things which display the *doxa* or glory of God, Luke 13.17) and *terata* ('wonders', John 4.48), but this aspect of the healing miracles is not emphasised in the gospels. It was not their character as wonders, but their significance as signs which was the concern of the gospel writers.[20]

## THE ADVERBS OF HEALING

To complete our survey of the words used in the gospels to describe healing we should mention the two Greek adverbs which are applied to it, and which are both usually translated 'immediately' in the English versions.

The first is the compound adverb *parachrema* which is used almost exclusively by Luke in the New Testament. In his gospel he uses it to describe four occasions on which instant healing occurred. These are the healing of Peter's mother-in-law (Luke 4.39), the woman with the flow of blood (Luke 8.44), the bent woman (Luke 13.13) and of Blind Bartimaeus (Luke 18.43).

The other adverb is *eutheos* which is a common word in Mark's gospel. There it is used of the healing of the advanced leprosy patient (Mark 1.42), the woman with the flow of blood (Mark 5.29), Jairus' daughter (Mark 5.42), the deaf mute (Mark 7.35) and of blind Bartimaeus (Mark 10.52). It will be seen that in three of these cases Luke replaces *eutheos* with *parachrema*.

It was the immediacy of the healing of these cases by Jesus which so impressed those who witnessed them. Most of these cases were chronic in nature and yet were healed instantly.

## THE VOCABULARY OF DEMON POSSESSION

The common verb used to describe demon possession in Matthew and Mark is *daimonizomai* usually in its participial form *diamonizomenous*. This is commonly translated 'demon-possessed', but is more literally rendered 'demonised'. In Luke and John the usual phrase is *echei daimonion*, 'to have a demon'. For example, our Lord was accused by the people of having a demon in John 7.20 and 8.48.

The verb most commonly used in the gospels for the casting out of demons is *ekballo*, 'to drive out'. The verb *exorkizo*, 'to exorcise', does not occur in the gospels, nor in the New Testament. The noun exorcist (*exorkistes*) does, however, occur once in the New Testament in Acts 19.13, where it is applied to certain itinerant Jewish exorcists. This is the earliest known occurrence of this noun in Greek literature.[21]

As we have already seen, the verb *therapeuo* is also used for the casting out of evil or unclean spirits in Matthew 17.18; Luke 6.18 and 7.21. On one occasion the verb *iaomai* is used with the same meaning (cp. Luke 9.42). If we compare the parallel accounts of the healing of the epileptic boy in the three synoptic gospels we find that the following words are used synonymously to describe the casting out of the evil spirit from him: *therapeuo* in Matthew 17.18; *ekballo* in Mark 9.28 and *iaomai* in Luke 9.42.

The possessing agent is defined as a *daimonion*, which is not the diminutive form of *daimon*, a demon, but the neuter form of the adjective *daimonios*, meaning 'pertaining to a demon'.[22] (The word *daimon* itself occurs in only two places in the gospels: Matthew 8.31 and Mark 5.12). The term *daimonion* is left unqualified except in one case (Luke 4.33), where it is spoken of as 'an unclean demon (*daimonion akatharton*)'. In both the AV and the RV of this verse it was mistranslated 'devil' which is more properly the name of Satan, the Devil (*diabolos*, 'the slanderer').

The other name for the agent of possession is *pneuma* or 'spirit'. This word may be used alone or more commonly be qualified by *akathartos*, 'unclean', or less frequently by *poneros*, 'evil'. In Luke 4.33 the names are combined in the unique phrase, 'having the spirit of an unclean demon', which describes the state of the demoniac in the synagogue at Capernaum.[23]

## Chapter 8
# THE APPROACH TO HEALING

Before we describe the methods by which Jesus healed the sick, there are a number of preliminary aspects of his healing activities which are important for a proper understanding of these activities. These form the subject of this chapter and include the question of who took the initiative in his healing of the sick, of what formed the context of this healing, of who were the witnesses of the healing, and finally of how far we can determine the motive or motives which lay behind his healing activity.

## THE INITIATIVE IN HEALING

On most occasions when Jesus healed sick people, the gospel records tell us who took the initiative. In only four out of the twenty-six occasions on which he healed individual sick people is this doubtful or unknown. These twenty-six occasions are classified in the following table which identifies those who appear to have taken the initiative in each case.

*I. Those in which Jesus himself took the initiative (4):*
1. The woman with the spirit of weakness (Luke 13.12).
2. The Bethesda paralytic (John 5.6).
3. The ear of Malchus (Luke 22.51).
4. The widow's son at Nain (Luke 7.14).

*II. Those in which the disciples took the initiative (2):*
1. Peter's mother-in-law (Mark 1.30).
2. The man born blind (John 9.2).

*III.Those in which the sick took the initiative (7):*
1. The two blind men (Matthew 9.27).
2. The ten leprosy patients (Luke 17.13).
3. The man full of leprosy (Luke 5.12).
4. The woman with the flow of blood (Mark 5.27).
5. Blind Bartimaeus (Mark 10.47).
6. The synagogue demoniac (Mark 1.24).
7. The Gadarene demoniac (Mark 5.6).

*IV. Those in which relatives took the initiative (5):*
1. The nobleman's son (John 4.47). His father.
2. The daughter of Jairus (Mark 5.23). Her father.

   3. The Syrophoenician girl (Mark 7.26). Her mother.

   4. The epileptic boy (Mark 9.17). His father.

   5. Lazarus (John 11.3). His sisters.

**V. *Those in which friends or master took initiative (2):***

   1. The paralysed man (Mark 2.3). His friends.

   2. The centurion's servant (Matthew 8.5). His master.

**VI. *Those in which opponents of Jesus took the initiative (2):***

   1. The man with the withered hand (Luke 6.6-7).

   2. The man with dropsy (Luke 14.1-3).

**VII. *Those in which unknown persons took the initiative (4):***

   1. The dumb demoniac (Matthew 9.32).

   2. The blind and dumb demoniac (Matthew 12.22).

   3. The deaf mute (Mark 7.32).

   4. The blind man of Bethsaida (Mark 8.22).

If we analyse the twelve records of the occasions when Jesus healed the multitude we find that on four occasions he took the initiative, on three occasions the sick themselves did so, and on four occasions it was other people, while in one case it is not mentioned who took the initiative.

The fact that our Lord so seldom took the initiative in healing comes as a surprise, but it is the clear impression given in the accounts of his miracles of healing. This means that the healing of the sick, the exorcism of demons and the raising of the dead were not the primary purpose or task of his earthly ministry. It is never recorded of him that he sought out the sick, only that he healed them when he saw them or when they were brought to him.

The most interesting record of all in this connection is the healing of the paralysed man by the pool of Bethesda in John 5.1-9. Around and between the twin pools at Bethesda, Herod the Great had built five stone porches to shelter the sick people who gathered there because of the healing reputation of the waters. In these porches 'lay many invalids - blind, lame and paralysed' (v.3 NRSV). Jesus comes into their midst and chooses only one of the multitude for healing, and then withdraws quietly and quickly after he has healed him. What an opportunity missed if healing had been his primary purpose. The fact that he did not take advantage of the opportunity presented by the crowd of sick people at Bethesda shows clearly that physical healing was not the primary reason why he had come into the world. He always taught the people, but he did not always heal the sick of their disease.

The number of cases in which it is recorded that Jesus took the initiative is too few from which to draw any firm conclusions, but there are several features about them which should be noted. It is Luke alone who records three of the cases and this may mean that he was particularly interested to know who it was who took the initiative in the miracles of healing. In each case except that of Malchus (Luke 22.51) a definite formula appears to introduce the miracle. This can seen by comparing the beginning of the three narratives:

1. The bent woman: '*And when Jesus saw her, he called her and said to her....*' (Luke 13.12).

2. The Bethesda paralytic: '*When Jesus saw him and knew that he had been lying there a long time, he said to him...*' (John 5.6).

3. The widow of Nain: '*And when the Lord saw her, he had compassion on her and said to her...*' (Luke 7.13).

In the case of the man born blind, John tells us that Jesus saw him (John 9.1), but he goes on to tell of the disciples' question about the origin of his blindness and not of what Jesus said. For this reason we have suggested that the initiative here came from the disciples who took up his case. However, it may be that this was another incident in which Jesus took the initiative as Barrett suggests.[1] It is worth noting that Jesus never took the initiative in a case of demon possession nor in any case where the sick was of non-Jewish race.

The source of the initiative in the two cases in which we have suggested that the opponents of Jesus were responsible is uncertain. The fact that Jesus' opponents were present and were particularly concerned to know what he would do about healing the sick on the sabbath day, makes it at least possible that they were responsible for the presence of the sick person on these occasions.

## THE CONTEXT OF HEALING

When Jesus unrolled the scroll of the prophet Isaiah which was handed to him in the Nazareth synagogue on that sabbath morning at the beginning of his ministry, he found the sixty-first chapter and from it read out to the assembled congregation the terms of his own commission (Luke 4.16-19). This commission included preaching and healing and Jesus combined these two activities throughout his ministry. The most explicit mention of this combination occurs first in Matthew 4.23 where we read:

And he went about all Galilee, teaching in their synagogues and preaching the gospel of the kingdom and healing (*therapeuo*) every disease (*nosos*) and every infirmity (*malakia*) among the people.

A similar statement to this occurs again in Matthew 9.35 and acts as a preface to the Mission Charge to the Twelve when Jesus sent them out to preach and to heal.

In general, there is a definite distinction between preaching and teaching in the gospels and throughout the New Testament as a whole.[2] Teaching (*didache*, from *didasko*, 'to teach') was the giving of systematic instruction such as in the Sermon on the Mount. This is an example of what Jesus taught his disciples and the listening crowds (Matthew 5.2, 28). This teaching was given both in the synagogue and in the open air and may be addressed to both believers and unbelievers.

By contrast, preaching (denoted by the verbs *euangelizo* or *kerusso*) is the proclamation of a definite message usually defined (particularly in Matthew) as 'the good news (*euangelion*)' of God (Mark 1.14) or of the kingdom (Matthew 4.23; 9.35). In the earlier part of his ministry Jesus is said to have preached in the Jewish synagogues (Mark 1.39; Luke 4.44), but later it was in the open air and in both cases it was to those who had not heard the good news. He is said to have sent out both the Twelve and the Seventy to preach the kingdom of God without mention of teaching (Matthew 10.7 and Luke 10.6 respectively). However, the distinction between teaching and preaching is not a rigid one for we find that the same activity may be referred to as both 'teaching' and 'preaching' (cp. Mark 1.21, 38), and what Matthew 4.23 calls 'teaching and preaching', Mark 1.39 and Luke 4.44 call simply 'preaching'.

While it is clear that our Lord's ministry combined preaching, teaching and healing, the relative proportions of these activities varied with the circumstances in which he found himself. However there are definite indications that the emphasis in our Lord's ministry is more on preaching and teaching than on healing. For instance, when Peter and the others interrupted Jesus at prayer early one morning above Capernaum with the news that everyone was looking for him, Jesus replied, 'Let us go on to the next towns, that I may preach there also; for that is why I came out' (Mark 1.38, cp. Luke 4.43). He had spent the previous evening healing all the sick and demon-possessed of Capernaum, and verse thirty-nine tells us that he went on from there preaching and casting out demons throughout Galilee, although he did not mention healing in his reply to Peter, only preaching. This emphasis on preaching and teaching is seen in the amount of space devoted to them by the gospels in comparison to that given to healing.

We have already seen how the amount of space given to recording our Lord's teaching varies from fifty per cent of Mark's gospel to seventy-five per cent of Matthew's gospel, while the amount of space devoted to healing ranges from nine per cent of Matthew's gospel to twenty per cent of Mark's gospel. The contrast is obvious and clearly indicates where the emphasis lies. This emphasis on preaching and teaching is also apparent when we examine the gospel accounts of our Lord's ministry more closely. For instance, there are three occasions where Matthew mentioned that healing was performed by Jesus but where Mark in recording the same incident speaks only of teaching. We can see this if we compare Matthew 9.35 with Mark 6.6; Matthew 14.14 with Mark 6.34; and Matthew 19.2 with Mark 10.1. The result of this comparison is rather surprising when we remember how we found that Mark gave much more space to healing compared with Matthew. There must, therefore, have been more miracles of healing than even Mark records (cp. John 20.30).

It appears then that, in general, healing is carried out in the context of preaching and teaching in the gospels rather than the other way round. In other words, healing as an activity of Jesus is practised in illustration of his preaching and teaching rather than as their text and occasion. There are, of course, exceptions to this general observation and it is of interest to note that they are found more often in the fourth gospel than in the synoptic gospels. Nevertheless, the point remains that physical healing was not the primary purpose for which Jesus came, and it is for this reason that preaching and teaching receive the primary emphasis in the gospel records.

The healing activity of Jesus had a very intimate connection with its context in his teaching and preaching. They were concerned with 'the good news of the kingdom', and so was healing. When Jesus and his disciples healed, the kingdom 'came near' to the sick people they healed (Luke 10.9), and when he cast out demons the kingdom of God 'came upon' those whom he delivered from their power (Matthew 12.28 and Luke 11.20). These acts of healing and deliverance were signs of the breaking into the human situation of the kingdom of God, and a foreshadowing of the time when God alone will reign. They were not indications of the glorious manifestation of the kingdom, for that was still future, but of its healing and saving power now visible in the present. In Jesus' preaching and teaching about the kingdom, people were given the opportunity of accepting the kingly rule of God and of fulfilling its demands. In his healing they were provided with a demonstration of its power and its potentiality.

## THE WITNESSES OF HEALING

The witnesses of the healing miracles of Jesus can be divided into three main groups - his disciples, the religious leaders of the community and 'the people'.

### The disciples

The term disciple (*mathetes*) is common in the gospels and the Acts where it usually means an adherent or follower of Jesus Christ. It may be used in a broader sense of all who believe in him (e.g. Luke 6.17 and John 6.60-69) or in a narrower sense when it refers to the twelve men whom he chose to be apostles (Luke 6.13). We may assume that some of his disciples accompanied him when he healed sick people, although they are not always mentioned in the record of these occasions. Thus, some disciples were certainly with Jesus when he healed the man born blind (John 9.2), but there is no mention of any at the healing of the Bethesda paralytic (John 5.1-9). The presence of the Twelve with him when he healed the sick was part of their training for, as we read in Matthew 10.1 and Mark 3.14, Jesus appointed the Twelve not only to be with him but also to be commissioned to preach and to heal the sick and cast out demons. Consequently every incident of healing at which the Twelve were present was another lesson for them in how to heal the sick, so that when they were sent out to heal they were able to do so by following Jesus' example (Mark 6.13 and Luke 9.6). Later, Jesus sent out seventy more of his disciples to heal the sick and to announce the coming of the kingdom of God (Luke 10.9), and they returned with joy and reported how they had been able to cast out demons (v.17).

Even those whom Jesus chose, were not always successful as we know from the case of the epileptic boy (Mark 9.18). On this occasion nine of the Twelve had failed to heal the boy and Jesus told them afterwards that they had failed because they had not prayed (Mark 9.29). It may be significant that it was only after this incident that the disciples came to Jesus with their request, 'Lord, teach us to pray' (Luke 11.1).

The presence of the disciples at the healing of the sick by Jesus explains why some of the records of healing by Jesus give the impression of being based on the accounts of eye-witnesses. One good example is the record of the healing of the epileptic boy in Mark 9.14-27 which we shall consider in detail in Chapter Ten. Another example is the account of the healing of the man born blind in John 9.1-41 which will be examined in Chapter Twelve.

## The religious leaders

The religious leaders of the Jews and their representatives form the second group of witnesses of the healing miracles of Jesus. They are described as Scribes and Pharisees and were the interpreters and upholders of the Jewish law. They were present at eight of the miracles of healing performed by Jesus. On the occasion of the healing of the paralytic at Capernaum, Luke tells us that Pharisees and teachers of the law (i.e., the Scribes) were present from every village in Galilee and Judaea including Jerusalem (Luke 5.17).

Although they saw so many of the miracles of healing which Jesus performed we are never told that they showed any amazement or astonishment at them. Their reaction was almost always recorded as hostile. They accused Jesus of breaking the law when he healed the sick on the sabbath day (Mark 3.2 and Luke 14.1-6) and we are told that they were furious and discussed how they might get rid of him after Jesus had healed the man with the withered hand on the sabbath day (Luke 6.11, cp. Mark 3.6). They accused him of blasphemy when he forgave the sins of the paralytic (Mark 2.6-7). When he cast out demons they said that he did this by the prince of demons and not by the power of God (Matthew 9.34; 12.24 and Mark 3.22). The fact that they were mainly hostile witnesses makes their testimony to the historicity of the healing miracles all the more valuable.

One reason why the Pharisees and Scribes showed no amazement at the healing miracles of Jesus may have been because they did not regard them as unique. They believed that such miracles could be performed by their own colleagues. This is suggested by the comment of the superintendent of the synagogue recorded in Luke 13.14. He was angry that Jesus had healed the bent woman on the sabbath and said to his congregation, 'There are six days for work. So come and be healed on those days, and not on the Sabbath'. This appears to imply that on those other days, people could be healed by himself or one of his colleagues as part of their routine 'work'. According to

Klausner, 'The people looked upon the Pharisees and Scribes as holy men and therefore miracle-workers. Both the Talmud and the Midrash give accounts of miracles performed by Rabban Yochanan ben Zakkai and R. Eliezer ben Hyrcanus, his disciple, who lived in the time of Jesus. But with the Pharisees miracles were only a secondary interest'.[3] Jesus himself admitted that there were those who could cast out demons in the Jewish society of his day (see Matthew 12.27; Luke 8.19; cp. Acts 19.13-16), but there are very few references to Rabbis performing healing miracles in the Talmud and Midrash and none at all in Josephus.[4]

The paucity of references to the various kinds of healing miracles could be explained by the fact that these Rabbinic miracles were so common as to be not worth recording, but this seems unlikely. It seems much more probable that the coolness and unresponsiveness of the Pharisees and Scribes towards the healing activity of Jesus arose not from the fact that they thought they could perform similar miracles and therefore those of Jesus were not unique, but from their hostile attitude to him and their wish to denigrate him in the eyes of the people.[5] They never attack him for his healing miracles but only on the basis of their accompanying circumstances, such as performing them on the sabbath day (e.g. Matthew 12.9-14; Luke 13.15-16) or claiming to forgive sins as well as heal physical disease (Matthew 9.2-7).

### The people

The third group who witnessed Jesus' miracles of healing were 'the people (*ho laos*)'. They came to Jesus in their thousands from all over Palestine and from beyond its borders (Matthew 4.25; Mark 3.7-8; Luke 6.17). They came to hear his teaching when they 'hung on his words' (Luke 19.48 NIV) and 'listened to him with delight' (Mark 12.37 NIV) for he taught with an authority which their Scribes did not possess (Matthew 7.29 and Mark 1.22). They watched in amazement as he healed the sick and cast out demons (Matthew 9.8; Mark 1.27; 2.12; 5.20; 7.37; Luke 4.36; 9.43; 11.14), with the result that they brought their own sick people to be healed by Jesus (Matthew 4.24; 14.35; 15.30; Luke 6.17-19). When they witnessed these cases of healing they usually glorified God (Matthew 15.31; Mark 2.12) and gave praise to his name (Luke 18.43). There was, however, sometimes another reaction for on three occasions we are told that when they witnessed healing, the people were afraid. This feeling of fear followed the healing of the paralytic man (Matthew 9.8; Luke 5.26), the resurrection of the son of the widow of Nain (Luke 7.16) and the exorcism of the Gadarene demoniac (Luke 8.37).

In every crowd of witnesses of unusual events there are always the committed, the critical and the curious but impressionable. So it was in New Testament times.

## THE MOTIVE FOR HEALING

In fewer than half the accounts of the healing miracles of Jesus is any indication of his motive given. As Richardson has pointed out, none of the four gospels is interested in the question of the motives of Jesus and their authors would not be interested in 'our modern discussion of what is sometimes crudely called "the psychology of Jesus"'.[6] Nevertheless it is possible to identify some motives which appear to underlie the healing activity of Jesus even though in most cases these are implicit rather than explicit. The following list is an attempt to identify and classify the motives which appear to underlie most of the healing incidents whether individual or group which are recorded in the gospels.

*I. An expression of compassion (4):*
1. The man full of leprosy (Mark 1.41).
2. The dead son of the widow of Nain (Luke 7.13).
3. Blind Bartimaeus and his friend (Matthew 20.34).
4. Healing after the return of the Twelve (Matthew 14.14).

*II. A response to a cry for mercy (5):*
1. The two blind men (Matthew 9.27).
2. The Syrophoenician girl (Matthew 15.22).
3. The epileptic boy (Matthew 17.15).
4. Blind Bartimaeus (Matthew 20.30).
5. The ten leprosy patients (Luke 17.13).

*III.An answer to faith (8):*
1. The centurion's servant (Matthew 8.10; Luke 7.9).
2. The paralysed man (Mark 2.5 and parallels).
3. The two blind men (Matthew 9.28-29).
4. The woman with the flow of blood (Mark 5.34).
5. The Syrophoenician girl (Matthew 15.28).
6. The epileptic boy (Mark 9.24).
7. The Samaritan leprosy patient (Luke 17.19).
8. Blind Bartimaeus (Mark 10.52; Luke 18.42).

*IV. A manifestation of glory (3):*
1. The nobleman's son (John 4.54, cp. 2.11).
2. The man born blind (John 9.3).
3. The raising of Lazarus (John 11.4).

*V. A fulfilment of Scripture (3):*
1. The evening healings at Capernaum (Matthew 8.16-17).
2. The demonstration to the Baptist's disciples (Matthew 11.2-6; Luke 7.18-23).
3. The healings by the seaside (Matthew 12.15-21).

In some cases, it is possible to identify more than one motive.

## An expression of compassion

Today, it is common to attribute our Lord's miracles to his feeling of compassion for the sick, and so it is surprising to find that this is not frequently done in the gospels. There are only four cases in which it is done explicitly and the word used in each case is the verb *splanchnizomai* which is derived from the noun *splanchnon*, and is the strongest word for pity in the Greek language. In its plural form *splanchna*, this noun is used to denote the inward parts of the body particularly the upper or nobler organs such as the heart, lungs and liver which were the seat of the emotions and the affections, in contrast to the *entera* or intestines which were regarded as the lower or ignoble organs by the ancient Greeks. The verb, therefore, means 'to be moved in the inward parts', i.e., to feel sympathy, pity or compassion for a person in the deepest part of one's being. As Lightfoot originally suggested, the word appears to have been a coinage of the Jewish dispersion for, apart from an isolated occurrence in a fourth-century BC inscription from the island of Cos, it is unknown before its occurrence in Biblical Greek.[7]

In the New Testament the verb is used only in the synoptic gospels where it occurs twelve times, including twice in parallel accounts. On seven of these occasions, compassion is attributed to Jesus by the gospel writers or by the one seeking help as in Mark 9.22. Before the feeding of the four thousand, Jesus himself described his feeling of compassion towards them because they were all hungry (Matthew 15.32 and its parallel Mark 8.2). The remaining three occurrences describe the attitude of figures who occur in his parables - the master of the unmerciful servant (Matthew 18.27), the good Samaritan (Luke 10.33) and the father of the prodigal son (Luke 15.20). In each of these cases the implication is that such compassion was what Jesus would like to see displayed by his disciples.

We find then that the compassion of Jesus was aroused by the presence of hunger (Matthew 15.32; Mark 8.2), by the condition of leaderlessness (Matthew 9.36; Mark 6.34), by the sight of mourning (Luke 7.13), and by sickness. In the four cases relating to sickness which we listed above, we are told that our Lord's compassion was directed to the relatives or friends of the sick. In the case of the widow of Nain it was the mother of the dead man who was the object of his compassion (Luke 7.13), and in the case of the group healing after the return of the Twelve from their mission we are told that Jesus had compassion on the crowd and healed their sick (Matthew 14.14). It is noteworthy that Matthew says here that Jesus had compassion on the crowd, not primarily on the sick amongst them. In the parallel reference of Mark 6.34 we are told that Jesus had compassion on the crowd, but there is no mention of healing, only of teaching.

The only individuals on whom we are told that Jesus had compassion because of their sickness were the leprosy patient of Mark 1.40-41 and the two blind men of Matthew 20.34.

The case of the leprosy patient needs further consideration for there is some doubt about whether he was in fact the object of the compassion of Jesus. The case is described in all three synoptic gospels and Luke adds the clinical detail that he was a very advanced case of the disease (Luke 5.12). Mark alone tells us that Jesus was moved with compassion (*splanchnistheis*, Mark 1.41) and stretched out his hand to touch and heal him, an action which would render Jesus unclean according to the Rabbinic regulations in the Mishnah.[8] There is a very impressive array of textual evidence for this reading of the original Greek text, but there is an alternative reading from the Western textual tradition which instead of speaking of Jesus' compassion speaks of his anger and reads *orgitheis*, being angry. Vincent Taylor and many other commentators on this verse accept this second reading on the well-established rule of textual criticism first laid down by the textual critic J.A. Bengel (1687-1752), that where there is a choice of readings the more difficult reading is more likely to be the correct one.[9]

It is certainly more difficult to understand why Jesus was angry when the man with leprosy came before him, than to understand why he felt compassion which would be much more natural in the circumstances. The standard Greek texts still retain the reference to compassion and put the reference to anger in the critical apparatus, and this is probably the correct procedure.[10] If we do accept the reference to anger as the correct text, then we accept a reading for which no satisfactory explanation has yet been given. Any acceptable explanation for the anger is rendered even more difficult when we realise that the man's disease was probably not leprosy as we know it today, and therefore not as disfiguring as that disease can be, but some variety of skin disease which showed the features which made the one who suffered from it ceremonially unclean according to the levitical regulations (Leviticus 13.1-3).[11]

## A response to a cry for mercy

On three occasions sick people, and twice their close relatives, approached Jesus with the cry '*Eleeson* (Have mercy)'. This cry for mercy recognised Jesus' power to heal and assumed his willingness to heal. It was an appeal to his feeling of compassion which we have seen he had towards the sick. When the gospels refer to this feeling of compassion, they do not use the verb *eleeo*, to have mercy, which is the one used by the sick in their plea for healing. They use the verb *splanchnizomai* which refers to that inner feeling of compassion of which acts of mercy and healing are the outward expression.

The cry for mercy is never used alone by those who seek healing from Jesus. It is always accompanied by a confession of faith in him which is a recognition of his power to heal. This confession and recognition is conveyed in the title by which Jesus is addressed along with the cry for help. These titles are five in number and none is identical with the others although they are made up of only four basic titles. The five titles are as follows:

**Lord**, used by the father of the epileptic boy (Matthew 17.15).

**Son of David**, used by the two blind men (Matthew 9.27).

**Lord, Son of David**, used by the mother of the Syrophoenician girl (Matthew 15.22).

**Jesus, Son of David**, used by Blind Bartimaeus (Mark 10.47; Luke 18.38).

**Jesus, Master** (*epistates*), used by the ten leprosy patients (Luke 17.13).

These titles all acknowledge the authority of Jesus and express different aspects of that authority. The title Lord (*kurios*) applied to Jesus in the New Testament has been the centre of much discussion,[12] but its use by the father of the epileptic boy must be more than a title of courtesy. He was expecting Jesus to do what his disciples had failed to do and this meant that he believed that Jesus had more power than they had. As if to remove any doubt on this matter, both Mark and Luke substitute 'Teacher (*didaskalos*)' for Lord, although they omit the cry for mercy (Mark 9.17; Luke 9.38).

The title **Son of David** is Messianic and clearly expresses the belief in Jesus as the Messiah.[13] Since the Messiah was to bring healing with him (Malachi 4.2) it was a very appropriate title on the lips of those who approached Jesus for healing and linked his healing activity with the expectations of the Old Testament.

The name of **Jesus** ('Saviour', Matthew 1.21) is the name most frequently used when our Lord is spoken of in the gospels, but it is used to address him on only four occasions and only by sick or demon-possessed persons. It is never used alone as the sole form of address. Twice it is used by demon-possessed persons who were disturbed at our Lord's presence when it formed part of the expression of their distress in his presence. The synagogue demoniac addresses him as 'Jesus of Nazareth' and goes on to recognise him as the Holy One of God who has power to destroy demons (Mark 1.24; Luke 4.34). In a similar manner, the Gadarene demoniac calls him 'Jesus, Son of the Most High God' (Mark 5.7; Luke 8.28) which also implies that he has power and authority over demons. In the other two cases in which the name of Jesus is used, it is associated with a cry for mercy. As we have seen, Blind Bartimaeus calls our Lord 'Jesus, Son of David' (Mark 10.47; Luke 18.38), and the ten men afflicted with leprosy address him as 'Jesus, Master' in Luke 17.13. This word 'Master (*epistates*)' describes one who has authority over others, but apart from this latter occasion it is only used by the disciples in addressing Jesus.

Of these four basic titles or names of our Lord, **Son of David** and **Master** are not used in the New Testament outside the gospels, and did not survive in Christian usage. There was in fact an attempt to revive the use of the term **Master** in certain circles of Anglo-Saxon Christianity in the nineteenth century but its meaning was not very precise and it again fell out of use.[14]

The other two titles, **Jesus** and **Lord**, did survive and are still in common use amongst us, enriched by centuries of Christian experience. In our present context all these four designations express the faith on the basis of which the sick approached our Lord with a cry for mercy and a plea for healing.

It is interesting that those possessed by demons never themselves approach Jesus with a request for mercy or for healing. They are either brought to Jesus by others or are disturbed by his presence near them (e.g. Mark 1.24 and 5.7). Also they never use any of the Messianic titles we have just discussed in addressing him. They usually use titles which acknowledge his deity as the Son of God (e.g. Mark 1.24; 3.11 and 5.7).

## An answer to faith

The writers of the gospels are not as interested in the role played by faith in the healing miracles of Jesus as writers would be today. Modern authors are often very concerned to determine the place of faith in our Lord's healing activity in order to decide whether he can be regarded as a 'faith-healer' or not. Out of the twenty-six accounts of individual healing miracles recorded in the gospels, faith is mentioned in only twelve, and amongst these there are eight in which it appears that Jesus healed in answer to faith. In four of these it was the faith of the sick person to which Jesus responded. These were the cases of the two blind men (Matthews 9.28-29), the woman with the flow of blood (Mark 5.34), the Samaritan leprosy patient (Luke 17.19) and Blind Bartimaeus (Mark 10.52). In the other four cases it was the faith of the friends or relatives which produced the response of Jesus. An exception to this may occur in the case of the paralysed man brought by his four friends, for we read that he was healed 'when Jesus saw their faith' (Matthew 9.2; Mark 2.5 and Luke 5.20). Modern commentators usually understand this to refer to the faith of the sick man and his friends, rather than to that of the friends alone, which was the view of the older commentators.[15]

The healing miracles in which there is no doubt that the faith referred to is that of the friends or relatives of the sick person are as follows:

1. The centurion's servant in Matthew 8.10 and Luke 7.9, where the faith is that of the centurion.

2. The Syrophoenician girl in Matthew 15.28, where the faith is that of the girl's mother.

3. The epileptic boy in Mark 9.24, where the faith is that of the boy's father.

The significance of this is that these cases cannot be labelled as psychoneurotic in nature nor their cure regarded as due to mechanisms of psychological suggestion. Furthermore, not only was the faith that of someone other than the sick, but in the two former cases the sick person was not even present when Jesus was asked to heal them and so was presumably not even aware of what was happening. The third case was that of the epileptic boy and here the sick person was present but was unconscious (Mark 9.26). These considerations make it all the more difficult to regard these cases as those of

psychoneurotic conditions responding to suggestion or the production of a
'psychic atmosphere' as Weatherhead describes it.[16]

The object of the faith to which Jesus responded by healing is not usually
explicitly stated. The sick or their relatives are exhorted to believe, but it is
not usually stated in what they are to believe, as we can see in such references
as Mark 5.36; 9.23; John 4.48, etc. In the case of the two blind men Jesus
directed their faith to his ability to heal by his question, 'Do you believe that
I am able to do this?' (Matthew 9.28). Also, he sought to elicit Mary's faith
in himself as able to restore her brother Lazarus to life before he actually did
so (John 11.25-26).

Although Jesus did not say what the object of the faith of the sick or their
relatives and friends had been, their faith must have been in his power and
ability to heal. This faith was sometimes expressed in the title by which Jesus
was addressed by the sick as we saw in the last section, but more often was
implied in the approach of the sick or their relatives to Jesus that they might
be healed.

## A manifestation of glory

Glory or *doxa* is another example of a Classical Greek word whose
meaning was completely transformed when it was adopted into Biblical
Greek and used in the Greek translation of the Old Testament. It originally
meant an opinion or a conjecture about something which might be true or
false. Then it was used for the honour or reputation of someone about whom
a good opinion was held, and in the Greek Old Testament it denotes the
honour, majesty and visible splendour of the presence of God which came
to have the special name of the *Shekinah* in Rabbinic theology.[17]

The motive of manifesting his glory is found most explicitly in the
account of the raising of Lazarus by Jesus in John 11.1-44. In this account it
is mentioned first in verse four which may be the actual message that Jesus
sent back to the sorrowing sisters. Later he appears to refer to this message
when he says to Martha, 'Did I not tell you that if you would believe you
would see the glory of God?' (v.40). In the case of the man born blind, Jesus
speaks of his healing as manifesting the works of God (John 9.3), which is part
of the revelation of his glory. To reveal the glory of God is to manifest his
power and majesty, and in John the signs (*semeia*) do just that. Not only do
they reveal the glory of God, they also reveal the glory of Jesus as the Christ,
the Son of God, for this glory is one and the same (John 1.14; 2.11; 11.4; 17.5,
22, 24). Thus for Jesus, the miracles he performed had evidential value and
bore witness to who he was, and so part of the motive behind them was to
show that he was sent from God. Therefore, in discussion and controversy
he would appeal to the works that he did to show who he was and whence
he came (John 5.36; 10.25; 14.11; 15.24), and others were not slow to
recognise their significance (John 3.2; 5.17-18; 9.33).

The miracles of Jesus were never performed simply to reveal the glory of God as a phenomenon for the world to observe and admire. In his rebuff to the court official in John 4.48, Jesus made it quite clear that he was not prepared to perform miracles simply as marvels. His miracles were never simply wonders (*terata*), but always signs (*semeia*).[18]

Although this idea is most obviously present in the fourth gospel, it also occurs in the synoptic gospels where the emphasis is not so much on the manifestation of our Lord's glory, but on the recognition of that glory by those who saw and experienced his healing power at work. We are frequently told by Luke that those who were healed 'glorified God' which means that they recognised and acknowledged his presence and power at work (Luke 5.25; 13.13; 17.15 and 18.43). Matthew and Mark do not speak of the healed individuals glorifying God as Luke does, but they record how the crowds who witnessed the healing miracles did so (Matthew 9.8 and Mark 2.12). It cannot be denied that there is an evidential aspect to the miracles of healing in the gospels for they do witness to the fact that Jesus is the Christ, the Son of the living God. Their occurrence caused the people to acknowledge that Jesus manifested the glory of God as he lived and walked amongst them on earth.

## A fulfilment of scripture

The earliest indication of a motive underlying his healing activity was given by Jesus when he read and applied to himself the lesson from the sixty-first chapter of the book of the prophet Isaiah. The record of this in Luke 4.16-21 is the earliest known account of a synagogue service.[19] The reading of the lesson from the prophets normally concluded the service and so was called the *Haftarah*, a Hebrew word meaning 'dismissal'. At this time the reader chose the passage he read and so Jesus found this chapter in Isaiah and proceeded to read it.[20] He then rolled up the scroll and returned it to the attendant and sat down to expound the meaning of the passage he had just read. To the surprise of the congregation he applied it to himself saying, 'Today this scripture is fulfilled in your hearing' (v.21). He had come to fulfil the scripture which had been written about him. He was the one of whom this scripture spoke and it described his work in terms of preaching, deliverance and healing. It is on this occasion that Jesus quoted the proverb, 'Physician, heal yourself' (v.23) and refers to the fact that he has already performed healing miracles at Capernaum where he had stayed with his family after his visit to Cana (John 2.12).

On two other occasions, Matthew quotes the book of the prophet Isaiah to show how the healing miracles of Jesus fulfilled what was written by the prophet about him. When Jesus spent an evening healing the sick and casting out demons, Matthew records this with the comment, 'This was to fulfil what was spoken by the prophet Isaiah, "He took our infirmities and bore our diseases"' (Matthew 8.17 quoting Isaiah 53.4).[21] Again, after the healing of the man with the withered hand, Jesus healed many sick people and as Matthew records this he quotes Isaiah 42.1-4 as the scripture fulfilled by this incident (Matthew 12.17-21).

There is no doubt that Jesus himself saw his healing activity as the fulfilment of the Messianic prophecies in the Old Testament. This is shown by his reply to the disciples of John the Baptist when they came from John after he had been imprisoned by Herod Agrippa, the tetrarch of Galilee. John had heard of all that Jesus was doing and he sent two of his disciples to Jesus with the question, 'Are you he who is to come, or shall we look for another?' (Matthew 11.3; Luke 7.19). By the phrase 'He that should come (*ho erchomenos*)', the Baptist meant the Messiah. Jesus replies to the question of the Baptist as follows, 'Go and tell John what you have seen and heard: the blind receive their sight, the lame walk, lepers are cleansed, and the deaf hear, the dead are raised up, the poor have the gospel preached to them. And blessed is he who takes no offence at me' (Luke 7.21-23). This description of Jesus' healing activities is derived from a combination of such passages as Isaiah 29.18-19; 35.5-6 and 61.1 where the work of the Messiah is described. Jesus is clearly appealing to his fulfilment of these prophecies by his healing and preaching activities in order to reassure John that he is indeed the Messiah who is to come. In a similar way Jesus tells his disciples that they are seeing and hearing what the prophets and righteous men of former times longed to see and hear (Matthew 13.16-17), i.e., that in his person and work what had been foretold was being fulfilled.

As we saw when we discussed the words for healing in Chapter Seven which are used in the New Testament, those which are used mainly by John for the healing miracles of Jesus are *erga* and *semeia*. On several occasions Jesus appeals to the witness of his works to substantiate his claim that he has come from God the Father (John 10.25, 38; 14.11; 15.24). In his gospel John also appeals to signs as the basis for belief in Jesus as coming from God (John 2.11; 3.2; 20.30-31).

When we suggest that the fulfilment of scripture was a motive behind the healing activity of Jesus, we do not mean to imply that miracles were performed for the express purpose of fulfilling scripture. That would be too naïve and unimaginative a view. But it is evident that whatever the primary motive was for which they were performed, once they had been performed, they could be seen to fulfil the scripture prophecies concerning the Messiah. Matthew in particular is anxious to point this out to his readers, but John also makes use of the healing miracles in this way and uses them as evidence of who Jesus was.

# Chapter 9
# THE METHODS OF HEALING

The methods used by Jesus in his healing activity cannot fail to be of interest to anyone who is concerned with the art and science of healing. His methods were simple and they were effective. They achieved a rate of cure which was beyond the capability of the medical skill available in his day, in cases which were both acute and chronic in character. The results were dramatic and caused people to glorify God.

His methods were basically two in number. In most cases he healed by word and by touch and we may classify his methods as follows:

1. Healing by word.
2. Healing by touch.
3. Healing by both word and touch.
4. Healing involving the use of saliva.
5. Healing at a distance.
6. Healing by excision.

There is no mention of the use of any medicine in this list for nowhere in the gospels are we told that Jesus used any medicinal agent. He certainly recognised the surgical use of olive oil and dilute alcohol in the treatment of wounds as we see from his parable of the good Samaritan (Luke 10.34). Also, according to Mark 6.13 we know that his disciples 'anointed with oil many who were sick and healed them'. On the basis of this verse Micklem has suggested that 'perhaps Jesus sometimes employed this remedy also', but this is to go beyond the evidence.[1]

## Healing by word

**In exorcism.** In his healing of demon-possessed persons by exorcism, Jesus addressed a word of command to the demon to leave them. This was the only method of exorcism recorded as used by him. He never laid hands on the demon-possessed. The words of command he used are preserved in three cases:

1. The synagogue demoniac: *'Be silent, and come out of him'* (Mark 1.25 'unclean spirit'; Luke 4.35 'demon').

2. The Gadarene demoniac: *'Come out of the man, you unclean spirit'* (Mark 5.8 'unclean spirit'; Luke 8.29 'demon'. Cp. Matthew 8.32 'demons').

3. The epileptic boy: *'Come out of him, and never enter him again'* (Mark 9.25 'spirit'; Matthew 17.18 'demon'; Luke 9.42 'demon' and 'unclean spirit').

In each case it is Mark who records the exact words used by Jesus in exorcising the demon, and in each the command is addressed directly to the demon, 'Come out (*exelthe*)!'. In the case of the synagogue demoniac, the demon is also commanded to be quiet for it had been announcing publicly who Jesus was. the Holy One of God. Jesus never accepted the testimony of demons and also sought to silence them by exorcising them as we see in the two cases of the synagogue demoniac and the Gadarene demoniac. In the two cases of exorcism which do not come from the Markan tradition, the details of the exorcism are not given. In the case of the deaf and dumb demoniac, Matthew says simply that Jesus healed him (Matthew 12.22, where the verb *therapeuo* is used to describe the exorcism), and Luke just says that he cast out the demon (Luke 11.14). In the case of the dumb demoniac Matthew tells us that the demon was cast out, after which the dumb spoke (Luke 9.33). The remaining case of exorcism of the six which are recorded in any detail is that of the Syrophoenician girl who was one of the people who were healed at a distance, and so no words could be spoken directly to the demon by Jesus in her case (Matthew 15.24-28; Mark 7.24-30).

The references to the group healings by Jesus frequently mention that he cast out evil spirits, but only Matthew 8.16 gives any indication of the method used. Here we are told that 'they brought to him many who were possessed with demons, and he cast out the spirits with a word'. Exorcism by word or command was the method used by Jesus. This method implies the existence and personality of the demons whom he thus addressed in words which they could understand. In the exorcisms carried out as part of the group healings we find that Jesus refused to allow the witness of the demons as to who he was and commanded them to be silent as he had done the demon of the synagogue demoniac. This is stated explicitly in Luke 4.41 where we are told that 'demons also came out of many crying, "You are the Son of God!" But he rebuked them, and would not allow them to speak, because they knew that he was the Christ'. It is interesting to find that even in our Lord's own lifetime others who were not his disciples were exorcising demons using his power and name (Mark 9.38 and Luke 9.49). Their word of command was the name of Jesus as in Acts 19.13-15.

**In physical healing.** In four cases of physical healing Jesus spoke a word to the sick persons themselves:

1. The paralysed man: *'Rise, take up your bed and go home'* (Matthew 9.6; Mark 2.11; Luke 5.24).

2. The Bethesda paralytic: *'Rise, take up your bed and walk'* (John 5.8).

3. The man with the withered hand: *'Stretch out your hand'* (Matthew 12.13; Mark 3.5; Luke 6.10).

4. The ten leprosy patients: *'Go show yourselves to the priests'* (Luke 17.14).

In each case the command of Jesus was to do something which the sick persons had been incapable of doing because of their sickness and its effects.

They were commanded to move powerless limbs which were incapable of movement after long years of paralysis and disuse, or in the case of the ten leprosy patients they were bidden to present themselves to the priests to be declared clean when the signs of the skin disease which made them unclean were still florid upon them. These signs would disappear as they went to present themselves to the priest.

In raising the dead. In two cases in which he raised the dead Jesus addressed a word of command to the dead person:

1. The widow's son at Nain: 'Young man, I say to you, arise' (Luke 7.14).
2. Lazarus: 'Lazarus, come out' (John 11.43).

It may seem odd that Jesus addressed words of command to the dead who could not be expected to hear them. John gives us the explanation of this in 11.42 where he records that Jesus said that he prayed so that the crowd might understand that his authority and power came from the Father. Similarly his word of command to the dead was spoken aloud so that there would be no doubt that it was Jesus who raised the dead by a deliberate act of power.

In the case of the raising from the dead of the son of the widow of Nain in Luke 7.11-17, we are told that our Lord touched the bier on which the young man lay dead, and then ordered him to get up. It has been suggested that Jesus' touch conveyed healing and revitalising power to the dead man through the bier, but this is unlikely. It is much more likely that he touched the bier to indicate to the bearers to stand still and set their burden on the ground. When they done this, Jesus spoke to the young man and raised him from the dead. Touch played no part in the miracle in this case.

## Healing by touch

We are told that Jesus healed by touch on seven occasions. In four he himself took the initiative:

1. The man with dropsy: 'He took him and healed him' (Luke 14.4).
2. The ear of Malchus: 'He touched his ear and healed him' (Luke 22.51).
3. The healing at Nazareth: 'He laid his hands on a few sick folk and healed them' (Mark 6.5).
4. The healing at evening: 'He laid his hands on every one of them and healed them' (Luke 4.40).

In three the sick themselves took the initiative:

1. The woman with the flow of blood: 'She touched the fringe of his garment and immediately her flow of blood ceased' (Luke 8.44).
2. The healings by the seaside: 'He had healed many, so that all who had diseases (mastigas) pressed upon him to touch him' (Mark 3.10, cp. Luke 6.19).
3. The healings at Gennesaret: 'As many as touched the fringe of his garment were made well' (Matthew 14.36 uses the verb diasozo, while Mark 6.56 uses sozo).

In the case of the man with dropsy we are given no clinical details but simply told he was hudropikos (Luke 14.2). The implication is that he suffered from *hudrops*, a word which lost its first syllable when it came into Middle English as 'dropsy'. This word is no longer in common medical use, but it was used to describe the swelling of some part of the body due to the accumulation of watery fluid in its cavities or tissue spaces, usually as a result of a chronic disease of the heart or kidneys. According to the Rabbis this condition was associated with sudden death in which people 'die even as they speak'.

The Rabbis also believed that dropsy was a punishment for sexual immorality.[2] There is no reason why we should not accept this case as one of classical dropsy due to systemic disease, but because dropsy is so difficult to cure, Micklem has suggested that this man really had what we call today angioneurotic oedema or giant urticaria.[3] This is a localised form of swelling of allergic origin which comes on more quickly than dropsy and passes off more rapidly. However, these two conditions are readily distinguishable and it is unlikely that Luke would have regarded the disappearance of the swelling of angioneurotic oedema as worth recording as a miracle. The fact that he did record it means that he did regard it as a miracle, for even with modern methods of treatment dropsy does not disappear immediately as the use of the aorist tense of the verb *iaomai* implies it did in this case.

It is not, however, unequivocally clear that Jesus did heal this man by touch. We are told that Jesus took hold of the man and healed him (Luke 14.4). The verb used is *epilambano* which in Mark 8.23 is used to describe how Jesus took hold of the blind man of Bethsaida by the hand and led him out of the village before spitting on his eyes and laying his hands on him to restore his sight. It is clear that Mark does not use this verb to describe healing and it may be that we should not understand it to indicate the method of healing in Luke 14.4. If this is so, then we do not know what method Jesus used in this case.

In each of the cases mentioned above, where the word 'touch' occurs, the Greek verb used is *haptomai* which is the strongest of the three Greek verbs which describe touch. It suggests the idea of a voluntary and deliberate effort to take hold of something.[4] It is significant that when Jesus speaks of what has healed the woman with the flow of blood he speaks not of her touch but of her faith (Mark 5.34; Luke 8.46), although it was her touch which caused power (*dunamis*) to flow into her from him (Mark 5.30; Luke 8.46).

While the commonest verb used in the gospels to describe the act of healing by touch is *haptomai*, to which we have just referred, two other verbs are used too. The second most common is *epitithemi* which it is used of healing is always used in the phrase *epitithemi tas cheiras*, 'to lay hands on'. This phrase is used five times of the action of Jesus in laying hands on the sick to heal them (Mark 6.5; 8.23, 25; Luke 4.40; 13.13). The phrase does not appear to have any technical application in the gospels such as it came to have in the history of the Church. It simply meant to touch a person with the hands in a deliberate and purposeful manner in blessing (as when Jesus blessed the children in Matthew 19.15) or more commonly in healing.

The least frequent phrase used of Jesus touching the sick is *krateo tes cheiros*, 'to take by the hand', where the verb is derived from *kratos* (strength), and the hand referred to is the hand of the sick person. This phrase can be ambiguous as it is not always clear whether it refers to the method of healing or simply to the physical assistance given to the healed person to help them to their feet again. It appears to be used in the latter sense where Jesus helps the epileptic boy to his feet after casting out the demon (Mark 9.27), since Jesus' method of casting out demons never involved physical contact with the demon-possessed. It may, however, be used in the former sense of the method of healing in the case of Peter's mother-in-law (Mark 1.31) and in the case of the daughter of Jairus (Matthew 9.25; Mark 5.41; Luke 8.54). In the latter case it should be noted that we are not in fact told that Jesus helped her up, but only that he grasped her hand.

However, these three verbs are on occasion used synonymously as when the Markan usage of *haptomai* in Mark 10.13 is changed to *epitithemi tas cheiras* in Matthew 19.13, and the use of *krateo tes cheiros* in Mark 1.31 is changed to *haptomai* in Matthew 8.15.

Healing the sick by touch or laying on of hands is not mentioned in the Old Testament nor in the Rabbinical literature, but it is mentioned once in the Dead Sea Scrolls. In a commentary on Genesis 12.10-20 found in Cave One at Qumran, Abraham is represented as praying for the Pharaoh of Zoan, the king of Egypt, who had taken Sarai, Abraham's wife, into his harem, and then laying his hands on the Pharaoh's head. The result of this was that the scourge departed from him and the evil spirit which afflicted him was expelled.[5]

According to the gospel records, touch was the main method by which Jesus healed the sick, whether touch alone or touch combined with a word. Healing by touch was well recognised as an effective method in New Testament times. This is shown by the following requests made to Jesus by those who sought his healing for others.

1. Jairus for his daughter: *'Come and lay your hands upon her, so that she may be made well* (sozo), *and live'* (Mark 5.23).

2. Friends of the deaf mute: *'They besought him to lay his hand on him'* (Mark 7.32).

3. Friends of the blind man of Bethsaida: *'They begged him to touch him'* (Mark 8.22).

As well as these specific requests for Jesus to touch the sick and heal them, we also find references to the sick people's belief that they could be healed by simply touching Jesus with or without his permission. Thus the woman with the flow of blood touched his clothes without his permission and was healed (Mark 5.27-29), while the friends of the sick by the Sea of Galilee sought Jesus' permission for their sick to touch 'even the fringe of his garment' so that they might be healed (Mark 6.56). On a third occasion we are not told if permission was sought, but the sick crowded round Jesus in order to touch him that they might be healed (Mark 3.10; Luke 6.19).

The gospel record does not usually tell us which part of the body Jesus touched when he healed the sick by touch. It would be natural to assume that he touched the part which needed healing and certainly this was the case on the three occasions on which the part is specified. Jesus touched the eyes of Blind Bartimaeus (Matthew 20.34), the ears and tongue of the deaf mute (Mark 7.33), and the ear of the injured Malchus (Luke 22.51). In other cases in which the disease was localised, we may imagine Jesus laying his hands on the place which was diseased. For example, it is probable that in the case of the bent woman he laid his hands on her spine (Luke 13.13). However, in most cases we are simply told that Jesus touched the sick person and the place he touched is not recorded.

What happened when Jesus healed a sick person by touch? This question is not answered explicitly, but only implicitly in the answer to the converse question of what happened when a sick person touched Jesus in search of healing. The most instructive case in this respect is that of the woman with the flow of blood which is recorded in the greatest detail in Mark 5.25-34 and who is traditionally known as Berenice or Veronica whose home was in Caesarea Philippi. Some authors have proposed the unlikely diagnoses of menorrhagia or dysmenorrhoea for this woman's condition,[6] but the most probable cause of her chronic uterine haemorrhage was the presence of fibroid tumours (leiomyomata) in the uterus which although benign in nature may cause chronic vaginal bleeding which would make her and anything she touched, ritually unclean (Leviticus 15.25-27).[7] There is, however, no mention of any ritual uncleanness in the case of this woman in spite of the obvious relevance of this levitical regulation. She is regarded by Jesus as a sick woman who needed healing and not also as an unclean woman who needed cleansing. He did not regard himself as unclean after she had touched him. Nor did he refer her to a priest to offer sacrifice for her cleansing as the Leviticus passage required.

Doctors had failed to cure her, and her condition was getting much worse for Mark tells us that her flow of blood (rhusis haimatos, Mark 5.25) had become a fountain (pege, v.29) comparable with the increased amount of blood lost after childbirth, which is called pege tou haimatos in Leviticus 12.7 (LXX). Her condition was described by Mark and then by Jesus as a mastix or scourge (vv.29 and 34). So when the woman heard reports about the healing power of Jesus, she felt that if she could touch even his clothes she would be healed (sozo). So she joined the great crowd around Jesus and worked her way through it until she came up behind him and touched the tassel of his cloak. He was immediately conscious of her touch and knew that it came from behind (v.27), and he turned round to see who had touched him (v.30). Mark tells us that he knew that her touch was different from that of the rest of the crowd because power (dunamis) had gone out of him and into the woman (v.30). The result was that her bleeding ceased immediately and she was healed. As we noted in Chapter Seven, the verb which Mark uses to describe her healing is *iaomai* in the perfect tense *iatai* (v.29) which meant that she was healed completely and for good without any possibility of relapse. When Jesus speaks of her healing, he uses the verb *sozo*, also in the perfect tense *sesoken* (v.34).

How then had she been healed? We may certainly dismiss the idea proposed by some authors that she was healed by autosuggestion or hypnotism.[8] She had been healed by touching Jesus, as a result of which the power (*dunamis*) that produced the healing passed from him and flowed into her body to stop the bleeding and rid her of the tumours which were causing the chronic loss of blood. The power is spoken of in an unusual way which requires careful translation. Most recent commentators accept the rendering first proposed by the RV as the most appropriate one, 'And straightway Jesus, perceiving in himself that the power proceeding from him had gone forth, turned about in the crowd, and said "Who touched my garments?"' (Mark 5.30).[9] The power referred to is the power which he possessed in himself as the Son of God. It is clear that this power went forth from Jesus himself and not from his clothes. No power resided in his clothes. Power to heal resided in him and was available to proceed from him as required, and it was this power which flowed out to this woman in response to her touch. Her healing was not by magic, nor was it independent of our Lord's will although the text appears to suggest that it was outside his knowledge until it was happening. The power which proceeded from Jesus was that of God himself and under God's control, and it was his will that the woman should be healed. To probe deeper is to become involved in suggestions derived from the internal relationships within the Trinity such as that which proposes that in this case the healing was carried out by God the Father without the direct intervention of God the Son.[10] Such suggestions do not seem either desirable or profitable. The woman was healed by the power of God which was available to sick people from Jesus for healing (Luke 6.19). It was this power that Jesus used in every method he employed for healing. Wherever he was, it could be said that the power of the Lord was present to heal (Luke 5.17).

The source of the healing power of Jesus becomes even more explicit in his casting out of demons. Even his enemies had to admit that he needed spiritual power to exorcise evil spirits, but they attributed his power to Beelzebul, the prince of demons and not to God.[11] However, Jesus had little difficulty in demonstrating the inconsistency of their argument, for demons would hardly cast out demons. He pressed his argument further by turning it back on themselves and asking by whom did they think that their sons cast out demons, if they maintained that he did this by the power of the prince of demons (Matthew 12.27; Luke 11.19). He was saying that they should judge him on the same basis as they would judge their own exorcists. Whatever they may think, he has no doubt about his own practice. He casts out demons by the finger of God (Luke 11.20), by the Spirit of God (Matthew 12.28). The phrase 'finger of God' denotes, as Schlier says, 'God's direct and concrete intervention'.[12]

## Healing by word and touch

Healing in the following cases was by a combination of word and touch.

1. Peter's mother-in-law: *'He touched her hand and the fever left her'* (Matthew 8.15 and Mark 1.31). *'He rebuked the fever and it left her'* (Luke 4.39).

2. The advanced leprosy patient: *'He stretched out his hand and touched him, saying, "I will; be clean"'* (Matthew 8.3; Mark 1.41 and Luke 5.13).

3. Jairus' daughter: *'Taking her by the hand he called, saying, "Child, arise"'* (Mark 5.41 and Luke 8.54).

4. The two blind men: *'He touched their eyes, saying, "According to your faith be it done to you"'* (Matthew 9.29).

5. The bent woman: *'He called her and said to her, "Woman, you are freed from your weakness". And he laid his hands upon her.'* (Luke 13.12-13).

6. Blind Bartimaeus: In this case Matthew 20.34 records the touch but not the word, while Mark 10.52 and Luke 18.42 record the word but not the touch.

In the case of Peter's mother-in-law and of Blind Bartimaeus not all the synoptic gospels record that healing was due to both word and touch. The case of Peter's mother-in-law is one of particular interest. She had contracted a febrile disease which was probably malaria carried by mosquitoes breeding in the fresh water of the Sea of Galilee near Capernaum. This produced a high temperature which had prostrated her on her bed (Mark 1.30). Luke calls the fever *puretos megas*, a high fever (Luke 4.38), which the Greek physicians recognised as a serious sign to be distinguished from the less serious *puretos micros* or low fever.[13] Modern medicine still recognises the distinction of *hyperpyrexia* and *pyrexia* as fevers with a temperature above or below 105° Fahrenheit or 40.5° Centigrade or Celsius respectively, and regards hyperpyrexia as a serious sign. Peter and the others were very concerned about her and asked Jesus to see her. Luke tells how he stood over her and rebuked the fever and it left her allowing to get up and serve them. Earlier in the same chapter (v.35) Luke had used the same verb *epitimao* to describe how Jesus had rebuked the demon in the case of the synagogue demoniac. Since the rebuke there was expressed in words, it is probable that it was similarly expressed here, thus making this miracle an example of healing by word and by touch.

The question remains, however, of what were the words in which the rebuke was expressed, and to whom or what was the rebuke addressed. The probability is that the words were a simple command to the fever to be gone. In view of the fact that the verb *epitimao* had previously been used to describe an exorcism, it is sometimes suggested that here too the rebuke of Jesus was directed to the demon believed to be causing the fever or even to Satan himself as the causal agent.[14] This need not necessarily be the case since the same verb in the same tense is used of Jesus rebuking the wind and the waves in the storm on the Sea of Galilee in Mark 4.39 and Luke 8.24. If it be maintained that in both cases Jesus was rebuking a demonic power behind the physical phenomenon, the problem remains of why he rebuked the phenomenon rather than its cause. In Mark 11.4 he spoke to the fig tree in terms which made it clear he was speaking to the tree and not to any spirit behind it, for a spirit could not bear fruit. As Taylor remarks, 'It is perverse to explain this language as a kind of primitive animism'.[15] It is rather an assertion of divine power and authority over the phenomena of physical nature, although it is undeniable that abnormal phenomena of this kind may have a demonic cause on particular occasions. It appears, therefore, that when we take the three synoptic accounts together, the healing of Peter's mother-in-law was not an exorcism but an example of healing by word and touch. Matthew 8.15 and Mark 1.31 record the touch but not the rebuke, while Luke 4.39 mentions the rebuke but not the touch.

In two of the cases he healed by word and touch, Jesus would have contracted ceremonial or ritual uncleanness by touching the body of the one he sought to heal. In the case of the man with advanced leprosy we are told by all three synoptic accounts that Jesus 'stretched out his hand and touched him' (Matthew 8.3; Mark 1.41; Luke 5.13). The combination of the verbs *ekteino*, 'to stretch out', and *haptomai*, 'to touch', in these verses is not found elsewhere in the New Testament and conveys the impression of a very deliberate and intense act of touching, more than that conveyed by the use of *haptomai* alone. On the other hand, the use of the first verb mentioned may simply indicate that the leprosy patient was keeping his distance from Jesus.[16] After he had touched the leprosy patient, Jesus betrayed no consciousness of having contracted ceremonial uncleanness and does nothing to purify himself by seeking cleansing from a priest. This is in contrast to his instruction to the healed man to show himself to the priest on duty and offer for his cleansing what the law of Moses required so that he could be pronounced clean (Matthew 8.4; Mark 1.44; Luke 5.14; cp. Leviticus 14.1-32). Only a priest could pronounce him clean and restore him to the life of the community and so add the social element to his healing. Jesus prefaced his instructions to the healed man about his cleansing with a stern warning not to say anything to anyone. Farrar suggested that this was because Jesus 'desired to avoid the Levitical rites for uncleanness which the unspiritual ceremonialism of the Pharisees might have tried to force upon Him'.[17] This explanation is unlikely, for the warning is more naturally understood as one to the man to avoid social intercourse with people before he had been declared clean by the priest.

The other case in which there was a danger that Jesus might contract ceremonial uncleanness was that of the daughter of Jairus, the ruler of the synagogue in Capernaum. This case is significant because her father would be very familiar with the regulations governing uncleanness by virtue of his position in the religious life of the community. He called Jesus to come and lay hands on his daughter who was at the point of death (Mark 5.23). In fact, she had just died according to Matthew 9.18 and yet he still wanted Jesus to come and lay his hands upon her that she might live (Matthew 9.25; Mark 5.31 and Luke 8.54). Jesus took her by the hand and restored her life. There is no suggestion that by this contact with her dead body he was regarded as ceremonially unclean and no mention of his need for the ceremonial cleansing required by Numbers 19.11-13.

The attitude of Jesus to ceremonial uncleanness illustrated by these two cases is in keeping with his teaching on what defiles a man in Matthew 15.1-20 and Mark 7.1-23. The medical interest of this teaching lies in the anatomical and physiological knowledge it reveals and which is derived from simple observation of the process of digestion. From these two passages it is clear that for Jesus uncleanness or defilement is not physical in origin or nature, but moral and spiritual; nor was it external but arose from the heart of a person. This explains why he did not concern himself with the failure of his disciples to wash their hands before meals which was a ritual requirement of the Jewish oral law or 'the tradition of the elders' (Mark 7.5). It also explains his unconcern about the ceremonial uncleanness which might be derived from contact with an unclean skin disease or with a dead body. The significance of Jesus' teaching is given by Mark when he commented, 'Thus he made all foods clean' (Mark 7.19). This principle laid down by Jesus applied to more than just food, but also to all physical things because personal moral uncleanness comes from within and not from without.

We have now discussed the main methods by which Jesus healed the sick and the demon-possessed and restored the dead to life. There remain two groups of cases in which he healed the sick in which his method included a special feature. In the first group he added the application of saliva to his touch, and in the second group he healed in circumstances in which the use of word, touch or saliva was impossible because the healing was carried out at a distance from the sick person.

## Healing involving the use of saliva

There are three cases in which Jesus made use of his own saliva (*ptusma*).

1. The deaf mute: *'He put his fingers into his ears, and he spat and touched his tongue; and looking up to heaven, he sighed, and said to him, "Ephphatha", that is, "Be opened"'* (Mark 7.33-34).

2. The blind man of Bethsaida: *'He took him by the hand, and led him out of the village; and when he had spit on his eyes and laid his hands upon him, he asked him, "Do you see anything?" And he looked up and said, "I see men; but they look like trees walking." Then again he laid his hands upon his eyes'* (Mark 8.23-25).

3. The man born blind: 'He spat on the ground and made clay of the spittle, and anointed the man's eyes with the clay, saying to him, "Go wash in the pool of Siloam"' (John 9.6-7).

The first thing to notice about these three accounts is that in none of them is the use of saliva the only method of healing which Jesus uses. In the case of the deaf mute it is not even clear that he applied saliva at all, for we are simply told that he spat. Wharton suggested that he spat to disperse the demonic forces, but this suggestion has no support in the gospel record either here or elsewhere.[18] One result of this uncertainty in the case of the deaf mute has been the production of a number of variant readings, all of which are aimed at making the method of use of the saliva more explicit, but the very existence of these attempts at explanation only serves to make the common reading more probable.[19]

Since in none of these three cases was saliva used alone, this excludes any suggestion that it was being used in any magical way. If it had been used magically, then it would been accompanied by a meaningless incantation and these would have been efficacious without the use of any other method. This form of healing played no part in Jesus' practice.

The saliva was applied in different ways in each of the three cases. In the case of the deaf mute it was probably applied to the tongue by the fingers of Jesus (Mark 7.33). With the blind man of Bethsaida, Jesus spat directly on to his eyes (Mark 8.23). In the case of the man born blind he spat on the ground and used the saliva to make a paste from the dust, and then applied this to the blind man's eyes (John 9.6). This absence of any uniformity in the application of the saliva suggests that no ritual pattern was being followed or prescribed for this type of case by Jesus.

The other healing procedures which were used by Jesus along with the application of saliva present some interesting features. In healing the deaf mute, Jesus did no less than seven other things in the production of this man's healing. He began by taking him away from the crowd to establish personal contact with him and to treat him in private. Then he put his fingers into his ears, which may suggest that the deafness had a physical cause and if this is so, it is the only case of physical deafness amongst the individual healing miracles. He spat, presumably on to his fingers. He then touched the man's tongue with his finger. After this he did something which is rarely recorded of him in his healing activities, he looked up to heaven. By this is probably meant that he prayed, for this same phrase clearly means this in Mark 6.41. As well as raising is eyes to heaven, we are told that Jesus sighed which Taylor regards as 'a sign of his deep feeling and compassion for the sufferer'[20] and Swete comments that this sign arose from his humanity.[21] The verb used is stenazo which is used for sighing as the expression of deep inward emotion and according to Cranfield 'it indicates the strong emotion of Jesus as he wages war against the power of Satan, and has to seek divine aid in urgent prayer'.[22] Finally he gives the command, 'Be opened' which Mark preserves in the original Aramaic transliterated as *Ephphatha* (Mark 7.34). Such a command is not appropriate to an exorcism and seems to be addressed to the physical organs which are the cause of the man's disability. This disability could have been due to some form of conduction deafness by which the pathway of the sound waves from the outside to the sensitive inner ear was obstructed, and to the condition of tongue-tie in which the tongue was bound down by a congenitally short frenulum which is the band which binds the front of the tongue to the floor of the mouth.[23] The fact that the man is described as speaking plainly immediately after he was healed (Mark 7.35) suggests that he had already learned to speak and so had not been born deaf, but had become deaf as a result of a childhood infection which affected both his ears. Mark 7.37 records that the people were 'astonished beyond measure (*hyperperissos*)' which suggests that they had not expected Jesus to heal this man.

The healing of the blind man of Bethsaida in Mark 8.22-26 is unique in the gospels for it is the only case in which Jesus had to lay his hands on a sick person twice before they were healed. This healing took place in private away from any emotional effect which a large watching and expectant crowd might produce. Jesus took the man and spat on his eyes and laid his hands on him. He then goes on to ask the blind man a most unexpected question, one which he had never asked in any other case. The question was, 'Do you see anything?' (v.23). The question reads like a request for information, but could be interpreted as implying doubt about whether the method of healing Jesus was using was being effective. The man looked up and said, 'I can see people. They look like trees - only they are walking about' (v.24 Phillips). His reply suggests that he had not been blind from birth, for he remembered what trees looked like. People carrying burdens on their heads resembled trees to his newly-returned but still blurred vision. This meant his near vision had returned and allowed him to recognise the gross outline of objects and their movements, but not the finer detail of these objects. So Jesus again laid his hands on the man's eyes and his distance vision was now restored and he saw everything clearly. This healing was not immediate, but took place in two stages. This fact alone is an indication of the truth of the incident, for no one would invent a story which suggested that Jesus had not healed a sick man completely the first time he had tried.

The blindness of the man born blind was cured by a combination of five procedures (John 9.1-7). First, Jesus spat on the ground. Then he made a paste of the saliva and the dust. This paste he applied to the man's eyes. He then told the man to go and wash the paste off at the pool of Siloam. The man did this and came back with his sight restored.

The function of saliva in these three cases of healing is not easy to assess because saliva has no recognised healing properties today. However, Barclay has reminded us that even today we instinctively put a cut or burned finger into our mouth to relieve the pain by the action of the saliva.[24] This, however, applies only to acute conditions and in the cases we are considering, the conditions were of long standing.

Suggestions have been made that the use of saliva made the cure of the speech difficulty or the blindness more personal and individual, but they do not seem to be very adequate in this context. There are indications that in the ancient world, saliva was believed to possess healing power, but this is usually of a magical nature which is not appropriate in the gospel record. The elder Pliny advises the application of fasting saliva (*saliva jejuna*) to the eyes each morning for the treatment of conjunctivitis.[25] Tacitus records how the Roman emperor Vespasian was credited with the restoration of man's sight at Alexandria in Egypt by moistening his eyes with saliva on the instructions of the god Serapis, the Egyptian god of healing.[26] However, this can hardly be compared with the healing activity of a humble Galilean peasant teacher. About a century later Galen, the famous Greek physician, attributed the cure of certain skin diseases such as psoriasis to saliva, and described how saliva, which he called *phlegma*, could destroy venomous creatures such as scorpions.[27] References to its use are infrequent in Rabbinic literature where its application is condemned, principally because of the magical practices which accompanied its use.[28] Whatever its significance in the healing practice of Jesus, he never used it alone and certainly never with anything resembling an incantation. Its use in healing did not persist in the healing practice of the Church, which indicates that it was not regarded as an essential part of any healing procedure even though it had been used by Jesus himself. The use of saliva or spittle has continued to form part of the Roman Catholic sacrament of baptism during which the priest applies his own saliva to the ears and nostrils of the child being baptised, although this is no longer a matter of obligation. The authority for this custom was based on our Lord's procedure in this case (Mark 7.33).[29]

## Healing at a distance

There are three cases in which Jesus is described as healing at a distance.

1. The nobleman's son: *'Go, your son will live'* (John 4.50).

2. The centurion's servant: *'Go, be it done for you as you have believed'* (Matthew 8.13).

3. The Syrophoenician girl: *'For this saying you may go your way; the demon has left your daughter'* (Mark 7.29).

Here we have three persons whom Jesus healed without touch or word and without even seeing them. It is not clear why he chose to heal from a distance for there were other cases which he could have healed from a distance but did not do so. For example, when Jairus asked him to heal his daughter, Jesus went with him to his house to restore her to life (Luke 8.41-42). It may be that the distances involved in the three cases in which Jesus did not go, were greater than in the case of Jairus' daughter. On the other hand,

Luke 7.6 suggests that Jesus was not a great distance away from the house of the centurion.

In each case Jesus was asked for help by the one who came to him; none of the sick persons sent a personal message direct to him. In each case there is mention of faith, and in the two cases in which it is mentioned most explicitly were concerned with persons of non-Jewish race. These were the Roman centurion whose faith was such that Jesus said he had never found any faith like it, not even in Israel among Jewish people (Luke 7.9); and the Syrophoenician woman whose faith he described as 'great' (Matthew 15.28).

In none of these cases is much clinical detail given. The centurion's servant was lying in bed paralysed and suffering great pain (Matthew 8.6). In addition Luke 7.2 describes him as being at the point of death. Trench has plausibly suggested that this man was suffering from tetanus.[30] The nobleman's son had a febrile illness which could be fatal (John 4.52), whose nature is impossible to determine, while the Syrophoenician girl is simply said to be severely demon-possessed (Matthew 15.22).

In these cases there was no word of command to the sick or to a demon. There was no touch of sympathy or opportunity for the transfer of healing power. There was no special method of healing at all, simply a command to the person who had come to seek help from Jesus that they should return, and an assurance that the sick one was well again. In the case of the nobleman's son we know from the record that the boy's fever left him at the very time that Jesus spoke the word of reassurance to his father (John 4.53).

The fact that in none of these cases was a word of healing spoken has been used by some commentators to suggest that they are not examples of healing, but of the possession by Jesus of special medical knowledge. In the case of the nobleman's son, for example, Bernard says that all that Jesus is represented as saying is, 'Your son will live', i.e. he will recover. He assumes that the father had described his son's symptoms to Jesus who recognised the identity of the disease and knew that it would not be fatal, and that even at that moment the crisis would be passing and the boy getting better.[31] What Jesus did was not beyond human power at that time, although it may have been beyond ordinary human knowledge. This explanation is not a very satisfactory one in view of the use of the word *semeion* in John 4.54. It is unlikely that John would have included this event amongst the *semeia* if it was simply the display of a superior knowledge of the nature and prognosis of the disease from which the boy was suffering. In all the other *semeia* there was a demonstration of supernatural power by Jesus, and this suggests that when Jesus spoke the word to the distraught father it was a word of supernatural healing power and not just a word of favourable prognosis which any Jewish physician might be able to give.

The suggestion is often made that the basis of the healing of the three sick people who were healed at a distance by Jesus was telepathy, but this does not shed much light on the method which Jesus used. The word *telepathy* was introduced by F.W.H. Myers in 1882 and he defined its meaning as 'the communication of impressions of any kind from one mind to another independently of the recognised channels of sense'. This definition is quoted in the Oxford English Dictionary as the standard meaning of the word.[32] Efforts to establish telepathy on a scientific basis and even to found a science of parapsychology based on extra-sensory perception or ESP have not succeeded in spite of the strenuous advocacy of J. B. Rhine (1895-1980) and his colleagues at Duke University in the U.S.A. and Arthur Koestler (1905-1983) in Britain.[33] Therefore the attempt to explain our Lord's healing of the absent sick on the basis of telepathy or extra-sensory perception is only to try and explain the unknown by the uncertain and leads nowhere. Furthermore, although investigators in this field have claimed to be able to transmit information from one mind to another, no one has reliably claimed to have cured cases of physical disease characterised by fever or paralysis, or cases of demonisation by methods which could be described as telepathic. To suggest that the method used by Jesus here was one of telepathy may give it a name, but does not help us to understand how it produced healing.

Trench likened the Syrophoenician woman to a living lightning conductor transmitting the power of Jesus to her sick daughter by offering in her faith a channel of communication between him and her distant daughter.[34] More recently, Weatherhead speaks of the cases of the nobleman's son and the centurion's servant (whom he regards as one and the same person) as cases in which 'at an unconscious level of the mind our Lord's mind actually made contact with that of the patient', and goes on to say that 'it is attractive to think that in a sense Jesus did go to the patient ... and that therapeutic forces in His mind flowed into the deep mind of the patient, achieving his recovery'.[35] Regretfully it has to be said that these attempts at understanding are but fanciful similes and do not advance our understanding of what happened in the cases of absent healing. However, there is no difficulty here if we believe in the fact and efficacy of prayer. In Christian experience throughout the ages the effect of prayer has never been limited by distance. What happened in the healing of the absent sick still occurs today when prayer for those who are absent from us is heard and answered. We may not know how it happens, but we can know that it does.

## Healing by excision

On two occasions Jesus recommended healing by excision, although he never practised this method himself. In the Sermon on the Mount he recommended the excision of the right eye or the right hand as the cure for lust (Matthew 5.29-30). If these were the cause of temptation which might end in sexual immorality then we were better without them. On a later occasion he recommended the excision of the eye, the hand or the foot if they were the cause of temptation and sin of any kind, for it were better to enter into the kingdom of God maimed than to remain whole and end up in eternal fire (Matthew 18.8-9; Mark 9.43-49).

Physical excision of disease is the method of the surgeon and occasionally in the history of the Church this recommendation of Jesus has been taken literally and surgically. The best known example of this is that of Origen, the third-century Biblical scholar and theologian of Alexandria, who on the basis of what Jesus said in Matthew 19.12, castrated himself so as to avoid sexual temptation in view of the fact that he had women as well as men amongst his students.[36] Afterwards Origen admitted that he had been wrong to do so, and such self-mutilation was subsequently forbidden by the Council of Nicea in AD 325.

It is quite clear, however, that Jesus did not intend these commands of his to be taken literally and physically. All three of the members of the body he mentions are paired and even if one of each pair were destroyed, the other one could still serve as the agent of sin. Also, none of these members is the source of temptation or sin for these come from the heart as Jesus reminds his disciples in Matthew 15.18. By the heart he does not mean the physical organ but the centre of a person's mental and moral life and activity, which cannot be excised or amputated.

By his use of this dramatic figure of speech, Jesus was not advocating 'a literal physical self-maiming, but a ruthless moral self-denial'. What he meant was: If your eye causes you to sin, don't look; if you are tempted to sin by your actions, don't do them; and if temptations come from the places you visit, don't go there. Act as though you had no eyes, hands or feet in these situations.[37]

Even though we may believe that these commands of Jesus do not require actual physical excision of parts of the body, they are a reminder that for Jesus, the mind and the imagination need healing just as much as the body, and that healing includes the prevention of physical and moral evil as well as their removal and forgiveness. However, healing by excision is a method which affected persons must apply to themselves. It was, for instance, the method Jesus recommended to the rich young man who came to him seeking eternal life. Jesus told him that he needed to excise his possessions from his life if he would inherit eternal life (Matthew 19.21).

Our survey of the methods which Jesus used in healing sick men and women is now complete, and this concludes our general examination of healing in the gospels. We have looked at the records which describe the healing work of Jesus and the description of this work which they contain. We have considered the context of his healing activity and sought to understand his motive for healing. Finally, in this present chapter we have discussed the methods by which he made the sick whole.

In the following chapters we proceed to study three of the individual cases of healing which are described in more detail in the gospels and show features of special interest.

# Chapter 10
# THE CASE OF THE EPILEPTIC BOY

An older generation of commentators spoke of this lad as 'the lunatic boy', taking their cue from the AV rendering of Matthew 17.15. The verb used in this verse (and also in Matthew 4.24) is *seleniazomai* which literally means 'to be moonstruck' and for which 'lunatic' is the literal translation which was adopted into English from the Vulgate's *lunaticus est*. The RV, however, boldly labelled him 'the epileptic boy', and has been followed by more recent English versions.

The RV did not escape criticism for its new rendering. Creighton tells us that the Revisers justified it on the grounds that 'epileptic' was a more scientific term than 'lunatic' and they quoted a seventh-century Greek medical writer.[1] However, Liddell and Scott give the gospel account of the healing of this boy as the earliest authority for their definition of the word *seleniazomai* as 'to be epileptic'.[2] The literal meaning of the word is derived from the popular belief (held by Galen and Calvin amongst others[3]) that the moon (*selene*) in certain of its phases, and especially when it is full or waning, is injurious to human beings and produces disease of a paroxysmal nature such as epilepsy. This belief may be referred to in Psalm 121.6 where Israel is promised that 'the sun shall not smite you by day, nor the moon by night'. We have no means of knowing whether this was still a living belief in New Testament times, or whether by then the word was used for epilepsy without any reference to its derivation.

In this chapter we are concerned to look at the justification for regarding this boy as epileptic, more particularly from a medical point of view. The account of his case will be found in Matthew 17.14-21; Mark 9.14-29 and Luke 9.37-43.

## THE CASE RECORD

As we see from the references just quoted, the case of the epileptic boy is recorded in all three synoptic gospels. It is one of the few incidents where the narrative of Mark is much fuller than those of Matthew and Luke. The wealth of detail given by Mark suggests its derivation from an eye-witness, and it is probable that this account comes from Peter whose eye for detail and ear for the memorable word we know so well in the gospel of Mark, who as Papias tells us, was regarded as Peter's interpreter (*hermeneutes*) and faithful reporter.[4] The incident is told from the standpoint of one who has returned with Jesus from the Mount of Transfiguration, rather than of one who was present with the nine disciples waiting below. This feature fits in with the traditional setting of the story as immediately following the Transfiguration, for we are told that Peter had gone with Jesus on that occasion along with James and John, while the rest of the disciples remained at the foot of the mountain.

Although this is a miracle of healing, Luke the medical evangelist does not give us the same detail of the miracle as Mark does. Nevertheless, his summary of the clinical features of the case in Luke 9.39 is a masterly example of compressed and relevant description. Matthew's summary of the case in 17.13 is much less medically informed, but his account gives us the *Kyrie eleison* which from the fourth century became the earliest and simplest form of response to a litany used in liturgical worship, often used in its original Greek form.

We are fortunate in this case to have not only the father's description of what happened when the boy had a convulsion, but also a description of an actual fit as seen by an independent eye-witness. This is the kind of case record which the physician hopes for in a case of epilepsy, but is not often able to obtain. Usually he is given a description of a fit by a relative or friend of the patient, but rarely sees an actual fit or obtains an eye-witness account of one from a reliable and independent observer. It is this which makes the account of the epileptic boy so valuable and so convincing to a medical reader. To such a reader there is no need to dissect the account into two distinct narratives such as Bultmann proposes.[5] The suggestion of Taylor that we have two accounts of the same incident is much more acceptable, for it is obvious that we have here intertwined the account of the father describing his son's fits in Mark 9.17-18, 21-22, and the account of the eye-witness describing the two fits which the boy had in his presence (Mark 9.20, 26-27).[6]

## THE HISTORY

In medical usage the term **history** means the information about the disease, its onset, its progress and its present manifestations which is derived from questioning the patient or his relatives and friends. There are some diseases in which the history is very important for establishing the diagnosis, and epilepsy is one of these. Often in cases of epilepsy we can see no signs of the disease or its effects on the patient, and since he loses consciousness during a fit he cannot be expected to help much in the description of what happens to him.

In this case we are very fortunate in having no fewer than seven descriptions of what happened to the boy when he had a fit, and each one of these adds new detail to the picture. Four of these descriptions are derived from the father's account of his son's seizures (Matthew 17.15; Mark 9.17-18, 21-22; Luke 9.39). The other three derive their details from the eye-witness whom we believe to have been Peter (Mark 9.20, 26-27; Luke 9.42). Beare comments on the exuberance of the story in Mark saying it is 'unusually full of detail, some of it repetitive, some irrelevant'.[7] No one who has listened to an anxious father describing the history of an afflicted son's illness could regard such repetitiveness as more than a true and natural characterisation of how this boy's father told his story to Jesus. Repetitive it may be, and that is understandable in the circumstances, but each repetition adds more detail to the picture, none of which can be dismissed as irrelevant in describing a condition such as epilepsy.

We learn from the father that his son has suffered from fits since childhood (*ek paidiothen*, Mark 9.21). This must mean that they probably began before he entered his teens for we are told that he was only a child (*pais*) when he was brought to Jesus by his father (Matthew 17.18; Luke 9.42). This means that he may have been about twelve years old as Jesus was when he was called a *pais* in Luke 2.43, but the New Testament usage of the word is not always as precise as this.[8] According to Hippocrates, *pais* commonly meant a boy of eight to fourteen years of age in Classical Greek usage.[9] Such an early onset of fits is a sign of true epilepsy rather than hysteria which occurs later in life.

The description of the condition makes it clear that it was paroxysmal or periodic in occurrence. The fits came on him without any prior warning, irrespective of wherever he may be (Mark 9.18). The command of Jesus to the unclean spirit never to enter into the boy again (Mark 9.25) also implies that the spirit had been in the habit of entering him periodically. We are given no indication of the frequency of the convulsions, for it is unlikely that the father's use of the verb *seleniazomai* was meant to indicate that they occurred monthly. Indeed, it is probable that he had his fits more frequently than this for his father told Jesus that his son suffered severely from the disease (*kakos echei* in Matthew 17.15) and uses the word 'often (*pollakis*)' to describe their occurrence (Mark 9.22).

As the father makes clear, the fits could occur in any place and had occurred in dangerous situations even throwing the boy into the fire or water (Matthew 17.15; Mark 9.22). His body may have borne the scars of burns he had suffered on some of these occasions. Because these incidents could have been fatal, some commentators have described the boy as having suicidal tendencies. However, it is well-recognised that epilepsy may endanger life if a convulsion occurs in a situation in which a sudden lapse into unconsciousness may result in its victim falling into fire or water. Death may then occur from severe burns or drowning, but this is not suicide, for the afflicted person is not in control of his actions during such a convulsion. The occurrence of such accidents due to a loss of consciousness as described by the boy's father is another indication that we are not dealing with a case of hysterical fits in this boy.

As well as being accused of having 'suicidal mania',[10] this boy has been described as mentally deficient, and even regarded as 'a low-grade moron'.[11] Neither of these suggestions can be justified from the facts which are recorded about him. There is nothing in the history or description of this boy's illness which would suggest to a medical reader that he suffered from any degree of mental handicap or instability. It is true, of course, that mental subnormality may be accompanied by epilepsy, and also that severe epilepsy may eventually be accompanied by some degree of mental deterioration, but we owe it to this boy to make clear that neither of these situations is even hinted at in the gospel narrative.

## THE CONVULSIONS

The gospel writers do not give us an exact medical description of the convulsions from which this boy suffered, such as we might find in a modern textbook of neurology, and we have no right to expect this from them. Even so, the details which are recorded, and the words in which these details are described, give us a very vivid picture of the seizures, and leave us in no doubt that this boy suffered from the major form of epilepsy or what the French neurologists of last century spoke of as *le grand mal*.

Before we examine the details set out in the gospel record, let us briefly summarise the different stages of a major epileptic fit as we recognise them in modern medical practice. Five stages are generally recognised:

1. The premonitory stage.
2. The stage of unconsciousness.
3. The stage of muscular convulsion:
       a. The stage of muscular rigidity, or the *tonic* stage.
       b. The stage of muscular jerking. or the *clonic* stage.
4. The stage of flaccid unconsciousness.
5. The stage of recovery.

This scheme is useful for the purposes of description, but it is not entirely satisfactory in practice because the stages are not all entirely distinct. Thus the second and the third stages begin together at the same point in time, while the unconsciousness of the second stage continues through the third and fourth stages.

### The premonitory stage

This stage does not occur in every case of epilepsy, but when it does occur it warns the afflicted person that an epileptic fit is about to begin. Sometimes this warning may precede the actual convulsion by hours or even days, but more commonly occurs only a few seconds before the fit. It consists of a brief subjective experience of some form of sensation and is usually called the *aura*. This term is the Greek term for a breeze. It was first used to denote the premonitory subjective symptoms of epilepsy by the Greek physician Galen who said that he got the term from a young patient of his who described these early symptoms as like a cold breeze rising from his body to his head.[12]

The premonitory stage is only momentary in duration, but the patients are now so taken up subjectively with what is happening to them that they becomes unresponsive to their surroundings, and this becomes even more marked when they lose consciousness with the onset of the second stage. Here we have the explanation of the father's description of the spirit which seizes him as 'dumb' (Mark 9.17), and also why Jesus addresses the spirit as 'you dumb and deaf spirit' (Mark 9.25). The spirit was not deaf for it heard and obeyed Jesus' command to come out of the boy, but it caused the boy to appear to be dumb and deaf as he went into an epileptic fit and became incapable of speaking or hearing during the period of unconsciousness. It is possible, of course, that the boy was a deaf mute, but the narrative connects his dumbness and deafness with the occasions when the spirit seizes him (Mark 9.17-18) rather than suggesting that they describe a permanent state. Also, the boy was brought to Jesus not as a deaf mute, but as an epileptic.

## The stage of unconsciousness

The loss of consciousness in epilepsy is sudden and complete. The affected persons fall rigid to the ground as they lose consciousness. This is described in the accounts in two ways. The boy is said to fall (Matthew 17.15 and Mark 9.20), and he is also said to be seized by the spirit and hurled to the ground (See Mark 9.18 and Luke 9.42 which use the verb *regnumi*, 'to throw or cast down'). We still speak of epileptic fits as 'seizures' and the term epilepsy is derived from the Greek verb *epilambano*, 'to take hold of', which is the verb used of the spirit seizing the boy in Mark 9.16 and Luke 9.38.

## The stage of muscular convulsion

The onset of this stage coincides with the loss of consciousness. It may be divided into two separate stages according to the condition of the muscles affected.

*1. The stage of rigidity or muscular contraction.* For the first thirty seconds or so of the convulsion, the muscles are contracted and the body held rigid. This stage does not appear to have been recorded in any of the seven descriptions of the fit we have, unless we may regard Mark 9.18b as a reference to it. However, we know that this stage did occur in this boy's case because one result of the sudden muscle spasm is a loud weird guttural cry which may be suddenly emitted at this stage of the fit. This cry is due to the forced expiration of air through the narrowed opening between the vocal cords which results from the spasm of the muscles of the larynx. This cry is referred to by the father in Luke 9.39 and by the eye-witness in Mark 9.26.

The verb used to describe the cry is *krazo* which was originally used as an echoism for the croak of the raven and so came to mean any inarticulate cry such as the spirit may have made. The later meaning of the verb for an articulate cry is illustrated by its use for the father's cry for help in Mark 9.24.

2. *The stage of muscular jerking.* The most striking stage of an epileptic fit is that in which contractions of the muscles of a part or the whole of the body produce strong jerking movements over a period of one or two minutes. This stage is described by the verb *sparasso* in Mark 9.26 and Luke 9.39, and by its intensive form *susparasso* in Mark 9.20 and Luke 9.42. During this stage patients may roll about on the ground as the result of the irregular unco-ordinated movements of the trunk and limb muscles. This is described by the eye-witness in Mark 9.20 where his use of the appropriate verb in the imperfect tense suggests that the boy kept on rolling about on the ground. In a fit, patients may also gnash their teeth as this boy did according to his father in Mark 9.18, and if the tongue happens to come between the teeth it may be bitten. Froth or foam may appear on the lips from the churning up of air and saliva by the jerking movements of the muscles of the mouth and the jaw, and the appearance of froth or foam is described by the father in Mark 9.18 and Luke 9.39, and by the eye-witness in Mark 9.20. As a result of the uncontrolled movements during this stage patients may knock against objects in their vicinity and so bruise themselves as this boy did in his fits according to his father's account in Luke 9.39 where the verb *suntribo* should be translated 'bruises' rather than 'shatters' (RSV) or 'mauls' (NRSV). In many cases the afflicted person ends this stage lying face downwards and may easily drown in quite a shallow depth of water.

## The stage of flaccid unconsciousness

When the muscular convulsions are past, patients remain limp and unconscious and a casual spectator may easily regard them as dead as we are told most of the crowd did when the boy's last fit reached this stage (Mark 9.26). The word used by the father to describe this stage of flaccid unconsciousness in Mark 9.18b is the verb *xeraino* and this word has given rise to some difficulty in translation. It commonly means 'to waste or wither away' and is used in Mark 3.1 to describe the state of the hand of the man who had probably suffered from acute anterior poliomyelitis in his youth. It is also used in Mark 4.6 to denote the dried-up condition of the seed which fell on stony ground. The meaning of wasting or withering is clearly inappropriate here for epilepsy does not interfere with the function of the nervous system or the nutrition of its victims. In their lexicon, Arndt and Gingrich propose 'becomes stiff' as the translation[13], and both the NRSV and the NIV render the verb as 'becomes rigid', a phenomenon which belongs to an earlier stage of the fit as we have seen above. However, it seems preferable to extend the meaning of the verb to include the result of the wasting, namely, lack of movement, and so to understand the father to mean that at the end of the fit his son is completely exhausted and motionless. This is the view of Cranfield who translates the verb as 'becomes exhausted'[14], and also of Taylor who suggests that it means 'the pallor of complete exhaustion'[15], while Bruce speaks of 'the final stage of motionless stupor graphically described as withering'.[16]

## The stage of recovery

When consciousness returns after an epileptic fit the person is usually dazed and confused, and commonly goes off into a deep sleep for several hours. The fit seems reluctant to leave them, and this explains the remark of the father that the spirit left his son only with reluctance (Luke 9.39). It was during this stage that Jesus took the boy by the hand and raised him up from the ground (Mark 9.27) and gave him back to his father (Luke 9.42).

## THE DIAGNOSIS

Our examination of the case record of this boy has left no doubt that he suffered from the major form of epilepsy. The RV and all the English versions which followed its lead were therefore fully justified in calling him *epileptic* rather than *lunatic*. However, some modern commentators on this story suggest that he was a case of hysteria rather than one of epilepsy, and so a short discussion of the differentiation of hysterical fits from those of epilepsy will serve to make the diagnosis even more secure in this boy's case. The relevant points of distinction between the two types of fit are set out below and compared with the description of the features of this boy's condition as given in the gospels.

| Hysterical fit | Epileptic fit | The boy's fits |
|---|---|---|
| 1. Onset in adolescence or adulthood. | Onset in infancy or childhood. | Onset in childhood (Mark 9.21). |
| 2. Fit begins slowly. | Fit begins suddenly. | Fit begins suddenly (Mark 9.20). |
| 3. No loss of consciousness. | Consciousness lost. | Boy became dumb and unresponsive (Mark 9.17). |
| 4. Injury does not occur. | Injury frequent. | Injuries reported (Matthew 17.15). |
| 5. Person normal after fit. | Person drowsy and exhausted after fit. | Boy exhausted (Mark 9.26). |

Once the features are set out in a table in this way, the distinction between hysterical and epileptic fits becomes quite clear. When we then compare with them the features described for the boy's fits, there can be no doubt that he suffered from fits which were epileptic in nature and not hysterical. We conclude, therefore, that not only is there no evidence that the boy suffered from mental deficiency, there is also no evidence that he suffered from neurosis in the form of hysteria. The fits with which he was afflicted were epileptic in nature. As van der Loos points out, the commentators show 'a surprising unanimity' about this diagnosis.[17]

## HIPPOCRATES ON EPILEPSY

Now that it is clear that we are dealing with a case of epilepsy in this boy, it is of interest to recall the classic description of this disease which has come down to us from the antiquity which preceded the Christian era. Hippocrates, the Greek physician of Cos (460-355 BC), wrote a book on epilepsy which he entitled *On the Sacred Disease*.[18] In this book he denies that epilepsy is a sacred disease due to a divine visitation, as was commonly thought in his day. On the basis of the ancient humoral theory of disease he believes that epilepsy is the result of an excess of phlegm or mucus collecting in the brain. When this mucus is prevented by some obstruction from draining away normally, it enters and obstructs the blood vessels and so prevents the normal circulation of air in the body. This cutting off of the brain from its air supply results in a fit.[19] In the course of his book, Hippocrates describes the features of an epileptic fit and this description is worth quoting in order to compare it with that of the fits we have been considering in the gospel which were exhibited by the epileptic boy.

According to Hippocrates, the features of an epileptic fit are 'loss of voice, choking, foaming at the mouth, clenching of the teeth and convulsive movements of the hands; the eyes become fixed and the patient loses consciousness, and in some cases passes a stool'.[20] He then proceeds to discuss each feature in detail and to explain how it might be caused, but the rest of the passage is too long to quote and does not add much to the description already given.

In this description, Hippocrates enumerates eight separate signs which are obviously the result of acute observation of persons seen during an epileptic fit. Of these eight signs only five are mentioned in the gospel accounts of the boy's fits. Those which are omitted by the gospels are choking, fixation of the eyes and the passage of a stool. Conversely, of the ten features of an epileptic fit recorded in the gospel account of the epileptic boy, only six are included by Hippocrates in his description. Those omitted by him are the history of previous injury during fits, the occurrence of a cry at the onset of a fit, the fact that the patient falls to the ground as he loses consciousness, and his rolling about in the clonic stage of the fit. We need to combine both descriptions to obtain the complete picture of an epileptic fit as a modern medical textbook would describe it, for both descriptions omit features which would be enquired for when a diagnosis of epilepsy was being considered today.

If we go further and compare the vocabulary used by Hippocrates with that used in the gospel accounts, a very interesting fact emerges. The only words which are common to the two descriptions are the nouns for froth (*aphros*) and teeth (*odous*). Luke uses the former word in 9.39 and Mark the latter in 9.18, but even Luke's word may be derived from Mark since he uses the verb *aphrizo*, 'to foam at the mouth' in Mark 9.18,20. This means that the Hippocratic description of the disease has not influenced Luke's description at all. Now Luke was a physician probably trained at the medical school at Tarsus, the chief city of Cilicia. The fact that he did not make use of the Hippocratic vocabulary in his description of this boy's fits suggests that he was trained, not in the Hippocratic tradition of Greek medicine but in some other medical tradition.[21]

In his book on the disease, Hippocrates uses the term *epilepsis* ('seizure') only once,[22] preferring to speak of 'the sacred disease (*hieres nosos*)', or simply of 'this disease'. In Roman medicine too the disease was called 'the sacred disease (*morbus sacer*)'. It also had four other names in the ancient classical world of which the most interesting were 'the falling sickness (*morbus caduceus*)' and 'the committee disease (*morbus comitialis*)'. This latter name was given to it because, if during a meeting of the *comitia* or public assembly a member had an epileptic fit, the meeting was immediately abandoned as the occurrence of a fit was regarded as a bad omen.[23] The Roman physician Celsus mentions the premonitory aura of an epileptic fit, and also describes some of the features of a fit but not in as much detail as Hippocrates.[24]

## THE CAUSE

The diagnosis of this boy's illness is not yet complete. Epilepsy is not a specific disease but a symptom-complex which results from the sudden discharge of energy by nerve cells in the brain. This discharge of energy may have many causes, and some medical writers have preferred to speak of 'the epilepsies' or 'the seizure disorders' rather than epilepsy. Having satisfied ourselves that this boy was afflicted by epileptic convulsions, we must now seek to determine their cause or we leave the diagnosis only half-made. This means that to arrive at the diagnosis of epilepsy in this boy's case does not automatically exclude demon possession as the cause of his disease as some commentators suggest.

If we investigate the causes of epilepsy we find that there is one group of patients in which an organic physical cause can be identified and in some cases removed. Into this group fall those who suffer from certain brain tumours or various acute and chronic infections of the brain as well as the after-results of head injury. These patients, who are mostly over the age of twenty-five years, are said to suffer from *secondary* or *symptomatic epilepsy*. When these cases have been separated out there remains a much larger group of patients in whom the cause cannot be determined, and these are said to suffer from *idiopathic epilepsy* which means epilepsy for which no organic physical cause can be found. If demon possession is a fact, then there is no reason why it could not be a cause of some cases of idiopathic epilepsy. We do not know enough about the spirit world and the activity of demons to disprove demon possession, nor enough about epilepsy to deny that it may be caused by such possession.

The existence of demon possession is usually denied on dogmatic grounds, but it would seem to be much more dogmatically congruous to recognise the existence of demons and the possibility of possession than to deny them. The Christian believes in the Holy Spirit and the possibility of his possessing the believer, and has therefore admitted the possibility of spirit possession (John 14.17, 23; Romans 8.9; 1 Corinthians 3.16 and 6.19). If evil spirits exist, and no one can deny that there is much evidence in the modern world that they do, may they not also possess and influence people? However, we do not wish to embark on the large subject of demon possession at this time, but merely to insist that to conclude that this boy suffered from epilepsy is not thereby to exclude the possibility that his illness was due to demon possession.

## THE CURE

Modern medicine knows no cure for idiopathic epilepsy. There are drugs which will control the convulsions by depressing the activity of the nerve cells of the brain, but there is no method of treatment which will cure an epileptic immediately and permanently. Fits may cease with the passage of time, but of no patient can we say with confidence that they will never have another fit. This is why the instantaneous cure of this boy is so striking from a medical point of view. Jesus told the spirit never to enter the boy again (Mark 9.25), and Matthew records that he was cured from that very hour (Matthew 17.18). There were plenty of eye-witnesses still alive at the time that Matthew wrote to contradict this statement if it were not true. Even modern medicine cannot cure epilepsy like that. Here indeed was 'the finger of God' (Luke 11.20).

# Chapter 11
# THE CASE OF THE BENT WOMAN

Jesus was on his last journey up to Jerusalem. He was passing through the tetrarchy of Herod Antipas which embraced Galilee and Peraea (Luke 13.22). On the Sabbath day he attended the service of worship in a local synagogue but we do not know where this synagogue was. Some believe that he was still in Galilee, and others say he had crossed into Peraea, but we do not know for certain.

We do know, however, that this was the last occasion on which he was allowed to enter and teach in a synagogue. It is possible that already many synagogues were closed to him and their elders would not allow him to preach in view of the fact that the Jewish hierarchy had become so hostile to him. This may in part explain the reaction of the president of the synagogue to our Lord's act of healing. The president's anger at the breaking of the Jewish law of the Sabbath may have been intensified by his feeling of apprehension that he had unwittingly become a party to it by allowing Jesus to preach in his synagogue, an act which many other synagogue presidents would not have allowed at this stage of our Lord's ministry.

As he taught in the synagogue, Jesus noticed in the women's section of the congregation a woman with a spinal deformity, and he called her to him and healed her. The account of this healing is peculiar to the gospel of Luke (Luke 13.10-17) and contains some special features which merit a closer examination than they usually receive in the commentaries. Most commentators regard this incident as primarily an illustration of the attitude of Jesus toward the law of the Sabbath, and spend more time and space on the attitude of the president of the synagogue than on the nature of the healing. When it is considered at all, there is no general agreement about the nature of her condition, whether it was one of physical disease or demon possession. Nor is much said about the activity of Satan in her case, apart from the suggestion that her disease may have been due to a sinful life.

It is our purpose here to examine these problems more closely and more especially from a medical point of view, and to endeavour to establish whether this healing of the bent woman was an exorcism or not.

We need not doubt the historicity of the story as it is recorded by Luke. Its atmosphere is wholly Jewish and its detail rings true to life. The deformed woman resigned to her deformity, the pharisaic attitude of the president of the synagogue, our Lord's logical refutation of his objection, and the crowd's delight in the discomfiture of his opponents and in his glorious works, are all set out clearly in the narrative and make it come to life in a very vivid way. Also, it is no valid objection to the truth of this story that it is recorded by Luke alone, for its medical interest would explain this, and also its illustration of the conflict between the need of healing and the man-made restrictions about the observance of the Sabbath. It is Luke alone who records all five of the healings performed by Jesus on the Sabbath and the controversy they aroused, which occur in the synoptic gospel tradition. Matthew records only two and Mark only three, while John adds a further two from his own experience making a total of seven for the four gospels.

## THE HISTORY

The woman was an Israelite, a daughter of Abraham (v.16). We know that there are some diseases to which people of Jewish race are more prone than those of other races, but none of these diseases produce the spinal deformity which this woman displayed. It is unlikely therefore that the reference to her race had any medical significance.

We are given no clue to her age other than that she is called an adult woman (*gune*, v.11). She had been incapacitated for eighteen years (v.11), but was still able to attend synagogue worship and so was not bed-ridden or completely crippled.

The only possible indication that we are given of the rapidity of the onset of her disease is in the use of the aorist indicative tense *edese*, ('bound') in verse sixteen. Here Jesus speaks of the woman as having been bound by Satan for eighteen years. The aorist tense normally means that the action denoted by the verb took place at a specific point in the past. Its use in this context, therefore, suggests two possibilities. Either her present spinal deformity suddenly appeared at a definite point in time eighteen years previously, or the disease began then and its progressive development produced her spinal deformity. From a medical point of view, the latter interpretation is to be preferred as the only cause of the sudden appearance of an abnormal spinal deformity in the absence of pre-existing disease would be an injury which produced a crush fracture of one or more spinal vertebrae. This is a possible cause of such a deformity in this woman, of course, but we would not expect it to be described as being bound by Satan when everyone knew that it was the result of an accident. Hysteria may also produce the sudden onset of deformity, but this deformity would not in the first instance be outside the range of the normal movement or position of the spine, although later when physical changes had occurred due to disuse of the part, the deformity might well become abnormal and permanent.

## THE DIAGNOSIS

The condition of the woman is described as one of *astheneia* in verses eleven and twelve. Most English versions translate this as 'weakness' or 'infirmity'. As we have seen in Chapter Seven, this word and its cognate verb *astheneo* are the common words for sickness in the New Testament, and presumably came to be applied to the state of sickness because sickness usually causes physical weakness. We need, therefore, to look for more specific terms to give us a clue to the nature of the disease in the case of this woman.

More specific information is given in verse eleven where we are told that the woman was 'bent over' (NRSV) or 'bent double' (REB). The verb used is *sunkupto* which is used only here in the New Testament. It is used in the LXX version of Ecclesiasticus of being crouched down in humility (12.11) or in mourning (19.26), and therefore must mean having increased curvature of the spine in a forward direction. The cognate verb *anakupto* is also used in verse eleven where the woman is described as unable to straighten herself up and stand upright. Such a state is called *kyphosis* in modern medical terminology and this word is derived from the verb *kupto*, although its modern medical meaning is not necessarily the same as that of its ancient Greek usage. It would seem that the deformity from which this woman suffered was a markedly increased curvature of the spine because of which the upper part of her body was bent forwards on the lower.

The degree of fixation of her spine is not clear as there is a grammatical ambiguity in verse eleven. Whether we understand her inability to straighten herself up to be partial or complete depends on which verb we decide to modify with the adverbial equivalent *eis to panteles* ('entirely'). The Latin Vulgate attached the phrase to the participle *me dunamene* ('not being able') and translated it by *nec omnino poterat sursum respicere*. Most English translations have followed the Vulgate and made the spinal rigidity complete so that the woman could not straighten herself up at all. This would emphasise the severity of her condition.[1] A minority of versions (including the RSV, but not the NRSV) have attached the phrase to the infinitive *anakupsai* and translated the clause to mean that 'she could not fully straighten herself up'. In other words she had some spinal movement left, but it was not complete.

From the description of the woman as 'bent double' we may assume that the site of her disease was the spine or vertebral column. Since she could not stand erect, the disease must have affected the bones, joints, ligaments or muscles of the spine. The presence of these two physical signs of spinal deformity and decreased spinal mobility narrow down our diagnostic field considerably.

Before we come to discuss specifically organic spinal diseases in our endeavour to reach a diagnosis in this woman's case, we must first consider the suggestion that her condition was one of hysteria as this diagnosis has been suggested by some authors. Weatherhead suggests a diagnosis of 'hysterical paraplegia', on the grounds of her immediate cure.[2] Paraplegia would mean that she would have paralysis of both lower limbs, but there is no suggestion of this in the narrative which implies she was able to attend synagogue worship and walk out to the front of the congregation when Jesus called her to him (v.12). Her trouble lay in her back, not in her lower limbs and so it is unlikely that she had paraplegia.

Did she, however, have hysteria? It is possible that her condition may have begun as a hysterical manifestation which showed itself in some disturbance of the position or function of the spine. This might explain the origin of her deformity, but after eighteen years of disuse there would be physical changes in the muscles, joints and bones of the spine resulting in atrophy or wasting of the muscles, stiffness of the joints and demineralisation of the bones. The result would be that while in the early stages the condition would be easily reversible, once the wasting of the muscles and the other changes had set in, it would no longer be immediately reversible, and certainly not after so long a period as eighteen years. Her healing, therefore, was not just the making of a hysterical woman do what she was perfectly well able to do, namely, to stand up straight. After eighteen years the physical changes which had occurred would prevent an instantaneous cure by ordinary natural means. It is on facts like these that the psychoneurotic theory of the nature of the healing miracles of Jesus breaks down, and we see no reason to suggest that the diagnosis in this case was simply one of hysteria.[3]

Although we do not have enough clinical detail to allow us to arrive at a diagnosis with absolute certainty, it would seem to be most probable that the disease of this woman was one which affected the spine. We may list as follows, the main diseases which produce kyphosis or an increased curvature of the spine causing a person to be permanently bent forwards.

*I. Infective diseases:*

    1. Tuberculosis of the spine.

    2. Spondylitis ankylopoietica or ankylosing spondylitis.

*II. Degenerative diseases:*

    1. Osteoarthritis of the spine.

    2. Osteoporosis of the spine.

Some authors use the term *spondylitis deformans* for the diagnosis in this woman's case.[4] However, this term simply means an affection of the spine which produces deformity, and it is applied to a number of different conditions, some of which are not very well defined. It is often used as a synonym for ankylosing spondylitis, but in view of the ambiguity which surrounds the usage of the term it is best to avoid it altogether. It is one of those descriptive terms which have survived from older medical usage and have not found a specific application to any particular disease in present-day usage in spite of the clearer differentiation of diseases in modern medicine. Consequently we have not used the term in our list above.

In general, we may say that infective disease of the spine affects younger persons, and degenerative disease affects older persons. Hence the importance of a knowledge of the age of this woman, but unfortunately this is not possible because her age is not specifically indicated in the narrative. Since the effects of the disease had already lasted for eighteen years when she met Jesus, it seems reasonable to suppose that she was in the younger age group when the disease began. The shorter expectation of life in ancient society would also support this suggestion. If this is accepted then it would appear more probable that her condition was due to an infective disease rather then to a degenerative one.

Tuberculosis of the spine is commonly called Potts' disease after the London surgeon Percival Potts (1714-1788) who described its features in the eighteenth century. This disease is a possible diagnosis in this case. Hippocrates appears to have been familiar with the disease and gives a clear description of its clinical features.[5] We know that tuberculosis of bones and joints existed in the ancient Near East, although most of the evidence has come from Egyptian mummies.[6] Evidence of its existence in Palestine, however, is only very rarely found in bones dug up in modern Israel.[7] When it does occur today, this disease destroys the front part or body of one or more adjacent vertebrae of the spine so that the vertebrae collapse in front. This collapse produces a local acute backward angulation of the spine in the area where the disease has developed. This acute angular deformity which tuberculosis may cause is probably greater than is implied by the verb *kupto* and its cognates which are used to describe the condition of this woman, and elsewhere in the gospels refer to stooping down (Mark 1.7 and John 8.6). They refer to a normal appearance of the spine which is quite unlike the acute local angulation produced by tuberculosis. Also, since she could neither straighten her spine nor lift up her head, it is unlikely that her disease was tuberculosis for this disease does not develop in two parts of the spine at the same time in the same person. Consequently, if she suffered from tuberculosis and could not straighten her back, she would still be able to lift up her head. If, therefore, she had a spinal deformity which affected both the thoracic and the cervical spine, as she appears to have had, then the probability is that it was not due to tuberculosis.

The other disease of the spine which may affect the younger age group is ankylosing spondylitis. This name is the English term for *spondylitis ankylopoietica* and it describes a disease which produces fusion or ankylosis of the spinal joints, hence its name. This name is used for a well-defined disease of the spine whose exact cause is unknown, but whose features suggest it is related to infection by some agent at present unidentified. Radiological studies of Egyptian mummies have shown that the disease occurred in ancient Egypt, but was not common.[8] Hippocrates describes its clinical features but does not give it a specific name.[9]

The disease as we know it today begins in early adult life and although it is commoner in the male sex, it does affect women too. It begins in the lower part of the vertebral column where it produces a progressively straight and rigid spine. To compensate for this straightness and immobility, the upper spine assumes an increased forward curvature which eventually becomes fixed and rigid. Later, as a complication, a further increase in forward bending of the upper spine may occur and the patients assume a permanent stooping position from which they cannot raise themselves. This position is more like that of normal stooping than of the acute angulation of the spine produced by tuberculosis, and is more appropriately described by the verb *kupto* and its derivatives, as we have already mentioned. Also since the rigidity affects the whole spine, patients are unable to straighten themselves up or raise up their head. It appears that this description fits the scanty details recorded in this woman's case better than any other disease, and that ankylosing spondylitis is the most probable diagnosis in her case.[10]

The degenerative diseases are much less likely to have been the cause of the woman's bent condition than the infective ones, because they begin later in life. However, they are the commonest form of joint disease found in bones dug up by archaeologists in modern Israel.[11] Osteoarthritis is a disease of middle and old age. Its main effect is limitation of movement of the spine, though it may also produce some degree of kyphosis. A more marked degree of kyphosis results from osteoporosis of the vertebrae in which their bony tissue becomes thin and decalcified, and then compressed vertically to produce what is known as senile kyphosis or 'the dowager's stoop'. The true nature of this condition has only been recognised in recent years, although Macalister suggested that this woman's case was one of senile kyphosis in 1900.[12] However, in terms of the medical knowledge of his day he understood this condition to be due to spinal osteoarthritis or 'chronic osteitis of the vertebrae' as he called it, and not to senile osteoporosis.

We have now completed our consideration of the possible diagnosis in this woman's case. The relevant details provided by the narrative are scanty, and the author's main interest in recording the case is not medical. Nevertheless it seems reasonable to suppose that the disease from which this woman suffered was that which today we call ankylosing spondylitis or spondylitis ankylopoietica.

## THE QUESTION OF DEMON POSSESSION

Now that we have considered the problem of the diagnosis of this woman's disease, a second problem arises which still divides commentators on the gospel of Luke. It is the question of whether or not the basis of her physical disease was demon possession. This problem perplexes not only commentators but also translators of modern versions of the New Testament, some of whom render the original of Luke 13.11 in a way which suggests that the woman was demon-possessed, in spite of the fact that all the original says is that she 'had a spirit of weakness for eighteen years'.[13]

We begin our discussion of this problem by outlining the case in favour of the presence of demon possession on this woman.

## The case in favour of demon possession

The case for the occurrence of demon possession as the basis of this woman's physical disease rests entirely on the interpretation of two phrases which are used to describe her condition in the narrative.

1. The *first* phrase speaks of the woman having 'a spirit of weakness' and is used by Luke in his initial description of her in verse eleven.

2. The *second* phrase was used by Jesus himself when he referred to her as 'this woman... whom Satan has bound for eighteen years' as recorded in verse eighteen.

We propose, however, to postpone further discussion of the meaning of these two phrases, and in particular whether they can be interpreted only in the sense of demon possession, until we have examined the case against the view that this woman was possessed by a demon.

## The case against demon possession

When we turn to examine the case against demon possession it is clear that there are numerous aspects of it which we must take into consideration.

1. The narrative does not employ the vocabulary of demon possession. There are six cases of individual exorcism described in the synoptic gospels, and if we examine their vocabulary we find that the following words are characteristic of these descriptions as we have already seen in Chapter Seven.

| Greek | English | Occurrence |
|---|---|---|
| *daimonion* | demon | in all six cases |
| *daimonizomai* | be demon-possessed | in four cases |
| *pneuma akathartos* | unclean spirit | in four cases |
| *ekballo* | cast out | in five cases |
| *exerchomai* | come out | in five cases |

It is significant that none of these words occurs in the account of the healing of the bent woman. In all four of the undoubted exorcisms which are recorded by Luke, the agent of possession is always called a *daimonion*. The absence of this word from the present narrative suggests that Luke wishes to avoid describing the woman as having a demon or being demon-possessed. It is true that he speaks of her as 'having a spirit', but he does not call the spirit an *unclean* spirit as he does in the three cases of exorcism in which he calls the agent of possession a spirit (See Luke 4.33; 8.29; 9.42). Nevertheless, several English versions including Barclay, Moffatt, the GNB and the TCNT have translated the word *pneuma* here as 'an evil spirit'.

2. The method of treatment used by Jesus was not that of exorcism. In this case he spoke directly to the woman and told her of her cure (v.12). In exorcism he always spoke directly to the demon and commanded that it leave the possessed person. Also, on this occasion Jesus laid his hands on the woman in order to heal her (v.13). This was a procedure that he never used in exorcism in order to cure a demon-possessed person. Even if it were clear that he laid hands on the woman after the demon had left her, it still remains true that he never did this in any case of undoubted exorcism, and therefore cannot be used as an argument in favour of exorcism here.

3. The description of the cure is not like that of an exorcism. Jesus described her cure as being loosed or freed from her weakness (v.12) or being released from a bond (v.16). The verb he used was *luo* which is never used of exorcism and is only used of the cure of disease here in the whole of the New Testament. It is too mild a term to denote the casting out of demons. In any case, it is important to notice that she was loosed from her weakness or her bond, and not from a spirit or demon. Then there is no dramatic description of a spirit or demon coming out of the woman as we normally find in the accounts of exorcism in the synoptic gospels, e.g. in Mark 1.26 and 9.26.

4. The presence of a recognised and well-known demon-possessed person in a synagogue service is unlikely. It is true that we are told of a demon-possessed man in the synagogue at Capernaum in Mark 1.23 and Luke 4.33, but he was presumably normal in appearance while this woman had an easily-recognised deformity. If this deformity was generally believed to indicate that she was demon-possessed, it was unlikely that she would be allowed to worship in the local synagogue. The fact that she was allowed to worship there suggests she was not regarded as demon-possessed by the people of the community in which she lived.

5. If the woman was possessed by a demon we might expect there to be a reaction by the demon to the presence of Jesus as recorded in Mark 1.24 and 5.7. It was the demon who reacted in these cases and since there was no record of any reaction in this woman's case this suggests that there was no demon involved.

6. The account of the healing of the bent woman is included amongst the narrative material which is peculiar to the gospel of Luke. This material does not contain any description of an exorcism although it does contain the accounts of five healing miracles, including that of the bent woman. The absence of any other account of an obvious exorcism in this material, when combined with the fact that the account of the healing of the bent woman

does not conform to the usual description and vocabulary of an exorcism as recorded elsewhere in the synoptic gospels, suggests that the healing of this woman was not of the nature of an exorcism.

Equally, of course, the fact that no case of exorcism is recorded in the special Lukan material means that we do not know what form or vocabulary would have been used by this author if he had described a case of exorcism. There is, however, no evidence that Luke has his own special vocabulary for exorcism narratives. When he includes in his gospel the account of an exorcism from Mark or the source usually called Q, he uses the same or a similar vocabulary as that used by Matthew or Mark. It may be presumed therefore that if he had described an exorcism from his own special source, it would have been in similar terms to those used by the other evangelists.

We have now considered the evidence for and against the occurrence of demon possession in this woman, It is obvious that the evidence against demon possession is much stronger than that in favour of it, and would warrant the conclusion that this woman was not the subject of demon possession. However, before we come to a final conclusion let us re-examine the argument in favour of demon possession, and look again at the two phrases in the narrative on which this argument rests.

## THE SPIRIT OF WEAKNESS

The phrase 'a spirit of weakness' in Luke 13.11 is the phrase more than any other in this passage which has given rise to the idea that this woman was demon-possessed. In view of this, the usage of the phrase in its context needs closer examination.

The first thing to notice is that the word 'spirit' occurs only once in this whole passage, and that is in this phrase 'a spirit of weakness'. Furthermore, it is not qualified by the adjective *akathartos* meaning 'unclean', nor does the word 'demon' occur as a synonym for it. This is in marked contrast to the usage in the narratives of the six undoubted cases of exorcism recorded in the synoptic gospels. In all these cases the word 'demon' is used of the agent of possession, and where the word 'spirit' is used, it is always made clear that it is an *unclean* spirit which is being described, (e.g. in Luke 9.42). When the word 'spirit' is used alone it does not imply an evil spirit or the presence of demon possession.

This conclusion is supported by the grammatical construction used in Luke 4.33. In this verse Luke describes the demoniac in the synagogue at Capernaum as 'a man having the spirit of an unclean demon'. Luke derives this story from the Markan tradition where the man is spoken of as 'a man with an unclean spirit' (Mark 1.23). Luke's construction here is therefore his own, and may be regarded as providing a parallel to the phrase we are considering. From this construction it appears that when Luke uses the phrase 'to have a spirit of', he does not mean that the person described is demon-possessed. What he means is defined by the noun in the genitive case which follows the phrase. In the case of the synagogue demoniac, the man was in fact demon-possessed, and so the noun in the genitive described the spirit as that of an unclean demon. In the case of the bent woman, however the noun in the genitive case defined her state as one of weakness without any reference to demon possession.

These considerations suggest that when Luke uses the word 'spirit' in this phrase, he does not refer to a spiritual being such as a demon, but to a state of mind or of the human spirit produced by the condition defined by the noun which follows it, as, for instance, in Luke 1.47. This condition may be demon possession or it may not. In this woman's case it was weakness, and therefore we interpret the phrase 'a spirit of weakness' as meaning that it was the weakness which produced the spirit, and not the spirit which produced the weakness. In more modern terms, we may say that the result of the long years of physical weakness was a state of profound mental depression. This is not to say that her disease was purely psychological as Phillips suggests by his rendering that the woman 'had been ill from some psychological cause'. Ronald Knox also in his note on this phrase suggests that the spirit may have been 'a morbid attitude of hysteria, which kept the woman a cripple, although she suffered from no organic disability'.[14] The record makes clear that she had a real organic disability which had affected her for eighteen years and produced her state of weakness. But superimposed on her physical disability was a state of mental depression, and it is this which Luke describes as the spirit which had resulted from her weakness.

We conclude, therefore, that the use of the phrase 'a spirit of weakness' by Luke in his description of this woman does not require us to believe that he was describing her as the subject of demon possession.

## THE BOND OF SATAN

In Luke 13.16 Jesus described this woman as bound by Satan. This description has been taken along with Luke's characterisation of her as having a spirit of weakness and made the basis of a diagnosis of demon possession. We have just seen that Luke's phrase in verse eleven need not carry this implication. What are we to say of our Lord's reference to the bond (*desmos*) of Satan?

Nowhere else in the New Testament do we read of anyone who was bound by Satan, and so we must seek the meaning of this phrase within its present context. Certainly we find that Paul speaks of delivering people to Satan in 1 Corinthians 5.5 and 1 Timothy 1.20, and uses the verb *paradidomi* which may mean handing a person over to bondage, but this usage is in the context of Church discipline and is not relevant here.

His healing of the bent woman had involved Jesus in an argument with the president of the synagogue about Sabbath observance. Jesus replied to his criticism with an *a fortiori* argument. If on the Sabbath day you untie the bond which has confined your animals in order to allow them to drink, how much more is it necessary to untie the bond of this woman who has been bound by Satan for eighteen years? The use of the words 'bound' and 'bond' by Jesus is therefore explained by the parallel which he draws for the purpose of his argument.

There is a further implication in the usage of the word 'bound' which is significant for the interpretation of the phrase we are considering. Bonds are put on from without, and not from within. This fact would argue against the condition being demon possession for this affects the personality and body of the possessed from within, not from without.

We come to the conclusion, therefore, that Jesus' reference to the bond of Satan does not mean that this woman was demon-possessed. What it does mean is that her condition is due to the activity of Satan as the primary cause of sin and disease. This idea appears elsewhere in the New Testament, notably in the case of Paul's 'thorn in the flesh' which we shall consider in a later chapter. In both cases, Paul and this woman suffered from a recognisable physical disease which may have had a discoverable physical cause, but nevertheless the origin of their disease is traced back to the activity of Satan.

We have now completed our consideration of the two problems presented by the case of the bent woman when it is examined from a medical point of view.

The *first* problem was the identity of the disease which produced her bent condition. The data are scanty and the conclusion cannot be certain, but the most probable diagnosis is that of ankylosing spondylitis or spondylitis ankylopoietica.

If this diagnosis is correct, it is the only case of a rheumatic disease which is identifiable in the Bible.

The *second* problem was the cause of her condition and the nature of her healing. Was the cause that of demon possession and the nature of her healing a case of exorcism? We suggest that the evidence is in favour of physical disease and against the presence of demon possession and the occurrence of exorcism in her case.

The main contribution which this account of healing of the bent woman makes to the Biblical view of health and disease is its clear implication that disease can be due to the direct activity of Satan. The cure of disease is therefore an illustration of the power of God over evil and over Satan which is revealed in the life, death and resurrection of Jesus Christ.

# Chapter 12
# THE CASE OF THE MAN BORN BLIND

From the consideration of two of the healing miracles of Jesus recorded in
the synoptic gospels, we now turn to one which comes from the gospel of
John. The record of the healing of the man born blind is the longest (and the
liveliest) of any miracle described in the gospels, occupying all the forty-one
verses of the ninth chapter of this fourth gospel. We begin our consideration
of it by noting some of the special features which characterise the records of
the miracles of healing in this gospel.

## HEALING IN THE GOSPEL OF JOHN

There are distinct differences in John's presentation of the healing activity
of Jesus when it is compared with that of the synoptic gospels.[1]

The first and most obvious difference is in the number of healing
miracles which each gospel records. As we can see from the following table,
John records far fewer than the other three do.

| Matthew | Mark | Luke | John |
|---------|------|------|------|
| 14      | 13   | 17   | 4    |

Another interesting difference is in the number of individual healing
miracles which are peculiar to each gospel. These are as follows:

| Matthew | Mark | Luke | John |
|---------|------|------|------|
| 1       | 2    | 5    | 4    |

Thus all four of the healing miracles which John records are peculiar to his
gospel. These four miracles are all of the healing of individuals. John does not
mention any of the group healings which are recorded in the synoptic
gospels, nor does he refer to physicians, who are mentioned in each of these
other gospels. At the end of his gospel John tells his readers that he has been
deliberately selective in the choice of which signs he would record. He chose
those which would lead people to believe in Jesus as the Christ and so find
life in his name (John 20.30-31).

These facts immediately raise the question of the relationship of John's
gospel to the synoptic record. Four possible relationships have been described.
The gospel may have been written to be supplementary to, independent of,
interpretative of or as a substitute for the synoptic gospels. If we were to
consider the healing miracles alone then we might say that the gospel is
supplementary to the record of the synoptic gospels because it adds four

more healing incidents to theirs. We might also say that John's gospel is interpretative of their accounts because it presents the healing (and other) miracles as *semeia* or signs (John 2.11, 23; 4.54; 12.18 and 20.30), an aspect of them which is not particularly emphasised in the synoptic gospels except for Matthew 11.2-6 and its parallel in Luke 7.18-23. However, when we consider the gospel as a whole, it is the supplementary theory which has most to be said for it and is the one most generally accepted today.[2]

The second difference between John and the synoptic gospels is in the description of the miracles of healing. In the latter they are called 'mighty works' (*dunameis*) which is a word which does not occur in John. The descriptive terms used in John are 'signs' (*semeia*) and 'works' (*erga*) which are not specifically applied to healing miracles in the synoptic gospels, except for Matthew 11.2 where it is said that the imprisoned John the Baptist hears of the works (*erga*) of Christ. In his reply to the Baptist, Jesus describes these in terms of healing miracles in the verses which follow (Matthew 11.4-5). We have already discussed the difference between these words in Chapter Seven.

A third difference is to be found in how the gospels describe the relation of faith to the miracles of healing. In the synoptic gospels, faith precedes the healing, which is a response to faith (e.g. Matthew 9.2 and parallels). In John, faith follows the healing, which is regarded as producing faith as we see in John 4.53; 7.31; 9.38; 10.38; 11.15, 45; 12.11; 14.11 and 20.30-31.[3]

A surprising fourth difference is the absence of all the words for compassion and mercy in John. In the synoptics we are told on several occasions that Jesus performed a healing miracle because he had compassion on the sick person, e.g. Mark 1.41 and Luke 7.13, but the motive of compassion or mercy is never mentioned in any account of a healing miracle in John.

A final observation may give us the clue to the reason for these differences. There is no mention of the healing of any cases of leprosy or demon possession in John.[4] A sufficient number of cases of these conditions had already been described in the synoptic gospels, and the reason for most of these differences probably lies in the fact that John's gospel was written some time after they were. This meant that John did not need to repeat what they had already recorded, but only to supplement it.

## THE DRAMA OF THE MAN BORN BLIND

Several of the incidents in the life and ministry of Jesus recorded in this gospel are readily cast in dramatic form, and this is certainly true of the incident of the healing of the man born blind. As Brown comments, 'no other story in the Gospel is so closely knit. We have here Johannine dramatic skill at its best'.[5] The result is that this blind man 'emerges from these pages in John as one of the most attractive figures of the Gospels'.[6] In contrast, we might add, to the surly and unimaginative paralytic at the pool of Bethesda (John 5.1-15) who is one of the least attractive.

The Prologue to the drama begins in the Temple at Jerusalem where Jesus is attending the feast of Tabernacles (John 7.2-14) which was the autumnal Jewish festival of harvest thanksgiving (Leviticus 23.33-43). He had gone up to the feast privately and in secret (v.10), but on the last day of the feast which was most probably the seventh day, he began to teach publicly in the Court of the Gentiles (John 7.37).[7] He discussed with the people who he was and after a hard-hitting discussion on both sides, the people took up stones to throw at him because they accused him of blasphemy when he called himself by the sacred name by which God had revealed himself to Moses, the name I AM (John 8.59, cp. Exodus 2.14).

One of the claims about himself which Jesus had made to the crowd which included some of the Pharisees was, 'I am the light of the world; he who follows me will not walk in darkness, but will have the light of life' (John 8.1). It was appropriate, therefore, that as he left the Temple he should see a blind man (9.1) and heal his blindness. Act One of the drama describes the healing of the blind man and Act Two the reaction of the neighbours which is to take him to the Pharisees for their opinion. Their investigations take up the whole of Act Three. In Act Four Jesus meets the man again, and the Epilogue brings in the Pharisees again.

The drama may thus be set out as follows:

>PROLOGUE: Jesus and the Jews (John 7.37 to 8.59).
>ACT ONE: Jesus heals the blind man (9.1-7).
>ACT TWO: The man and his neighbours (9.8-12).
>ACT THREE: The man and the Pharisees (9.12-34).
>>Scene 1: His first interrogation (9.13-17).
>>Scene 2: The interrogation of his parents (9.18-23).
>>Scene 3: His second interrogation (9.24-34).
>ACT FOUR: Jesus finds the man again (9.35-38).
>EPILOGUE: Jesus and the Pharisees (9.39-41).

The action begins as Jesus and his disciples leave the grounds of the Temple in Jerusalem through one of the two southern gates, which were those nearest to the pool of Siloam.[8] The gates of the Temple were favourite places for beggars to sit and solicit alms from the worshippers as they entered or left the Temple grounds. Begging was almost the only way that blind people could support themselves at that time and many of them sat at the gates of the Temple. There was one particular blind man sitting there who attracted the attention of Jesus and his disciples. He was there every day, even on the Sabbath when Jewish law forbad beggars to request or receive alms.[9] He was a well-known figure who lived with his parents not very far away from the Temple. Everybody knew that he had been born blind and they (and he) believed that nothing could be done to give him his sight (John 9.32).

Jesus saw him, but before he could say or do anything, his disciples asked him a question.

## THE DISCIPLES' QUESTION

'Rabbi', they said, 'who sinned, this man or his parents, that he was born blind?'

### The nature of the disciples' question

There are three things to say about the nature of this question. It was not logical, original or appropriate.

It was not **logical** for it committed a logical fallacy, the fallacy of the many questions in one. The form of the question is the same as the well-known, 'Have you stopped beating your wife yet?' Neither question can be answered unless you have first answered a prior question or questions. In the case of the wife-beating question you must first answer the questions, 'Do you have a wife?' and 'Do you beat her?' In the case of the disciples' question you need to have already answered the question, 'Is congenital blindness always due to sin?' Unless you have first answered this prior question, your answer to the main question will commit you to saying more than you mean to say. This is why Jesus begins his answer by saying simply, 'Neither this man nor his parents'(v.3).

Also, the question was not **original**. It had been asked many times before and the problem was often discussed in the Rabbinic schools. The Rabbis answered this question by quoting Exodus 20.5 which said that the iniquity of the fathers could be visited on the children to the third and fourth generation. This meant that the sin of the parents could leave its mark on an infant. They went further and said that it was also possible for a man to sin in his mother's womb before he was born. Their evidence for this was Genesis 25.22-26 where in verse twenty-two Jacob and Esau 'struggled against each other' (so GNB) in their mother's womb before they were born. From this description the Rabbis concluded that Jacob had tried to kill Esau while they were together in the womb of their mother Rebekah.[10] If this were so, then this man's blindness could be due to his own sin. When the Pharisees come on the scene later in the story we find that they hold the same view as the disciples: the man's congenital blindness was due to sin. They tell the man that he was born 'steeped in sin at birth' (v.34 NIV), but they do not say whose the sin was.

Finally, the question was not **appropriate**. As we have seen, just before this incident the disciples had heard Jesus say as he taught in the Temple, that he had come to bring light to the world (John 8.12) and claim that he was indeed the Son of God and therefore had the power of God at his command. Yet when they were confronted with a man who lacked that light and had with them someone who had the power to give him that light, they wanted to discuss theology and not therapy.

### The implications of the disciples' question

Even though their question was not logical, original or appropriate, its implications were very revealing about their attitude towards this man.

First, they saw the man as an object and not a person. He was an object to be discussed, not a sufferer to be relieved of his suffering. How disappointed Jesus must have been in them when he heard their question, a question which arose out of curiosity rather than compassion.

Second, they believed in an immediate personal connection between sin and disease or calamity. When they looked at the man and his physical condition, the first thing they thought of was sin. Now, there *is* a connection between sin and disease or calamity because there would be no disease or calamity in the world if there were no sin, but the connection is not necessarily immediate and personal. This is the point made by the book of Job in the Old Testament where it is made quite clear that Job was not suffering because of his personal sin.[11] Jesus also makes the same point clear in Luke 13.1-5 where he speaks of the violent death of some Galileans at the hands of Pilate as they offered sacrifice in the Temple at Jerusalem, and also the deaths of eighteen people who were crushed to death when a tower collapsed in Siloam. His hearers were not to think that these people were any greater sinners than others for everyone was a sinner and needed to repent.

Third, they ignored the healing resources which were available. They accepted that his blindness was congenital and therefore incurable. This was the current view which even the blind man accepted. Notice what he said in verse thirty-two, 'Never since the world began has it been heard that anyone opened the eyes of a man born blind'. But had the disciples not been listening when Jesus told the Jews in the Temple that he was the light of the world and had the power of God at his disposal? If they had been listening, then why did they it not occur to them that he might cure the man of his blindness? They had resources but they ignored them.

**The lessons of the disciples' question**

There are several lessons which can learned from the question asked by the disciples which concern any approach to healing.

First, in approaching a sick person who needs healing we must examine our presuppositions. There were three lying behind the disciples' question.
1. The man's blindness was due to sin.
2. The condition was incurable.
3. They had no resources to cope with it.

All these presuppositions were wrong. The result was they asked the wrong question and if Jesus had not been with them, there would have been no healing.

Second, we must examine our attitude to those who need healing. They are persons to be treated with care and compassion and not objects to be discussed whilst their suffering is accepted as incurable and ignored.

Third, we must recognise our resources for healing. Notice what Jesus said in verse four: 'We must work the works of him who sent me whilst it is day'. That 'we' includes the disciples of Jesus; they share with him in the work of healing, and his resources are available for them to call upon and use.

## THE PHARISEES' QUESTIONS

There are no fewer than sixteen questions in this ninth chapter of John and nine of them were asked by the Pharisees, to whom his neighbours had taken the man who had been born blind but was now able to see. This suggests that his healing posed a real problem for the Pharisees. Their real difficulty is summarised in the question in verse sixteen, 'How can a man who is a sinner do such miraculous signs?' (NIV).

The Pharisees were the religious party in Jewish society who steadfastly upheld the Jewish law and taught in the synagogues. They were the lay religious teachers of Israel and the recognised interpreters of the law and its meaning for everyday life.[12] They were a small party of about six thousand in all, scattered throughout the country (Luke 5.17).[13] When the ordinary people had a religious problem they consulted the Pharisees and that is why his neighbours brought to them the man who had been blind (v.13). They wanted the Pharisees to explain how it was that Jesus whom the Pharisees regarded as a deceiver (Matt 27.63), and certainly not the Messiah, could heal a man who was born blind.

Among the Pharisees were two leading schools of interpretation of the Mosaic Law. The school of Shammai was strict and conservative in its interpretation, while the school of Hillel was lenient and liberal. It is probable that the division which arose among the Pharisees over the significance of the healing of the man born blind was due to the conflicting views of these two schools.

### The issues for the Pharisees

So far as the Pharisees were concerned, their questions reflect the three issues which arose for them in the case of the healing of the blind man. These were the genuineness, the lawfulness, and the meaningfulness of the healing which the blind man claimed to have received.

1.    The **genuineness** of the healing. There were two questions to be settled about the genuineness of the healing:

(a) Had the man been born blind?

(b) Could he now see?

The best people to answer the first question were, of course, the man's parents and so the Pharisees sent for them (v.18). Yes, they said, their son had been born blind. The answer to the second question was obvious - he could now see. It was this fact that had made the neighbours take him to the Pharisees.

2.    The **lawfulness** of the healing. The second issue for the Pharisees arose from the fact that the healing had been carried out on the Sabbath day. Did this mean that Jesus had broken the law of the Sabbath? In other words, Was the healing lawful or unlawful?

The Jewish law of the Sabbath was based on the Mosaic law to remember the Sabbath day to keep it holy and the way to keep it holy was to do no work (Exodus 20.8-11; 31.13-14 and Leviticus 23.3). This raised the question of what constituted work, and in order to guide the people about this the Rabbis over the centuries had drawn up lists of what they regarded as work. If we examine those lists we find they forbid four of the things which Jesus had done in healing the man born blind.

First, healing of any kind was forbidden on the Sabbath except where life was at stake, and it is obvious that life was not at stake in this case.[14]

Second, kneading or pressing material such as dough and paste was forbidden on the Sabbath for it was regarded as work, and Jesus had kneaded together dust and saliva to produce a paste.[15]

Third, anointing the eyes with any substance was not allowed on the Sabbath, and Jesus had anointed the man's eyes with the paste he had made.[16]

Fourth, it was specifically forbidden to apply fasting spittle or saliva to the eyes on the Sabbath.[17]

In view of these four actions of Jesus, the Pharisees were perfectly justified in concluding that Jesus had broken the law of the Sabbath, and therefore was a sinner (v. 24). As Edersheim observes, 'there was abundant legal ground for a criminal charge'.[18] So the miracle of healing may have been genuine, but it was not lawful for it broke the law of the Sabbath. The vital question then was, Whose law of the Sabbath had Jesus broken?

The implication of Jesus' healing the blind man on the Sabbath was that the Rabbinic regulations we have just quoted belonged to the Jewish law of the Sabbath ('the traditions of the elders', Mark 7.8), and not to the Mosaic law as given by God. Therefore, although he may have broken the Jewish law of the Sabbath, Jesus had not broken the Mosaic law.

3. The **meaningfulness** of the miracle. This incident raised the further question: What did the miracle mean about the one who had performed it? The man who had been healed had no doubt. His healing meant that Jesus was from God. His argument was simple:

God does not hear sinners (v.31);

God heard this man because he gave me my sight;

Therefore this man must be from God. (v.33).

By contrast the argument of the Pharisees was different. They argued:

This man has broken the law of the Sabbath (v.16a);

A man who breaks this law is a sinner (v.16b);

Therefore Jesus is a sinner and cannot be from God (v.24).

The Pharisees were in fact divided among themselves (see v.16, cp. John 3.2 and 7.50), but the majority could only refer to Jesus as a man ('this fellow' v.29 NIV), as a man and a sinner. So they could not accept the real meaning of the healing and they avoided coming to a final decision on the matter by disposing of the problem and the evidence. They threw the man out from the place where they were met (v.34), and refused to listen to him any more.

Meanwhile the meaning of the miracle of healing was gradually dawning on the man who had been healed. We can trace this in the way in which he refers to Jesus. He begins by speaking of him to his neighbours as 'the man they call Jesus' (v.11). When he is put on the spot by the Pharisees he calls him 'a prophet' (v.17) which means that he was a man sent from God (v.33). When he meets Jesus after being thrown out of the synagogue and sees him with his own eyes for the first time, he addresses him first as 'Sir', a title of respect. Finally he calls him 'Lord', a title of reverence, and he kneels down and worships him. He accepts the claim of Jesus to be the Son of Man who came from heaven (v.38), a name which in this context means the Messiah, the Son of God. He has grasped the meaning which the Pharisees had either missed or refused to accept. His healing was now complete for not only were his physical eyes opened, but his spiritual eyes too. The healing of his body, therefore, now included the salvation of his soul.

## Lessons from the questions of the Pharisees

What then are the lessons we can learn from the questions of the Pharisees? There are three things we can learn about the nature of healing.

First, all healing comes from God. Both the man and the Pharisees are agreed on that. This was why the Pharisees had a problem for they could not agree that Jesus came from God.

Second, healing is a personal experience which cannot be denied. The Pharisees tried to deny it and called on the man's parents in the hope that they would deny it. Then they tried to shake the man's testimony by saying that Jesus could not have healed him because Jesus was a sinner and not from God. However, they could not deny the man's experience when he said, 'One thing I do know. I used to be blind but now I can see' (v.25).

Third, healing involves a personal relationship. The personal relationship in this case is described as obedience. As the man told his neighbours, 'the man they called Jesus told me to go and wash... so I went and washed, and then I could see' (v.11). It was not the paste of dust and saliva that healed him, but his obedience to the command of Jesus. If he had not obeyed that command he would never have been healed, no matter how long he had kept the paste on his eyes.

## THE ANSWERS OF JESUS

So far we have looked at the disciples' question and the questions raised by the Pharisees and now we consider how Jesus answered these questions.

There is also a third answer that Jesus gave which we must consider, and that is his answer, not to a spoken question, but to the unspoken challenge presented by the disability of the man born blind.

## His answer to the question of the disciples

The disciples had asked Jesus whether the man's blindness was due to his own sin or that of his parents. In his reply Jesus said that neither had sinned and the man had been born blind 'that the works of God might be revealed in him' (v.3 NRSV).

On a first reading, this statement of Jesus appears to present an ethical problem. It seems to mean that God decreed that this man was born blind so that at some point in his adult life he might be healed by Jesus to demonstrate the power of God; in the meantime he had to endure years of visual disability. This meaning is unlikely as it does not fit in with Jesus' teaching about the love and concern of God for people. How then are we to understand what Jesus meant?

The best way to understand the clause in question is to regard it as a *result* cause meaning that the healing of the man's blindness was not the purpose of his being born blind, but its result or consequence. In other words, Jesus is not saying that the man had been born blind in order that God's power and glory might be made manifest in his healing. What he is saying is, given that the man was born blind, the result will be that God's power and glory will be manifest in his healing. He denies the cause which the disciples have suggested in the sin of either the man or his parents, and turns abruptly from the cause of the blindness to its consequence, namely, the opportunity it provides to manifest the power and the glory of God.[19]

In his reply, Jesus is saying in effect to his disciples that they are asking the wrong question and therefore will miss the opportunity which the situation presents. He is saying to them that they should not be concerned with the sinfulness of the blind man, but with his need of healing. Knox paraphrases his reply in this way, 'Our job, yours and mine, is to put things right, not to argue about why they went wrong'.[20]

It is important to notice that in his answer to the disciples, Jesus includes them along with himself as those who must do the works that he has been sent to do by his Father (v.4).[21]

## His answer to the challenge of the man's blindness

We come now to Jesus' answer to the challenge presented by the condition of the man born blind. Jesus had claimed to be the light of the world (John 8.12) and now he was confronted by one who had never been able to enjoy that light as other men had been able to do. Of all those who were healed by Jesus and about whose healing we have sufficient detail, this man was the only one who was afflicted from birth. The phrase *ek genetes* (v.1) occurs only here in the New Testament and means that he was blind from the actual moment of his birth. He had never seen. His blindness cannot be due to some infection contracted during the process of his birth such as gonorrhoeal ophthalmia, as Creighton suggests.[22] This condition would not produce blindness from the moment of birth, but only after some days when the untreated infection had involved the cornea of both eyes. It could be due to some congenital malformation of the eyes but such malformations are very rare.

The most probable diagnosis in this case is that of bilateral congenital cataract in which the lens of the eye is opaque from birth. The cause of this condition is commonly unknown, but in recent years it has been discovered that an attack of German measles during early pregnancy in the mother may cause congenital cataract in the child.[23] In such a case the retina is normal and since the opaque lens can still transmit light, the blind person can distinguish day from night, but nothing more. It should be noted that blindness of this type cannot be explained on the basis of the psychoneurotic theory of the healing miracles of Jesus for hysteria cannot cause congenital blindness as this condition can only occur after birth and usually does not appear until adolescence or early adulthood. Nor can such blindness be cured by any method involving 'the mechanism of suggestion' as Weatherhead appeared to believe.[24]

In order to heal the man, Jesus makes a paste of dust and saliva and smears it over his eyes. This would, of course, make the blindness worse for it would prevent any light at all from reaching the retina at the back of the eye. As Calvin remarks, this would double the blindness.[25] Then he tells the man to go down the hill to the pool of Siloam and wash the paste off his eyes. So we may say that the healing took place in two stages. There was first the application of the paste and then its removal by washing with water. For the second stage he goes down to the pool and after washing off the paste, he comes back seeing. That was the answer of Jesus to the challenge of the man's blindness.

## His answer to the questions of the Pharisees.

We have already suggested that the most significant of all the questions asked by the Pharisees is that found in verse sixteen, 'How can a sinner do such miraculous signs?' In other words, the real problem of the Pharisees was to know who Jesus was.

In answer to the questions of the Pharisees, Jesus makes three points which make it quite clear that he came from God (v.39):
1. He had come to do the work of God, i.e., judgement (cp. John 5.22).
2. He had come to bring light to the world.
3. He had come to show up human blindness.

Jesus does not deal with the accusation of breaking the law of the Sabbath here, but he does elsewhere when he maintained that it was lawful to heal on the Sabbath (Matthew 12.10; Luke 13.16; John 7.23).

His most pointed answer comes when some of the Pharisees overhear what he has said to the man he had healed, and ask their final question, 'Are we also blind?' (v.40). The form of the question shows that they expected the answer to be 'No', because they used the Greek negative *me*, but Jesus in effect answers 'Yes'.

Of course, both Jesus and the Pharisees are now speaking in terms of spiritual blindness. Jesus had first healed the man born blind of his physical blindness, and then had healed him of his spiritual blindness so that he recognised who Jesus was and called him Lord and worshipped him. But Jesus and the Pharisees had different ideas of spiritual blindness. The sight of the Pharisees depended on the recognition of the law of Moses. They had said to the man born blind, 'We are disciples of Moses' (v.28). They claimed to see by the light of the Mosaic Law, but a new light had come into the world which they could not see. They were blind to this new light of the world (John 8.12 and 9.5). This was why they had not recognised who Jesus was and could not accept the plain meaning of the miracle of the healing of the man born blind. The man born blind had the organs of physical sight but he *could* not use them. The trouble with the Pharisees was that they had the organs of spiritual sight, but they *would* not use them. Had they wished, they could have seen what they really should have seen, namely, who Jesus was. They had no excuse. They more than all men claimed to see, but in fact they were blind and their insistence on being able to see when they could not see, made them guilty of sin, the sin of unbelief (v.41, cp. John 15.22).

## Lessons from the answers of Jesus

What then are the lessons of the answers that Jesus gave to the questions and to the challenge of the blindness of the man born blind?

First of all, healing demands compassion not curiosity; it demands action not discussion. As Jesus said in his answer to the disciples' question: 'We must do the works of him who sent me' (v.4). This work is now to become his disciples' responsibility. While he is on earth, he is the light of the world, but when he will no longer be on the earth, it is they who will be the light of the world as he told them in the Sermon on the Mount (Matthew 5.14). It is they who will do God's work then, to give sight to the blind and to bring light to those who sit in darkness and in the shadow of death.

Secondly, physical healing always has spiritual meaning and so it needs to be followed up. That is why Jesus sought out the man after he had been thrown out of the synagogue (v.35). Healing should affect the relationship of men and women with God. Therefore, when we take our leave of the man born blind we are not surprised to find him worshipping Jesus as Lord (v.38).

Thirdly, Christian healing always involves challenge. Jesus called it 'judgement (*krima*)' in verse thirty-nine, when he said that he had come into the world for judgement. When men and women come into contact with Jesus Christ through healing or in any other way they pass judgement on themselves. They reveal whether they are blind or whether they can see. If they are blind they see nothing in him and pass him by; if they are not blind they will see in him the Son of God and call him Lord and worship him. In other words, the reason for the coming of Jesus into the world was that men and women might be saved (John 3.16-17), but the effect of his coming was to pass judgement on those who would not believe (John 9.39). In fact, those who do not believe pass judgement on themselves by their refusal to believe and that was precisely what the Pharisees had done in this story. They knew so much and claimed to see so well, and yet they failed to recognise God's Son when he came.

# PART FOUR

# HEALING IN THE APOSTOLIC CHURCH

*THE CLIMAX of the gospel story of Jesus was reached in his death, resurrection and ascension. These events were unique in human history and revealed at one and the same time, the reason why Jesus had come, and the source of the power by which he healed people of disease and brought them forgiveness of sin.*

*After the gospels, the rest of the New Testament is concerned with the apostolic Church. If we ask when this Church or ekklesia came into being, then the evidence clearly points to the time after the death and resurrection of Jesus. All the early Christian writers use the word ekklesia only for those Christian communities which came into being after the close of the events which are recorded in the gospels. It was never used for the band of disciples which Jesus gathered round him and which frequently figured in the gospel narrative. With reference to the Christian community, Jesus used the word ekklesia twice in the gospel of Matthew but in terms of the future. In Matthew 16.18 he spoke in the future tense of its foundation, and in Matthew 18.17 he spoke of the spiritual responsibility which the future Church would exercise, as the subsequent verses reveal. Verse eighteen finds its parallel in Matthew 16.19 where the power of binding and loosing is said to be a future gift to Peter and is now extended to all the Twelve. Verse twenty contains Jesus' promise to be in their midst when two or three disciples gather in his name. This promise could only be fulfilled after the ascension of Jesus and the coming of the Holy Spirit. Jesus, therefore, does not use the word ekklesia of the original band of the Twelve nor of any group of his disciples during his earthly ministry, but only of the future Christian community which was to be established after his death and resurrection.*

*The question therefore remains of when the Church or ekklesia came into being. If Jesus spoke of it only in the future tense, at what point in the future was it established? It seems most natural to identify this point with the day of Pentecost for it was on that day, which was the Jewish Feast of Weeks, that the Holy Spirit came upon the disciples, now called apostles, so that Jesus' presence could now be with them wherever they met in his name (Acts 1.2-8 and 2.1-4). It was on this day of Pentecost that the apostles, whose qualification for their office was that they were witnesses of Jesus' resurrection (Acts 1.22), were invested with power (dunamis) from on high when the Holy Spirit came upon them (Luke 24.29 and Acts 1.8).*

As we have already seen, the word power or dunamis is used in the synoptic gospels to describe the works of healing which Jesus performed. These works were the outward expression of his power which came from God. The question which now arises is whether the power with which the apostles were invested when the apostolic Church was established included the authority and ability to heal. It is to this question that we address ourselves in Part Four of this book, and seek to answer it by a consideration of the healing activity of the apostolic Church in the book of the Acts of the Apostles and the epistles written by Paul and by James.

# Chapter 13
# THE RECORDS OF HEALING IN THE ACTS

The training of the Twelve is now over. Their Teacher has been put to death on a cross outside Jerusalem, and has been raised from the dead by the power of God. The book of the Acts of the Apostles opens with an account of his ascension to the right hand of God. Before his ascension Jesus gives them his final commission. They had been given one commission already, midway through their training. They had been sent out as miniature apostles or apprentice missionaries, to use the terms which Bruce applied to them.[1]

## THE GREAT COMMISSION

The content of their first commission was a threefold imperative bidding them to go, to preach and to heal (Matthew 10.5-8), and to equip them for their task they were given authority to cast out demons and to heal every disease and every infirmity (Matthew 10.1). In view of this specific command to heal given in the first commission, it is important to examine the terms of the final commission.

There is no common tradition of this commission. There are in fact no less than five different versions which were not all given on the same occasion. Together they form the final commission which Jesus gave to his disciples after his resurrection and before his ascension. Their content according to the four gospel traditions is as follows:

1. 'All authority in heaven and on earth has been given to me. Go therefore and make disciples of all nations, baptising them in the name of the Father and of the Son and of the Holy Spirit, teaching them to observe all that I have commanded you' (Matthew 28.18-20).

2. 'Go into all the world and preach the gospel to the whole creation. He who believes and is baptised will be saved; but he who does not believe will be condemned' (Mark 16.15-16, i.e. the long ending of Mark).

3. Then he opened their minds to understand the scriptures and said to them, 'Thus it is written, that the Christ should suffer and on the third day rise from the dead, and that repentance and the forgiveness of sins should be preached in his name to all nations, beginning from Jerusalem. You are witnesses of these things. And behold, I send the promise of my Father upon you; but stay in the city, until you are clothed with power from on high.' (Luke 24.45-49).

4. 'You shall receive power when the Holy Spirit has come upon you; and you shall be my witnesses in Jerusalem and in all Judaea and Samaria and to the end of the earth' (Acts 1.8).

5. Jesus said to them again, 'Peace be with you. As the Father has sent me, even so I send you'. And when he had said this, he breathed on them, and said to them, 'Receive the Holy Spirit. If you forgive the sins of any, they are forgiven; if you retain any, they are retained' (John 20.21-23).

It is clear from these versions of the final commission of Jesus to his disciples that they were to be empowered by the Holy Spirit to go out into all the world to preach the gospel of repentance and the forgiveness of sin. Those who accepted the gospel and believed were to be baptised and were to be instructed in the Christian way of life.

The only mention of healing in relation to the final commission of Jesus to his disciples is in Mark 16.17-18. These verses form part of the long ending of Mark (i.e. Mark 16.9-20) and they anticipate that those who believe as a result of the preaching of the gospel will cast out demons and lay hands on the sick so that they will recover. They do not form a specific commission to heal but are a promise and a prophecy that the eleven apostles and their converts ('those who believe') will cast out demons and heal the sick as a consequence and an indication (*semeion*) of their faith.

The long ending of Mark's gospel was probably not written by Mark, but appears to have existed from before the middle of the second century AD and even from the end of the first century. Whatever its origin and whoever its author was, this passage was accepted as authentic Scripture and attached to the end of Mark's gospel as a summary of the post-resurrection appearances of Jesus to his disciples. The passage would not have been preserved unless it described the experience of the early Christians, and would not have been included in the canon of Scripture unless it was believed to authenticate that experience as being what Jesus intended for his disciples.[2]

It is from a study of the book of Acts that we can discover how the disciples interpreted their commission and used the power with which they had been endowed by Jesus as he ascended into heaven and sent the Holy Spirit to be with them (John 16.7). From such a study we should be able to understand the place which healing occupied in the mission and ministry of the apostolic Church. There is no doubt that healing was a recognised activity of that early Church and is recorded for us by the author of the Acts of the Apostles whose records are made all the more significant by the fact that he was himself professionally trained in the art of healing.

## THE NARRATIVES OF HEALING

The space devoted to accounts of healing in the book of the Acts is much less than in any of the gospels. It amounts to only 4.5 per cent of the total in terms of verses.

If we now classify the healing narratives in the same way as we did for the gospels, the result is as follows:

### The healing of individuals

I. Accounts of physical healing

| | | |
|---|---|---|
| 1. The lame man at the gate of the Temple. | By Peter. | Acts 3.1-10 |
| 2. Paul's recovery of sight. | By Ananias. | Acts 9.17-19 |
| 3. Aeneas healed of paralysis. | By Peter. | Acts 9.32-35 |
| 4. Cripple healed at Lystra. | By Paul. | Acts 14.8-11 |
| 5. Cure of father of Publius. | By Paul. | Acts 28.8 |

II. Accounts of exorcism of demons

| | | |
|---|---|---|
| 6. The Philippian slave girl. | By Paul. | Acts 16.16-18 |

III. Accounts of raising of the dead

| | | |
|---|---|---|
| 7. Tabitha (Dorcas) at Joppa. | By Peter. | Acts 9.36-41 |
| 8. Eutychus at Troas. | By Paul. | Acts 20.9-12 |

### The healing of groups

| | | |
|---|---|---|
| 1. The sick in the streets of Jerusalem. | By Peter. | Acts 5.15-16 |
| 2. The sick in Samaria. | By Philip. | Acts 8.6-7 |
| 3. The sick at Ephesus. | By Paul. | Acts 19.11-12 |
| 4. The sick in Malta. | By Paul. | Acts 28.9 |

### Other general references to healing

| | | |
|---|---|---|
| 1. Wonders and signs in Jerusalem. | By apostles. | Acts 2.43 |
| 2. More wonders and signs in Jerusalem. | By all. | Acts 5.12 |
| 3. More wonders and signs in Jerusalem. | By Stephen. | Acts 6.8 |
| 4. Signs and wonders in Iconium. | By Paul and Barnabas. | Acts 14.3 |

## THE DISEASES HEALED

The narratives of the healing miracles can also be classified on the basis of the diseases whose healing they describe. In so far as we can identify the diseases involved we may classify them as follows:

### Physical diseases

*I. Acute conditions:*

| | |
|---|---|
| 1. Acute blindness. | Paul in Acts 9.8 |
| 2. Acute fatal head injury. | Eutychus in Acts 20.9 |
| 3. Acute bacillary dysentery. | Father of Publius in Acts 28.8 |
| 4. Acute fatal disease of unknown nature. | Tabitha in Acts 9.37 |

*II. Chronic diseases:*

1. Lameness or locomotor disability:
   a. The man at the gate of the Temple in Acts 3.2.
   b. The cripple at Lystra in Acts 14.8.
2. Paralysis due to neurological disorder:
   a. Aeneas in Acts 9.33.
   b. The paralysed and lame in Acts 8.7.

### Demon possession

1. Philippian slave girl in Acts 16.16.
2. The demon-possessed in Samaria in Acts 8.7.

These accounts of acute conditions and chronic diseases in the Acts include details and features which are of great interest from a medical point of view.

## THE ACUTE CONDITIONS

We begin our consideration of the accounts of the healing of the acute diseases with that of the sudden blindness which overtook Paul (or Saul as he was called then) on the road near Damascus (Acts 9.8).[3] It has been common to regard this blindness as psychosomatic in origin.[4] Carl Gustav Jung, the Swiss psychiatrist, took this view and went on to say that 'psychogenic blindness is according to my experience always due to an unwillingness to see, that is to understand and to realise something that is incompatible with the conscious attitude'.[5] In other words, Paul's physical blindness was due to his unwillingness to see in the person of Jesus, the one who was the Christ of Israel. This view would seem to be just playing with words and just too simple to be true. Even if it were true in cases of psychoneurotic illness, we cannot claim that Paul was such a case. Other writers have followed Jung in his simple correlation of physical and psychological blindness, but have attributed the blindness to more complex psychological influences. Thus, Harrison attributes the sudden onset of Paul's blindness to 'a state of profound psychological conflict' and 'intense emotional strain' resulting from 'the fundamental reorientation of his spiritual values involved in his conversion'.[6]

However, it seems unnecessary to seek a psychological cause when Paul himself mentions what could have caused the sudden onset of his blindness. In Acts 22.11 he is addressing the Jerusalem crowd from the steps of the Roman fortress of Antonia, which connected it with the northern part of the outer court of the Temple. He tells them of his experience on the road to Damascus and how he lost his sight because of the brightness of the light that shone around him. On another occasion, when he was speaking before Herod Agrippa he adds the significant detail that the brightness of the light was greater than that of the midday sun (Acts 26.13).

We know that looking into bright light can produce a condition called photo-retinitis or damage to the retina due to the brightness of the light, of which a good example is what is known as 'eclipse blindness' due to looking directly into the sun during a partial eclipse.[7] The resulting blindness may be temporary, but more often is permanent due to an actual burn of the retina caused by the infra-red rays of the sun's light. It seems very probable that Paul suffered from temporary retinal damage due to exposure to bright light and that this was responsible for his blindness. He saw the great light which shone around him and heard a voice, which made him look into the light to see where the voice came from in order to try and identify the speaker. His companions too saw the light, but they did not hear the voice (Acts 22.9) and so did not look into the light to see whence the voice came and so their eyes were not affected in the same way that Paul's were. When his sight returned, Luke tells us that 'immediately something like scales' fell from his eyes (Acts 9.18). The Greek phrase need not mean more than that the return of his sight felt to Paul as if scales had fallen off his eyes, but if it does mean more, then the scales may have been the crusts of dried secretion which would have accumulated in and around his eyes during the three days of his blindness. These would then break up and fall away as he opened his eyes to see once more.

Attempts have been made to connect this experience which Paul had on the Damascus road which the thorn in the flesh which affected him later and is described in 2 Corinthians 12.7. These attempts either regard both conditions as psychogenic in origin or assume that the blindness left some weakness of the eyes which formed the basis of the condition of the eyes which troubled Paul later. We shall discuss the identity of the thorn in the flesh later in this book, and so we content ourselves at this stage with the remark that it is unlikely that there was any connection between Paul's photogenic blindness and his thorn in the flesh.

Eutychus, in spite of his name, which means 'fortunate', was the victim of poor illumination and bad ventilation, to say nothing of the effects of overcrowding. He was a lad who had gone to attend Paul's farewell service at Troas (Troy) at the end of the apostle's week-long visit there (Acts 20.6-9). The service began after sunset on the Sunday evening for the lamps were already lit.[8] Many lamps were needed for each gave only a restricted area of light. They were in fact torches (*lampades*, cp. John 18.3) which were usually soaked in olive oil and when lit produced as much heat as light, and the smoke and hot air they generated eventually found their way out of the room through the small window-opening in which Eutychus was sitting, listening to Paul's long sermon. The warmth of the air combined with the lateness of the hour to make him sleepy. The verb tenses used by Luke reflect Eutychus' struggle to keep awake, but which ended in his falling into a deep sleep (v.9). As he relaxed he lost his hold on the window-sill and fell to his death out of a third-storey or second floor window of the tenement block in which the meeting was being held.[9] The most likely cause of his death was some form of head injury since he would land on his head as he fell backwards out of the window.

This account of the accident to Eutychus occurs in one of the 'we' sections of the Acts (Acts 20.5-15) which means that the author, i.e. Luke, was present (v.7). The clinical diagnosis of death was therefore an informed medical diagnosis and Eutychus was really dead when Paul was called to him. Once Paul had restored him to life, he was able to reassure the others that his life was now in him (v.10) and they were able to take him home (v.12). The original Greek clearly means that he was dead (*nekros*) and to object that Paul said there was life in him (v.10) is to miss the point that the apostle said this *after* he had 'bent over him and embraced him' and so restored him to life.[10]

The case of the father of Publius who was the chief man of the island of Malta appears to have been one of acute bacillary dysentery. He had fever and since the word translated fever is in the plural, we should probably speak of recurrent attacks of fever rather than a continued type of fever. Along with the fever he had *dusenterion* (Acts 28.8) which Wyclif in his English version of 1380 translated 'a blodie flux', a term which persisted in later versions until the RV supplied the word 'dysentery' in its place in 1881. The traditional diagnosis for this disease has been that of Malta fever,[11] but this diagnosis is excluded by the use of the term dysentery which clearly means that an intestinal disorder with pain and diarrhoea was present. These symptoms do not occur in Malta fever, for which the modern name is *brucellosis* in honour of Sir David Bruce who discovered its cause in 1887. The disease from which the father of Publius suffered was acute bacillary dysentery with fever and diarrhoea with blood and mucus in the stool, the result of his consumption of infected food or contaminated water.

## THE CHRONIC DISEASES

Luke appears to have had a particular interest in chronic disease. This is suggested by the higher proportion of records of this type of disease in the Acts when compared with the gospels. This impression is further deepened by the fact that he alone of the four gospel writers recorded two cases of the healing of chronic disease, namely those of the bent woman in Luke 13.11-17 and the man with dropsy in Luke 14.1-6. However, the number of case records is so small in both the gospels and the Acts that any conclusion from them can only be suggestive rather than significant of Luke's interest in chronic disabling conditions. Nevertheless, such an interest does harmonise with what we know of Luke's warm and sympathetic personality from his gospel where he is seen as one who is concerned for the sick and disadvantaged members of society.[12]

All three individual cases of chronic sickness which Luke describes in the Acts are unable to walk, and he recognises two causes of this condition, lameness and paralysis (Acts 8.7). The lameness is due to some disability or maldevelopment of the locomotor system made up of the bones and the joints, while the paralysis seen in the case of Aeneas (Acts 9.33) is probably neurological in origin due to some disease or injury of the central nervous system.

Lameness is described by the term *cholos* which like its English equivalent means disabled in the lower limbs. Both the cases of lameness described by Luke in the Acts are said to have been lame from birth or literally from their mother's womb (*ek koilias metros*, Acts 3.2 and 14.8). Their disability could not, therefore, be due to any infectious disease such as infantile paralysis or acute anterior poliomyelitis, nor to any state of hysteria. The cause of their lameness must have been either a developmental abnormality arising in the fetus before birth or an injury to the feet or ankles during the process of birth. It is difficult to see how a birth injury would produce a local injury to the feet of such a degree which would result in a complete inability to walk, and so a developmental abnormality seems to be the more likely diagnosis in these two cases. A possible diagnosis is a severe degree of club-foot, or what is known medically as *congenital talipes equino-varus*. In the case of the man at the gate of the Temple, this suggestion is made more probable by the clear indication in Acts 3.7 that the disability was in the feet and ankle bones.

The cripple at Lystra on the other hand had never stood upright on his feet or walked (Acts 14.8), and there is no mention of a local disability. The fact that he had survived to adulthood would exclude such congenital conditions as spina bifida as the cause of his lameness. In the condition of spina bifida the arches of the lower vertebrae fail to close over the spinal cord and there may be associated muscular paralysis of the lower limbs, but few complete cases of this condition reach their fifth birthday. However, it is possible that the diagnosis here is the same as in the case of the man at the gate of the Temple, namely, a severe degree of club-foot.

With regard to the race and religion of these two men, we may presume that the man at the Beautiful or Nicanor gate of the Temple was Jewish in race and religion.[13] In the case of the cripple at Lystra he was probably a Lycaonian Gentile who had become a Jewish proselyte and now was to become a Christian under the influence of Paul's preaching.[14]

In the case of Aeneas of Lydda in Acts 9.33, our data concerning his medical condition are very scanty. He was an adult male who was paralysed and had been bed-ridden for eight years. Luke describes him as *paralelumenos* which is the correct medical term for paralysis according to Hobart, as distinct from *paralutikos* which is the commoner and more popular term even though both words come from the verb *paraluo*, 'to weaken'.[15] The paralysis obviously affected the lower limbs since he was confined to bed. In an adult man such a paralysis could have been due to an infection such as tuberculosis of the vertebrae or have resulted from an accident in which the spine was fractured and the spinal cord damaged. However, we have no clue to the cause and are told simply that he was paralysed and so, apart from saying that his condition was due to some disease or damage to the spinal cord, we have no knowledge of the cause.

Before we leave our study of the records of these three individual cases of chronic disease or disability, we should note how careful Luke is to note how long each of the patients had been ill or disabled. The man at the gate of the Temple had been affected from birth and was now forty years old (Acts 3.2 and 4.22). The cripple at Lystra had been affected from birth and was now an adult man (Acts 14.8). Aeneas of Lydda had been bed-ridden for eight years (Acts 9.33).[16] These are the kind of details that a medically-trained person would always want to note down in any case records, and they form additional confirmation that the author of the Acts was indeed a physician.

## DEMON POSSESSION

The Philippian slave girl was possessed by 'a spirit of divination', whose alleged ability to foretell the future was exploited by her masters for financial gain (Acts 16.16). Luke was with Paul when the apostle met the girl, as we know from the occurrence of the incident in the first of the 'we' sections of the Acts. These are parts of the book of the Acts where Luke writes in the first person plural to indicate that he was with Paul on the occasion he is recording.[17] The girl is described by Luke as having 'a spirit, a Python'. This name derives from the python or she-dragon which used to guard the oracle at Delphi, the old name for which was Pytho. This creature was killed by the Greek god Apollo who succeeded to its oracular powers. The spirit of the python was then regarded as indwelling the priestess of Apollo at the oracle, who was called the Pythia or Pythoness and was believed to have the faculty of divination. There were several other oracles in various parts of the Greek world at which oracles were delivered by priestesses of Apollo. It was later believed that this same spirit could indwell other persons not associated with a special oracular place such as this girl, who would then be able to tell people's fortunes and supply them with information and advice about the future. These involuntary utterances were regarded as the voice of the god.[18]

In this girl's case it is usual to offer the alternatives of fraud or insanity as the basis of her soothsaying. Most authors choose the alternative of insanity and regard her as a case of mental illness. This diagnosis is not supported by the account of the incident. There are no indications of mental illness mentioned in the account such as we find in cases of demon possession in the gospels. In her case, demon possession was not manifested by physical or mental illness, but by the gift of divination or second sight. Once she came into contact with Paul and his companions, it became obvious what was the source of her faculty of prediction. It was a demon. This is the only case of demon possession recorded in the Acts and Paul exorcised the demon by charging it in the name of Jesus Christ to come out of her, in the same way that Jesus had exorcised the Gadarene demoniac (Luke 8.29).

## THE WORDS FOR HEALING

The three words which were commonly used to describe healing in the gospels are also the most frequently used to describe healing in the Acts. These are as follows:

*therapeuo* which occurs in Acts 4.14; 5.16; 8.7 and 28.9.

*iaomai* in Acts 9.34; 10.38 and 28.8,27.

*sozo* in Acts 4.9 and 14.9.

The verb *therapeuo* is always used in the passive voice in the Acts and is never used of our Lord's healing activity. This is contrast to the gospels where it is always used in the active voice and only of his healing activity. In Acts 17.25 Luke uses the verb in the only non-medical sense which occurs in the New Testament when he employs it to mean service given to a god. In our study of the vocabulary of healing in the gospels in Chapter Seven we found cause to regard the verbs *therapeuo* and *iaomai* as synonymous, and there is no reason why this should not be true of their usage in the Acts too. However, Harnack suggested that this was not true of the account of Paul's enforced sojourn in Malta recorded in Acts 28.1-10. Harnack would distinguish Paul's healing of the father of Publius by prayer and the laying on of hands for which the verb *iaomai* was used (v.8) from what he suggests was Luke's medical healing of the rest of the sick on the island for which the verb *therapeuo* was used (v.9).[19] He finds support for this suggestion in the fact that the gifts (*timais*) were given to both Paul and Luke according to the 'us' in verse ten, and that the word *timais* may also mean fees paid for medical attention.

This suggestion is unconvincing for several reasons. If Luke meant to record what Harnack suggests, why did he not do it more explicitly? Why should the verb *therapeuo* mean to provide medical attention in this context when in every other context in which it describes acts of healing by Jesus or his disciples, it means to heal by non-medical means? In no other place are we told that Luke practised healing by medical means. Also, in Acts 5.16 we find that Peter's healing by non-medical means is described using the verb *therapeuo* in the same voice, mood and tense. It appears more reasonable, therefore, to regard it as describing non-medical healing by Paul in Acts 28.9 rather than medical healing by Luke. We may agree with Lake and Cadbury who commented that Harnack's suggestion was ingenious but not convincing.[20]

When the medical author of the Acts was free of the constraints imposed by the use of written sources such as he had used in the writing of his gospel, it was to be expected that he would reveal that he commanded a more extensive vocabulary for the description of healing than was evident in that gospel. Even in the gospel he showed some dissatisfaction with the usage of his sources as can be illustrated by the three occasions in chapter nine of the gospel where he prefers to use *iaomai* instead of the verb *therapeuo* which Matthew had used in the corresponding passages of his gospel.[21]

Luke had used *sozo* fourteen times in his gospel. On nine occasions this usage referred to physical healing ('being made whole') and on five occasions it referred to deliverance from harm or danger. In the Acts, the verb occurs thirteen times and on two occasions it means physical healing (Acts 4.9 and 14.9) and on another two occasions to deliverance from harm or danger (Acts 27.20 and 31).

In the Acts we find several words for healing which are not used by any other New Testament author in a medical sense, but only by Luke. These may be listed as follows:

*stereoo* which occurs in Acts 3.7, 16, and also in a non-medical sense in 16.5.

*apallasso* in Acts 19.12 and in 5.15 (Western text). This verb is also used in a non-medical sense in Luke 12.58 and Hebrews 2.15.

*iasis* in Acts 4.22, 30. This word also occurs in a medical sense in Luke 13.32. It is derived from the verb *iaomai*.

The verb *stereoo* means 'to make firm, solid or strong'. Hobart notes that in medical usage this word was applied particularly to bones.[22] In Acts 3.7 it is used of the feet and ankle bones being made strong again. In Acts 16.5 it is used of the Churches being strengthened in the Faith.

The second verb, *apallasso*, means 'to set free or release' and according to Hobart is one of the words most frequently used of the cure of disease in the Greek medical writers and he quotes a number of instances of its use by Hippocrates and Galen.[23] The Western text attributes two further medical uses of this verb to Luke. One is in Luke 9.49 where the reference is to the exorcism of the epileptic boy, and the other is in Acts 5.15, a verse to which the Western text of the Codex Bezae adds a clause to say that the sick 'were being set free from every sickness'.[24] Whether these additional usages are significant will depend on how much value we place on the Western text, but they are at least interesting in our present context.

The third word is the noun *iasis* meaning 'the act of healing', which Hobart calls 'the great medical word' although it is used in non-medical writers as well.[25] Luke's use of it may reflect his fondness for the verb *iaomai* which we have already noted, and which is illustrated by the fact that out of the twenty-eight times this verb occurs in the New Testament, seventeen are to be found in his writings.

To complete our review of Luke's medical vocabulary in the Acts we should mention two further words which he uses to describe the state to which healing restored a person. The first is the adjective *hugies* which he uses in Acts 4.10 of the cure of the lame man at the gate of the Temple. We considered this word in Chapter Two when we reviewed the words used for the concept of health in the New Testament. We concluded then that it usually meant a state of physical soundness which was produced by healing. Although the cognate verb, *hugiaino*, is regularly used by the Greek medical writers for being in sound health, the adjective appears to be much commoner in non-medical writers and is not even commented on by Hobart.

The other word which Luke uses is the noun *holokleria* which occurs in Acts 3.16 where it is a *hapax legomenon*, i.e. its only use in the New Testament. The word means wholeness or soundness of an object in all its parts. Hobart was unable to find any instance of its use by the Greek medical writers who, however, frequently use the adjective *holokleros* in a general and a medical sense.[26]

A convenient summary of the words used for health and healing in the Acts is to be found in the account of the healing of the lame man at the Beautiful Gate of the Temple in the third and fourth chapters of that book. In this account, every word used by Luke in his gospel or the Acts with the meaning of either health or healing is used, with the exception of the verb *apallasso*, and also the verb *iaomai* unless we follow the Received Text which gives *iaomai* in Acts 3.11.[27] The chapters do, however, twice contain the noun *iasis*, 'healing', which is derived from the verb *iaomai*. The occurrence of the words for health and healing in these two chapters of the Acts is as follows in the NIV:

3.7: 'Instantly the man's feet and ankles became strong (*stereoo*).'

3.16: 'This man... was made strong (*stereoo*). Faith... has given this complete healing (*holokleria*) to him.'

4.9: 'How he was healed (*sozo*).'

4.10: 'This man stands before you healed (*hugies*).'

4.14: 'The man who had been healed (*therapeuo*).'

4.22: 'The man who was miraculously healed (*iasis*).'

4.30: 'Stretch out your hand to heal (*iasis*).'

The conclusion seems inescapable that since all these words describe the same state they are to be regarded as synonymous, or at least they must overlap each other in meaning in a large measure. It is clear, for instance, that *sozo* in 4.9 must mean physical healing. It is used in the perfect tense *sesostai*, indicating that he had been healed and remained healed. This is said to be the result of a good deed (*euergesia*) which suggests that it was a physical act of healing. The physical nature of this act of healing described by *sozo* is further supported by the use of *hugies* which indicates the healthy state of soundness to which he was restored. In view of this, it is of great interest that Peter goes on in 4.12 to use *sozo* in a much more comprehensive sense. This suggests that both physical healing and spiritual salvation are included in the *soteria* which is available only in the name of Jesus Christ of Nazareth. We take this also to mean that this man found more than merely physical healing in Jesus Christ. He had found a soundness and salvation which affected his whole being and made him truly whole.

# Chapter 14
# THE PRACTICE OF HEALING IN THE ACTS

## THE INITIATIVE IN HEALING

If we exclude the healing of Paul's blindness as a special case from which no conclusions can be drawn for our present purpose, we are left with seven cases of healing which are described individually in the Acts. In these cases the initiative in healing was mostly taken by persons other than those who were sick. This is shown by the following analysis:

I. *Case in which the sick person took the initiative:*
   1. The lame man at the gate of the Temple (Acts 3.3).

II. *Case in which friends of the sick took the initiative:*
   1. The raising of Tabitha (Acts 9.38).

III. *Cases in which an apostle took the initiative:*
   1. Aeneas at Lydda (Acts 9.34). Initiative by Peter.
   2. The cripple at Lystra (Acts 14.9). Initiative by Paul.
   3. The Philippian slave-girl (Acts 16.18). Initiative by Paul.
   4. Eutychus (Acts 20.19). Initiative by Paul.
   5. The father of Publius (Acts 28.8). Initiative by Paul.

In the group healings which are recorded in the Acts, it was usually the friends or relatives of the sick who took the initiative (cp. Acts 5.16 and 19.12), except in the case of the sick healed by Paul in Malta after he had healed the father of Publius. When the news of this became public, those who were sick appear to have taken the initiative in coming to him for healing (Acts 28.9).

The number of cases which Luke records is too small to allow any significant conclusion to be drawn from them, but certain comments appear to be justified. In general, the narratives give the impression that healing occurred on a casual basis. Cases of sickness were dealt with as they arose or were met with. Healing did not play any significant part in a strategy of evangelism and was not used to attract an audience for preaching. This is not to say that the opportunity to witness was not taken when it arose from a healing incident. The healing of the lame man at the gate of the Temple in the third chapter of the Acts provides an excellent example of how the apostles could use such an incident as a means of witness to both the people and the religious authorities when the opportunity arose.

It is striking how much more frequently the apostles appear to have taken the initiative in healing than Jesus did in proportion to the number of persons who were healed. However, the numbers of the sick healed in the Acts are fewer than those in the gospels, so no significant comparison can be made.

## THE CONTEXT OF HEALING

In the gospels, healing not infrequently occurs in the context of the preaching and teaching of Jesus. When we come to the Acts we find that this connection is not as obvious, although it is still present.

It appears in the teaching of the apostolic Church which recognised that preaching and healing were combined in the earthly ministry of Jesus. When Peter spoke to the company assembled in the house of the Roman centurion Cornelius, he reminded them of how Jesus preached the good news of peace and 'went about doing good and healing (*iaomai*) all who were under the power of the devil' (Acts 10.36-38 NIV). It occurs too in the prayer of the Church for Peter and John after the Jewish authorities had forbidden them to speak or teach in the name of Jesus. The Church prayed that the two apostles might have boldness to speak the word of God while God stretched out his hand to heal (cp. Acts 4.29-30, where the word *iasis* is used for healing).

This same combination of preaching and healing appears in the practice of the apostolic Church leaders. As a result of the persecution of the Christian community following the death of Stephen, the great missionary expansion of the Church began. Philip the evangelist went north to a city of Samaria and we are told that the people listened eagerly to his words and saw the signs (*semeia*) that he did (Acts 8.6). These signs included the exorcism of evil spirits and the healing of many who were paralysed or lame (v.7). Two other instances in which preaching and healing go together occur in the evangelistic activity of Paul in Asia Minor. As he preaches at Lystra, Paul sees a man lame from birth, who is listening to his words, and when Paul finds he has the faith to be healed (*sozo*) he calls on the man to stand up and he is healed and able to walk normally (Acts 14.8-10). Later, when Paul spent over two years in Ephesus proclaiming the word of God we are told that God worked healing miracles (*dunameis*) through him of an unusual kind by which evil spirits were cast out and sick persons were rid (*apallasso*) of their diseases (Acts 19.10-12).

However, it must be remarked that the connection of preaching and healing in the Acts is neither as definite nor as frequent as it was in the gospels. After Philip had preached and healed in Samaria, he went on a tour of the coastal towns between Azotus (Ashdod) and Caesarea and while we are told that he preached in all these towns, there is no mention of any healing activity (Acts 8.40). Also, a closer examination of the prayer of the Church for Peter and John in Acts 4.29-30 appears to suggest some separation between preaching and healing in the thought of the apostolic Church. The Church prays that Peter and John might be given boldness to speak the word of God while God stretches out his hand to heal. It is true that the two apostles had been forbidden to speak and teach in the name of Jesus (v. 18), but there had been no mention of a ban on healing. Nevertheless it cannot be without some significance that the Church appears to regard preaching as the main activity of the apostles with healing coming from the hand of God without any mention of their part in it.

We conclude, therefore, that although there is some evidence in the Acts of the occurrence together of preaching and healing, healing does not occur in the context of preaching in the same way or to the same degree as it did in the gospels.

## THE MOTIVE FOR HEALING

The accounts of healing in the Acts are not always as specific nor as clear-cut in their indication of the underlying motive as those of the healing activity of Jesus in the gospels. In about half the cases no indication of a motive is provided and we are left to guess at its nature.

Those cases in which some indication of a motive is given may be classified as follows in terms of the motive which they suggest.

I.   *A response to a request:*
   1. By the sick. The lame man at the Temple gate (3.2).
   2. By friends of the sick. Tabitha at Joppa (9.38).

II.   *A response to a need:*
   1. Aeneas the paralysed (9.33).
   2. Eutychus at Troas (20.10).
   3. The father of Publius (28.8)
   4. The sick on Malta (28.9).

III.   *A response to faith:*
   1. The cripple at Lystra (14.9).

IV.   *A witness to the gospel:*
   1. The healing of the sick in Samaria (8.5-7).

V.   *A reaction to vexation:*
   1. The Philippian slave-girl (16.18).

There are some significant differences between this list of motives and the list we compiled from the gospel records of healing in Chapter Eight. Here there is no mention of compassion and indeed the words for compassion or mercy do not occur in the Acts. It is not recorded of anyone that they cried to the apostles for mercy as they did to Jesus. The lame man asked for alms which is money given out of a feeling of mercy or compassion for the poor (Acts 3.3-6), and not for healing out of a feeling of compassion for the sick. Nor is healing represented as being performed in the fulfilment of Scripture as it was particularly in the gospel of Matthew in the case of Jesus (Matthew 8.17; 11.2-6 and 12.15-21). Faith, too, is by no means as prominent a feature in the records of healing in the Acts as it is in the gospels, and neither is the presentation of healing as a manifestation of the glory of Jesus Christ as the Son of God as it is in the gospel of John (John 11.4).

Although what we have just said is true, the differences between the Acts and the gospels in the matter of motives are not absolute. While it is true, for instance, that there is no mention of compassion in the Acts as a motive for healing, in so far as compassion is the response of Christian love to need, we cannot exclude compassion as the motive underlying healing in the four cases described as a response to need in the list given above. Also, it is clear that in some of the healing miracles in the Acts as in the gospels more than one motive may be discerned. While the healing of the cripple at Lystra by Paul is stated to have been when Paul saw he had faith to be made well and responded to it (Acts 14.9), it could also be regarded in the light of what followed, as a witness to the gospel which Paul preached. It undoubtedly played an important part in the planting of the Church in Lystra, and may even have played some part in the conversion of Timothy who lived there as we know from Acts 16.1. It is also important to notice that Luke uses the word *semeion* not uncommonly of the miracles of healing in the Acts. This word is not used specifically of any miracles of healing in his gospel, where he uses the word *dunamis* to describe miracles of healing in common with the other two synoptic gospels. As we saw in Chapter Seven, a *semeion* is a sign which points to something beyond itself. The motive behind a healing miracle may also be to draw attention to him in whose name and by whose power the sick were healed (See Acts 4.30; 8.6 and 14.3).

The outstanding example of a healing miracle in which more than one motive was present is that involving the lame man at the Beautiful Gate of the Temple in Jerusalem. In the third chapter of the Acts, Luke first portrays the miracle as the response to a request for alms by the man (v.3). If the account had stopped there, then we would be justified in identifying the motive as the response to a request for help, and nothing more. However, the account continues and records the events which followed the healing and incidentally uncovers several other possible motives which could have lain behind the response of Peter. It provides a salutary reminder that the motives which may lie behind any of the healing miracles are not always indicated in the brief narratives in which many of them are described.

If we now examine the narrative of the healing of the lame man and the events which flowed from it as recorded in the third and fourth chapters of the Acts, we shall discover no fewer than seven descriptions of the healing miracle and its results which may be regarded as providing possible motives for it. This is not to say that these were explicitly and consciously present as such to the mind of Peter when the miracle was performed. Nevertheless, the miracle is presented by Luke in his own record or in the words of the principal participants as the following:

1. A response to a request (3.3).

2. A response to a need of a cripple for healing (3.2).

3. A response to faith (3.16).

4. An opportunity to witness:
   a. To the people (3.12-16).
   b. To the religious authorities (4.5-12).

5. A sign pointing to the power of the name of Jesus (4.16, 22, 30).

6. An authentication of the preaching of the word (4.29-30).

7. A cause for people to glorify God (3.8-19 and 4.21).

There remains one unexpected and surprising motive for consideration. In the case of the Philippian slave-girl, we are told that she developed the habit of following the apostolic party, which at this point included Luke himself.[1] She did this each day as they went to the place of prayer beside the river Gangites at Philippi. As she followed close behind them she shouted out for all to hear, that they were servants of the Most High God proclaiming the way of salvation (Acts 16.16-17). Paul bore with her behaviour for many days, but finally was so vexed with her unsolicited testimony that he turned round on her and exorcised the spirit which possessed her.

The verb which expressed Paul's feeling of vexation is *diaponeo* and is used only here and in Acts 4.2 in the New Testament (except in the Western text of Mark 14.4).[2] Its use in Acts 4.2 gives us the clue to its meaning here for it describes the reaction of the Sadducees to the preaching of the resurrection by Peter and John in Jerusalem. The Sadducees did not believe in the resurrection of the body as we know from Matthew 22.23; Mark 12.18 and Acts 23.8, and they were annoyed at the apostles for teaching this doctrine to the people. Their annoyance was not petty or trivial, but arose from their firmly-held denial of the resurrection. In a similar manner, Paul's annoyance arose from his enmity towards all that was evil. It was directed not at the girl but at the spirit which possessed her. Like Jesus in the gospels, Paul was unwilling to accept the testimony of evil spirits even though this might help forward the task of preaching the way of salvation. The only answer the New Testament knows to demon possession is confrontation with Jesus Christ and a demand based on the power of his name that the demon should come out of the person whose personality it has possessed. That is what occurred here. Paul was annoyed at the spirit for its possession of the girl and its daily use of her to make Paul's presence and purpose known in the way that it did. It was this annoyance which prompted Paul to exorcise the spirit and release the girl from its domination.

# THE METHODS OF HEALING

The methods of healing used by the apostles and others in the Acts are similar to those used by Jesus in the gospels. As we found there, the principal methods were those of word and touch or their combination. We may classify the methods used as follows:

1. Healing by word.
2. Healing by touch.
3. Healing by word and touch combined.
4. Healing by other means.

There are, however, no examples in the Acts of healing by saliva and only one of healing at a distance.

## Healing by word

In exorcism. The only case of exorcism documented in the Acts is that of the slave-girl at Philippi. In her case Paul said to the spirit, 'I charge you in the name of Jesus Christ of Nazareth to come out of her' (Acts 16.18). In Luke 4.35 Jesus had used the same command to the spirit possessing the synagogue demoniac, and in Luke 8.29 he had addressed the spirit possessing the Gadarene demoniac in similar terms. In his charge to the spirit, Paul used the verb *parangello*, 'to charge', in what is usually interpreted as the aoristic present tense meaning that the spirit must come out that very instant.[3]

There were other cases of exorcism in the apostolic Church which are not recorded in detail but only mentioned incidentally. We may assume that these cases too were dealt with by a word of command addressed to the spirit. Some confirmation of this is provided by the account which Luke gives of the itinerant Jewish exorcists at Ephesus in Acts 19.13-20, who appeared to regard Paul as belonging to their own 'profession'. Luke instances the seven sons of Sceva, an otherwise unknown Jewish high priest. He may not have had any claim to this title but may have assumed it in the way that magicians and astrologers sometimes do today. His sons were exorcists of the itinerant kind and one day they attempted to exorcise a demon using the name of Jesus Christ. Their attempt failed and they were attacked and routed by the possessed man. They failed because they used the name of Jesus simply as a magical or theurgic formula relying on the pronouncing of the name itself as magic strong enough to overcome the demon.[4] But it was the person and authority which lay behind the name which was the important factor in exorcism. This can be seen in the reply of the evil spirit. It knew Jesus and Paul as persons who had authority over it, but these men had no faith in Jesus as a person nor any commission from him as their authority, and so it refused to obey them. The fact that they attempted exorcism by word alone suggests that this was the usual method in New Testament times.

**In physical healing.** Two cases are described in the Acts in which physical healing was performed by the use of word alone.

1. Aeneas: And Peter said to him, *'Aeneas, Jesus Christ heals you; rise and make your bed'* (Acts 9.34).

2. The cripple at Lystra: Paul said in a loud voice, *'Stand upright on your feet'* (Acts 14.10).

As in the gospels, the sick are commanded to do what their sickness had rendered them incapable of doing. In both cases their incapacity arose from a physical cause and cannot be explained on the basis of hysteria or other psychological cause. The cripple had never stood upright or walked, and Aeneas had been paralysed for eight years. No psychological cause can cripple a person from birth, and after eight years, physical atrophy and wasting will produce an incapacity which can no longer be attributed to purely psychological causes.

In the case of Aeneas, the word was more than a simple command. Peter first calls him by his name and then makes the statement, 'Jesus Christ heals you'. His name is Greek, well-known from the name of the hero of Virgil's epic poem, *The Aeneid*. The statement implies that he knew the name of Jesus Christ and had heard of his ability to heal. We are not told that he was a Christian, but at least he was familiar with Christian teaching, e.g. that Jesus was the Christ. He had been bedridden for eight years but Peter tells him that he is healed at the very moment that Peter is speaking to him, for the tense of the verb *iaomai* is another example of the use of the aoristic present.[5] Having told Aeneas that he was healed, Peter goes on to order him to make his bed (Acts 9.34). The exact meaning of the second part of this order is uncertain for the verb *stronnumi* may be applied either to make a bed on which to lie and sleep, or to prepare a couch on which to recline and eat at table (as in Mark 14.15).[6] Aeneas had been able to do neither for the past eight years, and so his doing either now would be a significant demonstration of his cure. Since he had been bedridden for so long, the making of his bed would seem to be the more probable reading, but Bruce points out that the alternative meaning would accord well with the Luke's interest in nourishment for convalescents (cp. Luke 8.55 and Acts 9.19).[7] However, there is no suggestion in the narrative that Aeneas had suffered from any lack of nourishment.

The cripple at Lystra had been unable to use his feet from birth (Acts 14.8) and so was unable to stand or walk. He had been brought each day to sit and listen to Paul preaching. On one of these days Paul saw that he had the faith to be made well (*sozo*) and looking intently at him, said in a loud voice for all to hear, 'Stand upright on your feet'. The Western text prefaces this command with a reference to the name of the Lord Jesus Christ, but this may safely be ignored as a probable assimilation to the account of Peter's healing of the lame man at the gate of the Temple in Acts 3.6.[8] The result was that the man leapt up in a single bound and began and continued to walk about as the tenses used indicate.[9] There are several touches in this record which suggest that it is based on the testimony of an eye-witness, and it may be that this eye-witness was Timothy who described the incident to Luke who then included it in his record of the visit of Paul and Barnabas to Lystra, Timothy's home town (Acts 16.1). The implication of the record of the miracle is that the man's feet were restored to their normal structure and function and for the first time in his life he was able to stand upright and walk.

**In raising the dead.** Tabitha was a Christian and when she died at Joppa (the modern Jaffa), the disciples there sent for Peter who was at Lydda (the modern Lod) about ten miles away from where he had just healed Aeneas. While their request may have been no more than an invitation for Peter to be present at the funeral ceremony, Marshall suggests that the fact they did not bury the body at once, but washed it and laid it out in an upper room indicated that they had some hopes that Tabitha might be raised from the dead.[10] However that may be, when Peter came and was shown the body all laid out for burial, he put everyone outside the room and after prayer, he turned to the body and spoke two words. He called Tabitha by her name and then ordered her to get up, using the same verb and verbal form he had addressed to Aeneas at Lystra. After she had returned to life and sat up, Peter took her by the hand and lifted her up and called in the disciples and presented her to them restored to life (Acts 9.36-41). This unexpected restoration of Tabitha to life had a profound effect in Joppa, for when it became known we are told that many believed in the Lord (v.42).

## Healing by touch

The only case in which touch alone was used in healing amongst those which are described in any detail in the Acts was that of the father of Publius, the chief man of Malta. Here we are told that Paul laid hands on him and healed him (Acts 28.8).

There are also three general references in the Acts which appear to describe healing by touch alone. These are as follows:

> Acts 5.12: 'Many signs and wonders (*semeia kai terata*) were done among the people by the hands of the apostles'.

> Acts 14.3: 'At Iconium... the Lord... bore witness to the word of his grace, granting signs and wonders (*semeia kai terata*) to be done by their hands' (i.e. those of Paul and Barnabas).

> Acts 19.11: 'God did extraordinary miracles (*dunameis*) by the hands of Paul'.

In each case the phrase *dia ton cheiron*, 'by the hands', is used and this may mean literally by the use of the hands in touching the sick, or it may be a Semitism for 'by the agency of' not necessarily involving the use of the hands at all.[11] However, there is no real reason why the phrase should not be understood literally as referring to healing by means of the active use of the apostles' hands rather than simply by their agency, especially when we recall that touch was the commonest healing method used by Jesus in the gospels.

## Healing by word and touch

There are two incidents of healing in the Acts in which word and touch are combined. The first is the cure of the lame man at the gate of the Temple in Acts 3.1-10. Peter first asked him to fix his attention on John and himself ('Look on us', v.4), and then ordered him in the name of Jesus Christ of Nazareth to walk. At the same time, he took the man by the right hand and helped him up, and as he did so, the man's feet and ankles were made strong and he was healed. Luke underlines the fact that he was healed by using no fewer than seven verbs to describe his activity immediately he was healed. These describe him as leaping up, putting his feet firmly on the ground and walking about. Then continuing to walk, he entered into the Temple courts with Peter and John still leaping about and now praising God for his healing (v.8). Four of these verbs are in the form of present participles which give an added liveliness to the narrative.

The second incident is the restoration of Paul's sight in Acts 9.17-19. In this incident, Ananias acting on instructions received in a vision, seeks out Paul (then called Saul) and lays his hands on him saying that he has been sent by the Lord Jesus in order that Paul may regain his sight. The result of this combination of word and touch is the restoration of Paul's sight.

## Healing by other means

We have now considered the methods which were used in most of the cases of healing in the Acts of which we have any detail. It has become evident that most cases were healed by word or touch, or by a combination of these, and as in the gospels, touch was the main method. There remain three incidents in which the methods used do not appear to fit into the categories of word and touch which we have used so far. These are the following:

1. The restoration of Eutychus to life (Acts 20.9-12).

2. The effect of Peter's shadow (Acts 5.15).

3. The healing by cloths from Paul's body (Acts 19.12).

We begin by looking at the account of the restoration to life of Eutychus by means which appear to resemble modern methods of resuscitation. Eutychus was a young man who was a member of the congregation which had gathered in a house in Troas (Troy) to hear Paul's farewell sermon on the Sunday evening before he left Troas never to return. Due to the unhygienic conditions in the meeting room which we mentioned in the previous chapter, he lapsed into a deep sleep and fell to the ground through a window of the third storey or second floor of the house. He was taken up dead and Paul went down and embraced him and life returned to his body (Acts 20.10).

Paul's words, 'His life (*psuche*) is in him', have been taken to mean that he was not dead, but Luke states quite clearly in verse nine that he was taken up dead, and Paul did not say that his life was *still* in him. As Marshall comments, 'There can be little doubt that Luke intended to portray Paul as being able to raise the dead (like Peter in 9.36-43); Paul's comment that the boy was alive refers to his condition after he had ministered to him. Luke would not have devoted space to the raising up of someone who was merely apparently dead'.[12]

Luke tells us that Paul fell on Eutychus as he lay on the ground and threw his arms round him, and since both verbs are in the aorist tense this would suggest that the actions they describe were performed once only. This means that the method Paul used was not artificial respiration as it is practised today, since to describe this repeated manoeuvre would require the imperfect tense. Neither was it the same as the methods of resuscitation used by the prophet Elijah in 1 Kings 17.21 or by the prophet Elisha in 2 Kings 4.34-35 with which it is often compared and which we have already considered in Chapter Five. The method used by Elisha appears to resemble the modern kiss-of-life type of resuscitation, but there is no suggestion that Paul used any similar method to restore Eutychus. That this was a miraculous and not a medical restoration to life is borne out by the fact that although Luke was present at the meeting at Troas, he was not called down to attend Eutychus and did not accompany Paul as he went down to see him either.

We know that Luke was present at the meeting because he uses the first person plural 'we' in describing events in the room (Acts 20.7-8). However, he then changes to the third person singular 'he' to describe what happened outside the room when Eutychus was taken up and Paul restored him to life (vv.10-11). In other words, Luke took no part in the healing at all. The explanation may lie in verse thirteen where Luke tells us that he went with the advance party to the ship in order to bring it round Cape Lectum in order to pick up Paul at Assos, in order to give him a longer time with the Christians at Troas. This would mean that Luke would not have been present when Eutychus fell to his death since he had already left the meeting to board the ship. If this were so, then the eye-witness account of how the young man finally lapsed into a deep sleep and fell out of the window came not from Luke, but from another member of the party who stayed on, possibly from Paul himself.

We now turn to consider the effect of Peter's shadow and its significance. After the healing of the lame man at the gate of the Temple, the apostles stayed on in Jerusalem and we are told that many signs and wonders (*semeia kai terata*) were wrought by their hands (Acts 5.12). Not surprisingly it was Peter who had the greatest reputation in this respect for it was he who had been instrumental in healing the lame man. The result was that the people laid their sick on mattresses and camp beds in the street 'that as Peter came by at least his shadow might fall on some of them' (5.15). The Western textual tradition adds the words, 'for they were all set free from every sickness which each of them had'.[13] Our difficulty in understanding this statement lies in the sparse detail which Luke gives us. Ramsay's comment on this verse was that Luke 'as a rule, carries brevity to the point of obscurity'.[14] Luke does not say that Peter's shadow was the means of healing the sick, and even the Western textual addition does not state this explicitly. Why then was Peter's shadow mentioned? First, to show how near to Peter the people brought their sick. They were near enough for his shadow to fall on some of them as he passed by. Second, to reflect the people's superstition that healing was to be found even in the shadow of an apostle. The shadow fell only on some of them, but all were healed (5.16). The explanation lies in verse twelve where we are told that the healing was performed by the hands of the apostles, and not by the shadow of any one of them. This record is therefore an account of healing by touch by the hands of the apostles.

In Acts 19.11-12 we are told that God did extraordinary miracles (*dunameis ou tas tuchousas*) by the hands of Paul. Luke uses the figure of speech called litotes not infrequently in the Acts and here he employs it to describe the miracles that God did through Paul at Ephesus as he tells us they were not of the ordinary kind. They were, in fact, of two kinds. The first kind was directly performed by Paul's hands. As we have already seen, the phrase *dia ton cheiron*, 'by the hands of', indicates not merely the agency of Paul but his personal activity and his contact with the sick.[15] The second kind was performed indirectly through the application of things which had been in close contact with the apostle. These were his sweat-rags or *soudaria*, the cloths he wore round his head to keep the sweat out of his eyes, and his work-aprons or *simikinthia* which he would wear to protect his clothes as he worked at tent-making with Aquila and Priscilla at Ephesus (cp. Acts 18.3,19). When these items were taken to the sick, the result was that they were rid of their diseases and evil spirits left them (v.12).

This account reminds us of the healing of the woman with the flow of blood who was healed by touching Jesus' clothes (Matthew 9.20-22; Mark 5.25-34 and Luke 8.43-48). Matthew records that 'she said to herself, "If I only touch his garment, I shall be made well"' (Matthew 9.21). She did touch his garment and was made well (Mark 5.27). We cannot dismiss this as an example of primitive mechanistic magic. For one thing there is no other record of healing in the gospels which lends itself to a magical explanation of this kind. Certainly the woman's own belief may have been superstitious and she may have been expecting some magical event to occur, but Jesus accepted her action in touching his garment and turned her superstitious belief into saving faith (Mark 5.34). His garment represented his presence symbolically and became the vehicle of his healing power. In the same way, here in Acts 19.12, Paul's clothes represented his presence and became the vehicle of the power of his risen Lord to heal the sick and cast out evil spirits. This verse records the two facts that items of clothing which had touched Paul's body were taken to the sick, and that the sick were healed. It makes no definite causal connection between them.[16]

Our consideration of the three accounts of healing in which means other than a word or touch appeared to have been used, shows that the method of healing in these cases was really one of touch. In the case of Eutychus, the touch was applied in a special way and was not simply by the laying on of hands by Paul but by his embracing young man's body in his arms (Acts 20.10). In the other two cases we are specifically told that healing was effected by the hands of the apostles (Acts 5.12 and 19.11). We do not therefore need to classify them in a separate category but can include them along with the other cases in which healing was by touch.

## HEALING IN THE ACTS AND THE GOSPELS

At the beginning of this chapter we noted that much less space was given by the author of the Acts to accounts of healing in comparison with that taken up by such accounts in the gospels. As we conclude our study of healing in the Acts of the Apostles it is appropriate to comment on the significance of this difference between the Acts and the gospels.

The first consequence of the difference is, of course, that we have much less material available for the study of healing in the apostolic Church as recorded in the Acts. This means that any conclusions we draw from such material are less certain than any we may have drawn from our study of the gospels.

The second observation which we may make about the difference, is that it means that the author of the Acts felt under no obligation to collect together a great number of stories of the miraculous in order to impress his readers with the case for Christianity. This appears first of all in the fact that the healing miracles of the Acts were not presented as a primary means of evangelism performed in order to impress their spectators and to persuade them to embrace the new religion. It is also reflected in the small number of miracles selected for more detailed record and the brief form in which these details were recorded. We know from incidental references in the course of the narrative of the Acts that many more healing miracles were performed than are recorded there.[17]

Finally, the difference in the amount of space devoted to healing in the Acts as compared with the gospels must mean that physical healing was not a major interest in the apostolic Church. In order to investigate this matter further, we now proceed to examine the other source of information about the apostolic Church, which is to be found in the epistles of the New Testament.

# Chapter 15
# HEALING IN THE EPISTLES

The book of the Acts of the Apostles is an account of the spread of the gospel outwards from Jerusalem through Judaea and Samaria, Asia Minor and Greece to Rome, the capital of the Roman Empire. In its progress from country to country, local Christian communities or Churches came into being. These Churches were at first minority groups in a pagan Hellenistic world and they faced problems of faith and practice for which they needed advice and guidance to solve. Sometimes such advice and guidance could be given by word of mouth, but at other times it was given by letter, and some of these letters, traditionally called 'epistles', have survived and are included in the New Testament. By their very nature, however, these letters rarely give us a complete picture of any situation, and they often produce more problems for today's readers than they resolve.

What these letters have to say about the healing activity of the Church in the early years of its existence forms no exception to this general statement. There are only a few tantalising references to sickness and healing and even these are scattered quite incidentally throughout the epistles, with no indication of whether these references describe only local situations and practices, or such as are general throughout the Church at large. There is no complete description or discussion of attitudes to sickness or methods of healing, so that we can never be certain that we have the whole picture before us. Nevertheless we can gain some valuable glimpses and insights into the thought and practice of the apostolic Church from a consideration of these scattered references.

The paucity of specific references to healing in the epistles is of great interest in view of the fact that these writings form over a third of the bulk of the New Testament. Some of them are contemporaneous with the events recorded in the Acts, whilst others are not, and it cannot be denied that they reflect a lessened interest in health and healing when compared with that book, as that book reflects a lessened interest in healing when compared with the gospels. It may be argued, of course, that the character of a letter does not lend itself to the mention of incidents of healing in the same way as a chronicle of events such as we have in the Acts. However, the Pauline letters in particular frequently deal with problems on which the local Christian communities have sought the apostle's advice and guidance and since it is only referred to in passing, we can only presume that healing was not a problem for them. Also, when we find that there are references in these same letters to illness which was left to the natural processes of recovery and not one reference to any case in which healing was obtained by supernatural means, it is only reasonable to conclude that there is a lessened interest in supernatural healing when the epistles are compared with the gospels, and even with the Acts.

When we look more closely at those references to healing which do occur in the epistles, we find that there are some striking differences between them and those which occur in the gospels and the Acts. The vocabulary used in the epistles is much more limited than it was even in the Acts. There is no reference to demon possession and exorcism, and no mention of raising the dead. Healing appears to be confined to within the Christian community unlike that recorded in the gospels and the Acts, and there is mention of gifts of healing which are not referred to elsewhere in the New Testament. Finally, we hear of Church leaders who are sick and yet nothing appears to be done to heal them. Some of these points will be discussed in this chapter, but we reserve for fuller treatment in later chapters the two topics of Paul's thorn in the flesh and James' instructions to those who became sick in the Christian community.

## THE WORDS FOR HEALTH AND HEALING

The words which express the different aspects of health in the New Testament all occur in the epistles although they frequently have a different emphasis and application from that found in the gospels. The verb *hugiaino* occurs in 3 John 2 with its literal meaning of being sound in health, but with this exception, its use is confined to the Pastoral Epistles where it is used metaphorically to describe sound doctrine.[1] This has been interpreted as meaning doctrine which makes people whole, whose goal is the health of the soul, but is more probably doctrine which is sound because it conforms to apostolic teaching. The word *eirene* occurs frequently in the epistles and describes that aspect of health which consists of a right relationship to God, and the serenity of mind and heart which flows from that relationship. The adjective *teleios* is used by Paul to express the idea of a person's complete maturity which he covets for all his readers in such verses as 1 Corinthians 14.20; Ephesians 4.13 and Philippians 3.15. The example and standard of this maturity is Jesus Christ himself.

The verb *sozo* is used in Paul's epistles 'only in connexion with man's relations with God' and has 'primarily an eschatological reference', seen in such verses as Romans 5.9; 1 Corinthians 3.15; 5.5 and Philippians 1.28. This is in contrast to the use of *sozo* in the gospels. The cognate noun *soteria* is hardly ever used in the gospels (Luke 1.69, 71, 77; 19.9 and John 4.22), but it is common in the epistles where it is never used of bodily healing, but only of spiritual salvation with a primary eschatological reference, as in Romans 13.11; Philippians 2.12 and 1 Thessalonians 5.8.[2] This is in contrast to the use of this word in the Greek papyri from Egypt where *soteria* is frequently used in the general sense of bodily health and well-being, both physical and general.[3]

There is one other word which should be noted. We met the noun *holokleria* in Acts 3.16 where it was used to describe the state of 'perfect health' (NRSV) or 'complete healing' (NIV) to which the lame man at the gate of the Temple had been restored. The noun occurs only there in the New Testament. However the cognate adjective *holokleros* occurs twice in the epistles, in 1 Thessalonians 5.23 and in James 1.4. This word is commonly used in the Greek papyri of physical soundness or completeness,[4] and is used by Paul to describe the complete soundness of spirit, soul and body as one entity which he wishes the Thessalonian Christians to enjoy now and until the Lord Jesus Christ comes again.[5]

As we saw previously, the common verb for healing in the gospels is *therapeuo*, but this verb does not occur in the epistles. The verb *sozo* is used only in James 5.15 in a sense which clearly indicates the healing of the sick. On the few occasions on which a word is required for healing in the epistles, the verb *iaomai* or one of its derivatives is used. These occasions are in 1 Corinthians 12.9, 28, 30; Hebrews 12.13; James 5.16 and 1 Peter 2.24.

## PAUL AND THE BODY

The question now arises of Paul's view of the body and physical health. It might appear from the last section that he had very little to say about the body, and yet John Robinson in his essay entitled *The Body* gives his opinion that 'one could say without exaggeration that the concept of the body forms the keystone of Paul's theology'.[6] This arises from the fact that *soma*, which is the common Greek word for the body may mean both the physical body and the whole person, and so may be understood individually and collectively. It is the collective sense which predominates in Robinson's own study. In the Pauline epistles, Stacey distinguishes no fewer than five different senses in which the word *soma* is used: 'There is the body as flesh, the body as the whole man, the body as the principle of redeemable humanity, the body as the means of resurrection, and the Body of Christ meaning the Church'.[7] Therefore, Paul uses this word in both a literal and a metaphorical sense.

There are more references to the body (*soma*) in Paul's first epistle to the Corinthians than in any other book of the New Testament. It is referred to there no fewer than forty-seven times out of a total of one hundred and forty-six times in the whole New Testament. Some of these references are literal, while others are metaphorical. The most important of the literal references are in 6.13-20; 7.1-4; 12.14-26 and 15.35-49. The metaphorical references are especially to the Church as the body of Christ (12.27) and to the communion bread as symbolising his body (10.16-17 and 11.24).

## The body is a unity

For Paul the body is a unity. It is an organism with an organic structure which is designed to exist and function as a unified whole. In his commentary on the epistle to the Ephesians, Armitage Robinson defines it as 'a living organism - a human frame with all its manifold structure inspired by a single life'.[8] This concept of the human body as a living organism appears most vividly in the metaphorical comparison which Paul draws between the body and the Church or the Christian community in 1 Corinthians 12.12-30. He speaks of the Church as 'the body of Christ' (*soma Christou* in v.27, cp. Ephesians 1.23; 5.30 and Colossians 1.24).

The body, then, is a unit made up of many members or organs which are dependent on their membership of the body for their life and activity. They are arranged in the body just as God wanted them to be arranged and are brought together by joints and held together by means of *sundesmon* (Colossians 2.19). According to Lightfoot, this latter word is a term which in its general sense 'denotes any of the connecting bands which strap the body together, such as muscles, tendons and ligaments'.[9] The members each have different functions but are still part of the body (1 Corinthians 12.14-16, cp. Romans 12.4-5). Because of their different functions, each member has its own contribution to make to the life of the whole. The unity of the body does not mean uniformity of the structure or function of its members and there is no schism or division in the body and no room for rivalry between the parts (1 Corinthians 12.25). In other words, the members are interdependent and complementary in their life and function, and form essential parts of the body. The consequence is that they all share in the health or suffering of the body as a whole (v.26) and its growth and development is controlled by the head (Colossians 2.19).

Paul uses this description of the body as an organism to illustrate how all Christians are members or organs of the body of Christ, the Church. They each have their own gifts and functions which contribute to the life and activity of the whole. They each have their own bodies, but these bodies are the members or organs of Christ's body, the Church, by which he continues to work in the world.[10]

## The organs of the body

There are not many specific terms in Paul's epistles for the organs of the body. These organs are collectively referred to as 'members' or 'parts' (*mele*) which God has arranged in the body according to his own design (1 Corinthians 12.18). The most obvious of these are the eye and the ear which are the organs of the special senses of sight and hearing. Paul mentions the sense of smell (v.17) but does not locate it in any organ.

Of the major organs, Paul mentions the heart (*kardia*), the stomach (*stomachos* or *koilia*) and the bowels (*splanchna*). With two exceptions these names are not used in a precise anatomical sense. These exceptions are in 1

Timothy 5.23 where Paul refers to Timothy's stomach (*stomachos*) as the possible site of his frequent illnesses and in 1 Corinthians 6.13 where Paul describes food as being intended for the stomach (*koilia*).

As in the Old Testament usage of the term, Paul does not refer to the heart as a physical organ, unless we can interpret 2 Corinthians 3.3 in that sense. He speaks rather in psychological terms of the heart as the seat of the will (1 Corinthians 4.5 and 2 Corinthians 9.7), the emotions (2 Corinthians 8.16), the intellect (2 Corinthians 4.6 and Ephesians 1.18), and the centre of a person's spiritual life (Romans 10.10 and 2 Corinthians 1.22).

The other anatomical term which Paul uses is *splanchna* which is usually translated 'bowels' in the English versions. This is a much more comprehensive term than the English one for in Classical Greek usage it covers the heart, the lungs, the liver and the kidneys with no specific reference to any one of these organs. It too was given a psychological meaning.[11] It was the seat of the emotions and affections, and in Christian usage denoted especially the source of love and compassion (2 Corinthians 7.15 and Philippians 2.1).

In 1 Corinthians 12.22-26, Paul distinguishes two types of parts or organs of the body. The first type he calls weaker (v.22), less honourable or less presentable (v.23); the second type by implication was therefore stronger, more honourable or more presentable. To the first type belong the eye and the head, and to the second belong the hand and the feet (v.21). Paul, however, says that all parts or organs are to be regarded as equal in honour for all are indispensable. In the same way, all members of the Church are indispensable and worthy of honour even though the gifts which the Holy Spirit has given to each individual member may vary in type and function.

## The body has needs and functions

An important aspect of the body is its physical needs. It requires food and drink or it will experience hunger and thirst (Romans 12.20; 1 Corinthians 6.13 and 11.21, 34). Paul himself had experienced hunger and thirst in the service of the gospel (1 Corinthians 4.11; 2 Corinthians 6.5; 11.27 and Philippians 4.12). The body also needs clothes, shelter and sleep (Romans 8.35 and 2 Corinthians 11.27). The body also requires exercise as Paul recognises in 1 Timothy 4.8, although the AV translation of this verse has often been used to justify lack of exercise.[12]

As we have just seen, the body is composed of different members and organs each with their own function (Romans 12.4). These include the foot for walking, the eye for seeing, the ear for hearing, the sense of smell for smelling (1 Corinthians 12.14-26) and joints for movement (Ephesians 4.16 and Colossians 2.19. The body is also the agent of sex for the procreation of life (Romans 4.19; 1 Corinthians 6.15-18 and 7.1-8).

## The body is subject to disease

We learn from the experience of Paul with his thorn in the flesh that the body is subject to disease, and from his mention of the illness of three of his colleagues (2 Corinthians 12.7; Philippians 2.25-30; 1 Timothy 5.23 and 2 Timothy 4.20). In some cases the body may recover from disease as in the case of Epaphroditus (Philippians 2.27). Nevertheless, the body is described as perishable and mortal, subject to decay and death in Romans 6.12; 8.11, 21; 1 Corinthians 15.42, 54; 2 Corinthians 4.16; 5.4 and Philippians 1.20.

## The body is the servant of the spirit

In 1 Corinthians 9.27 Paul speaks of his attitude to the body and uses the rare verb *doulagogeo* to describe it. The verb means 'to treat as a slave (*doulos*)'. The body is thus the slave of the spirit and does its bidding whether this is to righteousness or unrighteousness. The classic passage on this subject is Romans 6.12-23. The body carries out the will of the spirit whether this is righteous or unrighteous, as the slave carried out the will of his master. The body therefore shares in the dedication to God to which Paul exhorts the Roman Christians in Romans 12.1-2. It is also subject to possession by the Holy Spirit and is described as the dwelling place or temple of the Holy Spirit in 1 Corinthians 3.16 and 6.19 (cp. Romans 8.7, 11). Like the whole human being, the body was created to be dedicated to God and properly belongs to the Lord (1 Corinthians 6.13). God not only created it, he also redeemed it at the price of the death of his Son. We are therefore to honour and glorify God with our bodies (1 Corinthians 6.20),[13] even in our eating and drinking (Philippians 1.20).

## The body shares in redemption

In Romans 8.18-25 Paul describes the present suffering and future glory of Christians and how they and the whole creation are waiting for their final and complete adoption and the redemption of their bodies (vv.22-23). It is important to notice that Paul does not speak of redemption 'from' the body; that was a Greek idea which was alien to his thought. One of the central doctrines of the popular Orphic religion of Greece, taught that the soul was imprisoned in the body because of the previous sin of the individual, as an oyster is imprisoned in its shell.[14] The body was called 'the tomb of the soul (*soma sema*)'[15] and the redemption of the soul consisted of its release from the body which was then discarded. Thus the Greeks believed in the immortality of the soul but denied the resurrection of the body.[16] For Paul on the other hand, life after death was dependent on the resurrection of the body. In his previous paragraph he had reminded his readers that they were already adopted into the family of God (vv. 14-16), but the full realisation of their adoption and the completion of their redemption will only occur with the resurrection of the body. The body will then share in the redemption of the whole of the human being. It will no longer be 'a mortal body' for not only will it be alive, it will not be liable to death (Romans 8.11).

In 1 Corinthians 15.42-54 Paul describes the resurrection as a change from a *soma psuchikon* or a natural physical body to a *soma pneumatikon* or a spiritual body. This spiritual body is imperishable, glorious, strong, immortal and life-giving, in contrast to the natural body we now possess which is perishable, dishonoured, weak, mortal and merely living. The spiritual body is not subject to disease, decay or death. It is not a body of flesh and blood, for blood is only necessary to a body that is subject to decay in which the tissues require to be provided with materials for defence against disease, for the repair of damage due to injury or disease, or for the maintenance of normal growth and activity. In the natural physical body once the supply of blood to a part is cut off, that part decays and dies, but the spiritual body does not decay and therefore needs no blood to maintain or repair it. It is not without significance that when Jesus described his resurrection body to his disciples he said that a spirit did not have flesh and bones as they could see that he had (Luke 24.39). The natural phrase would have been 'flesh and blood', but his body did not now contain blood. His resurrection body is the only example we have of a spiritual body, and from the description given in the gospels it is clear that it resembled his previous natural body in form and could be recognised by those who had known him before death. It bore the scars of the wounds inflicted on it before death and could be touched and handled (John 20.25-27). It was capable of intelligible speech and of taking food (Luke 24.41-43), but the food was not for nourishment for nourishment implies decay and mortality. As Cyril of Alexandria said long ago, Jesus took food not to nourish his body but to strengthen the faith of his disciples.[17] His body bore a new relation to matter and could vanish and appear in a room at will even though the doors were shut (Luke 24.31 and John 20.19, 26).[18]

The attitude of Paul to the body is an indication of how, alone of all the spiritual religions of the world, Christianity takes the physical body seriously. This serious and realistic view of the body is the implication of the incarnation of the Son of God in human flesh, the atonement was made in his body (cp. 1 Peter 2.24) and his body was raised from the dead, and this view of the body is an essential element in the Christian Faith.

## HEALING AND THE CONGREGATION

There is no specific instruction about healing in the Old Testament. There, healing was regarded as the direct act of God which might on occasions be mediated through his servants the prophets. The priests had no mandate to heal, only to diagnose unclean states such as *sara'at*. Nor had the Israelite community any place in the healing of disease, although through their obedience to the law of God they had an important function in relation to its prevention as they observed the principles of hygiene which that law embodied.

In the New Testament this emphasis changes, as we can see particularly in the epistles. This change is foreshadowed in the gospels and the Acts. In the gospels not only did Jesus heal the sick, but also his disciples did as we know from the Mission of the Twelve (Mark 6.13) and the Mission of the Seventy (Luke 10.9). In the Acts too we read of incidents of healing by named disciples to which we have already referred in our previous chapter.

In the epistles there is a new emphasis and we find that healing may now take place within the Christian community or congregation and be practised by members of the congregation. This may happen in two ways. First, by the use of gifts of healing which may be given to individual members of the congregation (1 Corinthians 12.9) and second, by the sick members of the congregation calling on the elders to heal them (James 5.14).

Our next section deals with the gifts of the Holy Spirit of which the gift of healing is one, and we shall consider the place of the elders of the congregation in healing when we discuss the teaching of the epistle of James in Chapter Twenty. Meantime we note that the change in emphasis which gave the congregation a place in the practice was due to the coming of the Holy Spirit who gave the members of the Church the gift of healing and the power to heal in the name of Jesus Christ.

## THE GIFTS OF THE SPIRIT

The New Testament epistles contain six lists of what Paul calls 'spiritual gifts' (1 Corinthians 12.1), the gifts of the Lord to the Church.[19] Five of these lists occur in Paul's own writings and one in the first epistle of Peter. They may be classified as follows:

I. Those which describe the gifts in terms of function
(prophecy, teaching, healing, etc.):
   1. Romans 12.6-8.
   2. First Corinthians 12.8-10.
   3. First Peter 4.10-11.

II. Those which describe the gifts in terms of office
(apostle, prophet, teacher, etc.):
   4. First Corinthians 12.28.
   5. Ephesians 4.11.

III. Those which describe the gifts in mixed terms of office and function
(apostle, healing etc.):
   6. First Corinthians 12.29-30.

### The meaning of charisma

The word which Paul uses to denote the gifts is *charisma* which means a gift freely given, a gift or a present whose source is in the grace (*charis*), favour and goodwill of the giver. The word is a distinctively Pauline word for it is rare in Greek literature and apart from 1 Peter 4.10 occurs in the New Testament only in Paul's writings. He uses it in a general sense when he speaks of God's gift to humankind of eternal life in Romans 5.15-16 and 6.23. It is used in the Pastoral Epistles to describe the particular gift of ministry given to Timothy by the laying on of the hands of Paul and the elders in 1 Timothy 4.14 and 2 Timothy 1.6. The gift in Timothy's case seems to have been for the ministry of the word if we may judge from the context of the first reference. However, the most common usage of the word by Paul is to denote a gift given to individual Christians by the Holy Spirit for a specific ministry in the service of God, which may be described in terms of a function such as teaching, or in terms of an office such as that of a teacher.

We may, therefore, follow Stott and define a spiritual gift or *charisma* as 'neither a capacity by itself, nor a ministry or office by itself, but rather a capacity which qualifies a person for a ministry. More simply it may be regarded either as a gift and the job in which to exercise it, or a job and the gift with which to do it'.[20]

## The number of the gifts

About twenty different gifts are included in the six lists and there is no suggestion that these lists are exhaustive. No single gift occurs in all six lists and thirteen of the gifts occur in only one of the lists. The gifts in the lists are not said to be set out in any order of priority although Bruce suggests that in 1 Corinthians 12.8-10 they are placed in descending order of value according to Paul's judgement.[21] Also in 1 Corinthians 12.31 there is a reference to 'the higher or greater gifts' which may mean those which are placed at the top of the lists given earlier in the chapter. That prophecy is amongst these and is to be preferred to speaking in tongues is made clear in 1 Corinthians 14.1. Although the gifts are described in terms of both offices and functions, it is not always possible to equate office with function. It is easy to equate teacher and teaching, but no function is given corresponding to the office of apostle, and no office corresponds to generous giving (Romans 12.8).

If we ask to whom are these gifts given, the answer of both Paul and Peter is quite clear. If there are a large number and a wide diversity of the gifts, there is also a wide and even a universal distribution of them. The possession of the *charismata* is not the prerogative of the select few for the New Testament epistles indicate that every Christian has at least one of these spiritual gifts or capacities for service (Romans 12.3-6; 1 Corinthians 12.11; Ephesians 4.7 and 1 Peter 4.10). Thus, as Bittlinger reminds us,

> to *each* one gifts are given. The possession of spiritual gifts is therefore in no sense a measure of Christian maturity. Spiritual gifts are received as presents from God by every Christian who will accept them in childlike faith.[22]

We may recognise a spiritual gift by the three criteria or distinguishing marks which Paul gives in 1 Corinthians 12.3,7. The first one is that it must not deny the Incarnation for no one who is speaking by the Holy Spirit can say 'Jesus is cursed' (v.3a). The second is that it must recognise and uphold the Lordship of Jesus for no one can say 'Jesus is Lord' except by the Holy Spirit (v.3b). And the third criterion is that the gift must be one which can be exercised for 'the common good' (v.7), i.e. for the benefit of the whole Church and its members (cp. 1 Peter 4.10).[23] Such a gift is not given to members of the Church for their own glory or for their own private profit, although its use may deepen their own spiritual experience incidentally.

## The nature of a gift

The question now arises of the nature of a *charisma*. As we approach this question we need to be aware of a two-fold misunderstanding of the *charismata*. The first is the 'enthusiastic' misunderstanding which regards them as purely supernatural and miraculous and therefore an unnecessary addition to normal Church life. The second is the 'activist' misunderstanding which treats the *charismata* as purely natural in character, consisting of the normal activities and capabilities of a person so that a *charisma* is exercised whenever a Christian does anything within the Church. The first type of misunderstanding does not give individuals their true dignity as created by God, while the second ignores the result of the Fall. The truth must be that the *charismata* are both natural and supernatural.[24]

In these terms we may, therefore, define a *charisma* with Bittlinger as 'a gracious manifestation of the Holy Spirit, working in and through, but going beyond, the believer's natural ability for the common good of the people of God'.[25] The Holy Spirit does not work independently of individuals created by God, and the individual does not exercise a *charisma* except as a member of the Church which is the body of Christ. If we are to be faithful to the context of Paul's teaching on the *charismata*, we may only speak of a *charisma* if the words are spoken or the deeds performed in dependence on Jesus as Lord (1 Corinthians 12.3), in accordance with the measure of faith given by God (Romans 12.3), and as the expression and realisation of love (1 Corinthians 12.31 and 14.1).

What then is the relationship between spiritual gifts and natural talents? It is a matter of common experience that God has bestowed on some people, natural gifts of preaching and teaching, of leadership and administration, of helpfulness and generosity, and all these are mentioned by Paul in the lists of the *charismata* which he gives. When an individual with one or more of these natural gifts becomes a Christian, their gifts or talents as we commonly call them, are taken by the Holy Spirit and used in the ministry and work of the Church.[26] As we have already seen, Paul sums the matter up by saying that Christians collectively are the body of Christ and individually are members of that body (1 Corinthians 12.27). As members they may be limbs, organs or other bodily parts each with their own functions and gifts. Each brings their own gift or gifts whether natural or supernatural and all are integrated into the body so that these gifts are exercised within the organism of the body which is the Church.

## The persistence of the gifts

One question on which no guidance is given is whether these gifts were permanent or were only given for use in particular situations or even only for a particular period in the history of the Church. On the analogy of the possession of natural gifts or talents it would seem reasonable to conclude that the possession of spiritual gifts was permanent in the same way as natural gifts are. Both kinds of gift, of course, may be latent and lie dormant until called forth by some particular situation. In other words, we only realise that we have one or more gifts until we are called upon to use them. The gifts were given to be used. This is clear from 1 Corinthians 12.4-6 where in addition to being described as 'gifts' they are also described as 'services (*diakonion*)' and as 'activities (*energematon*)'.

The fact that Paul set no time limit on the existence of the gifts of the Spirit in the Church implies that these gifts are still available and present in the Church today as they were in Paul's day. This is borne out by the fact that it is obvious that there are still people in the Church who have been given one or more of these gifts and are using them for the common good and the upbuilding of the Church.

## The gift of healing

One of the *charismata* which is mentioned in all three lists in the twelfth chapter of First Corinthians, but in none of the others, is the gift of healing. The description in 1 Corinthians 12.9, 28 and 30 is literally of 'gifts of healings (*charismata iamaton*)' for both nouns are in the plural, although these gifts are given to one individual ('to another', v.9). This is usually interpreted as meaning that there is specialisation amongst the gifts of healing with different gifts for different diseases, and that no one person could heal all diseases.[27] It could also mean that a gift may be given to a particular individual for a particular occasion or situation only, as well as for a specific disease. In such a case the individual concerned might not be called upon for an ongoing ministry of healing. The healing of Paul's blindness by Ananias in Acts 9.17 could be an example of this.

The gift of healing was not given to all, but only to some as we learn from 1 Corinthians 12.30. Also, the gift of healing is always described as a function and never as an office, in so far as we may speak of an office and officers in these early days of the Church. The evidence for the exercise of the gift of healing in the apostolic Church is very scanty in the New Testament apart from the apostles themselves, and when Paul refers to his healing activity he includes it amongst the *semeia* or signs of an apostle (2 Corinthians 12.12, cp. Romans 15.19). There is no mention of a special gift of healing in the epistle of James where it appears that the elders of the Church are involved in healing by virtue of their office and their prayer for the sick (James 5.14-15), and where ordinary Church members can be agents of healing as they pray for the sick (v.16). The gift of healing is not mentioned in the lists of the *charismata* given in the epistles to the Romans and to the Ephesians, and it is of interest to note that two of Paul's colleagues who were sick, and were not healed by charismatic means, were sick in Rome and Ephesus. These were Epaphroditus (Philippians 2.27) and Timothy (1 Timothy 5.23). Does this mean that the Church in Rome and in Ephesus knew nothing of the gift of healing? If they did know, then it means that the gift was not always used when an obvious case for its use occurred.

What, then, was the nature of the gift of healing? Presumably the Church at Corinth knew, for Paul did not describe it in any detail, and even Calvin can say that in his day 'everyone knows what is meant by the *gift of healings*', and feel that he need make no further comment.[28] It is interesting to notice that Paul distinguishes the gift of healing from the gift of working miracles (*dunameis*) in 1 Corinthians 12.9-10, 29-30. Does this mean that he was referring to non-miraculous healing when he spoke of the gift of healing?

Today there is great interest in the gift of healing combined with a lack of understanding of its nature. If the definition of the nature of a gift which we quoted above is correct, then we must look for the basis of the gift of healing in the nature and characteristic of human beings who were created by God with certain aptitudes and capabilities. It is a matter of common experience that that some people are better at healing than others by virtue of their natural attributes of sympathy and compassion and their possession of natural skills and abilities. This is one reason why some people make better doctors and nurses than others do. When a man or a woman with these natural gifts acknowledges that 'Jesus is Lord' and so becomes a Christian and is incorporated into the Body of Christ, then the Holy Spirit intensifies and enhances their natural gifts and places them at the disposal of the Church.

What was the content of the gift of healing? Was it a special acquisition of knowledge about diseases and their cure, or of a special skill in surgical manipulation or procedures? The probable answer is that it was neither of these things, but consisted of a natural gift of sympathy or empathy combined with a capacity of knowing the right thing to do in any individual situation and with any individual sick person. This intuitive knowledge and sensitivity was sharpened and made even more sensitive by the operation of the Holy Spirit on the mind and had no necessary connection with medical knowledge or surgical training.[28]

How was the gift of healing exercised? Paul gives us no guidance on this matter, but if we are to judge from what we are told of his own practice in the Acts (Acts 28.8) and that of Peter (Acts 9.40), together with what is described in James 5.13-16, then it is clear that the gift was used in the context of prayer.

There is much more we would like to know about the gift of healing, but we are left with many of our questions unanswered. Why is the gift mentioned only in connection with the Church at Corinth and not elsewhere?

Why are those who healed sick people in the Acts not said to have a special gift of healing? Why is there no mention of such a gift in the epistle of James? Why, when such a gift existed, were leaders of the Christian community including the apostle Paul himself allowed to go unhealed? The existence of so many unanswered questions suggests that an understanding of the nature of the gift of healing is not necessary for the practice of healing. When we add to this the obscurity with which the gift of healing is described, and the fact that it is never specifically associated with any act of healing in the New Testament record, and is not mentioned in the explicit description of the Church's practice of healing given by James, it suggests that the gift of healing consists essentially of the application of earnest prayer together with the natural endowments of the members of the Christian community which have been enhanced by the Holy Spirit.

## SICKNESS AND THE LORD'S SUPPER

One of the matters on which Paul wrote to the members of the Church at Corinth was the proper observance of the Lord's Supper (1 Corinthians 11.17-34). In his letter he gave them an account of the institution of the Supper which he had received from the Lord himself. This account not only provided the warrant for the Church's observance of the Sacrament of the Lord's Supper, it also included the earliest written record of any of the actual words of Jesus for this epistle is earlier than any of the gospels. This is an indication of how important the proper observance of the Supper was to Paul and how concerned he was that the Corinthians Christians should observe it properly and reverently.

He tells them that they are not doing this. They are treating the Supper as an ordinary meal; eating and drinking the symbols of bread and wine unworthily. By this he did not mean that they were necessarily unworthy in themselves to partake of the Supper, but that they were treating it unworthily and irreverently by not recognising the meaning of the symbols and the need for unity and fellowship around the Lord's table. The result was that they were eating and drinking judgement on themselves and rendering themselves liable to the discipline of the Lord. This was why many of them were weak (*asthenes*) and sick (*arrostos*), and why a number of them had fallen asleep (v.30). Barrett suggests that these words are not to be understood metaphorically as referring to a weak and sickly spiritual condition, but literally to conditions of bodily weakness and sickness.[29] Findlay regards this as confirmed by Paul's adding the description of some of them as having 'fallen asleep', which may mean that they had died physically as the word *koimao* used here is frequently used metaphorically of physical death (cp. John 11.11; Acts 7.60; 1 Corinthians 7.39 and 1 Thessalonians 4.13).[30] Calvin understood the verse to mean that the Lord had sent some scourge or plague upon the members of the Corinthian Church to discipline them for their abuse of the Supper about the time that Paul was writing to them with the result that many of them had died from it.[31]

However, if we accept the literal meaning of the passage that the unworthy and indifferent reception of the elements of the Lord's Supper may result in physical sickness and even death, this describes a situation which is not referred to elsewhere in the New Testament and is not recognised in the life of the Church today. This explains why almost all commentators on this verse have little to say about its meaning.

It seems preferable, therefore, to understand the verse metaphorically referring to the spiritual weakness, sickness and even death which may follow the neglect or abuse of participation in the Lord's Supper. This still means that such neglect or abuse can affect their health, but not necessarily their physical health.

## THE FOUR WHO WERE NOT HEALED

One of the most significant facts about healing in the epistles is the occurrence of four cases in the apostolic Church who were not healed by the methods which Jesus used in the gospels and the apostles used in the Acts.

The first case is that of the apostle Paul himself whose thorn in the flesh was most probably some form of sickness and who asked God on three occasions that it should be removed, only to have his request refused on each occasion. This experience of Paul's is considered in detail in the next four chapters.

The second case is that of Epaphroditus who was a leader in the Church at Philippi and had brought gifts from that Church to cheer Paul in prison in Rome. He stayed on to serve Paul and the cause of the gospel in Rome, and contracted an acute infection from which he nearly died. When he recovered, he became homesick for Philippi and was especially concerned that the Christians there had heard that he was seriously ill. As Epaphroditus proposed to return home, Paul took the opportunity to write a letter for him to take to the Philippian Church, and so we owe the existence of the epistle to the Philippians to the illness of Epaphroditus (Philippians 2.25-30). The nature of the infection is unknown though it may have been some form of enteric fever. The interesting fact for our present purpose about the case of Epaphroditus is that, although he was in close contact with Paul, there was no suggestion that the apostle should use any special gift of healing to restore him to health. The disease was allowed to run its course and even to bring him close to death. This appears from Paul's description in Philippians 2.27 where he says that the illness of Epaphroditus made his companions despair of his life for it very nearly proved fatal.[32] His recovery, in other words, was the result of the operation of the natural healing processes of his body.

Timothy was the third case. In 1 Timothy 5.23 he is advised by Paul to take a little wine for the sake of his stomach and frequent sicknesses (*astheneiai*). Timothy was a young man but appears to have been ill frequently with some form of dyspepsia. Why then was he allowed to continue to suffer from these attacks, and not healed by someone who had the gift of healing amongst his colleagues, even by Paul himself?

The word which Paul uses for wine is *oinos* which normally means the fermented juice of the grape.[33] By virtue of its content of alcohol it had two internal medical uses in the ancient world. The first was preventive when in Greek and Roman times it was mixed with water in an attempt to render the water safe to drink.[34] Since Paul mentions the use of water too, it may be this prophylactic use of wine to which he is referring in 1 Timothy 5.23. According to this view, Timothy may have been drinking only water, which could often have been contaminated with pathogenic material or organisms and the cause of his gastric upsets. To add wine to the water would have an antiseptic effect and prevent, or at least reduce, such upsets.

On the other hand it is equally possible that Paul is referring to the second use of wine as a therapeutic agent when he advises its use in Timothy's frequent gastric illnesses. Alcohol in moderate doses has long been known to be a powerful stimulant of the gastric digestion of food and Paul may have suggested its use, believing that poor digestion due to chronic gastritis as the cause of Timothy's frequent illnesses. Whatever the clinical details of this case were, it is interesting to note that it was a case in which medical prophylaxis or treatment were preferred to charismatic treatment. We do not, of course, know the outcome of the treatment which Paul advised.

Finally, we come to the case of Trophimus, a Gentile Christian of Ephesus. His name was that usually given to a foster-child and so he probably lost his mother at birth. He was a travelling companion of Paul on his third missionary journey (Acts 20.4) and was with him in Jerusalem where he was the unwitting cause of Paul's arrest and imprisonment (Acts 21.27-34). He is sometimes identified with the unnamed brother who was famous throughout the Church for his preaching, whom Paul mentioned in 2 Corinthians 8.18-22. Even if this identification is incorrect, there is no doubt that Trophimus was a close associate of Paul, and it is therefore all the more surprising that Paul left him behind in Miletus sick, as he says in 2 Timothy 4.20 in explanation of why he was not with him as he wrote. His sickness was presumably an acute one but no clue is given about its nature. Again the problem arises about why no one exercised a gift of healing and restored Trophimus to health, so that Paul did not need to leave him behind because he was sick. Furthermore, Luke was with Paul when he informed Timothy that Trophimus was sick at Miletus (2 Timothy 4.11) and there is no suggestion that he might have gone to Miletus to treat Trophimus medically. As in the case of Epaphroditus, his recovery was left to the natural bodily process of healing and neither medical nor charismatic methods were applied.

194

It is sometimes suggested that there was a fifth Christian leader in the New Testament who was sick and yet remained unhealed. This was the Gaius to whom John addressed his third epistle. John wishes that all may go well with Gaius and that he may enjoy good physical health (*hugiaino*), as John knows he enjoys good spiritual health (v.2). However, this wish occurs very frequently at the beginning of letters amongst the Egyptian papyri, so that its use here may be merely conventional without any implication that the addressee of the letter was physically sick in any way.[35]

The subject of health and healing in the epistles poses more problems than it solves, and yet what is written there allows us to draw a number of conclusions. Health concerns the whole person, body, soul and spirit, but is not fully attainable in this present life. In fact, the Christian concept of health provides a powerful argument for the life which is to come, for complete health or wholeness is only possible after the resurrection of the body from the dead. One result of this is that healing is not always the answer to illness in the epistles. Disease may be allowed to take its natural course as in the case of Epaphroditus, or to become chronic and recurrent as in the case of Paul. Some members of the Church were given a gift of healing, but this does not appear to have been universally used for the healing of the sick. Finally, the sick may call upon the ministry of the elders of the local congregation to pray over them as we shall see when we consider what James has to say in a later chapter.

What is clear from the epistles is that Christian faith and experience provide no immunity against disease. What it does provide is most fully illustrated by the experience of Paul with his thorn in the flesh, which we now proceed to consider in the next four chapters.

# Chapter 16
# PAUL'S THORN IN THE FLESH: ITS OCCURRENCE

Throughout the Christian centuries the whole Church has had cause to be grateful to the young Christian community in Corinth whose lively relationship with the apostle Paul provoked his Corinthian correspondence, some of which still survives in our New Testament. This correspondence is concerned with the practical problems faced by a young enthusiastic Church living in a pagan cosmopolitan city whose very name was a synonym for immorality. The Greek verb *korinthiazomai* means to practise immorality and this sense still persists in the now archaic English verb 'to corinthianise' which is derived from it, meaning 'to live voluptuously and licentiously'.[1]

One of the many problems which this young Church raised for Paul was the question of his own authority as an apostle of Jesus Christ. The result was that throughout his correspondence with them he constantly asserts his apostolic authority, which he claimed was ultimately based on the call to be an apostle he had received from God himself (1 Corinthians 1.1 *et passim*). On several occasions, however, he appeals also to his own experience in the service of God and of his Son Jesus Christ as displaying his credentials as an apostle and his fitness to exert pastoral authority over the Corinthian Church.

It is in the course of one of these autobiographical passages that Paul speaks of an experience of heavenly visions and ineffable revelations which had come to him, and which had been followed by what he called according to the common translation, 'a thorn in the flesh' (2 Corinthians 12.7).[2] It is with some reluctance that he speaks of these experiences to demonstrate the basis of his authority. He calls it 'boasting' and uses the verb *kauchaomai* which is a characteristic word of the Corinthian epistles in which it occurs twenty-six times. Boasting in this context does not mean the self-glorification which springs from pride, for to Paul that would be of the essence of sin. Paul's boasting is not the glorification of himself, but of God. Twice he quotes Jeremiah 9.24, 'If a man must boast, let him boast of the Lord' (1 Corinthians 1.31 and 2 Corinthians 10.17). Paul, therefore, speaks of his experiences not to glorify himself, but to glorify God who had given him these experiences which served to validate his call to be an apostle.

It is in the eleventh chapter of the second epistle to the Corinthians that Paul speaks of the wonderful mystical experience which he had had fourteen years previously. It was an experience of surpassing wonder which would amply justify pride and boasting of the baser sort had he wished to indulge in it. However, in order to forestall such pride and boasting, God had given Paul 'a thorn in the flesh', which continued with him like a messenger of Satan to recur at intervals throughout his life.

The passage in which he describes this thorn in the flesh and which forms the basis of our present consideration of it, is translated as follows in the NIV:

> To keep me from becoming conceited because of these surpassingly great revelations, there was given me a thorn in my flesh, a messenger of Satan, to torment me. Three times I pleaded with the Lord to take it away from me. But he said to me, 'My grace is sufficient for you, for my power is made perfect in weakness.' Therefore, I will boast all the more gladly about my weaknesses, so that Christ's power may rest on me. That is why, for Christ's sake, I delight in weaknesses, in insults, in hardships, in persecutions, in difficulties. For when I am weak, then I am strong.        (2 Corinthians 12.7-10)

## THE MEANING OF THE PHRASE

The phrase 'a thorn in the flesh' is a metaphor and not an exact literal description. Plummer suggested that the phrase could be derived from the LXX rendering of Numbers 33.55 which describes the discomfort which the inhabitants of the land of Canaan would cause Israel if they were not entirely driven out when Israel occupied their land.[3] However, this suggestion does not seem very likely and has not been accepted.

In the original Greek, the phrase is *skolops te sarki*. The word *skolops* is an uncommon word and occurs only here in the New Testament. It means something which is pointed, and in Classical Greek denoted a pointed stake on which the heads of one's enemies were impaled after their decapitation,[4] or which was used in the construction of a defensive palisade.[5] It could also be the instrument used in execution by impalement.[6] In Hellenistic Greek it came to mean a thorn or a splinter stuck in the body, and one of its earliest usages in this sense is in the LXX where it is always used in the sense of thorn or splinter and never of stake (cp. Numbers 33.55; Ezekiel 28.24; Hosea 2.6 and Ecclesiasticus 43.19).[7]

In translation, therefore, the choice lies between a large pointed stake or a small sharp thorn for the rendering of *skolops* in this passage. Both meanings can muster impressive lists of New Testament scholars in their defence, but it must be realised that the opinion of many of those who proposed 'stake' as the meaning of the word here, dates from before the time when it was recognised that the New Testament was not written in bad Classical Greek, but in the Hellenistic or *koine* Greek spoken by the ordinary people of the Graeco-Roman world. Had this fact been recognised earlier than it was, it is probable that many more scholars would have favoured the translation 'thorn', rather than 'stake'.

This is suggested by an examination of the English versions of the New Testament published after the year 1900. When we examined forty of these, no fewer than thirty-two of them were found to give 'thorn' as the preferred rendering, while only two gave the translation 'stake'; the rest gave paraphrases or interpretations of the meaning.[8] There seems to be no doubt, therefore, that we should prefer the meaning 'thorn' in translating the word *skolops* in the present passage.

There is another consideration which would favour the translation 'thorn'. It appears that Paul is deliberately minimising the serious effect of this experience on his health and activity. If we look back to 2 Corinthians 11.23-28 we find Paul describing his experiences in the service of the gospel. He has been in prison, been flogged, been beaten and stoned, shipwrecked, hungry and thirsty, but these things were as nothing compared to the thorn in the flesh.[9] He never prayed to have these experiences removed as he did the thorn in the flesh. They never interfered with his ability to preach the gospel as it did. This suggests that the thorn was a much more serious and disabling condition than any of them were. Yet he played it down and dismissed it as not really serious - a mere thorn in the flesh, 'a mere scratch' as we might say today!

In contrast to *skolops*, the second word in the phrase is a common word, for *sarx* occurs almost one hundred and fifty times in the New Testament and is one of the characteristic words of Paul. It has various meanings and our choice of its meaning here will depend on our view of the nature of the thorn. Consequently we find that *sarx* or 'flesh', which basically means the soft, muscular parts of the animal body has been interpreted of the whole physical body, of human nature either in contrast to the divine or in its lower aspect, and of the relationship of persons to their fellows by birth.[10] Undoubtedly the commonest interpretation of the word here is that which refers to the human body, but the relevance of the other interpretations will appear when we discuss the identity of the thorn in the next chapter.

The relationship between the thorn and the flesh depends on the significance of the dative case in which the word *sarx* is expressed. The translation 'for the flesh' (a dative of disadvantage) has been suggested as on the whole more probable than 'in the flesh' (a dative of location), because of the absence of the preposition *en*, 'in'.[11] There is little difference in meaning between these two phrases except that 'in the flesh' might suggest a more permanent attachment of the thorn, while 'for the flesh' suggests that it might only be attached to the flesh on occasions. However, the eventual result is the same whether the thorn be 'in the flesh' or 'for the flesh', and the latter phrase is only infrequently used in modern European versions, where the favoured translation is 'a thorn in the flesh'.

We end where we began, with the phrase 'a thorn in the flesh' firmly established as the most probable translation of the Greek *skolops te sarki*. We cannot improve on the common translation although it is patently a metaphorical description of the condition from which Paul suffered. The meaning and interpretation of this phrase will occupy us for the rest of this chapter and the following three chapters.

## THE FEATURES OF THE THORN

Paul had been reluctant to mention the matter of visions and revelations from the Lord at all, and only did so because it illustrated the basis of his apostolic authority in his relationship with the God and Father of the Lord Jesus Christ. The result is that he gives but scanty details of his experience, and this true also when he comes to speak of his thorn in the flesh. There are, however a number of features of the thorn which we may discover by a closer examination of his description. These are the details of its onset, its occurrence, its character and its effects. Consideration of these features will help us to come closer to an identification of the nature of the thorn, and it to this examination that we now turn.

1. **Its onset.** The onset of the experience which Paul calls a thorn in the flesh was sudden and acute. It was given to him at a specific point in his life. This is suggested by the verb form *edothe* ('there was given') in verse seven, the first aorist passive form of the verb *didomi*, 'to give'. It began when he was 'a man in Christ' (v.2), i.e., when he was already a Christian. It followed the experience in which Paul had received visions and revelations in such a way and at such an interval that he realised that it had been given him to prevent his becoming too elated or conceited by them (v.7). It does not however appear to have been part of that experience, but was distinct from it.

2. **Its occurrence.** The only clue to the first occurrence of an attack of the thorn in the flesh is the mention that the preceding experience of visions and revelations from the Lord took place fourteen years before he wrote the twelfth chapter of Second Corinthians which is commonly dated about AD 56.[12] This gives the year AD 42 as the approximate time when this experience happened to Paul. Since his conversion is usually dated some eight years previously, i.e., AD 34, this experience of visions and revelations cannot be identified with his experience on the road to Damascus. Such an identification, of course, is also excluded by Paul's statement that he was already a Christian when he received the visions and revelations. We have no details of the time or place of the first attack of the thorn in the flesh, but it is clear that it was recurrent and might attack him at any time.

He calls it the messenger (*angelos*) of Satan and says that it was sent to beat and bruise him. The word he uses is *kolaphizo*, which means 'to beat with the fist (*kolaphos*)'. This word was used in Matthew 26.27 and Mark 14.65 to describe the beating of Jesus by his guards. It is used here by Paul in the present tense which indicates that he was still suffering such attacks.[13] It is clear that he was not affected by them all the time or he could never have accomplished all the work he did in the service of the gospel. The condition must therefore have been recurrent in nature. The present tense also suggests that it was a permanent affliction or 'a very steady companion' as Denney terms it.[14] This is also suggested by the tense in which Paul gives the Lord's reply to his request for the removal of the thorn. This was given in the perfect tense which meant that it was to be the Lord's permanent answer for the rest of Paul's life, no matter how often he was afflicted by the thorn.

3. **Its character.** The thorn in the flesh was personal to Paul. Although he began this chapter in the third person by describing himself as a man in Christ (v.2), he soon changes to the first person and says that the thorn was given to him personally to keep him from elation and conceit (v.7). It was therefore something which was personal to him and not shared with anyone else. According to the common interpretation, the thorn had to do with the physical part of him, his flesh in the sense of his body, and so its character was physical. We have already seen, however, that this view is not universally held, particularly by earlier commentators, and we shall discuss this in more detail in the next chapter.

Many of these earlier commentators describe the character of the condition as painful, and some prefer the translation of *skolops* as a stake precisely because it suggests a greater intensity of pain than thorn. But there is no explicit mention of pain in the passage and the painful character is assumed by the commentators rather than described by Paul. Certainly the description of a thorn sticking into the flesh suggests a painful experience, and the use of a word which likens the experience to being beaten with a fist (*kolaphizo*) supports this suggestion. The fact remains, however, that Paul did not particularly emphasise the painful character of his thorn in the flesh.

4. **Its effect.** It was in terms of its effect that Paul described his thorn and not in terms of any painful character, and its effect was to produce weakness and humiliation. It was debilitating (v.9) and produced a weakness in which Paul was supported by God's strength (vv.9-10). It was also humiliating because it not only showed his weakness, it also prevented him from being too elated at the abundance of visions and revelations which God had given to him (v.7).

We may now summarise the features of the thorn in the flesh in so far
as we can discover them from the passage in which Paul describes them.

1. It began when Paul was a mature adult and a Christian.

2. Its onset was sudden and acute.

3. Its course was chronic and recurrent.

4. Its character was personal and painful.

5. Its effect was debilitating and humiliating.

## OTHER POSSIBLE EVIDENCE OF THE THORN

If this condition was part of the experience of Paul and affected him as much
as he suggests it did, then it is reasonable to suppose that there may be further
references to it either in the Acts or in his own epistles. A number of
references have been regarded as providing other possible evidence of this
kind and these fall naturally into four groups.

### 1. References which are expressed in general terms

'I was with you in weakness and in much fear and trembling' (1
Corinthians 2.3).

'We are weak, but you are strong' (1 Corinthians 4.10).

'We do not want you to be ignorant, brethren, of the affliction we
experienced in Asia; for we were so utterly, unbearably crushed that
we despaired of life itself. Why we felt that we had received the
sentence of death' (2 Corinthians 1.8-9).

'For they say, "His letters are mighty and strong, but his bodily
presence is weak"' (2 Corinthians 10.10).

'For we are glad when we are weak and you are strong' (2 Corinthians
13.9).

'You know that it was because of a bodily ailment that I preached the
gospel to you at first; and though my condition was a trial to you. you
did not scorn or despise me' (Galatians 4.13).

'I bear on my body the marks of Jesus' (Galatians 6.17).

'I rejoice in my sufferings for your sake, and in my flesh I complete
what remains of Christ's afflictions for the sake of his body, that is,
the church' (Colossians 1.24).

It is improbable that most of these references cast any further light on Paul's thorn in the flesh. It is tempting to regard his near-fatal experience in Asia which he mentions in 2 Corinthians 1.8, as an example of an attack of the thorn in the flesh, but as Barclay comments, 'the most extraordinary thing about this passage is that we have no information at all about this terrible experience which Paul went through at Ephesus', and so we must resist the temptation.[15] However, both Alexander and Allo suggest this was an attack of serious illness.[16]

The marks (*stigmata*) of Jesus to which Paul refers in Galatians 6.17 are neither signs of disease nor what we mean by the stigmata today, namely, the appearance on a person's body of the wounds of Jesus which resulted from his crucifixion. Nevertheless, it has been maintained that Paul was a hysterical visionary who received the stigmata by an autosuggestive reaction to the passion of Jesus.[17] In fact, it is far more likely that they were scars on Paul's body, the visible result of the personal violence he experienced in the service of the gospel and which he describes in 2 Corinthians 11.24-25. Bultmann called them Paul's 'battle-scars as a soldier of Christ'.[18]

The only reference amongst those given above which might refer to the thorn in the flesh is Galatians 4.13. Here Paul reminds his readers in Galatia that the reason he was able to preach the gospel to them on the first occasion he did so, was because he developed an acute illness which incapacitated him for travel and caused him to visit and stay in Galatia for some time. We shall have to take account of this reference when we come to consider the identity of the thorn in the flesh.

## 2. References which may indicate that Paul suffered from an eye affliction

'For three days he was without sight' (Acts 9.9).

'Paul, looking intently at the council, said...' (Acts 23.1).

'Paul said, "I did not know, brethren, that he was the high priest"' (Acts 23.5).

'Though my condition was a trial to you, you did not scorn or despise me, but received me as an angel of God, as Jesus Christ. What has become of the satisfaction you felt? For I bear you witness that, if possible, you would have plucked out your eyes, and given them to me' (Galatians 4.14-15).

'See with what large letters I am writing to you with my own hand' (Galatians 6.11).

It is doubtful if any of these verses taken individually would suggest that Paul had an affliction or infection of the eyes, and even their cumulative information and force is no more than suggestive. Each reference is explicable on some basis other than than that of a disease of the eyes. Paul's loss of sight on the Damascus road lasted only three days after his exposure to a blinding light brighter than the sun, was completely healed and did not recur (Acts 9.9, cp. 26.13). The verb *atenizo* which describes Paul's concentration of his attention on the members of the Sanhedrin in Acts 23.1, is used on twelve occasions by Luke and twice by Paul. It never indicates any difficulty in seeing which might be due to a disease of the eyes, but refers to a special intensity of looking at a person as shown by its use in Luke 4.20; Acts 1.10; 3.4 and 14.9.

Although the failure of Paul to recognise the high priest according to Acts 23.5 is surprising, there are several possible explanations other than that which suggests he suffered from poor eyesight due to eye disease. The high priest may not have been wearing his official robes because the council had been hurriedly called together by the tribune Claudius Lysias. Paul may not have known the high priest, having been only a few days in Jerusalem. Ramsay's suggestion that the tribune was in the chair and the high priest at the side with the other members of the council and so not readily distinguished, is possible but unlikely.[19] Finally, Paul may have been speaking ironically, expressing surprise that anyone who ordered a defendant to be struck on the mouth whilst giving evidence in his own defence, could be a high priest.

As in the previous section, the Galatian references appear to be the most promising and relevant. Paul in Galatians 4.13 speaks of 'a bodily ailment', as the RSV translates his phrase *astheneia tes sarkos*, which he had suffered from and which appears to have been the reason why he paid his visit to Galatia. This had been a condition which produced a repulsive physical appearance in him, as a result of which he thought that the Galatians would have been justified in regarding him with loathing and disgust (v.14). In verse fifteen he makes a more specific reference to the possible nature of his disease when he says that the Galatians would, if it had been possible, have plucked out their own eyes and given them to him. Does this mean that Paul's bodily ailment at this time was one which affected his eyes, and that in their concern for his recovery the Galatians would have been willing even to gouge out their own normal eyes in order to give them to Paul to replace his diseased ones?

It certainly could mean this and we shall have to examine this possibility when we come to discuss the identity of the thorn in the flesh in more detail. The reference to 'large letters' in Galatians 6.11, however, need not imply poor eyesight. Paul did not usually write his own letters as we know from Romans 16.22 and it may be that at this point he took up the pen and wrote the concluding paragraph in larger letters than his amanuensis had used. In this final paragraph he sums up the essential issue of the letter and the large script would emphasise its importance.

## 3. References which may suggest that Paul suffered from a fatal disease

'I die every day' (1 Corinthians 15.31).

'We are... always carrying in the body the death of Jesus' (2 Corinthians 4.10).

'We are always being given up to death for Jesus' sake' (*Ibidem* v.11).

'Death is at work in us, but life in you' (*Ibidem* v.12).

'We are treated as ... dying, and behold we live' (2 Corinthians 6.9).

'I am ... often near to death' (2 Corinthians 11.23).

'That I may... share his sufferings, becoming like him in his death' (Philippians 3.10).

These verses do not refer to a fatal disease and neither do they lend any support to the notion that Paul thought he was suffering from one. They clearly refer to the constant exposure to violence which he faced in the course of his travels and preaching. This frequent possibility of injury is reflected in Romans 8.35 and is given in more detail in his Corinthian letters (1 Corinthians 4.9-13; 2 Corinthians 4.7-12; 6.4-10 and 11.23-28). It is significant for our present purpose that none of these passages includes a mention of disease. Indeed his survival of such violence argues for his extreme physical fitness which allowed him to withstand such violent treatment. The fact was that Paul constantly faced death in the service of his Lord, and was in danger of dying by violence in the same way that Jesus had died. This is the force of the unusual word *nekrosis* used by Paul in 2 Corinthians 4.10, unless we accept Denney's suggestion that Paul is saying that his apostolic work and sufferings were 'killing him'.[20]

## 4. A reference which mentions hindrance by Satan

'We wanted to come to you - I, Paul again and again - but Satan hindered us' (1 Thessalonians 2.18 NIV).

Paul regarded his thorn in the flesh as the messenger of Satan sent to harass him (2 Corinthians 12.7). This verse in First Thessalonians has some times been interpreted as referring to this thorn since it suggests a recurrent obstruction to his visiting the Church at Thessalonica. But the reference is too indefinite to provide any real clue to the nature of the hindrance which Satan continually placed in the way of Paul and his companions to prevent their going to Thessalonica.

It is evident from this review of the other references which might have some bearing on the identity of the thorn in the flesh, that few of them provide much further help, with the possible exception of the references in the epistle to the Galatians. We shall have occasion to return to these in the course of the next two chapters where we consider the possible identity of the thorn in the flesh.

## Chapter 17
# THE THORN IN THE FLESH: ITS IDENTITY (I)

At the outset of our consideration of the identity of Paul's thorn in the flesh, we do well to remind ourselves that we cannot know its precise identity. The very multiplicity of theories about its nature only serves to underline this fact. Deissmann in his book on Paul points out that a small library could be collected of all the books and articles which have been written on Paul's illness, and many more have appeared since he wrote his book.[1] In the same vein, the Danish philosopher Soren Kierkegaard commented that this passage on the thorn in the flesh 'seems to have afforded an uncommonly favourable opportunity for everyone to become an interpreter of the Bible'.[2]

Merrins has suggested that if one day a contemporary statue of Paul were unearthed by the spade of an archaeologist somewhere in the eastern Mediterranean area, we might then be able to recognise some particular appearance which would allow us to identify the thorn in the flesh.[3] This is extremely unlikely, however, since almost all the suggested identifications of the thorn are of such a character that they would not be obvious in the gross delineation of the facial features of a statue. Also, since the thorn affected him only from time to time, it is most improbable that a likeness would be made of him during an attack when his appearance would be somewhat abnormal, if we accept the reference in Galatians 4.14 as relevant. The point remains theoretical for we do not have any evidence of the existence of any contemporary picture or sculpture of Paul.

The best known early description of Paul is in the late second-century apocryphal Acts of Paul and Thekla. According to this book a man named Onesiphorus went with his family to meet the apostle on the road from Lystra to Iconium in Asia Minor. He had not met Paul before and when Paul arrived he found that he was,

> A man of small stature, with a bald head and crooked legs, in a good state of body, with eyebrows meeting and nose somewhat hooked, full of friendliness; for now he appeared like a man, and now he had the face of an angel.[4]

This translation is that of the Syriac version of the Greek original. The Armenian version adds that Paul had blue eyes and crisp or curly hair.[5] There are similar descriptions of his appearance from later centuries, but none of them gives us any clue to the identity of his thorn in the flesh.

It is not even clear that the Corinthian Christians knew its precise identity. Stanley suggested that the very obscurity of the nature of the thorn to us was occasioned by the fact that it was plain to Paul's contemporaries.[6] This, however, need not be so. Paul is boasting, albeit reluctantly, of things which support his claim to be an apostle and to have apostolic authority. He is appealing to evidence with which the Corinthians would not be familiar. They did not know about his experience of the surpassingly great visions and revelations, and need not have known about the experience of the thorn in the flesh which followed them.

## THEORIES ABOUT ITS IDENTITY

In the absence of any contemporary evidence about the nature of the thorn in the flesh we are left in the realm of conjecture, and it must be said at the outset of our review that we do not lack theories. These range from the bizarre and improbable to the reasonable and possible. They include suggestions which have no contact with the text and bear no relation to the metaphors which Paul uses to describe his experience. It is obvious that some of the suggestions have simply been snatched from the air and are without any foundation in reality at all. Lightfoot suggested that many of them have arisen from the circumstances of their originators who saw in the apostle's experience a more or less perfect reflection of the trials which beset their own lives.[7] A list of the conditions which have been proposed for the diagnosis of the identity of the thorn in the flesh reads like the index of a medical textbook.

For the purpose of discussion, however, the theories conveniently divide themselves into two main groups. On the one hand there are those theories which identify the character of the thorn as non-physical, and on the other hand those which regard it as physical in character.

### I. Theories which identify the thorn as non-physical in character

1. Religious opposition:
   a. By an individual.
   b. By a Jewish or pagan group.

2. Mental oppression:
   a. Exaggeration of a normal state of grief or remorse.
   b. Neurosis, e.g. anxiety state or hysteria.
   c. Psychosis, e.g. depression or paranoia.

3. Spiritual temptation:
   a. Pride.
   b. Doubt.
   c. Sensuality.
   d. Ill-temper.

## II. Theories which regard the thorn as physical in character

1. Physical defect:
    a. Stammering.
    b. Deafness.
2. Bodily injury.
3. Organic disease:
    a. A painful disorder.
    b. A nervous disease.
    c. An affection of the eyes.
    d. An infective disease.

# THEORIES OF ITS NON-PHYSICAL CHARACTER

The theories which belong to this group dominated the exegesis of the passage on the thorn in the flesh from the fourth to the eighteenth century, and any group of theories which endures for fifteen centuries demands respect and discussion. However, these theories are not much favoured today for most commentators prefer to regard the thorn as physical in character. One of the main reasons for this loss of favour is that most of these theories are not based on a careful examination of what Paul actually said, nor upon a natural understanding of the meaning of the words which he used. Many of the theories are examples of *eisegesis* rather than *exegesis*, of reading a meaning into the text rather than drawing one out of it. This is the significance of the remark made by Lightfoot about the influence of the circumstances of the originators of many of these theories, which we have already quoted.

The group as a whole can be divided into three sections according to whether the precise nature of the thorn was regarded as religious opposition, mental oppression or spiritual temptation.

1. **Religious opposition.** This was the view held by John Chrysostom and the Greek Fathers in general. Chrysostom begins his exposition of the passage by denying that the thorn could be a headache inflicted by the Devil as some had said, because 'the body of Paul could never have been given over to the hands of the Devil, seeing that the Devil himself submitted to Paul at his mere bidding'. He went on to draw attention to the Hebrew name Satan in the phrase 'a messenger of Satan' which Paul had used (v.7). Because this name meant an adversary, Chrysostom believed that the use of the name here meant that the thorn in the flesh was the work of opposition by adversaries such as Alexander the coppersmith (2 Timothy 4.14) and what he calls 'the party of Hymenaeus and Philetus' (2 Timothy 2.17).[8] Amongst modern commentators, Ronald Knox regards Chrysostom as 'Paul's best

interpreter', and prefers his theory that the thorn was the opposition of adversaries, but admits that it 'does not impose itself on the mind'. He thought that the opposition came from Paul's own flesh and blood.[9] Tasker also favours this theory after reviewing and dismissing the other ones. He points out that there is nothing so calculated to deflate spiritual pride as opposition encountered during the preaching of the gospel, and because of this 'it is not unlikely that Chrysostom's interpretation is nearer the truth than any other'.[10]

We know, however, from Acts 9.23 that Paul encountered religious opposition immediately after his conversion and so this began some time before he was given his thorn in the flesh. Also, religious opposition was an experience common to all Christian believers and was not peculiar to Paul. He would not have prayed to be delivered from an experience which was the common and expected lot of all who shared his faith. It appears unlikely, therefore, that the thorn in the flesh was the religious opposition which Paul encountered in his preaching, and so it is not necessary to discuss whether this came from an individual or a group.

2. **Mental oppression.** Numerous mental states have been proposed for the diagnosis of the thorn in the flesh, but it is unnecessary to enter into a detailed discussion of their nature or relevance. Some of the descriptions used are too imprecise to define what their proposers intended in terms of modern medical knowledge, e.g. the use of the words 'neurasthenia' and 'depression' without any further explanation. In most cases the suggestions are so widely at variance with what we know of the character and mind of Paul, that they are not worth discussing. For instance, whoever would entertain the thought of the diagnosis of hysteria for the thorn in the flesh lacks insight alike into the character of Paul and the nature of hysteria. Modern authors who have thought that the thorn was some form of mental affliction include Weatherhead who regarded it as 'some form of psychosomatic disorder'.[11]

Amongst those who regard the thorn as the persistence of a normal state of grief or remorse, the most recent is Menoud who suggests that it was Paul's great sorrow at the unbelief of his own people, the Jews. Paul's prayer for the removal of the thorn was therefore a prayer that he might evangelise and convert them.[12] However, it is difficult to see how this view of Menoud and others explains the precise dating of the onset of the thorn some years after his own conversion and its connection with his own experience of visions and revelations. Also, this view requires a very specialised and improbable interpretation of the phrase 'in the flesh' which sees in it a reference to the Jewish people, 'my flesh' as Paul calls them in Romans 11.14 (cp. Romans 9.3). Finally, it is difficult to see how such a sorrow could find a place in the list of the weaknesses which Paul gives in 2 Corinthians 12.10.

3. **Spiritual temptation.** The final category of theories which identify the character of the thorn in the flesh as non-physical, consists of those which derive it from spiritual temptation. This identification is given some plausibility by the description of his bodily ailment as 'my temptation' in Galatians 4.14 according to the AV rendering which was based on the Textus Receptus. However, the better textual tradition reads 'your temptation', and so removes any basis for this type of theory which has been found in the text on the assumption that it refers to the thorn in the flesh.[13]

Calvin preferred to interpret the thorn in the flesh as including every temptation by which Paul was assailed. He paraphrases Paul's meaning as 'to me there has been given a goad to jab at my flesh, for I am not yet so spiritual as to be exempt from temptations according to the flesh'.[14] In Calvin's view, the flesh does not mean the body, but the part of the soul which is not yet regenerate. The only temptation Calvin mentions specifically is pride, but it is clear that he is not very interested in exploring the possible identity of the thorn further than his general statement we have just quoted. He is more concerned with the significance of the thorn in the apostle's spiritual experience, and its lessons for us. Pride is an unlikely identification for the thorn if only because it was given to Paul specifically to save him from pride in the special visions and revelations which God had given him, as Paul himself tells us in 2 Corinthians 12.7. It is of interest that in his note on Galatians 4.13, Calvin does not link the infirmity of the flesh spoken of there, with the thorn in the flesh. He interprets the flesh mentioned there as meaning Paul's outward appearance, and explains the infirmity of the flesh as 'whatever might make him mean and despised'.[15]

**Doubt** appears to be an improbable diagnosis for the thorn in the flesh. Paul had just been given greater visions and revelations than others had been, and these would reinforce his faith rather than produce doubt.

**Sensuality** or concupiscence would also appear to be an unlikely identification for the thorn, in view of the fact that Paul has already explained how he came to terms with this problem in the seventh chapter of First Corinthians where he regarded himself as having the gift of celibacy from God (1 Corinthians 7.7-9). This has been a popular identification in Roman Catholic exegesis and was set out in authoritative fashion in the seventeenth century in the celebrated commentaries on the epistles of Paul by William Estius[16] and Cornelius à Lapide.[17] As Lightfoot points out, the latter author 'almost exalts this interpretation into an article of faith'.[18] Luther attributed the popularity of this view to the Vulgate rendering of *skolops tei sarki* by *stimulus carnis* which meant 'a goad for the flesh', with the flesh being understood as the carnal or sensual nature of man.[19] This interpretation is usually mentioned by modern Roman Catholic commentators, but is not now commonly adopted by them. It has not often been accepted by Protestant writers, but its existence in Scotland is illustrated by its occurrence in Robert Burns' cynical poem, *Holy Willie's Prayer* (1785):[20]

> May be thou lets this fleshly thorn
> Beset thy servant e'en and morn
> Lest he owre high and proud should turn,
> That he's sae gifted;
> If sae, thy hand maun e'en be borne,
> Until thou lift it.

Finally, the suggestion that the thorn in the flesh consisted of an infirmity of **temper** or fits of anger has been made by Lias,[21] and more recently by Holmes Gore.[22] These authors point to Paul's disagreements with Peter at Antioch (Galatians 2.11) and with Barnabas at the outset of his second missionary journey (Acts 15.37-40) as evidence of Paul's outbursts of anger. However, it cannot be said that this identification of the thorn in the flesh as fits of anger is at all convincing. It is difficult to explain why they began so late in Paul's life, and why they should follow an intense spiritual experience as the appearance of the thorn did.

The main objection to all these theories which regard the thorn as some form of spiritual trial or temptation is that God would hardly have told Paul to stop praying for its removal if it were of this nature. Temptation of various kinds is the lot of all Christian believers and Paul would not have expected to be exempt from it. Equally, it is unlikely that the apostle would regard spiritual temptations as something to boast about and be content to suffer as he does in 2 Corinthians 12.9-10. In so far as these suggested identifications are defects in Paul's character or of his psychological make-up, they make strange bed-fellows with the insults, hardships, persecutions and calamities of verse ten of this passage, and this would imply that the thorn was not of the nature of spiritual temptation in any form. Finally, if Galatians 4.13 refers to the same condition as the thorn in the flesh then it is difficult to see how a spiritual temptation could be the cause of Paul's preaching of the gospel to the Galatians on the first occasion that they heard it from his lips.

So far we have not mentioned Luther's views on the nature of the thorn in the flesh although they also fall into the category of those which maintain the non-physical character of the thorn. This is because they underwent a change in his lifetime. His earliest view is contained in his earlier commentary on the epistle to the Galatians published in 1519, where in his comment on Galatians 4.13 he identifies the infirmity of the flesh and the thorn as religious opposition and persecution. In his later and fuller commentary of 1535 he still believes that the two phrases refer to Paul's trials and and temptations, but he now makes a distinction between outward trials and inward temptations. By the infirmity of the flesh Luther now understands Paul to refer to the religious opposition and persecution of his enemies which may issue in physical violence and bodily injury. The thorn in the flesh, on the other hand, he now believes to refer to inward and spiritual temptations such as Jesus experienced in the garden of Gethsemane before his arrest; these consisted of depression, anguish and terror. His final view is given in his Table Talk where he speaks only of spiritual temptations as the nature of the thorn in the flesh and refers no more to outward opposition and persecution.[23]

The conclusion of our review of the theories which propose a non-physical character for the thorn in the flesh which affected Paul must be that such a character is unlikely. This has emerged as we have considered the different types of theory individually, and is reinforced by a consideration of the theories as a group. In spite of recent attempts to revive them in one form or another, no new evidence has been produced and it is not surprising that they have fallen out of favour today for 'modern exegetical opinion generally opts for some physical malady'.[24] As we shall see, this represents a return to the early interpretation of the thorn in the flesh which appears to have been dominant until the fourth century when the idea that it was some form of bodily suffering was rejected or lost sight of by most writers.[25]

# Chapter 18
# THE THORN IN THE FLESH: ITS IDENTITY (II)

## THEORIES OF ITS PHYSICAL CHARACTER

As a prelude to a more detailed investigation of the theories which regard the character of Paul's thorn in the flesh as physical, we take up certain general considerations. These consist of a number of observations on the two passages relevant to our discussion, which when taken together do at least create a presumption in favour of the general thesis that the thorn in the flesh was physical in character.

### Observations on 2 Corinthians 12.7-10

1. The metaphor embodied in the phrase 'a thorn in the flesh' (v.7) is one which is derived from the physical world, and so may be presumed to be intended to describe an experience which was physical in nature.

2. The primary and literal meaning of *sarx* or flesh is physical and denotes the material which covers the bones of a human or animal body.[1] It is true that the word may also be used in an ethical sense to mean the human carnal nature but, as Hughes points out in his commentary on this epistle, Paul ordinarily reserves the ethical usage for a doctrinal-ethical context in which the flesh is opposed to the spirit. In a narrative context such as our passage, it is more likely to be used in a physical sense.[2]

3. The situations of weakness which include the thorn in the flesh and are listed in verse ten are all predominantly physical. Most commentators speak of only four kinds of weakness described in this verse, but there are five words in the description and it is more natural to take them as specifying five different kinds of weakness under the general heading of 'the weaknesses' in verse nine. Here *astheneiai*, 'weaknesses', is used with the definite article to denote the class of things which make Paul weak and in which God's power makes him strong. In verse ten, five of these things are listed and the first one is *astheneiai*, 'weaknesses', but this time without the definite article. It is possible that we should translate this second use of the word as 'sicknesses' for it forms part of a list of those things which make Paul weak. The other things are 'insolent maltreatment' (*hubris*, here in the passive sense), 'hardships' (*anankai*), 'persecutions' (*diogmoi*), and 'desperate straits' (*stenochoriai*, literally this word refers to narrowness of space). All these things make Paul

weak and unable to cope, but God's power makes him strong even in the situations which these words describe and that is why he glories in their occurrence.

## Observations on Galatians 4.13-15

It is customary to associate Paul's thorn in the flesh with this passage in the epistle to the Galatians, but this association is not absolutely certain as Tasker reminds us when he writes that in verse thirteen of this passage:

> Paul speaks of 'an infirmity of the flesh'. There is no definite article and there is no personal pronoun; he is not, in other words, referring to 'that constantly recurring trouble of mine which elsewhere I call my thorn in the flesh'. It may well have been a rather exceptional illness which had caused him to journey into Galatia at that particular time.[3]

It is only fair that we should remind ourselves of this possibility that the Galatian passage might be explained on another basis, because once we have associated it with the passage from Second Corinthians which we have just considered, then the case for the physical character of the thorn in the flesh becomes much stronger. We can see this from the following observations:

1. The meaning of the phrase *astheneia tes sarkos*, 'a weakness of the flesh', in verse thirteen in this context is most naturally taken as physical and translated 'bodily illness' (REB) or 'physical infirmity' (NRSV). However, the same phrase occurs in Romans 6.19 where Paul uses it to denote the defective spiritual insight of the Roman Christians. It is clear that these two meanings are not interchangeable in their respective contexts. The meaning in Romans would not fit the Galatian context for this latter context demands a physical meaning.

2. The condition which Paul here calls a weakness of the flesh made him unable to travel, and obliged him to stay and rest in Galatia for some time until he was fit again. This would be most naturally understood of a physical illness.

3. The nature of this condition which caused Paul to visit Galatia was obvious to the Galatians in his physical appearance ('in my flesh'), which was repulsive to behold (v.14).

4. The reaction of the Galatians to his repulsive appearance was to wish to do something physical to help him such as plucking out their eyes to give them to him (v.15). This too suggests that his condition was physical in nature.

These preliminary observations have served to set forth the general case in favour of regarding the character of the thorn in the flesh as physical. We now proceed to consider the various theories which have been proposed for the specific identity of the thorn.

## CONSIDERATION OF SPECIFIC THEORIES

### 1. Theories of Physical Defect

a. *Stammering* It would appear unlikely that an effective evangelist like Paul suffered from a defect of his speech such as stammering, but this has been suggested as the character of the thorn in the flesh. A convenient statement of this view is by Lowther Clarke in his book *New Testament Problems* where he suggests that the apostle was 'a victim to nerves' and suffered from a stammer.[4] Although in the concluding paragraph of his discussion he indicates that this view may be thought fanciful he claims support for it in two verses in Second Corinthians. The first is in 10.10 where Paul quotes his opponents as saying that his bodily presence was unimpressive and his speech of no account (*exouthenemenos*). The second is in 11.6 where Paul admits, perhaps ironically, that he may be unskilled in speaking, and uses the word *idiotes* ('unskilled' RSV or 'untrained' NRSV) meaning that he is an amateur rather than an expert in rhetoric. It must be admitted that no one reading these verses in their context would think that they meant that Paul had a speech defect. It is very improbable that his thorn in the flesh was of this nature although Barrett appears to accept it.[5]

b. *Deafness* A defect of hearing was suggested by Knapp as the identity of Paul's thorn in the flesh.[6] It is, however, very difficult to find any evidence of this in the New Testament. Deafness is a permanent state and Paul clearly indicates that the thorn in the flesh affects him only intermittently. This suggestion does not explain any of the features of the attack described in the Galatian passage, and must be discarded as a possible diagnosis for Paul's condition.

### 2. Theories of bodily injury

a. *Physical violence* There is no doubt that the opposition which Paul encountered often expressed itself in physical violence which led to his bodily injury. Incidents which resulted in bodily injury are mentioned in Acts 13.50; 14.19 and 16.23, and he gives details of others in 2 Corinthians 11.23-27 (cp. 4.9 and 6.5). It is unlikely, however, that bodily injury constituted his thorn in the flesh for violence against his person began some time before he had the ecstatic experience which preceded the appearance of the thorn.

An attempt was made by Marcus Dods to identify the thorn in the flesh, or at least the weakness of the flesh which Paul describes in Galatians 4.13, with what happened to the apostle at Lystra immediately before he went to Galatia.[7] At Lystra Paul was stoned and left for dead according to Acts 14.19. This stoning would result in bodily weakness and produce a repulsive appearance such as he suggests the Galatians saw in him (Galatians 4.14). If this appearance was an example of his thorn in the flesh, it could very well have been the result of personal violence resulting in serious bodily injury.

b. *Crucifixion* An even more dramatic suggestion has been made by Turner. According to this suggestion, Paul was actually crucified at Perga in Pamphylia by Jews who resented his charges that the Jewish people had crucified their Messiah. This occurred just before Paul went inland to visit Galatia and Turner finds support for his suggestion in the following references in the epistle to the Galatians:

'I have been crucified with Christ' (Galatians 2.20).

'The cross of our Lord Jesus Christ, by which the world has been crucified to me, and I to the world' (6.14).

'I bear on my body the marks (*stigmata*) of Jesus' (6.17).

Turner expects the suggestion of Paul's crucifixion to be regarded as fantastic, and it is difficult to take it seriously.[8] There is no mention of violence in the record of Paul's visit to Perga in Acts 14.25, and if the Jews there had crucified Paul it would have been so unusual and significant that Luke would surely have mentioned it in his account. Paul's language in his references to crucifixion in the epistle to the Galatians is clearly metaphorical, and refers back to the crucifixion of Jesus and its significance in the spiritual experience of Paul and the Christian believer.

If we take the Galatian passage by itself, the suggestion that Paul is describing the result of a violent assault upon his person is possible, although it must be said that to describe the result of an assault as 'a weakness of the flesh' reads strangely. If, however, we take it along with the passage in Second Corinthians, then the suggestion of bodily injury as the character of the thorn in the flesh becomes very improbable.

## 3. Theories of organic disease

We are left, then, with the view that Paul's thorn in the flesh was physical in character and probably due to some identifiable syndrome or specific disease. This return to the earliest views held about the nature of the thorn may have several causes. For instance, there has been an increasing understanding of the nature of both mental and physical disease in modern times and it may be that this has had some influence on the change of opinion. Also, the more recent views do try to do justice to the meaning of the passages in which the thorn in the flesh is described, and this may be attributed to the development of critical Biblical study and scholarship in the nineteenth century and after. Whatever the cause may be, the fact remains that many modern commentators accept the physical character of the thorn in the flesh, although they are not agreed on any one specific physical identity for it. Numerous suggestions for this have been put forward with varying degrees of plausibility.

**a.** *A painful disorder* The earliest recorded tradition about the physical nature of the thorn in the flesh was current in the second century AD and is quoted by Tertullian (c.AD 160-240) in his Montanist work *De Pudicitia (On Modesty)* written about AD 217. In chapter thirteen of this work he writes that Paul's elation of spirit was restrained by what 'they say' was earache or headache (*dolor auricular vel capitis*), a description which might suggest that Paul suffered from the condition of trigeminal neuralgia.[9] Jerome (c.AD 346-419) also mentions in his commentary on Galatians, written about AD 386, the tradition that the physical weakness of Galatians 4.13 was a very severe headache (*gravissimus capitis dolor*).[10] How authentic this tradition was, is now impossible to say, but it does not of itself bring us much nearer a solution of the problem since headache is only a symptom and not a disease.

Other more specific suggestions have been toothache due to dental caries, pain from some condition of the locomotor system such as gout, sciatica or rheumatism. However, as we have already mentioned, from the fourth century onwards the tradition of pains in the head or bodily suffering of any kind is rejected by most authors, and persecution becomes accepted as the most likely nature of the thorn. Finally, we have the conjecture of Aquinas (AD 1225-1274) that the thorn was a recurrent renal colic caused by the presence of a urinary stone in the kidney or ureter (*morbus iliacus*).[11] These suggestions are either too imprecise or improbable to justify their further investigation. It is very probable that the thorn in the flesh was painful, but it is doubtful if we can reach any definite conclusion about its identity by a consideration of pain alone.

**b.** *A nervous disease* The two principal nervous diseases which have been proposed for the diagnosis of the thorn in the flesh are migraine and epilepsy.

The characteristic feature of **migraine** is a recurrent headache which occurs on only one side of the head. The name is a corruption of the term *hemicrania* used by the Greek physician Galen (AD 130-210) because of the unilateral distribution of the pain.[12] Support for the theory of migraine as the thorn in the flesh came from Johnson who appeared to have described an attack of this disease from her own personal experience and saw in it an explanation of what happened to Paul on the road to Damascus. She did not however, relate her explanation very closely to Paul's descriptions in his two letters, but assumed that his conversion experience was the same as his thorn in the flesh, a name which she thinks he gave the affliction because he did not know the technical medical term for it.[13] The most recent attempt to identify the thorn in the flesh as 'migraine without aura' comes from the Department of Neurology of the University of Kiel in Germany, but it adds little to what has been said already about this possible diagnosis.[14]

Migraine as we know it today does not readily agree with Paul's experience. This condition usually begins at puberty and its attacks become less frequent and less severe in middle age. Paul is quite clear that the thorn was given to him when he was about forty years of age and that he had never had an attack before. As we have already seen, he experienced his first attack some nine to ten years after his conversion on the road to Damascus. Migraine attacks last only a few hours or in its most severe form only a few days, and would be unlikely to interfere with the apostle's travelling plans as the thorn in the flesh did, if it was the condition referred to in the epistle to the Galatians.

It is significant that medical commentators have rarely been satisfied with the classical diagnosis of migraine in Paul's case. but have regarded it as a special type. For instance, Adolf Seeligmüller was the Professor of Neurology at Halle University who in 1910 published a booklet with the title *War Paulus Epileptiker?* (*Was Paul an epileptic?*). In this booklet he agreed that the apostle might have suffered from migraine but of a special variety which he called *Augen-migräne* or ophthalmic migraine. He described the features of this type of migraine and included amongst its features, loss of consciousness and the occurrence of fits. This made it clear that he was describing epilepsy and not migraine at all. It is therefore possible that other authors who put forward the diagnosis of migraine, and did not describe its features in detail, were in fact thinking of epilepsy and not migraine. When we compare the features of migraine with the experience of Paul it would appear that his thorn in the flesh was not migraine as we know it today.

The most popular identification of the thorn in the flesh in the nineteenth century was that of **epilepsy**.[15] This identification appears to have been first made in 1804 by K.L. Zeigler of Göttingen in the publication *Theologische Abhandlungen*. This suggestion was accepted and popularised in Britain by Lightfoot in his commentary on the epistle to the Galatians, the first edition of which appeared in 1865.[16] It was taken up in Germany by Max Krenkel in an article published in 1873 and then in a book which appeared in 1890. After its introduction to Biblical scholarship by these authors, it was widely reproduced and accepted.

The evidence that Paul may have been an epileptic is based on the description of his conversion experience in Acts 9.3-9; 22.6-11 and 26.12-18, and on his account of the experience of visions and revelations in 2 Corinthians 12.1-4. We must therefore look at this evidence before we consider whether the thorn in the flesh could have been epilepsy.

The essential features of Paul's experience on the Damascus road can be summarised by saying that he saw a bright light, fell to the ground, heard a voice speaking to him and was blind for three days afterwards. There is little positive evidence in these features for the diagnosis of epilepsy, and a great deal of negative evidence against it. This latter we may set out as follows:

(1) The bright light was also seen by his companions according to Acts 22.9 and could not therefore have been the premonitory aura of an epileptic attack as has been suggested.

(2) His companions fell to the ground along with him according to Acts 26.14 and so shared this experience too.

(3) They also heard the sound of the voice but could not distinguish the words, as we are told in Acts 9.7 and 22.9.

(4) At no point did Paul lose consciousness, which is the essential feature of a major epileptic fit.

(5) There was no loss of memory for events which happened during the experience such as commonly occurs after an epileptic fit.

(6) Blindness does not usually follow an epileptic fit and if it did, it would not be complete nor last as long as three days as it did in Paul's case.

(7) The experiences of an epileptic during an attack, in so far as they may be remembered (which is rarely the case) do not show a rational pattern nor have objective significance as they had in Paul's case.

(8) A profound change of personal belief and character such as occurred in Paul's case does not occur during or after an epileptic fit.

When we look at the second experience which Paul had and which he describes in 2 Corinthians 12.1-4, we find that the evidence for its being an epileptic fit is even less convincing than it was for his conversion experience. The evidence against epilepsy in this second case is as follows:

(1) There was no loss of consciousness during this experience.

(2) There was no loss of memory for what happened during it.

(3) Epileptic attacks could never add to a person's knowledge of God as Paul's experience of visions and revelations did.

In the light of all the evidence we have considered, it is clear that neither Paul's conversion experience nor his experience of visions and revelations were epileptic in nature.

What are we to say then of the thorn in the flesh? Was it epileptic in nature? The first thing to notice is how carefully Paul distinguishes the thorn in the flesh from the ecstatic experience in his description in 2 Corinthians 12.1-10. It was given to him after that experience in order to counteract its possible elating effect on him (v.7). Consequently it was not of the same nature as that and if we had concluded that the ecstatic experience was epileptic in nature, this would mean that the thorn in the flesh was not. However, there are several considerations which make the epileptic nature of the thorn unlikely.

(1) The thorn in the flesh and the weakness of the flesh are not described in terms which would suggest a diagnosis of epilepsy.

(2) The thorn in the flesh is usually regarded as a painful experience, but the clinical features of epilepsy do not include pain.

(3) The majority of persons who develop epilepsy do so before the age of thirty, but Paul was over forty years of age when the thorn first troubled him.

(4) An epileptic fit normally lasts only a few minutes and would not normally lead to an alteration in plans such as Paul suggests his illness did in Galatians 4.13.

The only exception to the first of these considerations which could be made is found in the use of the word *exeptusate* in Galatians 4.14. This is the only use of the verb *ekptuo* in the New Testament. Its literal meaning is 'to spit out' and it was suggested by Krenkel in his book of 1890 already mentioned that it referred to the custom of spitting at the sight of sick people in order to ward off the sickness from oneself (cp. Job 17.6). Paul is commending the Galatians for not observing this custom and so not rejecting him because of his disease. The disease in which this custom was observed more than for any other was epilepsy. The Roman comedy playwright Plautus (c. 254-184 BC), for instance, calls epilepsy *morbus qui sputator* ('the disease which is spat upon') in one of his plays.[17] However, Plautus wrote in the late third century BC and by New Testament times the designation was applied to other diseases than epilepsy. For example, we find Pliny the Elder (AD 23-79) recording that even the sight of a person with a lame right foot provoked spitting in his day.[18] The observance of the custom of spitting was not therefore diagnostic of epilepsy. Schlier[19] defends the literal meaning of the word in Galatians 4.14, but it seems preferable to take it metaphorically and believe that, as its literal application widened, so it came to be used in a metaphorical sense of rejection without any necessary accompaniment of the physical act of spitting. In its literal usage it was a pagan word describing a pagan custom, and it is unlikely that Paul would use it in this sense to the Christians of Galatia. It is more likely he used it simply to mean that they did not despise or reject him because of his altered physical appearance produced by his illness. However, even if the literal meaning is insisted upon, the word does not require the diagnosis of epilepsy for, as we have seen, it may be applied to other diseases as well. In the absence of any unequivocal supporting evidence, we conclude that the use of the word *ekptuo* here does not necessarily imply a diagnosis of epilepsy.

The final argument we must notice in favour of the epileptic nature of the thorn in the flesh is at least as old as Nietzsche (1844-1900),[20] and has appeared frequently in the literature since his day. This argument is that since great men of history like Alexander the Great, Julius Caesar, Muhammad,

Cromwell and Napoleon were all epileptic, there is a strong possibility that Paul was too. The fallacy of this argument becomes apparent when we express it in the form of a syllogism:

Paul was a great man;
Some great men have epilepsy;
Therefore Paul had epilepsy.

The evidence for the diagnosis of epilepsy in the case of almost all the great men of whom it is alleged is very scanty. In the case of Napoleon, for example, Allo mentions that the diagnosis is based on one page in the *Mémoires* of Talleyrand where the author describes how one day in Strasbourg in 1805, the Emperor Napoleon fainted from fatigue and indigestion.[21] Our conclusion must be that the argument which this instance illustrates has no firm foundation in fact, and is not worth considering amongst those used to support the case for the epileptic nature of Paul's thorn in the flesh.

By this time it should be clear that there is no real evidence either that Paul was an epileptic, or that his thorn in the flesh was epilepsy. This was also the verdict of Paul Wendland in his book on *Hellenistic and Roman Culture* published in 1912. He said that the suggestion that Paul was an epileptic was 'a thesis of historians ignorant of medicine, and of doctors ignorant of history'.[22]

Before we leave our consideration of nervous disease as a possible cause of the thorn in the flesh, we should refer to a modern attempt to explain both Paul's conversion experience and his thorn in the flesh in terms of the same condition in much the same way as epilepsy has been used. Hisey and Beck, two physicians of Alabama, have suggested that Paul's conversion experience was due to a small acute brain haemorrhage which occurred in the occipital area of the cerebral cortex which is concerned with sight and hearing. The permanent sequel to this haemorrhage was a unilateral loss of vision (hemianopsia) and perhaps minor epileptiform attacks, either of which, or both of them together constituted his thorn in the flesh.[23]

This theory is open to most of the objections we have already urged against the view that the thorn in the flesh was epilepsy. The fact that at his conversion, Paul's sensory impressions of light and sound were shared by his companions excludes any cause intrinsic to himself. Cerebral haemorrhages like epileptic seizures do not produce profound religious changes in their victims and do not inspire them to turn the world upside down as Paul was accused of doing at Thessalonica in Acts 17.6. The description of Paul's thorn in the flesh is not given in terms which would suggest the effects of brain haemorrhage, and so we must conclude that this theory too can be safely discounted as an explanation of both Paul's conversion and his thorn in the flesh.

c. *An affection of the eyes*  The view that an affection of the eyes constituted Paul's thorn in the flesh was originally advanced by Lewin in 1851 when he published the first edition of his two-volume work *The Life and Epistles of St Paul*.[24] This view was adopted by Farrar in his book *The Life and Work of St Paul* first published in 1879, although he appears to accept the possibility that the thorn was epilepsy and that Paul suffered from eye disease and epilepsy concomitantly.[25] The basis for this view is found in certain references in the epistle to the Galatians and it assumes that the illness Paul mentions there was identical with the thorn in the flesh described in Second Corinthians. The references are Galatians 4.13 which is interpreted as meaning a physical illness; 4.14 which means that the condition was obvious to the Galatians when they saw him; and 4.15 which suggests it had something to do with the eyes. Both Lewin and Farrar refer to verses in the Acts and Galatians which might mean that Paul suffered from defective vision and to which we have already made reference above. In a later edition of his book, Lewin added a further point when he derived the noun *skolops* from the words *skello*, 'to dry up', and *ops*, 'the eye', and suggested that *skolops* therefore meant something which withered the eye and affected the sight. Needless to say, this derivation did not prove acceptable to later authors.

Lewin's original suggestion, which was accepted by Farrar, was that the disease of the eyes was ophthalmia, which we would call conjunctivitis today. He suggested that Paul's eyes had been inflamed and weakened by the bright light on the Damascus road, and in Damascus he had contracted an infection of the eyes which never left him and whose acute exacerbations incapacitated him from time to time. Farrar suggests that one of these exacerbations occurred when he was in Arabia and exposed to desert conditions there.[26] A more specific identification of the nature of the disease as trachoma or granular conjunctivitis due to an organism of the *Chlamydia* group is preferred by Short, who claims that the features of trachoma 'correspond exactly' with those of the thorn in the flesh.[27] This disease was known in the nineteenth century as 'Egyptian ophthalmia' because it was brought to Britain by soldiers returning from the campaign against Napoleon in Egypt in 1801.

This theory sounds plausible until it is examined more closely. To place its origin in Damascus, as both Lewin and Farrar do, is to forget that the first appearance of the thorn was some years after Paul's Damascus experience. To find support for the theory by adducing apparent examples of poor vision is to place an interpretation on certain incidents which might not otherwise have occurred to commentators. Finally, to interpret Galatians 4.15 of an affection of the eyes is to misconstrue the emphasis of that verse.

The theory that the thorn was a disease of the eyes depends solely on the mention of the eyes in this verse in Galatians. Here Paul says to the Galatian Christians in the words of the AV translation, 'I bear you record that, if it had been possible, you would have plucked out your own eyes, and given them to me'. The question arises whether the reference to eyes in this verse requires us to understand that Paul's disease was one of the eyes or can be explained in some other way.

Lightfoot's comment on the argument that this disease was one of the eyes is that 'the stress of the argument rests on what I cannot but think is a mistaken interpretation of Galatians 4.15'.[28] He goes on to point out that the emphasis is not on **your** eyes but on your **eyes**, i.e., not on your healthy eyes as opposed to my diseased ones, but on your eyes as your most precious possession which you would have been willing to give up to make me well again. The NEB adopts this interpretation when it translates this verse, 'I can say this for you: you would have torn out your very eyes and given them to me, had that been possible'.

If this interpretation is correct, and it appears to be very reasonable and satisfactory, then there is no real basis here for the theory that Paul's thorn in the flesh was an affection of the eyes. This finds confirmation in the fact that the other evidence quoted from the Acts and elsewhere in the epistle to the Galatians to suggest that Paul suffered from defective eyesight, can be explained just as adequately on other grounds. Also, as Ramsay points out, the power of Paul's eyes which is described by Luke in Acts 13.9; 14.9 and 23.1 does not support the view that he suffered from any affection of the eyes or weakness of his vision.[29] We conclude, therefore, that there is no real basis for the view that the thorn in the flesh was an affection of the eyes.

d. *An infective disease* The final category of physical disease which has been proposed to explain the nature of the thorn in the flesh is that of infective or communicable disease. A number of the conditions suggested can be safely set aside as improbable identifications. These include leprosy, smallpox and lice infestation.[30] However, a recurrent infective febrile disease is a strong possibility and appears to have been considered as early as the time of Chrysostom (AD 347-407) who was himself a sufferer from 'ague-fever'. In his twenty-sixth homily on Second Corinthians he comments on the tenth verse of chapter ten of that epistle and gives his opinion that Paul, in speaking of the kind of infirmity he had, did not speak of fevers, nor of any intermittent disease (*periodos*), nor of any bodily ailment.[31] Since Chrysostom believed that the thorn in the flesh consisted of persecution, we may assume that he is here denying those theories which held it to be a recurrent febrile disease, and therefore witnessing to their existence in his own time. Whether this deduction is valid or not, there is no doubt that a febrile disease has been suggested as Paul's thorn in the flesh by modern authors. The two most common ones proposed are brucellosis and malaria.

**Brucellosis** is the modern name for Malta or undulant fever. We met with this disease earlier in this book when we considered the identity of the infection from which the father of Publius suffered according to Acts 28.8.

The cause of this disease is the *Brucella* group of micro-organisms which infect humans through the milk of affected goats or cows. It occurs around the shores of the Mediterranean Sea and in some other parts of the world. It is characterised by a chronic variable fever which persists for about a year and then clears up, and is accompanied by weakness and sweating with aches and pains in various parts of the body.

In 1904 W.M. Alexander, who was a medically-qualified theologian occupying the chair of divinity in the Glasgow College of the Free Church of Scotland, wrote two articles in the *Expository Times* in which he identified Paul's thorn in the flesh as brucellosis.[32] He began this article by rejecting eye disease, epilepsy and malaria as possible identifications, and went on to describe what he regarded as three attacks of illness from which Paul suffered. The first attack was in Cilicia and is described in 2 Corinthians 12.2-8; the second one was at Antioch in Pisidia (Acts 13.13-14); and the third at Troas is described in 2 Corinthians 1.8-9. Alexander claimed that these attacks were of brucellosis and constituted the three occasions on which Paul prayed to be rid of his thorn according to 2 Corinthians 12.8. The article concluded with a table which compared the effects of brucellosis, which the author called Malta fever, with the features of Paul's thorn in the flesh. However, neither the details in this table nor the accompanying comments in the article explain the features of Paul's illness any better than malaria can, whilst malaria can explain other details which brucellosis cannot explain. We conclude. therefore, that brucellosis is a less probable diagnosis than that of malaria in the case of Paul's thorn in the flesh.

The diagnosis of **malaria** was first suggested by Sir William Ramsay as the one which best explained the nature of Paul's thorn in the flesh in his book *The Church in the Roman Empire before AD 170* which was first published in 1893.[33] The suggestion arose out of Ramsay's own experience as a traveller and archaeologist in Asia Minor. In his experience, malarial fever was endemic on the coastal plain of Pamphylia where he believed that Paul had contracted this disease at Perga on his first missionary journey.[34] His comments on the disease are all the more interesting because they were made before Sir Ronald Ross had finally demonstrated the transmission of the malaria parasite to human beings by the bite of the spotted-winged anopheline mosquito in India on August 20th 1897.[35]

We know that malaria was widely prevalent in the lands of the eastern Mediterranean from at least the fourth century BC. It played an important part in the history of both Greece and Rome and is blamed by some historians for the decline of both these civilisations in turn. Jones points out that malaria was one of the commonest diseases among the ancient Greeks and suggests that when they spoke of 'fever (*puretos*)' they usually meant malaria. Its characteristic features of periodic fever and enlargement of the spleen are frequently described by the ancient Greek physicians.[36]

We believe that of all the diseases we have so far considered, malaria best satisfies the requirements of the two passages in which Paul's sickness is described. This can be seen by setting down these requirements down one by one and comparing them with the effects of malaria. We begin with the requirements of the passage in chapter twelve of Second Corinthians.

## Second Corinthians 12.1-7

(1) The disease should be a physical one, for the thorn was 'in the flesh' (v.7). No special comment is necessary here, for malaria is a physical disease caused by the various species of the malarial parasite.

(2) It should produce pain like a thorn does, and also aches such as those which follow a beating about the head and body with fists (*kolaphizo*, v.7). Headaches and aches in muscles, bones and joints are typical of malaria.

(3) It should produce depression as opposed to elation (v.7). Untreated malaria with its intermittent fever, chills and sweating soon produces a profound state of misery and depression in its victims.

(4) It should not be connected with Paul's conversion experience because it occurred some years after it as we know from the date mentioned in verse two. Malaria would not be connected with such an experience if its onset was some years after it had occurred.

(5) It should not be of the same nature as the ecstatic experience described in the first four verses of the chapter. Although malaria may produce dreams and even hallucinations, it never produces an ecstatic experience such as Paul describes and out of which comes the apprehension of new truth about God which he calls 'revelations' (*apokalupseis*, vv.1 and 7).

(6) It should have a definite point of onset in time which could be described by the aorist tense as in verse seven where Paul says that there was given (*edothe*) to him a thorn in the flesh. About ten days or so after the bite of an infected mosquito, the first attack of malaria begins with a sudden rise of temperature and shivering.

(7) It should be recurrent and should return to affect him from time to time. This is the implication of the present tenses in which the two verbs *huperairo*, 'to be elated', and *kolaphizo*, 'to beat with the fists', are given in verse seven. The type of malaria which Paul probably contracted was benign tertian or vivax malaria, for this variety is commonest in the Mediterranean area, and where this is untreated it is notorious for producing relapses at intervals of weeks or months, and even for years after the initial infection.

(8) It should be a chronic disease lasting at least fourteen years. Untreated malaria is a chronic disease and has been known to persist for many years. Also, in Paul's case there would be the possibility of constant re-infection as he journeyed in lands where malaria was endemic.

We now turn from an examination of the requirements of the passage in Second Corinthians to consider those of the account of Paul's infirmity of the flesh in the fourth chapter of the epistle to the Galatians.

## Galatians 4.13-15

(1) The disease is again required to be a physical one for it is described as a weakness 'of the flesh' (v.13) and its effects were visible in the flesh (v.14). As we have noted already, no special comment is needed here for malaria is clearly a physical disease.

(2) It should be a disease which could be contracted in Pamphylia because, immediately prior to his first visit to Galatia, Paul had been on the low-lying plain of this region which lies between the Taurus mountains and the sea on the south coast of Asia Minor (modern Turkey). In summer this well-watered plain was hot, humid and fever-ridden and mosquitoes infected with the malaria parasite bred in its swamps and marshes. Paul in the course of his first missionary journey had come from Paphos in Cyprus and had sailed up the River Cestris to land at the port of Perga (Acts 13.13). As we have seen, it was here that Ramsay suggests he contracted malaria.

(3) It should be a disease of sudden onset which lasts long enough to result in a change of plan for an enterprise such as Paul and his companions were engaged on. It was, therefore, not a condition of short duration as an epileptic fit would be, but one which could be expected to last some days if not weeks, and which would call for a period of convalescence. This requirement fits in with the picture of malaria.

(4) It should be a disease in which the removal of the patient from a hot humid climate to a cooler mountain atmosphere would normally be advised, if this were possible. It was well-recognised that patients suffering from malarial fever were more comfortable in a cool mountain climate and ran less risk of further infection when removed from beside the swamps of a fever-ridden plain. This would explain Paul's change of plan which caused him to cross the high Taurus mountains to reach Antioch in Pisidia which stood at an altitude of 3,600 feet above sea-level (See Acts 13.14). If he had not contracted malaria he would not have sought a cooler climate and higher ground, and so he was able to say to the Galatians that his first visit to them was the result of illness (v.13). This illness had caused him to change his plans which did not originally include a visit to Galatia, but because of his illness such a visit became a medical necessity.

(5) It should be a disease which could produce contempt or scorn in those who came into contact with anyone suffering from it (v.14 NIV). This verse has usually been understood to refer to the possible reaction of the Galatians to the apparently repulsive character of Paul's physical appearance during an attack of his disease, due perhaps to dehydration and suffering. However,

Ramsay has suggested another more plausible explanation. In pagan belief, fever was regarded as a chastisement or punishment from the gods who sent fire from the underworld to produce fever in the victim. If Paul's condition were one of fever, then the Galatians might have thought him to be the subject of the displeasure of the gods and so regarded him with contempt and abhorrence. On the contrary, Paul says that they welcomed him as if he were an angel or messenger of God.[37]

(6) It should be a disease whose cure was at that time unknown, and whose course was unaffected by even the greatest expression of sympathy by the patient's friends. In the case of the Galatians that sympathy was expressed by their willingness to tear out their very eyes in order to help Paul (v.15). Although malarial attacks were described by Hippocrates and other Greek and Roman writers,[38] its cure was unknown for many centuries after their time. Sympathy might have influenced the course of a mental illness, but could have no effect on the course of malaria.

(7) It should be a disease from an attack of which the patient would recover and be able to travel for even long distances and preach between its attacks and relapses. Malaria is such a disease.

In our statement of the case for malaria being the most probable identification for the thorn in the flesh we have followed Ramsay's presentation of the theory in his various publications. Although we believe this identification to be the most acceptable, there is one difficulty in the way of our total acceptance of the details of Ramsay's theory. This is not in the identification of the thorn as malaria, but in the date and location of Paul's contracting this infection. As we have seen above, Ramsay suggested this happened at Perga in Pamphylia during Paul's first missionary journey. This journey is commonly dated to AD 47-48. However, Paul said he experienced the visions and revelations fourteen years before he wrote Second Corinthians. Since this epistle is usually dated to AD 56, this means that these experiences occurred about AD 42.[39]

Ramsay further suggested that the thorn in the flesh was given to Paul not long before he visited Galatia for the first time, and that the attack in Pamphylia may perhaps have been the first one he had experienced.[40] If this were so, there could have been a period of some five to ten years between the experience of the visions and the appearance of the thorn.[41] Such an interval makes the close association of the two events which Paul clearly makes in 2 Corinthians 12.7 very unlikely. It is much more reasonable to suppose that the interval was very much less than this and that thorn was given very shortly after he had had the visions and revelations. Lightfoot comments that the language Paul uses to describe his experience of the thorn in the flesh implies that the two events were 'nearly coincident'.[42]

Presuming, then, that the thorn was given to Paul shortly after he had the visions and revelations, this would mean that the time of the appearance of the thorn would fall in the silent period of about ten years in Paul's life about which we know very little beyond what the apostle himself tells us in Galatians 1.15-21. There he tells us that after his conversion he went from Damascus into Arabia (which may mean the Nabatean kingdom to the south of Damascus. See 2 Corinthians 11.32). On his return to Damascus he spent three years there, at the end of which he went up to Jerusalem to see the apostle Peter (Galatians 1.18). Later he went to the Roman imperial province of Syria-Cilicia where he spent most of the period AD 35-46 (Galatians 1.21).[43] During part of this time he was in his home town of Tarsus in Cilicia (Acts 9.30), and it was here that Barnabas found him in AD 46 and enlisted his services for the supervision and upbuilding of the Church at Antioch in Syria (Acts 11.25). It would, therefore, be during this silent period and somewhere in the province of Syria-Cilicia that he contracted malaria. As malaria of the benign tertian or vivax type occurs in this area there is no reason why he could not have contracted it there, just as readily as in Pamphylia.

It would also be more probable that it was in this period that he received the special visions and revelations from the Lord of which he speaks in Second Corinthians 12.1. In this so-called silent period he was being prepared for his life's work in the service of the gospel and engaging in the evangelism which led to the foundation of the churches in Syria-Cilicia (Galatians 1.23, cp. Acts 15.41). It would be entirely appropriate, therefore, that such visions and revelations should be given to him as part of his preparation and validation for the wider work that lay ahead of him as an apostle to the Gentiles (Galatians 2.8).

In the circumstances, no conclusion can be final, but it seems reasonable to conclude that a diagnosis of malaria is in keeping with the features required of the thorn in the flesh as set out in the two passages we have just considered, more than that of any other disease which has been suggested. It also has the advantage of harmonising with the earliest tradition which described headache as the nature of the thorn, for headaches which can be very severe and disabling are a characteristic feature of malaria.

## Chapter 19

# THE THORN IN THE FLESH: ITS SIGNIFICANCE

### ITS SIGNIFICANCE FOR PAUL

Whatever the identity of the thorn in the flesh may have been, Paul leaves us in no doubt about its significance for him and his spiritual experience. This appears from the description of the thorn and its effects which he gives in 2 Corinthians 12.7-10, where he has the following things to say about it:

### 1. It was a given thing (v.7).

The appearance of the thorn in the flesh was not an accident due to chance, for chance had no place in Paul's thinking. The thorn was given to him at a definite point in time with a specific relationship to another event, namely, the ecstatic experience he had just described in the previous six verses of the chapter. He tells us that to prevent him from being too elated or conceited after that experience, 'there was given (*edothe*)' to him a thorn in the flesh. Paul uses an impersonal passive form of the verb as though he was reluctant to say who gave it to him.[1] It is clear, however, that he means us to understand that the thorn was given to him by God, for its purpose was a preventive one to keep him from spiritual pride.[2] Realising who gave it to him helped him to accept it and understand its purpose.

### 2. It was a messenger of Satan (v.7).

Although it was given by God, it was provided by Satan. What God willed for a good purpose, was provided by Satan for an evil one. The word for messenger here is *angelos* not with its technical meaning of angel, but simply meaning an ordinary messenger carrying out the orders of Satan as the agent of God. The thorn is personified, but that it not to say as Barth understands Paul to say, that 'like a thorn in the flesh, an angel of Satan stands at his side to buffet him'.[3] The thorn in the flesh was sent by Satan to remind Paul of his weakness, and was allowed by God in order to preserve him from spiritual pride. Physical disease is clearly associated with Satanic activity in Scripture. The supreme example in the Old Testament is the affliction of Job (Job 2.1-7), and the outstanding New Testament example is found here in Paul's thorn in the flesh.

### 3. It provided a recurrent source of harassment (v.7).

The thorn came like an enemy to fight with Paul and to belabour him as an opponent might do with his fists. This is the sense of the verb *kolaphizo* which Paul uses to describe the effect of the thorn. The present tense of the verb suggests that it harassed him repeatedly, whenever he was over-elated by his memory of the the abundance of the visions and revelations he had been given. It was a source of weakness to him, for its attacks sapped the strength of both his body and his mind. As we learnt from Paul's experience in Galatia, it affected his plans for it was an attack of the thorn which resulted in the evangelisation of Galatia, an area which had not been in Paul's original plan (Galatians 4.13). Indeed we may go so far as to attribute the epistle to the Galatians to his thorn in the flesh, for had he not turned aside into Galatia to recover from his illness he would not have preached to the Galatians, and so there would have been no reason for him to write a letter to them afterwards. This is another example of how God controls the evil intention of Satan in order to produce good. Every thing which happens to the Christian believer is not good, but 'we know that in everything God works for the good of those who love him' (Romans 8.28 NIV).

### 4. It was an antidote to spiritual pride (v.7).

Paul gives this as the primary purpose of the thorn in the flesh and makes this observation twice in the same verse as though to give it special emphasis. The word he uses to describe his temptation to spiritual pride is *huperairomai* which means 'to exalt oneself exceedingly', or 'to be puffed up' (so GNB). It was this state to which the thorn in the flesh was to form the antidote. The tense of the verb is again in the present implying that the temptation to excessive elation still recurred even though it first came to him fourteen years previously (v.2). Paul does not say that he had more than one experience of visions and revelations, although there is no reason why he should not have had. However, the thorn was given to him as antidote to spiritual pride and not to the ecstatic experience which was its cause. Excessive elation or spiritual pride could result simply from the recollection of the experience of ecstasy, and so occur more frequently than the ecstatic experience itself. The antidote was the thorn in the flesh which produced in Paul a feeling of weakness and depression which counteracted his feeling of over-elation and pride. The fact that the thorn was to prevent excessive elation indicates that even if Satan provided it, God still controlled it. Left to himself, Satan would have wished to cripple Paul completely and made him incapable of continuing his work of preaching the gospel, but God prevented this and did not allow Satan to do more than check Paul's spiritual pride.

### 5. It provided a subject for prayer (v.8).

Paul tells us that he prayed on three occasions that the thorn might be removed from him and there is no reason why we should not take this number literally. However, commentators from Chrysostom[4] to Barrett[5] have understood this verse to mean that Paul prayed earnestly and repeatedly about his thorn and not only on three occasions. We have no record of the three occasions on which he prayed, but we may presume that they were related to recurrent attacks of his thorn. His prayers were directed to the Lord by whom he clearly means Jesus Christ (cp. v.9), and this makes his prayer more personal for it was not simply to God through Jesus Christ, as in chapter one (v.20), but directly to Jesus Christ personally. As Denney comments, we may be sure that the Lord had full sympathy with those prayers for he had himself prayed three times that his cup of suffering might pass from him (Matthew 26.39-44).[6] Paul had to persevere in prayer for he did not receive an answer to his first two prayers, or if he did, he did not recognise or accept it. After his third prayer he was in no doubt about the Lord's reply and recognised that reply as final. He describes the reply in the perfect tense *eireken* ('he has said'), which means that what the Lord had said was his answer to Paul when he prayed, was his answer at the time he wrote to the Corinthians and would remain his answer until the end of his life. The matter was closed so far as both the Lord and Paul were concerned and Paul would not pray about it again, even though it had not been settled in the way that he would have expected and preferred.

## 6. It produced an accession of strength (vv.9-10).

The Lord's answer to Paul's prayer was the unexpected one that he would not remove the thorn in the flesh which was causing the weakness, but would always supply enough strength to counteract the weakness caused by the thorn. As we have already seen, Paul quoted to his readers the actual words used by the Lord in his reply: 'My grace is all you need, for my power is greatest when you are weak' (v.9 GNB). Grace here is not to be identified solely with strength (*dunamis*) for that would be to impoverish the concept of grace. Grace not only commissioned Paul as an apostle, it also continually supported him in his apostolic ministry. On this occasion it was grace which provided the strength which Paul needed, and it would have much more to provide when other occasions with other needs arose. Both the verbs in this statement are in the present tense to indicate this. The all-sufficiency of grace and the perfect provision of strength applied not only to Paul's immediate situation but for the rest of his life. So Paul tells us he will continue to boast of his weaknesses secure in the knowledge that in his times of weakness he will be clothed by the strength and power of God. He uses the rare verb *episkenoo* which means 'to pitch or spread a tent (*skene*) over'. This may be a reminiscence of how the glory and power of the Lord descended upon the Tabernacle (*skene* in LXX) in the wilderness according to Exodus 40.34-38. In the same way as the *shekinah* or glory of the Lord filled the Tabernacle of old to reassure the Israelites of God's presence and power and guidance, so his strength and power would fill the frail tent of Paul's earthly body and strengthen him in his times of weakness. Alternatively, we may understand it to mean that in Paul's time of weakness, God would spread his power or strength over him like a tent.

## 7. It was a reason for boasting (v.9).

In this section of Second Corinthians, Paul is boasting of certain things which demonstrate the basis of his authority as an apostle of Jesus Christ. He has in mind those whom he calls false apostles in 11.13 and who are at work in the Church at Corinth and are boasting of their credentials to be apostles. He answers their boasting by boasting himself, but he finds this distasteful and does it only reluctantly and because the Corinthians have forced him into it (v.11). His boasting, however, ends in irony. He begins by mentioning visions and revelations of the Lord probably because the false apostles at Corinth had claimed to have them, but he refuses to boast about them, preferring to boast about his weaknesses instead (v.5). He then describes the appearance of the thorn in the flesh and its antidote in the grace and power of the Lord, and concludes that he would now rather boast of the things which caused his weakness than ask the Lord to remove them (v.9). The reason for this unexpected attitude is to be found in the Lord's reply to Paul's prayer, in which he was assured of the strength he needed whenever weakness came upon him, so that he could say that when he was really weak was the time when he was truly strong (v.10). So he boasted of the thorn in the flesh, not because of the weakness it produced, but because of the accompanying experience of divine strength. It was this experience which really demonstrated how closely he lived to the Lord, who was the source of his calling and apostleship.

## 8. It caused a change of attitude (v.10).

As the ground of his boasting had changed from that of having special ecstatic experiences to that of experiencing weakness so that he might know the power of Christ (v.9), so his attitude to those things which caused his weakness had changed. No one could be expected to welcome sickness, ill-treatment, hardship, persecution and distress even when they were experienced for the sake of Christ, but this is now Paul's attitude to all these things. The word he uses is *eudokeo* which means 'to take pleasure in'. Paul had asked for the thorn to be removed, but the Lord had not agreed and had shown him how the weakness it produced could be overcome by the strength provided by divine grace. This changed his attitude to those things he called his weaknesses, so that he did not now ask for them to be removed nor did he resign himself passively to endure them, but he welcomed them and took delight in them for they revealed more to him of the grace of God and the power of Christ than otherwise he would have known. His change of attitude is seen in the final statement of the passage where he declares that he now welcomes those things which cause weakness because he realises that the weaker he gets, the stronger he becomes (v.10).

## 9. It witnessed to a special relationship (v.4).

The most significant aspect of the thorn of the flesh is its witness to the special relationship of close fellowship which Paul had with his Lord. This is implied by the fact that he was given an experience of an abundance of visions and revelations from the Lord (vv.3-4). Paul said that he had been given these visions and revelations in Paradise (v.4). This word 'paradise' comes from old Persian and denotes a garden enclosed by a wall.[7] 'When a Persian king wished to confer a very special honour on someone specially dear to him, he made him 'a companion of the garden' and gave him the right to walk in the royal garden with him in intimate companionship.'[8] In addition to this honour, Paul's special relationship to the Lord was also witnessed to by the Lord's concern that Paul would not fall into the sin of spiritual pride, and it was to prevent this that the Lord gave him the thorn. Although to remove the thorn at Paul's request would thwart the Lord's purpose in giving Paul the thorn, he was nevertheless willing to provide an antidote. Out of all this came a new and deeper experience for Paul of the function and effectiveness of divine grace and also a witness to his special relationship with his Lord.

There can be no doubt that the experience of the thorn in the flesh had great significance for the apostle Paul. In his brief account of it we are taken into his confidence and told of something which was at once a cause of weakness and a source of strength. This paradox of spiritual experience found expression in the words already noted that Paul quotes as the very words of the Lord to him: 'My grace is enough; it's all you need. My strength comes into its own in your weakness'.[9] With the general principle that grace was all-sufficient, Paul was already familiar, but he was now able to see how it applied to his particular situation, to his state of weakness in which grace was to provide strength.

The result was that when he was writing to the Church at Philippi from his Roman prison some five years later, he could tell them that he had learned to be self-sufficient (*autarkes*) in all circumstances because his sufficiency was of Christ who was the source of his strength (Philippians 4.11-13). It was experiences like that of the thorn in the flesh which lay behind Paul's confidence in his Lord and his contentment in his service whatever that service may involve.

## ITS SIGNIFICANCE FOR US TODAY

Our discussion of Paul's thorn in the flesh so far could be dismissed as merely antiquarian in nature and historical in interest, but that would be to misunderstand the real significance of the thorn in the flesh for those who suffer today. It not only had meaning for Paul; it also has meaning for us today. Its meaning is all the more relevant because we do not know the identity of the thorn with any certainty. If it were certain that the disease which Paul contracted was malaria, then it could be argued that his experience was only relevant for those who suffered from malaria, and not for those who suffered from other diseases. The fact that Paul did not describe the nature of his illness in any detail, but dwelt mainly on the fact that he became ill, makes his experience all the more relevant and meaningful for us today in any situation of sickness in which we may find ourselves.

Paul's refusal to go into details about his thorn in the flesh illustrates a basic difference between the Biblical attitude to events in life and the attitude which often characterises the modern secular approach to them. The Bible is concerned with the primary causes of events and usually ignores the secondary ones, while modern secular thinking usually remains satisfied with information about the secondary causes and does not enquire about the primary ones. As we saw when we discussed disease in the Old Testament in Chapter Four, the Bible is more interested in the 'why' than in the 'how' of events, while the modern mind is more concerned with the 'how' and does not ask about the 'why'. Thus, if Paul suffered from malaria, then people today would be satisfied to know that he had been exposed to the bite of an infected mosquito in an area where malaria was endemic, because he had not taken the recognised precautions to prevent this. The Bible, on the other hand, is interested in knowing why he fell ill. This difference in approach explains why the Bible is not specially interested in identifying the disease or answering those questions which we today would regard as of interest and significance.

## 1. It is an explanation of sickness.

The first thing we can learn from Paul's experience of the thorn in the flesh is that sickness has a meaning which is deeper than the merely physical and pathological. Sickness is a universal human experience and our natural instinct is to deny that it belongs to the ideal scheme of things. We could dismiss Paul's experience with a comment such as this and fail to realise that in this experience of Paul's, the veil is temporarily lifted for us and we are allowed to glimpse something of the context and purpose of human sickness.

The first thing to notice is that Paul fell ill at all. He was subject to disease and sickness like other people and had he not been executed, he would have eventually died of some disease or injury. It is important to notice this because the view still prevails in some quarters that when a person becomes a Christian they need never again suffer from any illness, and if they should do so, this is a sign that they lack real faith. Those who hold this view maintain that Jesus Christ came into the world to save people not only from sin, but also from its physical effects which included disease. Paul's thorn in the flesh gives the lie to this view. It is important, therefore, to notice that when Paul was given his thorn in the flesh he was already 'a man in Christ', i.e., a Christian, according to 2 Corinthians 12.2.

The second matter which arises from Paul's experience is that there is always a reason for sickness and an explanation of the time at which it occurs. Its onset is not an accident. Even if Paul's disease was malaria and was due to the bite of an infected mosquito, it was not an accidental occurrence which resulted from his neglect of anti-malarial precautions as we might say today. It was given to him at a particular time as an antidote to personal pride and spiritual conceit. In Paul's case the reason for his sickness was revealed to him, but it is not often revealed to us when we are sick. This is not to say, however, that a reason does not exist.

The third point to notice has to do with the origin of sickness. We have already mentioned our natural instinct which refuses to accept disease and sickness as part of the ideal scheme of things, and there is no doubt that such an instinct is right. The Bible associates disease with evil and suggests that disease in the physical realm corresponds to sin in the moral and spiritual, and that disease spoils physical health just as sin mars spiritual holiness. This is what Paul means when he regards his disease as a messenger of Satan. It was supplied and sent by the Great Adversary of God and goodness, just as it was in the case of the patriarch Job in the Old Testament (Job 2.7). If there were no evil in the world there would be no disease. There were those in Judaism who believed that all sickness was the result of the personal sin of the one who was sick and that there was no such thing as innocent suffering. Rowley, however, has shown that this was not the orthodox Israelite view and that it was not characteristic of the Old Testament as whole.[10] It certainly receives no support from Paul's experience, for his thorn in the flesh did not arise from his own personal sin. His thorn was not the result of pride but was given to him in order to prevent him from succumbing to the temptation to be proud because of his special relationship to the Lord, which had resulted in his experience of visions and revelations. This was the explanation of Paul's sickness. It formed part of his spiritual experience and development.

## 2. It provides an illustration of providence.

The thorn in the flesh also provides a good illustration of the working of divine providence. The word providence does not occur in Scripture, but the fact of providence is reflected on every page as we see how God provides for his creation and his creatures. In the case of Paul's thorn in the flesh we may distinguish several different aspects of providence.

a. **The control of evil.** The thorn in the flesh was given to Paul by God for a beneficent purpose, but Satan supplied it for a malicious one. That malicious one was overruled and kept in check by God. Instead of the thorn crippling Paul permanently, it was allowed to operate only periodically as it was required to prevent him from falling into sin. It never got out of God's control.

**b. The prevention of sin.** Paul makes it very clear that the thorn was given to keep him from falling into the sin of spiritual pride from becoming too elated at his visions and revelations. It was not given to him as a punishment for sin as in the case of Miriam in Numbers 12.9-15 or Gehazi in 2 Kings 5.27, nor as a test of faithfulness as in the case of Job in Job 2.3-8. It was given to him as a preventive against the sin of spiritual conceit and pride.

**c. A provision of strength.** God in his providence actively supplies us with what we need in our different situations, and this is illustrated by his reply to Paul's prayer. There is never a shortage of grace; it is always sufficient to cope with any situation and it provided the strength which Paul needed to overcome his weakness and to counteract the effect of his thorn in the flesh. This applies equally to us today for it is an expression of a permanent principle of the Christian life. Paul accepted the assurance of God's help and the implication that the experiences he describes as weaknesses will continue, secure in the knowledge that in his time of weakness he would be clothed with God's strength (cp. 1 Corinthians 10.13).

## 3. It is a lesson in prayer.

Prayer is the natural response of the Christian to sickness and here Paul gives us a example of how we should pray. His prayer was specific, aimed at the removal of his thorn. It was also persistent for he prayed three times to the same end. He did not at first agree with God's answer to his prayer, but after he had prayed three times he recognised what God's answer was and accepted it and that was the end of the matter. He never prayed about the removal of the thorn again. The matter was closed.

We can also learn from Paul's experience that a Christian's prayer is never unanswered. We tend to forget that 'No' is as much an answer to prayer as 'Yes'. When Paul did not receive the answer he wanted, he thought his prayer was unanswered, but this was not so. God was saying 'No' to his request that the thorn should be removed because he was going to deal with Paul's problem in another way. He was going to provide an antidote of the effect of the thorn, not to remove it.

## 4. It is a lesson in healing.

Paul's experience of his thorn in the flesh is not only a lesson in prayer, it is also a lesson in healing. We see from his experience that healing does not necessarily mean cure, if by cure we mean the removal of the disease. We see too that there is more than one method of healing and this has already become obvious in our studies of healing in the New Testament. Paul's healing was not left to the natural healing processes of his body as it was in the case of Epaphroditus (Philippians 2.27), nor was it dealt with by the exercise of any gift of healing, but by the provision of an antidote of grace to counteract the debilitating effect of his thorn in the flesh.

## 5. It is a source of reassurance.

The fifth way in which Paul's experience of the thorn in the flesh has significance for us today is as a source of reassurance and encouragement. It is not usually given to us to have the curtain drawn back to reveal the context and purpose of our experience of illness as it was for Paul. It is noteworthy that even in his case it was not drawn back at his first request for help, or he would not have needed to persist in prayer. However, he has recorded his experience for our encouragement so that when illness comes to us we can be reassured that it has a providential context and that in our experience of weakness we, like him, can expect to know the strength which God's grace in Jesus Christ can provide. This grace working through the various methods which God has provided and revealed to us may produce healing. If it does not result in the removal of the disease which afflicts us, as it did not in Paul's case, then it will still be true that God's power will increase in us as our strength declines. For us, as for Paul, it is still true that God's power comes to its full power in weakness, so that we experience the paradox of grace that when we are really weak is the time when we are truly strong.

In a world where people still suffer from sickness and disease, this record cannot be dismissed as either simply antiquarian or irrelevant. In the hour of pain and suffering, Christians can know that their experience is not an accident outside the purpose of God resulting from a suspension of his providence, but a situation in which God is active for good with everything under his control. From this we can draw encouragement and reassurance as we face our own experience of illness and suffering, and follow the example of Paul and seek healing and strength from the Lord.

# Chapter 20
# HEALING IN THE EPISTLE OF JAMES (I)

The epistle of James is one of the most Jewish of the letters of the New Testament and yet is written in excellent idiomatic Greek. Its language is 'purer and more cultured than in any other New Testament book'.[1] The epistle is traditionally ascribed to James the half-brother of Jesus (Matthew 13.55 says 'brothers') and there is no decisive argument against this traditional view and no more credible alternative to it.[2] The epistle must, therefore, have been written before James died a martyr's death in AD 62,[3] and will reflect the thought and practice of the apostolic Church in Jerusalem where James was one of the Church leaders (Galatians 1.19).

The epistle is described by Hunter as pithy, prophetic and practical.[4] It is written in a simple vivacious and direct style with its meaning often expressed in aphorisms and epigrams, and illustrated by apt similes from nature and from human life. It breathes a prophetic passion and his attitude to the rich in 1.9-11; 2.1-7 and 5.1-4 has earned James the name of the Amos of the New Testament. The practical character of the epistle is shown by the fact that its one-hundred-and-eight verses contain no less than fifty-four imperatives, giving an average of one imperative for every two verses. It is, therefore, an epistle of exhortation and practice.

This epistle is the least theological of all the New Testament epistles with the exception of Paul's epistle to Philemon. As a consequence it has long lain under the undiscerning condemnation of it by Martin Luther as 'an epistle full of straw' containing little to feed the Christian soul because it contained nothing about the gospel when compared with the other books of the New Testament.[5] He thought so little of the epistle that according to the record in his Table Talk he said, 'Some day I will use James to heat my stove', i.e., burn it.[6] In fairness to Luther, however, it must be said that he agreed that it contained many good sayings and he thought highly of its emphasis on the law of God. Although we can understand the reason underlying his attitude to the epistle, we can also be glad that it has been preserved in the New Testament canon to remind us that the Christian life may begin and continue in faith, but unless the daily life of believers exemplifies their faith, then that faith is not a living reality.

Every commentator on this epistle remarks on the difficulty of reducing its contents to a logical plan. Hunter describes it as 'the despair of the analyst", and Luther says that its author 'throws things together so chaotically',[8] whilst Calvin more tactfully speaks of it as 'a rich source of varied instruction'.[9] The epistle appears to consist of a series of sayings and admonitions without any apparent order or connection, although the repetition of themes and catchwords has been recognised as giving a measure of unity to the whole.[10] This feature has led to the suggestion that it is basically a sermon in the Jewish tradition and one which shows many parallels with the Sermon on the Mount for, as Knox remarks, 'James has always kept the Sermon on the Mount well in view'.[11] Another theory regards the epistle as essentially an exposition of the contents and implications of the *Shema* of the sixth chapter of Deuteronomy. More recent study has recognised a substantial literary coherence in the epistle combined with a carefully-styled opening thematic statement (1.2-27) and an equally carefully constructed closing section (5.7-20).[12] Turner has drawn attention to the chain of words which proceeds throughout the book, with one word providing the link between two short discussions or sentences. These connecting words appear to have a didactic purpose facilitating the committing to memory of the teaching of the book.[13]

Our present concern is with one short paragraph of the closing section of the epistle, namely, James 5.13-18, which is translated as follows in the NRSV:

> Are any among you suffering? They should pray. Are any cheerful? They should sing songs of praise. Are any among you sick? They should call for the elders of the church and have them pray over them, anointing them with oil in the name of the Lord. The prayer of faith will save the sick, and the Lord will raise them up; and anyone who has committed sins will be forgiven. Therefore confess your sins to one another, and pray for one another, so that you may be healed. The prayer of the righteous is powerful and effective. Elijah was a human being like us, and he prayed fervently that it might not rain, and for three years and six months it did not rain on the earth. Then he prayed again, and the heaven gave rain and the earth yielded its harvest.

This paragraph provides one of the few glimpses into the healing practice of the apostolic Church that we have in the New Testament. As we have already seen from our study of Paul's mention of the gift of healing in his Corinthian correspondence, it is not easy to construct a coherent picture of the healing activity of the apostolic Church. The few references we have to it in the Acts of the Apostles and the epistles only raise more questions than they answer.

## WHAT JAMES SAID

When we turn to the paragraph in question, we note first of all that its main subject is that of prayer. The key verse of the paragraph is found in verse sixteen in the words, 'The prayer of the righteous is powerful and effective'. The topic of healing is thus dealt with in the context of prayer. It is worth emphasising this fact because many commentators have obscured it. Even so sane and learned a commentator as Alfred Plummer introduced his remarks on this paragraph by saying, 'Two subjects stand out prominently in this interesting passage - the elders of the Church and the anointing of the sick'.[14] These two subjects became very prominent in the later history of the Church, but we cannot feel that they were as prominent in the mind of the author or of his readers as Plummer suggests. Other commentators characterise the contents of this paragraph as simply a list of miscellaneous Church activities, and fail to notice the occurrence of the word 'prayer' in each verse of the paragraph which ends with the great example of Elijah as someone whose prayer was powerful and effective in his day. The intention of the author is to underline how prayer is the basis of all the activities of the Church, and its healing ministry is no exception to this.

The passage before us readily divides into the following three sections:

1. Three groups of people are characterised and advised what to do (vv.13-14a).

2. The advice for the third group (the sick) is described in more detail (vv.14b-16).

3. The effectiveness of the recommended procedure is illustrated from the experience of Elijah (vv.17-18).

## The three groups

The three groups of people consist of those who are suffering, those who are cheerful and those who are sick.

### 1. Are any among you suffering? (v.13)

The verb is *kakopatheo* which means 'to be in trouble of any sort, to suffer misfortune'. The cognate noun has already been used in verse ten to describe the example of the prophets in suffering affliction. Here in verse thirteen, the emphasis seems to be neither on the misfortune nor on the suffering but on the feeling of unhappiness or depression which these produce. The Vulgate was therefore correct in translating this question as *Tristatur aliquis uestrum?* which Knox translates in his English version as 'Is one of you unhappy?'[15] This feeling of unhappiness is in contrast to that of happiness in the latter part of the verse. The first group of people consist, therefore, of those who are unhappy or depressed because they are in trouble of some kind. This need not be because of their faith as it was in the case of the prophets in the previous paragraph, but because of the misfortune which is the common lot of those who live in this world.

## 2. Are any cheerful? (v.13)

The AV has 'merry' which is not a good translation as this word refers to outward hilarity rather than inward cheerfulness. The verb is *euthumeo* and like *kakopatheo* it is used only three times in the New Testament. The other two occasions are in Acts 27.22 and 25 where Paul exhorts his companions to take heart as they face the wreck of the ship on which they are sailing with all the danger to life and limb which that entailed. The verb can therefore refer to being in good heart (so REB here) in spite of facing misfortune and trouble, and thus indicates an attitude of mind rather than a specific situation in life. James has no particular situation in mind, but has in view all those whose present lot is happiness as opposed to the unhappiness of which he has just spoken in the previous verse.

Everybody falls into one or other of these groups. They are either happy or unhappy, in trouble or out of it, facing good fortune or misfortune. It might seem that James had included everyone in these two groups, but he goes on to speak of a third category of people.

## 3. Are any among you sick? (v.14)

This third category may be regarded as a special section of the first. Here the misfortune or the suffering is due to sickness, and so the unhappiness or distress has a physical cause and this justifies the recognition by James of a third category, those who are sick.

### The advice given

Each of these three groups is recommended to do something. Those who are unhappy as they face misfortune or are in trouble are advised to pray (v.13a). There is no promise that this will remove the cause of the unhappiness, but it will remove the unhappiness itself. Those who are happy and cheerful are recommended to sing hymns of praise to God. In both cases the tense of the verb is the present imperative which implies that the action of praying or praising should become a habit and go on constantly.

The first verb is *proseuchomai* which is the common one for praying in the New Testament and always means praying to God. The second verb is one of the three Greek verbs used for singing. There is not as much about singing in the New Testament as we might expect. The three verbs are only used thirteen times between them and the corresponding nouns only nine times. The verb used here is *psallo* which originally meant to play on a stringed instrument, and ultimately to sing praise to God without necessarily specifying any instrument or type of hymn (cp. 1 Corinthians 14.15 and Ephesians 5.19).

### The case of the sick

The procedure recommended for the third group is significantly different from that which was recommended to the first two groups. In their case the procedure did not necessarily involve anyone but the person concerned. The third group, however, were to call in the elders of the Church. This may well have been the reason why James separated the sick into a third group rather than leaving them in the first group, since the Church had a special responsibility for the sick. Harnack regarded this verse as 'a clear proof that all aid in cases of sickness was looked upon as a concern of the Church'.[16] As if to underline this difference in procedure where the sick are concerned, James changes the tense from the present imperative to the aorist imperative which implies that the action of the verb is to be done immediately and on one occasion only. The third significant difference in the procedure is that it is prescribed in more detail than in the case of the other two groups. This leads us on to the second section of the paragraph.

## The procedure for the sick

The sick person is to call for the elders of the Church and when they come they are to do two things. They are to pray over the sick person, and they are to anoint them with olive oil (*elaion*) in the name of the Lord (v.14b). These two actions are based on the recognition that it is God who is the source of healing. Of the two procedures, prayer is the more significant. This is indicated by the fact that 'pray' is the main verb in this clause and 'anoint' is a subordinate participle.

It is difficult to be certain of the time relationship of these two activities. The instruction to anoint the sick with oil is expressed by an aorist participle, which usually means that the action it describes precedes that of the main verb which in this case concerns prayer. This is why the RSV margin translates the clause, 'Let them pray over him, having anointed him with oil in the name of the Lord'. However, since there are numerous examples where the aorist participle appears to denote a simultaneous action, it is probable and more natural to understand the anointing and the prayer as occurring simultaneously.[17] It should be noted that James gives no guidance about where on the body the sick person should be anointed.

The elders are to stretch out their hands over the sick person and pray for their healing as they lie in bed. The type of prayer which would be effective is defined in verse fifteen as 'the prayer of faith'. In response to this believing prayer, the sick person will be saved (*sozo*), raised up by the Lord and be forgiven any sins they have committed. James does not instruct the sick person to confess their sins to the elders and so there is no justification here for the practice of auricular confession to a priest. The fact that the prayer of faith will result in healing for the sick shows that it is not offered in anticipation of death, but of recovery.

In verse sixteen, James appears to ignore the elders as he goes on to say that all members of the congregation can take part in healing. They should confess their sins to one another and pray for one another and they will be healed (*iaomai*). These imperatives are again in the present tense implying that both confession and prayer should be the usual activities in the circumstances of sickness. This encouragement of mutual confession and prayer for each other is an indication of the close sympathy and fellowship which existed between members of the early Christian community. It is noteworthy that there is no mention of anointing with oil in this verse. This appears to be reserved for the elders alone to do.

## The place of prayer

The final sentence of this second section (v.16b) is the key to the whole paragraph. Here James defines the kind of prayer which is most effective in healing. It is the earnest prayer of one who is righteous. There has been much debate about James' comment on prayer here, and in particular about the meaning of the present participle *energoumene* ('being made effective').

Apart from a brief mention in the sixth verse of his first chapter, James speaks of prayer only in this paragraph of his epistle and with only one exception he always uses the verb *proseuchomai* or its derived noun *proseuche*. The one exception is in our sentence where he uses the noun *deesis* which is a less common word for prayer than *proseuche*. *Deesis* denotes prayer which springs out of a definite need, a specific petition for help in a particular situation. He goes on to say that when this kind of prayer is prayed by a righteous man it is powerfully effective. This is the plain meaning of James here, but debate has centred round the participle *energoumene*, whether it should be construed as in the passive or the middle voice. Mayor, who wrote the classic commentary on this epistle, argued strongly for the passive meaning, namely, that the prayer of a righteous man is powerful in what it is enabled to do by the Holy Spirit (cp. Romans 8.26).[18] The meaning of the middle voice, on the other hand, is that the prayer of a righteous man is powerful in what it is able to do by itself, without any special enabling by the Holy Spirit, and this is the meaning which is preferred by most modern translators and commentators.[19]

## The example of Elijah

James goes on to give an example of one who was righteous and whose prayer was powerful and effective. He chooses Elijah, an example which is not obviously related to the subject of healing and which is a reminder that the subject of the paragraph is prayer rather than healing. Elijah had come to hold a special place in Jewish thought.[20] This is shown by the twenty-eight references to him in the gospels, or nineteen if we exclude the nine parallel references, as well as in Ecclesiasticus 48.1-9. James reminds his readers that Elijah was one of like nature with themselves and then goes on to give them an example of his effective prayer.

If we turn to the Old Testament record of the incident to which James alludes in this passage, we find that he has deduced from it certain matters which are not explicitly stated in the text.[21] We are not told in the text, for instance, that Elijah prayed for drought. We are told in 1 Kings 17.1 that he was able to declare on the authority of the God of Israel that there would be a drought, and we may deduce the fact of his prayer from the phrase 'before whom I stand'. The reference in James 5.17 to the length of the drought, which is also mentioned in Luke 4.25, is a deduction from 1 Kings 18.1 which speaks of the third year of the drought. Finally there is no reference to Elijah's prayer for the end of the drought in the Old Testament narrative, although it may be assumed that such a prayer was offered by Elijah.

## WHAT JAMES MEANT

In the previous section we have seen what James said in his short paragraph. We now turn to ask what he meant by what he said. His injunctions to the first two groups of people, those who were unhappy and in trouble and those who were cheerful even though they might be in trouble, are clear. Prayer and praise cover all life's situations and sanctify both sorrow and joy for God's people.

In the case of the third group, those who were sick, James' meaning is not immediately clear. There are several words and phrases that he uses which need closer examination in order to discover their meaning.

### Sickness

First of all, we must ask what James understood about the nature and cause of sickness. He uses two different words for sickness in this paragraph and both of them describe the physical effect of sickness rather than sickness itself. This is typical of the words used for sickness in most languages, for such words are descriptive of the effect of sickness rather than indicative of its nature. This derives from the fact that people experience the symptoms which sickness produces before they reflect on its nature and explains why the traditional names for many diseases are descriptions of their symptoms, rather than indications of their nature or cause.

The first word James uses is the verb *astheneo* which occurs in verse fourteen. Its basic meaning is 'to be weak' and presumably it came to applied to sickness because of the bodily weakness it caused. As we have already seen, this verb and its derivatives form the commonest words used for physical illness in the New Testament. We may therefore assume that it is physical sickness is referred to here since it is contrasted with mental distress and treated with a physical remedy (olive oil).[22]

The second word used by James is the verb *kamno* which occurs only three times in the New Testament. The present participle of this verb is employed in verse fifteen to describe the sick person on their bed. It is also the word used for the sick in the Hippocratic oath.[23] The verb originally meant 'to work', then it meant 'to be weary as the result of constant work' as in Hebrews 12.3 and Revelation 2.3, and finally 'to be weary from sickness' as here.[24]

Although these two words have different etymologies, there is no valid reason for distinguishing between them in usage. They both mean 'to be sick'. Outside the New Testament, however, a further extension of meaning of *kamno* occurred and the verb came to mean 'to die' as in Wisdom 4.16 and 15.9, and this has been used to justify the basing of the practice of extreme unction on verse fifteen. Tasker remarks that the verb used in its past tenses has been used as a description of the dead, 'but as there is no instance of the present participle conveying the meaning of "the dying", it is most improbable that is the sense here, and that the writer means to suggest that the sick person is *in extremis*'.[25]

Even apart from the question of tense usage, the context would appear to exclude any extension of the meaning of *kamno* here. If we accept the extended meaning of the verb in verse fifteen as given in the lexicons,[26] then the meaning of the passage would be that, although Christians should call in the elders of the Church for all sickness (v.14), only those who were actually dying would be healed. This is unlikely to be what James meant, and so we see no real reason for distinguishing between the meaning of the two verbs in this context.

What kind of sickness did James have in mind? This question is important because some authors maintain that what James describes here is exorcism and not the healing of physical disease. In his commentary on this passage, Dibelius concludes that 'the whole procedure is an exorcism' in spite of the complete absence of any such indication in the text.[27] The main clue lies in the usage of the verb *astheneo* and its derivatives, as we may ignore the rare verb *kamno* in this case. A close examination of the usage of the verb *astheneo* and its derived forms in the New Testament will show that these words are always applied to physical disease when they are used in a pathological sense and do not simply mean weakness. In at least three cases the condition they describe is carefully distinguished from demon possession. These are in the verses Luke 4.40; 8.2 and Acts 5.16. In view of this clear indication of usage, we feel that we are justified in concluding that James meant physical sickness when he spoke of anyone being sick (*asthenes*) in the community to which he wrote. The nearest we can còme to an understanding of the kind of sickness he had in mind is to say that it appears to have been acute in onset and have confined the sick person to bed or confined them to their house so that the elders had to be called to them (v.14).

The important question here, however, is the relationship between sickness and sin. It is frequently maintained that the Old Testament view is that sickness is due to personal sin, and that this is the view that James sets forth in this passage. Neither of these suggestions can be sustained. As we have already mentioned, Rowley points out that the rigid equation of desert and fortune or of sin and suffering is 'nowhere characteristic of the Old Testament as a whole'.[28]

Likewise whoever insists that James teaches such a rigid doctrine has missed the significance of the particle 'if' in verse fifteen. James says that if the sickness is the result of some personal sin, then this sin will be forgiven the sick person in response to the prayer of faith of the elders. Thus Mayor suggests that the final clause of verse fifteen should be interpreted as 'if he has committed sins which have given rise to this sickness' he will be forgiven.[29] The clear implication of this is that there are some illnesses which are due to personal sin, and some which are not. It is certainly true that there is an organic connection between sickness and sin for there would be no sickness in the world if there were no sin, but we may not go on to conclude that an individual's sickness is always due to their own personal sin. This is contrary to human experience and certainly not what James says here.

## Healing

James speaks of healing only twice in this paragraph and uses a different word each time. In verse fifteen he uses *sozo* and in verse sixteen he uses the verb *iaomai*. When we discussed the meaning of *sozo* in Chapter Seven, we saw how in the gospels this verb included both physical healing and spiritual salvation and therefore could be used for the complete healing of the whole person. Since spiritual salvation in the form of forgiveness of sin is specified separately in the same verse, James appears to use *sozo* here in the sense of physical healing. On the other hand, the verb *iaomai* was used exclusively for physical healing in the gospels except for one instance when it was used of exorcism (Luke 9.42). It is clear that in this paragraph this verb is used to include both recovery from sickness and forgiveness of sin for healing is associated with the confession of sin where this is appropriate.

Verse fifteen provides the three basic components of the Christian definition of healing. Here we are told that in response to the prayer of faith three things will happen:

1. The sick person will be made well (*sozo*).

2. They will be raised up by the Lord.

3. They will be forgiven any sins they may have committed.

The first part of the definition refers to physical healing for, as we have just suggested, it is the sense of physical healing which predominates in James' use of the verb *sozo* here.

The second part of the definition says that in response to the prayer of faith, the Lord will raise up the sick person. The word *egeiro* is the usual one used for the physical resurrection of our Lord from the dead, but it is plainly not used of raising the dead in our paragraph. In Mark 1.31 it is used of the healing of Simon Peter's mother-in-law and in Matthew 9.6 of the healing of the paralytic. We therefore take it in a physical sense here. The Lord not only heals the sick of their disease, he also raises them up from their bed to put them on their feet again with new strength and vitality (cp. Mark 9.27 and John 5.8).

The final part of the definition is clearly spiritual and so completes the definition of healing by extending it to the whole of the human being. If the sick person has committed sins they will be forgiven by God (v.15). There is no suggestion that the sick person may never have sinned, but only that their present sickness may or may not be connected with their sins. The tense of the verb is the perfect which suggests that the sick person may have committed some sin of which the present condition is the consequence. If this is so, then its healing will include forgiveness.

Healing, then, in the Christian understanding of the term may be summed up in the following three propositions:

1. The removal of physical disease.

2. The restoration of bodily strength.

3. The forgiveness of sins.

James is quite clear that healing is always more than physical for it includes the whole being of the human person.

## The elders of the Church

The sick person was to call for 'the elders of the Church'. Who and what were these *presbuteroi*? We may be quite sure they were not priests in the sacerdotal sense because the New Testament word for this office is *hiereus*, which is never applied to a separate class of people but only to saints or Christian believers in general. In this sense all Christian believers are priests (1 Peter 2.5; Revelation 1.6; 5.10 and 20.6). Having said this, we must add that we know very little about the elders of the apostolic Church in spite of all the intensive study of the origins of the Christian ministry in recent years. In contrast to his account of the appointment of deacons in Acts 6.1-6, Luke tells us nothing about how elders came to be appointed. This suggests that they were not a novelty in the Church and when we put this together with the fact that it is at Jerusalem that we first hear of elders (Acts 11.30), it seems probable that the apostolic Church originally organised itself along the same lines as the synagogue. We may conclude, therefore, that the synagogue custom of choosing a body of senior men or elders to have oversight of its worship and well-being was also followed by the early Church. It is a body such as this that James has in view in this passage. The *ekklesia* or Church of which they were the elders was the local Christian community or congregation which was the local embodiment and expression of the Church Universal, as in Philemon 2. Thus the NEB translation calls them 'the elders of the congregation'.[30]

Why were the elders called in? Were they called in as representatives of the Christian community they led, or did this healing function belong to their office as elders? These are important questions for the healing ministry of the Church today. In so far as the office of the elder is defined in the New Testament there is no suggestion that healing the sick was a specific function of this office. There is no reference to healing as a function of elders or bishops in the Pastoral Epistles, where these terms describe the same office. Apart from these epistles there is no mention of elders in the epistles of Paul. Thus in the lists of offices and functions given in First Corinthians there is no mention of the office of elder and the gift of healing was given to those whom the Holy Spirit willed to give it (1 Corinthians 12.9, 28, 30). Even in our present passage, James says that healing is possible for all members of the Church to practise in verse sixteen, while in verses fourteen and fifteen he associates healing with the elders alone. The most probable view is that the elders were called in as representatives of the congregation and not because of any healing function which belonged to their office as elders. There is no evidence to support Dibelius' suggestion that 'they must be bearers of miraculous power by virtue of the fact that they are the elders'.[31] Intercession for others was part of their pastoral care and duty certainly, but it was a duty which was shared by all members of the congregation as they prayed for each other (v.16).

The elders were to be summoned as a body, and it is of interest to note that Luke in the Acts always refers to the elders as a body and never as individuals. James does not envisage an individual elder acting as a healer in private, but only of healing as a corporate function of the body of elders of a congregation. Bengel in his comment on this passage speaks of the elders as the highest Medical Faculty of the Church (*Ecclesiae summa Facultas Medica*) and deplores its loss in his own day because of the lack of faith.[32]

## Prayer

As we have indicated, prayer is the main topic of this paragraph and in verses fifteen and sixteen it is specifically stated that prayer will heal the sick. It is important, therefore, that we should understand what type of prayer James means here. He sets this out in the following three phrases:

'The prayer (*euche*) of faith' (v.15).

'The prayer (*deesis*) of the righteous' (v.16).

'He prayed fervently (*proseuche proseuxato*)' (v.17).

We may deduce the type of prayer which James regards as being effective for healing from an examination of these phrases. It is to be prayer based on faith and proceeding from faith without doubting (cp. James 1.6). Since it is the elders who pray it is their faith which is in view and not the faith of the sick person. It is to be the prayer of a righteous person, one who is in a right relationship to God and able to stand in his presence before him as Elijah did. It is to be specifically related to the need out of which it arises. This is the significance of the word *deesis* used in the second phrase. It is to be a specific prayer for the healing of the sick person to whom the elders have been called, and not vague intercession for the sick in general. Finally, if the prayer is to be effective it is to be made fervently. This phrase in verse seventeen is one of the few Hebraisms in the epistle of James, reflecting the infinitive absolute in Hebrew. *Proseuche proseuxato* means literally that Elijah 'prayed with prayer' and is a means of expressing the great intensity of his prayer. We may summarise the type of prayer which James regards as effective in healing as that which is earnest and believing, which is specifically directed to its object, and which springs from the offerer's close relationship to God. It should be noted that the prayer arises out of the faith of the elders; there is no mention of faith on the part of the sick person, although faith of some kind is implied in their calling in the elders in the first place.

The unqualified nature of the two statements in verses fifteen and sixteen that prayer will result in healing is worth noting. However, we may not draw from this unqualified relationship of the prayer of faith and healing, the apparent corollary that if healing does not occur then either the prayer has not been earnest enough or the faith has not been strong enough. This apparently sound logic is not the logic of faith, for there are other reasons why healing has not occurred. This is why most commentators tone down these statements by saying that we must understand the unexpressed qualification that healing will only occur if it is the will of God. This is a legitimate qualification and is in accord with the teaching of the rest of the New Testament. For instance, we have already seen how Paul prayed three times to be healed of his thorn in the flesh according to 2 Corinthians 12.8, but healing was not granted. God had another reason why his affliction should continue and so healing in his case did not include the removal of his disease, but a new use for it in Paul's relationship to God and his fellows.

# Chapter 21

# HEALING IN THE EPISTLE OF JAMES (II)

## WHAT JAMES MEANT *(CONTINUED)*

### Anointing with oil

We come now to one of the most interesting questions associated with our passage, although it cannot be regarded as the most important. When the elders were called in by the sick person they were to anoint them with oil. James gives the impression that this was not a new procedure he was suggesting, but simply what he would expect to be the normal custom with which his readers would be familiar. Had it been something new, we would have expected him to give more details about it and explain its significance.

The oil specified was olive oil (*elaion*) obtained by crushing the fruit of the olive tree (*Olea europaea*) which was widely cultivated in Palestine in Biblical times. The oil would be freely available in the Mediterranean world of the first century AD, as it is today. It would be readily available in every household where it was used for culinary, toilet and medicinal purposes, as well as in domestic lamps and religious rites. There is no suggestion that the elders took special oil with them when they were called to the house of the sick person; we may presume that they found it readily available there.

This ready availability of olive oil in the homes of ancient world and its common use as a domestic and even as a professional remedy creates a presumption in favour of the view that James was here referring to the medicinal use of the oil rather than the religious one. In the very nature of the case, the religious and ritual use of anointing with oil would be much rarer than its medicinal use. This raises the problem of the real significance of the anointing of the sick with oil which James recommended. To a consideration of this problem we now turn.

Two different words are used in the New Testament for the application of oil to the body. *Aleipho* is the humbler non-sacred word and almost always means to apply oil to the body for toilet or healing purposes as in Matthew 6.17 and Mark 6.13. The other word is *chrio* which is the sacred and official term for anointing with oil but is never used in the New Testament for the physical act of anointing with oil, only in the figurative sense of anointing by God to denote his commissioning of an individual such as he gave to his Son Jesus Christ (See Luke 4.18; Acts 4.27; 10.38 and Hebrews 1.9). Here in

James the humbler word *aleipho* is used. In the New Testament this distinction in usage is strictly maintained, but this is not true of the usage of the two words outside the New Testament.[1]

There have been two views of the significance of anointing the sick in this passage. The first view is that it was a medical procedure in which the oil was used medicinally. In other words, James was saying that normal medical methods should be used in the name of the Lord along with believing prayer. On this view we should translate the clause in verse fourteen in modern terms such as those suggested by Sugden, 'Let them pray over the sick person, giving them their medicine in the name of the Lord'.[2] If it be objected that this instruction of James could not now apply to all cases of sickness for olive oil could have a specific effect in only a few, then the evidence is that in the first century AD anointing with oil was a common supportive procedure in many cases of systemic illness. Thus the elder Pliny observes that 'olive oil has the property of imparting warmth to the body and protecting it against cold, and also of cooling the head when heated'.[3] Josephus records how Herod the Great in his last illness was lowered into a bath of hot oil by his physicians in order to warm his body.[4] According to the Mishnah, anointing the body with oil (but not scented oil) was one of the procedures allowed to Jews on the Sabbath for pain in the loin, which may have been the severe pain of renal colic.[5] In addition, the Jerusalem Talmud allows anointing of the head with oil for headache on the Sabbath.[6]

Our most complete information on medical practice in this period, albeit from a Roman source, giving an account of Greek medical practice, comes from the Latin treatise *De Medicina (On Medicine)* to which we have already had occasion to refer many times in this book. It was written in the first century AD by Aulus Cornelius Celsus who is sometimes called the Roman Hippocrates. In the first four books of this work there are numerous references to the use of anointing with oil (*unctio*) in the treatment of different systemic diseases, and a general statement that 'it is desirable that even in acute and recent diseases the body should be anointed and then gently stroked, but only during remissions and before food. But prolonged rubbing is unsuitable in acute and increasing diseases'.[7]

Anointing with oil with or without massage is not to be regarded as a panacea or cure-all. It is essentially a supportive measure and the oil is not used because it is believed to be a universally specific remedy with some inherent healing property.

The second view regards the anointing with oil as a religious act with no medical significance. Those who hold this view usually regard the act of anointing as partly or wholly sacramental in character, and so this view found its ultimate development in the Roman Catholic sacrament of extreme unction. This name refers to the anointing given by a priest to one who is *in extremis* and in danger of death. In fact, this practice has no warrant in this passage, which speaks of anointing the sick in anticipation of healing, and not of anointing the dying in anticipation of their death. In recognition of this fact, the Second Vatican Council (1962-1965) suggested that the name 'anointing of the sick' might replace that of 'extreme unction'.[8] However, after an examination of this change of name, Dickinson concluded that the original doctrine of extreme unction was in no way basically altered, but only modified by being extended to cover not only those who are at the point of death but also those who are seriously ill.[9]

Calvin rejected both the view that the oil was used as a medicament and that which regarded the anointing as a sacrament, and accepted the view that the use of the oil had a religious significance. He believed that it symbolised the Holy Spirit and witnessed to God's healing presence and power during the process of anointing the sick.[10] This view has recently been maintained by Shogren who appeals for support to the custom of pouring or smearing oil on the head which was an ancient ritual in Israel. Such anointing was used in the setting apart of priests, kings and prophets in the Old Testament. Shogren maintains that these cases indicate that oil is 'a general symbol of God's special presence, election and good favour'.[11] The difficulty with this view is that healing may also take place at the instance of the Church members without any anointing with oil (v.16). If we accept this view then it would appear to imply that God is not specially present in cases of healing where oil is not used.

This description of the ritual use of oil for anointing as a symbol of God's presence at the ceremony and his approval of what was being done, does not appear to be an adequate explanation of its use in the Old Testament. The dominant idea behind its use there is that of the consecration or setting apart of persons or things to a special office or function. Thus we find anointing described at the consecration of priests (Exodus 30.30), kings (1 Samuel 10.1; 16.13; 1 Kings 1.39; 2 Kings 9.6 and 11.12) and prophets (1 Kings 19.16 and Isaiah 61.1), and at the dedication of the Tabernacle and all the objects associated with it (Exodus 30.26-29). It is difficult to recognise this concept of anointing as a setting apart in James 5.14 unless we accept Motyer's suggestion that 'the oil may signify a separating off of the sickness from the patient to Christ' such as is referred to in Matthew 8.17.[12]

In only two places in the Old Testament is anointing specifically associated with the presence or activity of God. In the account of David's anointing with oil by Samuel we are told that 'the Spirit of the Lord came mightily upon David from that day forward' (1 Samuel 16.13). In Isaiah 61.1 the prophet describes how 'the Spirit of the Lord God is upon me because the Lord has anointed me to bring good tidings to the afflicted'. Jesus applied this verse to himself after he had read the passage during the synagogue service at Nazareth (Luke 4.16-21). He had been anointed and sent to preach good news to the poor and to proclaim the acceptable year of the Lord. There is, however, no account of his being physically anointed with oil as he begins his ministry, only an account of his baptism by John when the Holy Spirit descended upon him (Matthew 3.16-17; Mark 1.9-11 and Luke 3.21-22). The word 'anointed' thus appears to be used metaphorically for his consecration as the Messiah ('The Anointed One') as represented by his baptism.

In the New Testament epistles, an 'anointing' is spoken of which means the coming of the Holy Spirit on individual Christian believers. It should be noted, however, that in these epistles there is no association of this anointing with baptism as there was in the case of Jesus. The significance of this anointing is that it marks them out as belonging to the people of God (2 Corinthians 1.21-22) and is the source of their knowledge of Christian truth (1 John 2.20, 27, cp. John 16.13). This means that this anointing is to be distinguished from that of which James speaks. In the first place, the words which describe the anointing are the verb *chrio* and the noun *chrisma* which is derived from it. As we have seen already, the verb used by James here is *aleipho* and not *chrio*. Secondly, the purpose of the anointing is for the identification and the enlightenment of the Christian believer and not for healing as it is in James. Finally, there is no mention of the use of oil, for the references are clearly metaphorical and spiritual, and not literal and physical.

In spite of this, the association of anointing with the coming of the Holy Spirit upon a person has led to the suggestion that James 5.14 should be interpreted in these terms. The involvement of the Holy Spirit in healing is said to be implied by the use of oil. In this way, healing as described by James might be linked up with the gift of healing spoken of by Paul in 1 Corinthians 12.1-11 as one of the gifts of the Holy Spirit. However attractive such a suggestion might be, there is no doubt that anointing with oil and the use of a special gift of healing from the Holy Spirit are never associated together in the New Testament. Jesus never used oil in healing and did not mention its use when he commissioned the Twelve to heal, although they said that they had used it (Mark 6.13).[13] Paul never mentions the use of oil and James never mentions the use of a special gift of healing. It is advisable, therefore, to regard them as separate procedures both of which are appropriate in their own sphere, and not to seek to bring them together.

In order to determine the significance of the use of olive oil recommended by James, we must consider what uses are described for it elsewhere in the New Testament. It was used in lamps to provide illumination (Matthew 25.3-8); in cooking to prepare food (Revelation 6.6 and 18.13); for toilet purposes (Matthew 6.17 and Luke 7.46), and for the purpose of healing (Mark 6.13 and Luke 10.34). The only one of these uses which is appropriate to the mention of the use of oil in James is that of healing. This suggests that this was the use which James meant here. As we have already mentioned, nowhere in the New Testament is physical anointing with oil associated with the the presence or activity of the Holy Spirit. If we are to accept such an association here then we must explain why anointing with oil is not associated with any other activity of the Holy Spirit in the New Testament and why it was not used when the Holy Spirit was given to the disciples at Pentecost or to the Gentiles in the house of Cornelius (Acts 10.44-46).

The fact that it was only to be used for healing suggests that it had a unique application to situations of sickness, and the only satisfactory way to explain this is to recognise that this unique application was a medicinal one. This would explain why anointing with oil is not mentioned in connection with any other of the gifts of the Holy Spirit even though his activity is also responsible for their exercise as it is for that of the gift of healing.

There is probably not enough evidence in the passage to allow us to decide definitively whether the anointing with oil is to be regarded as medicinal or religious in character. However, a fuller analysis of the usage of the verb *aleipho* in the New Testament appears to support the medicinal view rather than the religious one. This verb is used nine times, once here in James and eight times in the gospels. It is never used in the gospels of anointing for a religious purpose, but usually for toilet or medicinal purposes. In seven instances it is used for smearing or rubbing the body with oil for toilet purposes (e.g. Matthew 6.17 and Luke 8.46), or for the preparation of a body for burial (Mark 16.1). In these cases the oil acted as a solvent or vehicle for the various spices, incenses and aromatics used as perfumes and cosmetics.[14] The remaining instance of the use of the verb is in Mark 6.13 where it refers to anointing for healing by the disciples. Here Mark tells us that 'they cast out many demons, and anointed with oil many that were sick and healed them'. This may simply mean that they used the medical procedure of anointing with oil along with the healing power and authority which Jesus had given them when he sent them out on their mission (cp. Luke 9.1).

There is a distinction in Mark 6.13 which should be noted. In spite of several contrary opinions, including that of Schlier,[15] anointing with oil is never used as part of the practice of exorcism in the New Testament. In this verse the healing of many sick people by anointing them with oil is carefully distinguished from the casting out of demons. This means that anointing with oil was used only for the healing of physical disease in the New Testament. This fact would be difficult to explain on the view that such an anointing was religious in nature with the oil symbolising the presence of the Holy Spirit. Thus we find Jesus specifically describing his driving out of demons from possessed persons as performed by the Holy Spirit (Matthew 12.28; the parallel reference in Luke 11.20 speaks of 'the finger of God'[16]), and yet we find no mention of oil being used in exorcisms carried out either by him or his disciples.[17]

Even though Mark 6.13 mentions the use of anointing with oil in the healing of the sick by the disciples, we have still to explain why the use of this procedure is never mentioned in any individual case of the healing of the sick by Jesus which is recorded in the gospels, or by the apostles in the book of Acts. On the religious view of its meaning, such an omission would mean that the Holy Spirit was not regarded as present at the particular healing being described, while the medicinal view of its significance would suggest that oil was not being used in the treatment and healing of the disease in that particular case.

In his comment on Mark 6.13, Swete regards the anointing with oil as perhaps serving to differentiate the miracles performed by the disciples from those performed by Jesus.[18] However, as there is no mention of anointing with oil in connection with cases of healing in the Acts of the Apostles nor any mention of this procedure in the epistles (except for James 5.14), this suggestion seems unlikely.

In the history of the Church there were several changes in the practice of anointing the sick with oil, which are more readily understood if the oil is regarded as a medicine rather than the symbolical material of a religious rite. One very significant change came in the ninth century AD when anointing of the sick was finally restricted to the priesthood of the Roman Catholic Church by the second Council of Chalon-sur-Saône (AD 813).[19] This restriction soon became universal throughout the Church. Prior to this, the anointing of the sick had been performed freely by lay members of the Church who were either sick themselves or were friends or relatives of the sick. The late origin of this restriction to presbyters or priests in the history of the Church is difficult to understand, if from the beginning it had been regarded as a religious rite. It would mean that for almost eight centuries the practice of the Church was in conflict with the clear instruction of James that the presbyters or elders of the Church should anoint the sick and the lay members of the Church should not. The practices of prayer and confession was all that was required of them for their healing of the sick (v.16). For the Church to leave the anointing to be carried out by lay members was contrary to what the instructions of James required. This would suggest that the anointing of the sick with oil was not regarded by the Church as a religious rite to be practised only by elders or priests, and whose exact observance was binding on it from the beginning and for all time.

There were also two further changes in the practice and usage of anointing which indicate an acceptance of the fact that the anointing with oil frequently failed to heal. Such an acceptance is more readily understood if the oil was regarded as a medicine which could fail to heal, rather than a symbol of the presence of the Holy Spirit whose involvement would not be expected to result in a failure to heal. The first of these changes was the introduction of measures which were designed to boost or supplement the efficacy of the oil. By the third century, the oil came to require special consecration before it was used for the purpose of anointing the sick. At first this could be carried out by a lay person, but eventually in the fifth century, Pope Innocent I who was pope from 401 to 417, decreed that the oil must be consecrated by a bishop.[20] However, once it was consecrated, the oil could be used by any Christian, ordained or lay, in the anointing of the sick. The oil might be taken from lamps used in Churches (cp. Exodus 27.20), or might be stored in martyrs' tombs or mixed with the relics of saints, all in order to increase its efficacy.[21] The second of these changes was the association of the anointing with oil not with healing, but with dying. This occurred about the middle of the twelfth century when the sacrament of extreme unction ('the last unction') was so named by Peter Lombard (c.1100-1164) as the fifth sacrament of the seven recognised by the Roman Catholic Church.[22] This view was officially adopted and promulgated by the Council of Trent at its fourteenth session in 1551. This marked the final loss of faith in the oil as a medicinal agent. This loss of faith reflected a change in contemporary medical opinion about the oil, which would have had no effect on the practice if it had been regarded only as a religious rite with no medical significance.

We cannot escape the feeling that a reference by James to what was a contemporary medical practice, made in order to illustrate the principle that both medical and non-medical methods of healing were valid methods for the treatment of the sick, has been mistaken for a binding instruction on the Church which confines its ministry of healing to only one method. We believe that James held that healing should be by a combination of medical and non-medical methods. In illustration of this, he referred to the contemporary medical method of anointing the sick with oil, and said that the elders should now combine this with prayer in the name of the Lord Jesus Christ, although ordinary Church members need not do so. The illustration has been taken to mean that the contemporary medical method of the use of oil described by James should be a permanent feature of the healing ministry of the Church, even though it would eventually fall out of use in medical practice as more effective medicines and procedures were discovered and used. But Jesus never used this method of healing and never specifically commissioned his disciples to use it, and James attributed healing to the prayer of faith which accompanied it, rather than to the application of the oil. The fact is not without significance that the Church did not appear to understand the practice of anointing and eventually came to change its meaning from that of a prelude to healing to that of a preparation for death. This would explain why the modern Church commonly neglects the practice altogether and often shows some embarrassment when the subject is raised.

One final relevant point should be made about the understanding of the anointing of the sick with oil which James recommends. If he intended it to be a religious and ritual act to apply for all time to come, then it may be argued that there is no place in the Christian ministry of healing for any of the modern medical and surgical procedures without which many sick people today would not be cured of their sickness. If on the other hand he intended it to be a medical procedure then the Christian ministry of healing may include such procedures, so that this ministry can adopt a comprehensive and holistic approach to sickness and disease.

## In the Name of the Lord

The instruction of James about how the anointing with oil should be done has immediate relevance to the point that we have just discussed. The fact that it was to be done 'in the name of the Lord' implies that such a procedure could be carried out without invoking the name of the Lord. If the procedure were a purely religious one, then it would have no meaning apart from such an invocation. If on the other hand, it was a medicinal procedure then it would still be meaningful even if it was not done in the name of the Lord. This suggests that James is saying that prayer and medical treatment should be combined and carried out 'in the name of the Lord'. Thus verse fourteen should be interpreted in the way suggested by Sugden and which we mentioned above, namely, that the elders should 'pray over the sick person and give him his medicine in the name of the Lord'.

The phrase 'in the name of the Lord' has given rise to some discussion on account of the questions which arise about its interpretation.[23]

The first question which has been raised concerns the identity of 'the Lord'. Is he God or Jesus Christ? Already in this chapter the name Lord has been used of Jesus (vv.7-8) and of the God of the Old Testament (vv.10-11). To the Christian there is no problem for Jesus Christ is God. Moreover, Jesus encouraged his disciples to pray in his name (Matthew 18.19-20; Mark 9.39; John 14.13-14; 15.6 and 16.23-26) and to do things in his name (Matthew 18.5 and Luke 10.17). In the latter verse we see how the Seventy disciples had used his name effectively in casting out demons. In addition, we read in the book of Acts, of healing carried out in the name of Jesus Christ (Acts 3.6; 4.30 and 16.18). There seems to be no doubt that James means Jesus Christ when he speaks here of the Lord.

A second question is whether the use of the name of the Lord is a request for the healing power of Jesus to be revealed, or a declaration of the authority on the basis of which that request is made. In fact, of course, the incidents of healing recorded in the Acts of the Apostles are both revelations of the healing power of Jesus and demonstrations of the authority which Peter and Paul possessed to heal in his name. To heal 'in the name of the Lord' means, therefore, both to heal by his power and to use the authority of Jesus Christ to use that power.

The final question is whether the use of the name is part of the prayer or a separate form and type of utterance. This question arises because we know that the name of Jesus was used as an incantation or magical formula by professed healers as mentioned, for instance, in Acts 19.13. Also, about the year AD 110 a controversy arose amongst the Jews of Palestine about whether persons might allow themselves to be healed in the name of Jesus.[24] In a Christian context it would seem most natural to regard the use of the name as included in the prayer which the elders prayed over the sick person (v.14). However, in the accounts of healing in Acts 3.6 and 16.18 there is no prayer (and no anointing) but a direct order in the name of Jesus Christ to secure the healing.

The use of this phrase 'in the name of the Lord' in this context has several implications. First, it expresses the confidence that the healing of the sick person comes from God who will raise them up from their beds (v.15). Second, it makes the healing procedure 'indisputably Christian'[25], and thirdly it assures us that both physical and spiritual methods find a place in the Christian approach to healing. It has also been suggested that the use of this phrase means that the act of anointing is to be regarded as a religious and ritual act rather than a medicinal one as we have suggested. However, this need not necessarily be so. Medicine can also be prescribed and given in the name of the Lord, and may even be psychologically more effective if given in this way.

It will be noted that the phrase is used only with reference to what the elders are to do. However, the Lord promised all his disciples that he would give them whatever they asked in his name (cp. John 14.13-14). We may presume, therefore, that the prayer of the members of the Church for the healing of their fellow-members which is referred to in verse sixteen would also be 'in the name of the Lord', although it is not explicitly stated that it should be.

## WHAT JAMES DID NOT SAY

In any study of healing in this epistle, significance must also be given to what James did not include in his description of what should be done in cases of sickness. When we consider his omissions, it is clear that he did not intend to give a complete account of the healing practice of the apostolic Church. This was for the very good reason that he was writing to those who were already familiar with such practice. It is unfortunate for us that we are not in a similar position today. The topics omitted by James include the following:

1. **The laying on of hands.** James makes no mention of the common method of touching or laying on of hands for the healing of sickness used by Jesus in the gospels and the apostles in the Acts. According to the records in these books, this method was used far more often than anointing with oil. James must have seen hands being laid on the sick to heal them, but he does not include this procedure in his advice to the sick and those who sought to heal them. Some authors have interpreted James' instruction to the elders

that they should pray over the sick person, 'to mean prayer with the laying on of hands'.[26] However, if James meant this he surely would have said so and we should not import this meaning into an otherwise clear description of the healing procedure he recommends. It is true, of course, that anointing involves touching the sick and so it may be argued that James did recognise touching as a means of healing. However, the method he described was not the simple one of the laying on of hands that Jesus has used, but one which involved in addition the application of oil to the body.

2. **Demon possession.** We have noted already that there is no mention of demon possession or exorcism in this passage. The sick are described by the verb *astheneo* which is never used in the New Testament to describe those who are demon-possessed. Exorcism in the the New Testament never includes touching the possessed person, and since anointing with oil would involve touching the possessed person, it would not be used in exorcism.

3. **The gifts of healing.** As we have seen, Paul in 1 Corinthians 12.9 spoke of 'gifts of healing' and how these were bestowed by the Holy Spirit on whom he will, and how they were to be used for the benefit of all members of the body of Christ. James does not mention such gifts, but appears to assume that all elders and even all members of the Church can heal. His emphasis is on the place of prayer in healing rather than on special gifts to individuals. There need be no real contradiction here. The presence of some with a special gift of healing does not mean that healing is necessarily confined to them, nor that all cannot share in healing. In any case, we do not know how extensively these gifts were present in the apostolic Church, for they are only mentioned in connection with the Church at Corinth. The fact is that James does not mention them here. The suggestion of Riecke that 'in the present passage in James, the elders are described as having extraordinary spiritual gifts, which enable them to heal the sick' is not supported by a careful study of the passage.[27]

4. **Anointing with oil.** James did not say that anointing with oil was essential for healing. It was to be carried out by elders when they were present, but healing could occur when elders were not present and when it would occur at the prayerful request of Church members (v.16). This apparently optional nature of the anointing with oil would appear to argue against its being regarded as a religious rite and certainly not a sacrament. It would also explain the absence of any record of its use in healing from the pages of the Acts and the epistles in the New Testament.

5. **Sin and sickness.** In James' view there is no absolute connection between personal sin and personal sickness. He leaves the connection open by saying if the sick person has sinned then he will be forgiven (v.15). There may be cases in which sin is the cause of the disease or is a hindrance to the occurrence of healing, and in these cases it should be confessed to fellow members of the Church community (v.16).

6. **Healing and Church Services.** In the ministry of healing as envisaged by James no place is given to services of public worship or celebrations of the Lord's Supper. This ministry is provided by a group of elders of the congregation to individual sick people who call them to their homes to carry out such a ministry in private.

7. **The duration of the ministry of healing.** Finally, James gives no indication of how long the practice of prayer and anointing with oil for the healing of the sick should continue in the Church. As Paul did not indicate how long the gift of healing would continue in the Church, so James does not say for how long the practice of prayer and anointing which he prescribes should continue to be practised.

## WHAT JAMES TEACHES

There are several principles concerning the Church and the healing of the sick which are embedded in this paragraph we have been considering.

### The Church and Healing

1. **The Church has a concern for the sick.** This is the clear implication of James' instruction to the sick person to send for the elders of the Church and to the ordinary Church members to pray for the sick that they may be healed. Both groups are to be involved because both are concerned. This is the first obvious deduction from this passage.

It is true that the primary application of the instruction is to the sick of the Christian community, just as the original commission of Jesus to his disciples was to heal the sick of the lost sheep of Israel according to Matthew 10.5-8. In practice, however, the Church has never been able to confine its healing ministry to its own sick. This appears in the Acts and has increasingly appeared in the history of the Church, especially in missionary situations.

In the minds of many people in western society today, the concern of the Church is one which is essentially peripheral to the main task of healing. The minister stands aside while the doctor does the real work of healing. Finally, when the doctor has done all he can, the minister is allowed to come in with the assumption that no more healing is possible and that all the minister can do is to prepare the sick person for death. This is not the view James takes here, for the clear implication of the passage is that the concern of the Church is not peripheral but central.

2. **Healing is part of the normal work of the Christian Church.** There is no suggestion in this passage that the healing work of the Church is something abnormal or extraordinary. It was part of the normal routine of the life of the Church. If someone fell ill, they sent for the elders of the Church and they came without any apparent reluctance or embarrassment to carry out a recognised procedure which was normally expected to result in the recovery of the sick person who had called them.

## Healing and the Church

1. **Healing is based within the Christian community.** In the epistle of James healing is based within the Christian community. It is to be practised by the elders and by the ordinary members of the Church and it is to be done in the name of the Lord. This continued to be the case for many centuries of the history of the Church. It was only with the rise and organisation of the medical and nursing professions that the basis of healing moved out from the Church to the community at large. It is this change which has resulted in so much uncertainty in the Church's attitude to healing and produced the tendency for the Church to withdraw from its healing ministry or to identify it with the practice of certain procedures which are usually included in the category of 'faith-healing'.

2. **The healing ministry of the Church includes all methods of healing.** If our interpretation of the reference to anointing with oil in this passage is correct, then James is here recommending the employment of both physical and non-physical methods of healing and their application in the name of the Lord. Even if this interpretation is not correct, the point still remains in view of all the benefits of modern medical healing. These benefits are the gift of God to suffering humanity and are to be used in the service of the sick. They are applied by Christian doctors in the course of their daily work and are therefore included in the healing ministry of the Church through its members. The Church uses all methods of healing in its ministry of healing, whether they be medical or non-medical. The method used in any particular case will depend on the skill and training of the person concerned. Methods which need medical knowledge and skill can only be applied by those who are medically trained. Every method of healing is represented amongst the members of the Church, and when those members are practising the method of healing for which they are trained they are sharing in the healing ministry of the Church. All methods of healing are thus available for the healing ministry of the Church and should be included within it.

## The Wholeness of Healing

1. **Sickness and healing always have more than a physical dimension.** James reminds us that there are more dimensions in healing than the purely physical. This is implied in the need for prayer and forgiveness, and the involvement of the Christian community in cases of sickness. The other dimensions have been obscured by the Cartesian separation of body and soul which still dominates popular thought today. Sickness always has more than a physical dimension even though it be so minor as the common cold. It always has mental, social and spiritual dimensions, and this paragraph of James reminds us of all of these. Similarly, healing cannot be confined to the physical or medical dimensions, but must include all the other ones too.

2. **Prayer and healing**. We end where we began by insisting that this whole paragraph is primarily concerned with prayer. Prayer is the basis of Christian healing when it is made in the name of Jesus Christ. It is also the bond which binds together all forms of healing and makes them effective in restoring wholeness.

In spite of all that we have said above, it may be inappropriate to try to distinguish between the medical and religious elements of James' description of healing. All the elements he describes are but part of the single event of healing which is bound together by the prayer which is the Christian response to human sickness, in the name of the Lord.[28] Thus there is a wholeness about healing as there is a wholeness about health because God is involved in both.

The paragraph in the epistle of James which has formed the basis of our study in this and the previous chapter is short, but its exegesis reveals that much has been based on it and much read into it. It has provided the main proof-text for auricular confession to a priest, unction and extreme unction by a priest, and faith-healing. It would be tragic if the Church continued to treat this passage as it has treated it in the past and missed what we believe to be its clear teaching.

We may summarise that teaching in the following terms. The Church has a healing function to perform in all cases of sickness. This function includes the use of all forms of healing through those who are professionally qualified and those who are not. All methods are to be applied in the name of Jesus Christ and supported by prayer. In this way and in other practical ways, all members of the Christian community can share in the healing of the sick. This healing is not confined to the repair of the body or the saving of the soul but includes both in the redemption of the whole person in every aspect of their being.

# PART FIVE

# HEALING IN THE MODERN CHURCH

OUR STUDY of the teaching and practice of the apostolic Church in Part Four has shown that the apostles and others associated with them healed men and women of disease, and also on occasion raised them from the dead. It follows, therefore, that they had the authority and ability to heal which they must have derived from Jesus Christ, their risen Lord.

Nevertheless, we have also seen that their use of this power to heal was not a prominent feature of the life of the apostolic Church, and was not always manifest even when a clear indication for it was present. Miracles of healing were not such a marked feature of the book of the Acts of the Apostles as they were of the gospels, even though the period of activity of the apostolic Church recorded in that book was about ten times longer than that of the earthly ministry of Jesus. Also, we did not read in Acts of any failures such as occurred in the case of the epileptic boy in the gospels, where it was said of the apostles in Matthew 17.16 that 'they could not heal him'. However, in the epistles it is recorded that Paul and three of his colleagues remained unhealed even though other members of the Church had the power to heal them.

The question now arises whether the modern Church still possesses the authority and ability to heal men and women of disease. All down the centuries of the history of the Church there have been claims that men and women have been healed just as they were in the gospels and in the apostolic age. The early Christian apologists pointed to the miracles of healing performed by the Church as proof of the divine origin of Christianity, and the Roman Church has recognised and accepted them as the required proof of sanctity prior to its beatification and canonisation of some faithful member of that Church.

In dealing with the question of healing in the Church today we begin by discussing in some detail the healing commission which Jesus gave to the Twelve and the Seventy disciples as this is recorded in the gospels. We do so because of the frequency with which this commission to heal is referred to in the modern literature on the ministry of healing of the Church. Having decided about the validity of this commission for the Church today, we then go on to consider the healing ministry of the modern Church in the light of the principles and practice of such a ministry which are set forth in the New Testament.

## Chapter 22
# THE HEALING COMMISSION TO THE DISCIPLES

Jesus commissioned his disciples to heal the sick on two separate occasions. The first occasion was in the Mission Charge to the Twelve and the second was in the Mission Charge to the Seventy.

## THE MISSION CHARGE TO THE TWELVE

The record of the Mission Charge to the Twelve is given in the synoptic gospels in Matthew 10.5-14; Mark 6.7-12 and Luke 9.1-5. The record varies in length and detail between the three gospels, but there can be no doubt of its authenticity for it was written and published within the lifetime of at least some of those to whom the charge was given. Of the Mission itself, T.W. Manson writes that it is 'one of the best-attested facts in the life of Jesus'.[1] Its importance is shown by the fact that it is recorded in all three synoptic gospels.

### Power and authority for the Mission

In each of these gospels we find that the terms of the Mission Charge are preceded by a description of the power and authority which Jesus gave to his twelve disciples in preparation for the task which lay before them. These descriptions differ slightly from each other verbally, but all mean the same.

Matthew says that Jesus gave his twelve disciples 'authority over unclean spirits, to cast them out, and to heal every disease and every infirmity' (Matthew 10.1).

Mark says that Jesus 'gave them authority over the unclean spirits' (Mark 6.7).

Luke says that Jesus 'gave them power and authority over all demons and to cure diseases' (Luke 9.1).

The important words in this authorisation of Jesus are power (*dunamis*) and authority (*exousia*). By the former word, which is given by Luke alone, is meant the absolute power of God to do anything he wishes to do, and by the latter word, the right or authority to use that power.[2] In other words, Jesus is delegating to his disciples the power he has been given by his Father. In their case and on this occasion, however, the use of this power is limited to the casting out of demons and the healing of the sick.

It is significant that such power and authority is not applied to preaching and teaching, but only to healing. In healing the disciples were confronting the power of evil and needed the power of God to oppose it and overcome it.

## The content of the Mission Charge to the Twelve

The version of the Charge which we shall consider is that given by Matthew because he gives it in its fullest form, and his version is the one which is most frequently quoted in the literature on healing. He places the Mission Charge in the context of the compassion of Jesus. Jesus saw the crowds harassed and helpless because they were leaderless and without a shepherd (Matthew 9.35-38). They were like a harvest without labourers to gather it in, and so Jesus proceeds to appoint his twelve disciples as labourers and give them their instructions. It is these instructions which constitute the Mission Charge.

The content of the Mission Charge consists of the following seven imperatives:

1. **Go.... to the lost sheep of the house of Israel** (Matthew 10.5-6). The commission of the disciples was confined to the house of Israel as Jesus' own original commission was according to Matthew 15.24. They were not so much as to set foot on any road which led to a Gentile centre of population, such as a city of the Decapolis. They might use a road which led to a Samaritan city but they must pass by the city when they reached it and go only to the lost sheep of the house of Israel. As Jesus was most probably in Galilee when he spoke these words, the Mission of the disciples was in effect confined to this region. There were Gentiles to the north in Phoenicia and Syria, to the east in the Decapolis, and there were Samaritans to the south. The roads of Samaria were open to them so they could reach Judaea if they wished, but it is unlikely that they went there. It was in Galilee that they attracted the attention of Herod Antipas the tetrarch, who attributed their doings to a resurrected John the Baptist (Mark 6.14-16).

The unexpected exclusiveness of this command is a mark of its authenticity. No one would put a restriction on the Mission of the disciples if Jesus had not actually done so himself in his Mission Charge. The restriction may have been imposed on the grounds of a lack of time for the Mission as Matthew 10.23 may suggest. The reference to 'the lost sheep of the house of Israel' is not a further restriction by Jesus as though he meant only the criminal class of the population, but a reference to the whole house of Israel represented by the crowds he had just seen looking like sheep who were lost, because they were without a shepherd (Matthew 9.36).

2. **Preach as you go** (v.7). The first purpose stated for their going was to preach. The theme of their preaching was to be, 'The kingdom of God is at hand' combined with a call to repentance according to Mark 6.12. This message was the same as the Baptist had preached up and down the Jordan valley (Matthew 3.2) and which Jesus had already preached in Galilee

(Matthew 4.17). In view of this it is difficult to derive from the Mission Charge a new sense of urgency as though Jesus had suddenly come to the realisation of an imminent crisis in his ministry and was preparing for it, as Taylor suggests in agreement with Albert Schweitzer.[3] There was no new message but new and more messengers as the natural development in the expansion of the Christian movement.

3. **Heal the sick** (v.8). The second purpose of their going was to heal the sick. This command is the first of what we may call the four clinical imperatives in which their task of healing the sick is more specifically defined. This fuller definition is given by Matthew alone, and not by Mark or Luke. Mark does not mention the command to heal the sick in his account, but he records how the disciples did heal when they went out (Mark 6.13). The verb in Matthew is *therapeuo* which Luke changes to *iaomai* (Luke 9.2) in line with his preference for this latter verb, which we have already noted. The command is a simple one with no details of how the disciples were to heal. The only indication of the methods they used is given in Mark 6.13 where we are told that 'they anointed with oil many that were sick and healed them', where the verb used is *therapeuo*.

4. **Raise the dead** (v.8). Jesus raised the dead and here he gave his disciples the authority to do the same. The existence of no fewer than five variant readings for this clause clearly shows the difficulty that the early Church had with this command. In some manuscripts it is omitted, whilst in others its place in the commission varies.[4] Its omission suggests that those who omitted the command took the Mission Charge as valid in their own day but doubted the authenticity of this part of it. The manuscript evidence, however, leaves little doubt that the command is authentic. The command has caused difficulty in our own day too, and has sometimes been interpreted as meaning the raising of the spiritually dead from sin to goodness.[5] Nevertheless, there is no real need to avoid the plain meaning of the words if we accept that Jesus had the power to raise the dead which is so clearly set out in the gospel record. Also, it should be noted that Jesus does not speak of people being dead in sin as Paul does, and so any reference Jesus made to raising them from the dead would be in a physical and not a spiritual sense.

5. **Cleanse the lepers** (v.8). At first sight this command to cleanse lepers appears to be anomalous. Jesus is commanding his disciples to do what he did not do himself, and in fact what they could not do because they did not belong to the levitical priesthood. It is clearly laid down in the fourteenth chapter of Leviticus that only a priest could perform the ceremony of cleansing a leper. Jesus himself observed this regulation and when he cured lepers of their leprosy, he was always very careful to send them on to a priest to fulfil the levitical law (Matthew 8.4; Mark 1.44 and Luke 17.14). The explanation of this apparent anomaly lies in the fact which we mentioned in Chapter Seven, namely, that the verb 'cleanse (*katharizo*)' can refer to both

the physical cure of the leprosy and the ritual cleansing of the leper, or to each separately. Our Lord's command to his disciples on this occasion was therefore not anomalous or contrary to the levitical law. He healed the physical disease but did not carry out the levitical ritual, and his command was that his disciples should do the same.

6. **Cast out demons** (v.8). In verse one, the disciples were given authority (*exousia*) over unclean spirits and were commissioned to cast them out of those whom they possessed. Demon possession is clearly distinguished from sickness and from leprosy, and its treatment is to be of a different character. Jesus does not call this 'exorcism', for by derivation this word means the casting out of demons by oaths, incantations and magic. The disciples were to cast out demons in the name and by the power of Jesus Christ.

7. **Take no gold... no bag** (vv.9-10). Money, haversack, sandals, staff and a spare tunic were all items which prudent travellers would provide for their journey, but the disciples were to go as they were and not put off time to collect these things before they left. It has often been pointed out that the Mishnah tractate *Berakoth* directs that a man 'may not enter into the Temple Mount with his staff or his sandals or his purse'.[6] This part of the Mission Charge may therefore mean that the Mission was to be undertaken as a sacred task comparable with the setting out to worship in the Temple at Jerusalem. This parallel is interesting, but it is doubtful if it is significant, since the disciples are to lay aside more than the three articles mentioned in the Mishnah, and a sufficient reason for doing so is to be found in their need to travel light as well as the short period they are to be away. This imperative implies that Jesus expected the Twelve to be supported and accommodated by those to whom they ministered (vv.10b-11). The disciples were to respond graciously to those offered them hospitality (vv.12-13).

From this brief survey of the contents of the Mission Charge to the Twelve, it will be noted that four out of the seven imperatives which make up the Charge are concerned with healing. There is no doubt, therefore, that the Twelve were given a healing commission as they set out on their first experimental Mission without Jesus. One implication of the inclusion of these healing imperatives in the commission of Jesus to his disciples is that this confirms that he himself engaged in the same kind of healing activities as he commissioned his disciples to carry out.

## The report on the Mission of the Twelve

To a modern reader, one of the most interesting features of the two Missions on which Jesus sent his disciples is the result of their preaching and healing on these occasions, but the record of this result is not very detailed. However, we must accept that the gospels were not written simply to satisfy our curiosity and to supply our modern demand for statistical information and systematic evaluation.

Although Matthew gives us most detail about the commission which Jesus gave to the Twelve (Matthew 10.1-16), he gives us no indication of whether they carried it out, nor even whether they actually went out on their Mission. This is left to Mark and Luke. The latter tells us that they 'set out and went from village to village, preaching the gospel and healing people everywhere' (Luke 9.8 NIV). Mark tells us more but even his report is very brief and factual: 'They went out and preached that people should repent. They cast out many demons, and anointed with oil many who were sick and healed them' (Mark 6.12-13).

The pattern of their missionary activity is much the same as that of Jesus, namely, preaching, casting out demons and healing the sick. There was, however, one significant difference. They anointed the sick with oil (Mark 6.13), which Jesus never did according to the gospel record. As we indicated in our study of the epistle of James in the previous chapter, we take this reference to anointing with oil to be to the medicinal treatment of sickness which was commonly practised in the contemporary world of the New Testament. If this is true, then the disciples combined medicinal and spiritual methods in their healing of the sick.

The word used for the preaching of the Twelve in the gospel accounts of the Mission, with one exception, is the verb *kerusso* which means 'to act as a herald (*kerux*)'. The message was not their own, it belonged to the one who had sent them. They were his heralds (Matthew 10.7; Mark 6.12 and Luke 9.2) announcing his presence and proclaiming his message which was concerned with repentance (Mark 6.12) and the kingdom of God (Matthew 10.7 and Luke 9.2). The exception is in Luke 9.6 where the word used is *euangelizomai*, 'to preach good news'. The theme of their preaching was the same as that of John the Baptist and of Jesus himself. It was that people should repent and believe the good news of the coming of the kingdom of God (Mark 1.4, 15).

With regard to their healing activity on the Mission, Swete has pointed out a possible significant change of tense in Mark 6.12-13. The verb *kerusso* is in the aorist tense suggesting that the preaching went on all the time and is therefore spoken of as a whole. By contrast the verbs describing the casting out of demons (*ekballo*), the anointing with oil (*aleipho*) and healing (*therapeuo*) are all in the imperfect tense suggesting that these activities did not go on all the time, but only from time to time in the course of the preaching.[7]

At the end of their Mission, the disciples (now called apostles, i.e., missionaries or 'those who had been sent', Matthew 10.2) returned to be with Jesus. They told him all that they had done and taught (Mark 6.30 and Luke 9.10). There had, in fact, been no instruction to teach in their original commission, but preaching inevitably involves teaching and so we need not be surprised that Mark says that they had taught.

The brief and meagre character of the record of the return of the Twelve to Jesus has been contrasted by Farrar with that described for the return of the Seventy in Luke 10.17-24. On the basis of this contrast he infers that the Mission of the Twelve was not so successful as that of the Seventy, and that the training of the Twelve was still imperfect.[8] This seems to be a precarious inference, although it appears to be shared by Taylor who regards the Mission as having failed.[9]

When the Twelve returned to Jesus at Capernaum, he took them across the Sea of Galilee to a quiet place near Bethsaida hoping to be able to relax with them there, but the people heard where he was and thousands followed him. In spite of his desire to be alone with his disciples, Jesus welcomed the people and proceeded to do for them what he had instructed his disciples to do on their Mission, to speak about the kingdom of God and to heal sick people (Luke 9.11). This was another lesson in their training and allowed them to compare what they had done on their recent Mission with how Jesus would have done it, whether or not the suggestion of Farrar is true that their Mission had been less than successful.

## THE MISSION CHARGE TO THE SEVENTY

Luke alone records the Mission of the Seventy, and this fact has led to the conjecture that he was himself one of their number. This is improbable for in the prologue to his gospel (Luke 1.1-4) he indicates that he was not an eye-witness of the events he recorded, but only a compiler of the experiences of others. The same fact has also led to a denial of the authenticity of the Mission since the instructions contained in the Mission Charge to the Seventy are very similar to those which were given to the Twelve. As a result some scholars have taken the view that Luke's account of the charge to the Seventy is but a doublet of the charge to the Twelve and has been created by Luke using the material in which that charge was described.[10] However, as Marshall points out, Luke tends to avoid doublets.[11] Also, any similarity between the two Mission Charges can be explained by the similarity between the two Missions. Plummer concludes that the view which regards the two Missions as one and the same, 'will not bear criticism'.[12]

As Eusebius pointed out long ago, no list of the Seventy existed even in his time. He mentions a number of traditions about the identity of some of them, of whom only one (Thaddaeus) was an apostle.[13] It has been suggested that the Twelve also were included amongst the number of the Seventy.[14] However, this seems to be unlikely in view of the description of the Seventy as 'others' (Luke 10.1).[15] The Twelve formed a definite and recognisable body of people who were chosen by Jesus that they might be with him and available to go out to preach and heal (Mark 3.14-15). By contrast, the Seventy were brought together for their Mission on one occasion only and are not referred to again. Significantly, they are not called 'apostles' as the Twelve were (Luke 9.10).

In the case of the Mission of the Seventy there is no specific delegation of power and authority to cast out demons and to heal diseases as there was for the Twelve (Luke 9.1). On the other hand Jesus made it quite clear that these seventy disciples were going forth as his personal representatives. According to Luke 10.16 (NIV), he tells them 'He who listens to you listens to me; he who rejects you rejects me; and he who rejects me rejects him who sent me'. Nothing could be clearer than that.

## The content of the Mission Charge to the Seventy

The Mission Charge given by Jesus to the Seventy is recorded in Luke 10.1-11, and while it is not set out as systematically as that to the Twelve in Matthew, the main terms of the Charge are clear enough.

1. **Go your way** (v.3). Here there is no restriction to the house of Israel and no mention of the Gentiles. Luke's editorial comment is that the reason for the sending out of the Seventy was that they might prepare the way for Jesus' own visit to the places which he was about to include in his own itinerary (v.1). As in the case of the sending of the Twelve, they were to go out two by two (v.1, cp. Mark 6.7). The mention of Bethsaida, Chorazin and Capernaum (vv.13-15) suggests that the Seventy were being commissioned in Galilee as the Twelve had been, but their Mission was not to be confined to Galilee as that of the Twelve had been. Jesus had at this time set his face to go up to Jerusalem for the last time and since the Samaritans had refused to receive him (Luke 9.51-53), he would have to pass through the towns and villages of Peraea and Judaea and so it would be in these places that the Seventy would carry out their Mission.

2. **Say to them** (v.9). The message they were to declare to those they healed was, 'The kingdom of God has drawn near to you'. This was the same message as that given to the Twelve in Matthew 10.7. The nearness of the kingdom 'is the local nearness of a present reality, not the chronological nearness of a future reality'.[16] The implication of this message is that its hearers can accept or reject the kingdom or the rule of God; it does not come on them automatically or forcibly. When they hear it, that is their day of opportunity and decision. It is important to notice that this message is here linked to the healing of the sick. Also, its use is not specifically described as preaching, and there is no mention of preaching when they reported to Jesus on their return (Luke 10.17).

3. **Heal the sick** (v.9). The verb is *therapeuo* as in the Mission Charge to the Twelve in Matthew 10.8, although in Luke's version of that charge he changed the verb to *iaomai* as we see in Luke 9.2. No details are given, only the bare command. There is no mention of the casting out of demons, although we know from the report of the disciples when they returned from their Mission that they did cast out demons in the name of Jesus (v.17). There is also no mention of raising the dead in the commission to the Seventy and

Cowan has pointed out that 'only Apostles in the special sense are ever represented in the New Testament as raising the dead' (Acts 9.20 and 20.9-10).[17] It is significant, however, that on this occasion the commission to heal was extended to include others than the Twelve.

**4. Carry no purse, no bag, no sandals** (v.4). This instruction is similar to that given to the Twelve in their commission, and it suggests that the Seventy like them were being sent on a short preaching and healing Mission to prepare for the coming of Jesus on a later occasion, as indeed is indicated in verse one. They were to take with them none of the things which travellers might regard as indispensable. Their needs would be supplied as they proceeded on their Mission.

## The report on the Mission of the Seventy

As we have already mentioned, when the Twelve returned from their Mission, they told Jesus 'all that they had done and taught' (Mark 6.30), but we are given no details of what they said. By contrast, the report of the Seventy was given by Luke, albeit briefly, in their own words. They said to Jesus, 'Lord, even the demons submit to us in your name' (Luke 10.17 NIV). In addition, we are told of the response of Jesus to their report which was not indicated for the report of the Mission of the Twelve, except for the mention of his realisation that they needed to rest (Mark 6.31).

The first thing we are told about the Seventy after their Mission was that 'they returned with joy' (Luke 10.17). They had gone out not knowing what to expect, and they were now returning delighted with their experience. Calvin suggests that this would seem to imply that when the seventy disciples originally set out they 'did not have a full and firm faith in Christ's words' in spite of the power and commission which had then been given to them.[18]

The second thing was that they had possessed greater spiritual power than they had realised, so that even demons had submitted to them. They had not expected this for they had not been commissioned to cast out demons, only to heal (*therapeuo*) the sick (v.9). They knew now from their own experience that the casting out of demons was part of healing too. The word they used to describe the submission of the demons was *hupotasso*, which is a military term meaning 'to be of a lower rank'. In other words they found they could give orders to demons and they would obey them. This was the source of their great delight.

The third thing was that they realised that the source of this power over demons was Jesus himself whose name they had used to cast out the demons (v.17). When he had commissioned them, Jesus had designated them his own personal representatives and allowed them the use of his name and power.

The response of Jesus to the report of the Seventy is to share their joy at the conquest of the demons. His joy at hearing about this was even greater than that of the disciples. Of them, Luke says simply that they returned with joy (*meta chara*), but he speaks of Jesus being 'thrilled with joy' (so Moffatt) using the verb *agalliaomai* (v.21).[19] He first reaffirms the authority over Satan and the demons which he had given to them and confirms the defeat of Satan through their Mission (vv.18-19), but goes on to warn his disciples that the source of real and permanent joy is the knowledge that their names are recorded in heaven, and not the possession of the ability to overcome demons (v.20). Jesus then thanks his Father for the things that he has revealed to the disciples in the experiences of their Mission just completed (vv.21-22, cp. Matthew 11.25-27). He ends by turning to his disciples in private and saying how blessed they are to see and hear what is being revealed in their day (vv.23-24).

## THE MODERN VALIDITY OF THE HEALING COMMISSION

The question which now arises is whether the terms of the healing commission which was included by Jesus in the two Mission Charges to his early disciples are still valid for the Christian Church today. This is an important question because the commission to heal the sick is commonly regarded as the justification for the medical missionary movement which arose in the Protestant Churches in the late eighteenth and early nineteenth centuries and still continues to the present day.[20] Also, as we have already mentioned, it is frequently appealed to as the basis of the modern healing ministry of the Church.[21] The only way to answer this question is by a closer examination of the details of the healing commission which the two Mission Charges contained.

### The Mission Charge to the Twelve

The first significant point to note about the first Mission Charge is that its terms restrict the activity of the disciples to 'the lost sheep of the house of Israel' (Matthew 10.6). This point alone raises and even may be held to settle the question of the modern application and validity of the terms of this Charge. Today the mission of the Church is to all peoples, and not only to the house of Israel.

The next thing to notice is that the message which the disciples were to preach was defined in pre-crucifixion and pre-resurrection terms. These terms were 'the kingdom of God' and 'repentance'. They were not the terms used in the final commission of Jesus to the disciples or in the *kerugma* or preaching of the apostolic Church. The preaching of the apostolic Church was in terms of the death and resurrection of Jesus Christ and the salvation which flowed from these two events. Obviously the terms of the message of the Mission Charge could not be other than they were, for they came before the great events of the gospel. The character of the message which the disciples were to preach is therefore another indication that the terms of the

Mission Charge referred to the original circumstances in which it was given and not to the post-resurrection Church.

Furthermore, two of the clinical imperatives of the Mission Charge are not the common practice of the Church today. The first of these is the command to raise the dead. So far as we know, the disciples did not raise any dead person to life again before the ascension of Jesus although they were given authority to do so on this occasion. In the book of Acts both Peter and Paul are each recorded as having raised a dead person to life again (See Acts 9.36-41 and 20.9-12), but since that time this command has rarely if ever been fulfilled. It was the realisation of this non-fulfilment which presumably led to the attempts to remove the command from the text, which we have already noted. The fact that this command is not observed by the modern Church, suggests that the Church today does not regard itself as having the necessary power and authority to raise the dead.

The second clinical imperative not commonly observed by the Church today is the command to cast out demons (Matthew 10.8). On this there is less certainty however. On the one hand there is the not uncommon denial of the existence of demons and demonic phenomena which would render the command meaningless. On the other hand there is an increasing modern acceptance of the reality of demons and their activity in human life and society. This is accompanied by a rise in the interest in a deliverance ministry in which the reality of demon possession is recognised and its cause and effects are countered.[22]

However, such a deliverance ministry has not been accepted by the main branches of the Church as part of their normal activity. This suggests that the Church today has not generally felt this clinical command of Jesus to be binding on it.

The modern relevance of the command to cleanse lepers has been questioned on the ground that the leprosy of the New Testament is probably not the disease which we know by that name today.[23] Most of the evidence on this subject comes from the detailed descriptions in the thirteenth and fourteenth chapters of the book of Leviticus and raises the problem of the identity of the disease referred to as leprosy in the New Testament as no descriptions are given there.[24] Harrison goes so far as to say that in the New Testament, the word *lepra* 'appears to be restricted to specific dermatological conditions exclusive of true leprosy'.[25] If it is true that the leprosy of the New Testament is not the disease which we recognise today as caused by the leprosy bacillus which was first discovered by Armauer Hansen of Bergen in 1871, then this provides a further reason for doubting the modern validity of the terms of the Mission Charge, of which one was the command to cleanse lepers.

The final aspect of the Mission Charge to the Twelve which bears on its modern validity is the minimum provision which the disciples were required to make for their preaching and healing tour (Matthew 10.9-10). This provision envisaged only short-term activity on their part and does not suggest that Jesus was laying down the terms of their permanent activity.

In a section which is peculiar to Luke's gospel, Jesus refers to an occasion on which he sent out the Twelve with 'no purse, or bag or sandals' (Luke 22.35). It is after the institution of the Lord's supper and in anticipation of a situation which the disciples are going to find more difficult than in the past, that Jesus asks them if they lacked anything when he sent them out at that time. They replied that they had not. The actual previous occasion which Jesus had in mind is not specified. On the basis of the words he used, some commentators have identified the occasion with the sending out of the Seventy, for only on that occasion was the wording used by Jesus in his instructions to the disciples the same as that used in this later reference. It was the Seventy who were told to 'carry no purse, no bag, no sandals' (Luke 10.4).[26] However, Jesus was now speaking to the Twelve and it would appear more natural for him to refer to the Mission Charge which he had given to them rather than to the Seventy who, as we have already seen, were carefully distinguished from the Twelve by the word 'others' in Luke 10.1.[27] In Matthew 10.9-19, the Twelve were instructed to take no money (so that they needed no purse), no bag and no sandals. If Luke 22.35 is a reference to the Mission of the Twelve, as we think it must be, then Jesus clearly envisages that Mission as a distinct event with its own separate instructions which Jesus now contrasts with those he is about to give for the new situation described in Luke 22.36-38. In other words, the instructions given to the Twelve prior to their previous Mission were for that Mission alone and were now no longer valid.

The conclusion seems inescapable that the terms of the Mission Charge given to the Twelve applied only to the situation and circumstances in which these were originally given. Its terms were not a permanent requirement applicable to the Church in all ages and in all places.

## The Mission Charge to the Seventy

The terms of the Mission Charge to the Seventy can also be seen to be local and temporary. Luke in his editorial comment says that Jesus appointed the Seventy and sent them out, two by two. There is no restriction to the house of Israel, only a geographical restriction to those towns and places which he was about to visit (Luke 10.1).[28] The message they were to proclaim concerned the kingdom of God and was in pre-crucifixion terms. They were to carry no baggage, to engage in no elaborate greetings on the road, and not to spend time eating in different houses each day (Luke 10.4-7). These features of the Mission Charge to the Seventy indicate that, like that to the Twelve, its terms were not a permanent requirement of the Church in all ages. Their local and temporary nature is further suggested by the fact that

Luke records the completion of the Mission of the Seventy after a period of time which is not specified, but could have been several months according to Arndt. In Luke 10.17-24 it is suggested that their Mission was now complete and had been strikingly successful although Jesus' comment on it was that 'the highest thing in life is not spectacular outward success but the assurance of possessing God's favour'.[29]

Our conclusion, therefore, must be that the terms of neither the Mission Charge given by Jesus to the Twelve and recorded in Matthew 10.5-15 and Luke 9.1-5, nor that given by him to the Seventy and recorded in Luke 10.1-11, were intended to be permanently valid and binding on the Church. Nevertheless we know from past history and modern experience that the Church today does have a healing ministry and it is to a consideration of the history of that ministry we now turn in our next chapter.

# Chapter 23
# FROM THE COMMISSION TO THE MINISTRY

The phrase **The Ministry of Healing of the Church** is a modern one and does not occur in the New Testament, nor in the literature of the Church before the nineteenth century. The earliest occurrence of the shorter term **The Ministry of Healing** we have been able to trace is as the title of a tract published in 1881 by the Revd Adoniram J. Gordon, DD (1836-1895), a Baptist minister of Boston, Massachusetts. In the following year he used the phrase again as the title of a book which was published first in the United States and then in Britain.[1] This book was the first extended study of healing in the Church to appear, although the author confined his attention to miraculous or non-medical healing, as indicated by the subtitle he gave his book of *Miracles of Cure in all Ages*. We cannot say if Gordon coined the phrase, but it is one which has come into common use in recent years. Many prefer it because it begs fewer questions than other terms which are often used such as 'faith-healing', 'divine healing' and 'spiritual healing'.[2]

## THE HISTORY OF THE MINISTRY OF HEALING

Gordon may have given a convenient name to the practice of healing by the Church, but it was a name for a phenomenon whose history was as old as that of the Church itself.

Most of this present book so far has been concerned with the origins of that practice in the healing activity of Jesus Christ and of the leaders of the apostolic Church. From these beginnings, the practice of the healing ministry of both a medical and a non-medical nature has continued in the history of the Church. The full history of this practice still remains to be written, although it has been sketched by such authors as Phyllis Garlick[3] and Morton Kelsey.[4] A more detailed study of the place of healing in the Ante-Nicene Church has been published by Evelyn Frost giving full quotations from Christian writers of the first three centuries of the existence of the Church.[5]

The Church's ministry of healing was at first concerned with healing in its comprehensive sense. It comprised natural healing, both folk and professional, as well as healing through prayer and spiritual ministration. To provide healing according to natural principles the Church founded hospitals and infirmaries where the sick were nursed and treated in accordance with these principles, and where the aged and disabled could find shelter and care. The herb-gardens of monasteries provided healing remedies which were applied to the treatment of diseases and injuries on an empirical basis. The staff of the monasteries also appear to have provided a community care service for the sick by visiting them in their homes.

In the Middle Ages, the Church began to withdraw from the practice of medical healing. Early in the twelfth century, monks were forbidden by Church councils to practise medicine.[6] In 1123 the First Lateran Council forbad monks to visit the sick and in 1139, the Second Lateran Council forbad them to study medicine on the grounds that their proper function was the cure of souls and not to be physicians of bodies. Then in 1163 the Council of Tours prohibited churchmen from practising surgery on the grounds that *Ecclesia abhorret a sanguine* (The Church abhors the shedding of blood). This resulted in surgery becoming the province of the barbers and it was from their ranks that the surgical profession developed. The guilds of the barber-surgeons were the first of the professional organisations to be established in Europe for the supervision and control of the practice of medicine and surgery. The emergence of a distinct medical profession which this reflects, meant that healing of a medical nature became increasingly their province and no longer that of the Church.

Uncertainty also arose about the place of anointing in the healing of the sick. As we saw in Chapter Twenty-one, by the twelfth century the procedure for the anointing of the sick for their healing had officially become the preparation for their dying, and not a means of their healing as it was in the epistle of James.

The gift of healing which the apostle Paul had regarded as one of the gifts given to the Church by the Holy Spirit was increasingly ignored and rarely exercised. Origen in the third century, Basil the Great and his brother Gregory of Nyssa in the fourth century and Chrysostom in the fifth century, all believed that the Church still had the power to heal.[7] On the other hand, Augustine and Aquinas at first denied that the Church still possessed this power, but later in life they came to accept that it did and that supernatural healing did occur.[8] This was true of Luther too until the year 1540 when he saw his colleague Philip Melanchthon restored to health through prayer.[9] In 1545 he even wrote out instructions for an order of service for healing based on the fifth chapter of the epistle of James.[10] Calvin, on the other hand, was quite convinced that the Church no longer possessed the gift of healing in his day and consequently, although he consulted doctors for his various diseases, he never sought non-medical healing from his colleagues.[11]

However, the practice of healing by the Church never entirely died out. In the eleventh century, evangelists of the Waldensian Church practised both medical and non-medical healing. In Britain, healing was associated with the ministries of George Fox (1642-1691),[12] the founder of the Society of Friends ('The Quakers') and John Wesley (1703-1791), the founder of Methodism.[13] We know that Wesley practised both medical and non-medical healing. In 1746 he opened the first free medical dispensary to be established in England for the treatment of the sick poor. In the following year he published a book of practical medical advice with the title *Primitive Physic, or an Easy and Natural Method of Curing Most Diseases*. This work was very popular and remained in print for a whole century.[14]

## THE MODERN INTEREST IN THE MINISTRY OF HEALING

The modern interest in the ministry of healing of the Church can be traced to two main sources. The first is to a reaffirmation of the teaching of the New Testament so far as non-medical healing is concerned. The second is to the rise of the medical missionary movement in the Protestant Churches of Europe and America in the nineteenth century so far as medical healing is concerned.

### The Teaching of the New Testament

In previous chapters we have considered in some detail the healing ministry of Jesus as recorded in the gospels. Jesus set his disciples an example of healing activity which in itself constituted a sufficient inspiration and authority for them to follow, and we have seen from the book of Acts how they did follow his example in the apostolic Church. That example still applies to the modern Church.

In addition to the example of Jesus, there were two indications in the New Testament epistles that the Church still had a ministry of healing after the apostolic period. These indications were in the passages which we have already discussed in some detail, namely, 1 Corinthians 12.1-11 and James 5.13-16. It remains now to see how important these passages were in the renewed interest in healing which has characterised the modern Church.

### 1. The Prayer of Faith (James 5.15)

One of the most prominent names in the revival of interest in the ministry of healing of the Church in Europe is that of Dorothea Trüdel (1810-1863) of Männedorf on Lake Zurich in Switzerland. Miss Trüdel was the eleventh child of a drunken father and a beautiful and pious mother. The family were often reduced to poverty by the father's drinking habits and when her mother died, an uncle encouraged Dorothea to learn artificial flower-making. This she did, and then proceeded to open a factory for flower-making in Männedorf to give employment to local women and girls.

In 1847 she became very concerned when four of her employees fell ill and their illness did not respond to medical treatment. When she turned to prayer and the study of the Bible she recalled the passage James 5.14-15. She could find no elders of the Church who were willing to act as this passage required, and so she herself prayed at the bedside of her sick employees with the result that they recovered. This marked the beginning of her healing ministry and eventually a hospital was built to accommodate those who came to her for healing from France, Germany and Great Britain. The only methods she used for healing were those described in the Bible, namely, prayer, the laying on of hands and anointing with oil.

Although she did not deny doctors and medical treatment a place in healing, she encountered professional opposition to her work from the local doctors who invoked the law against her on the grounds that it was illegal to heal without a physician. A court order was obtained closing her hospital but this order was revoked on appeal, when it was proved that she had been able to cure many sick people the medical profession had given up as incurable. She died in 1863 from typhus fever contracted from one of her patients.[15] After she died, her work was continued by her colleague Samuel Zeller with the assistance of his sister and others of her former colleagues.

In Germany the most famous work of healing was that of Johann Christoph Blumhardt (1805-1880), a Lutheran pastor, and his son Christoph Friedrich Blumhardt (1842-1919) at Bad Boll in south Germany. Blumhardt senior had studied theology at Tübingen and in 1830 joined the teaching staff of the missionary training institution in Basel, which had been founded by his uncle Christian Gottlieb in 1815. Then in 1838 he became pastor of Möttlingen, a village in Württemberg on the edge of the Black Forest. In 1843 he exorcised the two sisters Gottliebin and Katharina Dittus, who had exhibited the signs of demon possession.[16] This was the beginning of Blumhardt's healing ministry and of a movement of spiritual revival in the local Lutheran Church.

However, in 1845 the Lutheran Church authorities forbad him to include healing in his ministry, but they relented when he pointed out that he could not stop healings from happening during his ministry even though he did not seek them. Eventually in 1852 he resigned his pastorate when he purchased the defunct sanatorium which had been built beside the sulphur springs at Boll near Göppingen, twenty miles east of Stuttgart. Here he established the Bad Boll sanatorium as a centre of Christian healing which became famous throughout Europe and America. When asked about his healing methods, Blumhardt usually replied by saying, 'My remedy is simply prayer'. He did not use anointing with oil and only rarely used the laying on of hands, but healed in the context of divine worship which included the proclamation of the healing word of God and prayer. Like Miss Trüdel he was not against the employment of doctors or the use of medicines.[17] He was assisted in his work of healing by Gottliebin Dittus and his own two sons. When their father died in 1880, one of them, Christoph Friedrich Blumhardt, succeeded him at the sanatorium at Bad Boll.

News of these healing activities in Europe reached North America where the origin of the interest in the ministry of healing of the Church is usually associated with the Holiness Movement, and in particular with the name of Dr Charles Cullis (1883-1892).[18] Cullis was an Episcopalian layman who qualified in medicine at the University of Vermont and then established a very successful medical and homoeopathic practice in Boston, Massachusetts. He was very impressed with the work of Dorothea Trüdel and wrote her biography in 1872. Each summer, Cullis organised holiness conferences in New Hampshire and Maine which included the theme 'Faith cures through Prayer'. Two of those who attended these conferences were Albert Benjamin Simpson (1843-1919) and William Edwin Boardman (1810-1886) who were also involved in the Holiness Movement which had arisen in America in the 1830s and owed much to the perfectionist teaching of John Wesley.[19]

Simpson was originally a Presbyterian minister in Canada who moved to the United States in 1873. In 1887 he established two bodies known respectively as The Christian Alliance and the Evangelical Missionary Alliance, which ten years later were combined to form The Christian and Missionary Alliance. This was the first modern Christian body or denomination to emphasise spiritual healing as an integral part of its ministry. It was Simpson who introduced the slogan 'Christ our Saviour, Sanctifier, Healer and Coming King' which became known as the Fourfold Gospel.[20] In 1915 he published a book with the title *The Gospel of Healing* which was very influential in the Healing Movement in America. He died of cerebrovascular disease at the age of seventy-five years.

Boardman was also a Presbyterian minister who was at first involved in the Holiness Movement in the United States. In 1858 he published a book called *The Higher Christian Life* in which he set forth his views on personal holiness in terms of entire sanctification. Later in life he became more interested in healing and wrote his book *The Great Physician: The Lord that Healeth Thee* which was published in 1881. He moved permanently to Britain in 1875 and established the Bethsan Institute of Healing in London. It was through Boardman that the interest in healing spread to Britain where he organised a series of conferences on healing in London which attracted representatives from America and Europe. These included Simpson from New York and pastors from Switzerland amongst whom was Pastor Otto Stockmayer, the head of a healing institute in Hauptwal similar to that established at Männedorf by Dorothea Trüdel.[21]

The Healing Movement spread to South Africa through the ministry of Andrew Murray, a prominent minister of the Dutch Reformed Church there, and one who was influenced by the Holiness Movement. As a student he had visited Bad Boll and seen the work of the Blumhardts. He had read

Boardman's book on healing soon after it was published, but was not specially impressed by it. In May 1882 he came to Britain seeking relief from a severe chronic laryngitis which had led to a medical ban on his regular preaching for most of the previous two years. In London he sought out Boardman and spent three weeks as a patient in his Bethsan Institute, which were followed by some weeks of medical treatment until in April he was allowed to begin preaching again. He attended the 1882 healing conference in London where he met Stockmayer with the result that he visited Switzerland and saw the work at Männedorf, now in the charge of Samuel Zeller. On his return to South Africa, Murray's interest in healing continued and in 1884 he published a small book in Dutch which was then translated into English under the title *Divine Healing*. This book had a wide circulation in Britain and the United States.[22]

The modern practice of healing whose origins and early development we have just sketched still continues in the Church. The books we have mentioned above are still in print, although they were published well over a century ago. In 1992, the books on healing by Gordon, Simpson and Murray already mentioned were published together in a single volume as providing 'solid, biblical teaching on the subject that today's church needs to hear'. The Introduction to this volume notes that none of these three men 'allowed healing to become the central focus of his ministry'. For them 'the healing ministry was just a matter-of-fact addition to their everyday pastoral duties'.[23]

As we mentioned at the beginning of this section, the leaders of this movement based their ministry of healing on the statement in James 5.15, 'The prayer of faith will save the sick'. The verb used in this sentence is *sozo*, which we have seen in Chapter Seven includes both physical and spiritual healing in its scope.

## 2. The Gifts of the Spirit (1 Corinthians 12.1)

The other New Testament passage which provided a source for the renewed interest in the ministry of healing in the modern Church was 1 Corinthians 12.1-11. In this passage Paul speaks of the different gifts given to the Church by the Holy Spirit. Amongst these is the gift of healing. We have already discussed the nature of these gifts in some detail in Chapter Fifteen and in this present chapter we are concerned with the understanding of these gifts, and in particular the gift of healing, in the modern Church.

The movement in the modern Church which emphasised the ministry of healing as a gift of the Holy Spirit to the Church is usually called Pentecostalism, although the recognition of this ministry and the exercise of this gift is not confined to the Pentecostal Movement. The members of Holiness Movement, which has been described as a near cousin to Pentecostalism, also practised healing as we have seen in the case of Charles

Cullis and the others mentioned in the previous section. However, it was the Pentecostal Movement which brought healing to the notice of the mainstream Churches, often in very dramatic ways.[24]

The source of the emphasis on the charismatic healing of the sick in the Pentecostal Movement is usually traced to the influence of the Revd John Alexander Dowie (1847-1907). Dowie was born in Edinburgh and when he was thirteen he emigrated along with his family to Australia, where he was engaged in business for eight years in Adelaide. He then returned to Edinburgh to study divinity from 1869 to 1870. Whilst he was a student, he acted as an honorary chaplain to the Royal Infirmary of Edinburgh. His experience in this institution made him disillusioned with the medical profession and he became opposed to all forms of medical treatment of the sick. Later (in 1895) he was to publish a sermon entitled 'Doctors, Drugs and Devils; or the Foes of Christ the Healer', in which he described all these three agencies as the instruments of Satan.[25] Dowie's theological studies were cut short by his father's financial difficulties and he had to return to Australia, where in 1870 he was ordained to the ministry of the Congregational Church and then served as the minister of congregations in Alma and Sydney.

During an epidemic of plague in 1876, Dowie discovered that he possessed the gift of healing and two years later he resigned from the ministry of the Congregational Church and formed an independent congregation in Sydney. He moved to Melbourne in 1882 where he founded the Free Christian Church and built a large independent tabernacle to accommodate his congregation. In the same year he established the International Divine Healing Association. He was invited to the 1885 healing conference organised by Boardman in London but was unable to attend. In 1888 Dowie went to the United States and spent two years organising Church congregations and missions in the San Francisco area. He then moved to Evanston and in 1893 he settled in Chicago where he built a large tabernacle with special rooms for divine healing. Three years later he established a new denomination called the Christian Catholic Church in Zion. In 1901 he purchased six thousand acres of land on the shore of Lake Michigan, about forty miles north of Chicago, where he founded Zion City with about five thousand of his followers. This city was a utopian theocratic colony where, in accordance with Dowie's views, no doctor or veterinarian was allowed to practise and the use of pork, alcohol, tobacco and drugs was forbidden. Dowie was partially paralysed as the result of a stroke in September 1905 and in the following year, whilst he was absent on a visit to Mexico, he was deposed by his followers from the leadership of the Christian Catholic Church. He died at Zion City in March 1907, 'an abandoned, broken and sick man'.[26]

The classical Pentecostal Movement traces its origin to New Year's Day 1901 when a student named Agnes Ozman spoke in tongues at the Bethel Bible College in Topeka, Kansas. This event created a great interest in the gifts of the Spirit, of which speaking in tongues was one.[27] Although the gift of speaking in tongues is usually regarded as the main characteristic feature of Pentecostalism, another of these gifts was that of healing. As we have just mentioned, it was Dowie who was responsible for bringing healing to the forefront of Pentecostalist teaching by his influence on the founders of the Pentecostal Movement. These included Charles Fox Parham (1873-1929) who had founded the Bethel Bible College in 1900. Two years earlier he had established the Bethel Healing Home, also at Topeka. He had already had experience of his own personal healing during an attack of rheumatic fever. Under the influence of Dowie he began to emphasise the importance of the gift of healing and encouraged his colleagues in the Movement to do the same.[28]

It will be clear from our description so far, that the modern interest in the ministry of healing of the Church was at first confined to bodies outside the mainstream Christian Churches. The result was that those people who pioneered this ministry often encountered opposition from their own Churches and in some cases felt they had to leave their membership. Those who remained within the mainstream Churches began to establish special groups for those of their members who were interested in the ministry of healing. In Britain the first of these groups within the Church of England was the Guild of Health which was founded in September 1904 by Percy Dearmer and others. This was followed by the establishment of the Society of Emmanuel by James Moore Hickson in October of the next year, which in 1933 was renamed The Divine Healing Mission. The Guild of Health became ecumenical in 1914 with the result that the Guild of St Raphael was formed in 1915. At first this body restricted its membership to members of the Church of England who regarded the ministry of healing as primarily sacramental in nature. However, in 1996 the Guild of St Raphael too became ecumenical in its membership. Eventually almost every main Christian denomination had its own healing group and in 1943 Archbishop William Temple of the Church of England suggested that a new national body should be set up to co-ordinate the work of these groups and to promote closer co-operation between doctors and ministers. The result was the establishment in April 1944 of the Churches' Council for Health and Healing which included representatives of the Royal Medical Colleges together with those of the Churches, and had its headquarters in London.[29]

Meantime there had been a parallel development of healing groups in North America. The first of these was the Emmanuel Movement which was founded in 1905 by Elwood Worcester, the rector of Emmanuel Episcopal Church in Boston, Massachusetts. This Movement brought together physicians and ministers who developed a psychotherapeutic approach to mental illness. It also inspired the establishment of other groups, notably the Order of the Nazarene and the Order of St Luke the Physician. The latter Order was founded in 1947 by Dr John Gaynor Banks and soon established a Chapter in Britain where it is still active. In 1930 a group was founded by Glenn Clark with the title of The Camps Farthest Out, whose healing conferences became very popular.[30]

The work and success of these healing groups in both Britain and North America, and then the formation of the new ecumenical and interdisciplinary council in Britain, constituted a challenge to the mainstream Churches in these countries which they could not ignore. In due course, each of these Churches came to reconsider their attitude to healing. During the decade 1958-1967, almost all of the mainstream Churches in both Britain and North America appointed special committees which produced reports on the ministry of healing for the guidance of their membership, some of which are listed in the bibliography at the end of this book. The result was that a number of Churches set up special committees and organised conferences to provide guidance for their members about the ministry of healing.

Although we have distinguished different sources for the modern interest in the ministry of healing and described its early development by separate paths, these distinctions are not absolute. They are more of the nature of differences of emphasis than of contradictions in theory and practice. Thus both the main movements we have described, laid great stress on the use of prayer for healing. Both recognised the gift of healing, though they might differ about how it was given to individuals in the Church and how it should be exercised in the Church.

There is, however, one important difference within their approach to the ministry of healing which is displayed by the various groups engaged in this ministry, and that is the place they give to medical healing within it. Some groups in the Pentecostal Movement are opposed to the use of medical healing at all and depend entirely on non-medical methods of healing by prayer and the laying on of hands. On the other hand, those who followed Dr Cullis accepted that there is a legitimate place for medical treatment and agreed that it may be combined with non-medical methods of therapy in the healing of the sick.

## The Medical Missionary Movement

It is not surprising that the Church eventually came in modern times to reassert its right to practise both medical and non-medical healing, and to reject the view which restricted its responsibility and activity to healing of only one part of the human being, namely, the soul. This did not occur as the result of any dramatic gesture or even at a single stroke, but through the gradual introduction of medical practice into the overseas missionary activity of the Church. It is not without significance that those who practised non-medical methods of healing had strong links with the modern medical missionary movement in the Protestant Churches. This is illustrated by the connection of the Blumhardt family with the Basel Mission and its training institution.

It was through the modern medical missionary movement that the Church regained its place in the practice of medical healing and came once again to include both medical and non-medical healing in its ministry of healing.[31] Medical missionaries were trained in the methods of modern scientific medicine and used those methods in the name of the Church and in the service of humanity.[32] It is of interest to note how this happened without its real significance being realised by the Church initially. This is shown by an examination of the nature of the literature which arose out of the work of medical missionaries. The books and articles which were written by them or about their work were all purely descriptive, and only rarely was any attempt made to relate that work to a theological concept of health and healing, or to regard it as part of the healing ministry of the Church.[33]

The hospitals and community health care services which were established by medical missionaries have made an important contribution to the health care of the populations they serve.[34] It has been estimated that by the year 1910 well over two thousand hospitals and at least twice that number of health centres were being operated by the missionary agencies of the Protestant Churches. In the next fifty years many more were established and their management has now become the responsibility of the local Churches which were founded by the missionary agencies. Through these institutions and their staff the local Churches are providing medical treatment and health care services for the local population as part of their total ministry of healing.

Modern health care services, especially in their institutional form, became increasingly expensive to provide. It was not, therefore, surprising that in the 1960s these local Churches found themselves faced with financial and staffing difficulties as they continued to run them. They appealed for help to the World Council of Churches who called together a consultation first at Lagos in Nigeria in 1963, and then at the German Institute for Medical Missions at Tübingen in May 1964.[35] The report of the Tübingen consultation was issued in the following year under the title of *The Healing Church* and included its unanimous finding that the Church has a specific task in the field of healing based on God's plan of salvation for mankind.[36] Some three years later in September 1967, a second consultation was held in Tübingen to consider the medical and theological aspects of the Church's involvement in the ministry of healing and more especially the role of the congregation in such a ministry.[37] Following these two consultations, the Christian Medical Commission was set up by the World Council in 1968 to assist the Churches in exercise of their ministry of healing.[38]

In the years since it was established, this Commission has made a significant contribution to the theology and practice of the Christian ministry of healing in the Churches throughout the world. It has also played an important part in the secular debate about the health care of the peoples of the world conducted under the auspices of the WHO and the member states of this Organisation. As a result, the Churches have become much more aware of the nature and importance of healing, and the secular health care agencies have come to recognise the great contribution which the Christian Churches make to the health and health care of the world's populations.[39]

The result of all the developments in the theory and practice of the Church's ministry of healing which we have now outlined, is that there is no Christian Church today that is unaware of its involvement in the healing ministry. This involvement may range from the simple activity of a worship service in which participants are reminded of the healing which is to found in the gospel, to the provision of advanced professional health care services under the auspices of the Church.

As we have mentioned, all the mainstream Churches have commissioned reports or appointed standing committees to advise their members on the theology and practice of the Christian healing ministry. In addition, numerous consultations and conferences on the same subject have been held throughout the world. This means that the recognition and practice of the healing ministry of the Church are now worldwide.

What then is the basis of this ministry and how is it to be practised today? It is to a consideration of these questions that we turn in the final chapter of this book.

## Chapter 24
# THE PRACTICE OF THE HEALING MINISTRY
# TODAY

In Chapter Twenty-two we considered the two Mission Charges which Jesus gave to groups of his disciples, both of which contained a healing commission. We came to the conclusion that neither of these Charges could be regarded as permanently valid or binding on the Church because of the terms in which they were originally given to the disciples.[1] Does this mean, then, that the Church today has no commission to heal the sick?

It has been suggested that Jesus did in fact include a commission to heal the sick in his final commission to his disciples. He told them to teach those who would become his disciples through their preaching, that they should obey everything that he had commanded them (Matthew 28.20). As we have seen in Chapter Twenty-two, he commanded his disciples to heal the sick on two occasions and therefore it is maintained that this command to heal was one which was now binding on all future disciples. This would appear to be precarious exegesis, for both of the Mission Charges in which a healing commission was included had certain restrictions placed on them, which would not apply to any later healing activity of the Church. The Mission Charge to the Twelve was restricted geographically to Galilee and ethnically to the house of Israel (Matthew 10.5-6), while that to the Seventy applied only to the towns and villages which Jesus was about to visit (Luke 10.1).

In spite of the apparent absence of any explicit healing commission which might apply to the Church today, the Church has nevertheless believed that it has the authority to heal those who may be sick in body, mind and spirit.

## THE AUTHORITY TO HEAL IN THE CHURCH TODAY

The modern interest in the healing ministry of the Church and its practice makes the question of its basis and authority a very important one. We begin our consideration of healing in the Church today by examining this question.

We have already seen that the evidence suggests that the the two Mission Charges each included a healing commission which was no more than local and temporary. We have also seen that neither Paul nor James set any time-limit on the ability of the Church to heal whether by the exercise of a gift of healing or by the use of prayer and anointing. We would suggest, therefore, that there are a number of reasons on the basis of which the Church today is entitled to believe that it does possess the authority and power to heal in the comprehensive sense in which we have defined healing in this book. These are as follows:

1. **The intention of Jesus.** It is clear that Jesus intended that his disciples should heal the sick. This is shown by the fact that he included a healing commission in the two Mission Charges. Although the commission in these Charges was restricted to specific situations, its inclusion in them reflects a general desire and intention on his part that the disciples should heal the sick as he had done.

2. **The promise of Jesus.** The disciples were promised by Jesus that after his ascension they would be able to do the same works as he had done whilst he was with them. In John 14.12 he says to Philip, 'He who believes in me will also do the works that I do; and greater works than these will he do, because I go to my Father'. These works (*erga*) of which Jesus speaks include his works of healing for as we saw in Chapter Seven this word is commonly used of his miracles of healing in the gospels.

3. **The practice of the apostles.** We have noted that there was no explicit mention of healing in the final commission of Jesus to the apostles, with the possible exception of Mark 16.17-18, a passage whose status we discussed in Chapter Two. However, we know from the book of Acts that the apostles did heal the sick after Jesus left them at the Ascension. This suggests that they understood that it was the intention and desire of Jesus that they should do so. They would not do what they had no authority to do. The fact that they did continue to heal the sick must mean that they believed that they still had the authority to heal the sick in Jesus' name. Their example is therefore part of the basis and authority for the Church to engage in its ministry of healing today.

4. **The scope of the gospel.** Healing the sick was part of the gospel which the apostles and the Church were commissioned to preach. This is another implication of the fact that the apostles and others did heal the sick after the ascension of Jesus. The gospel included the healing and salvation of the whole human being in body, mind and spirit. It is the same gospel that is still entrusted to the Church to proclaim today, and since it included healing of the sick in apostolic times, it still does so today.

5. **The power of prayer.** The main agent in the Church's ministry of healing of the sick is prayer, and that is still available to the Church today. After Jesus promised his disciples that they would do the same works as he did, he goes on immediately to say, 'Whatever you ask in my name, I will do it, that the Father may be glorified in the Son' (John 14.13). This suggests that when they came to do the same works as he had done, they could request

the power to do them through prayer. We have examples of this in the book of the Acts of the Apostles where prayer preceded healing in the case of the raising of Tabitha by Peter (Acts 9.40), and in the healing of the father of Publius by Paul (Acts 28.8). When James writes of healing in the fifth chapter of his epistle, he does so in the context of prayer, and he recommends the elders and the Church members to pray for the healing of the sick (James 5.14-18). Healing occurred in the apostolic Church in response to the prayer of faith, and there is no reason that what happened then, should not happen still in the modern Church.

6. **The presence of healing gifts.** Within the Church today there are people who possess undoubted gifts of healing. Many of these people use these gifts as part of the ministry of healing which the Church is able to offer. These gifts would not exist unless the Church had a healing ministry in which they could be exercised.

7. **The vocation of the Christian.** The Church is involved in the ministry of healing through its corporate and individual vocation. The corporate vocation of the Church is the expression of the general vocation of its individual members, who are called to love and serve their neighbours. Its responsibility is, therefore, to promote their health and to encourage and produce healing in situations where this is required. The vocation of individual Church members may be to accept and use a gift of healing which is given to them. That vocation may also be to undergo professional health care training and so share in the healing ministry of the Church in a professional medical way, whether they serve in Christian or secular institutions or health care schemes.

These reasons provide the basis on which the Church today may legitimately claim that it has the authority to heal the sick and to engage in the ministry of healing.

## THE CONTEMPORARY CONTEXT OF HEALING

When we turn from the New Testament scene to look at the situation today we soon become aware of several features in the contemporary scene which are very different from those of the first-century Hellenistic world. It is important to remind ourselves of these features because they profoundly affect the modern attitude to healing and the concept of the role and involvement of the Church in healing.[2]

### 1. The loss of the spiritual dimension of life

One marked difference between New Testament and modern times so far as the western world is concerned is the loss of the spiritual foundation of private and community life. In western society today the emphasis tends to be on the physical and material with the result that the health of the body takes precedence over the health of the soul. This is in marked contrast to the world in which the healing ministry of the Church began, and in marked contrast to the life and thought of African, Asian and other non-western communities of the modern world.

This is clearly a difference of which the practice of a healing ministry by the Church must take account. This ministry will be rendered more difficult in a situation where an inadequate view of human nature and destiny prevails, and the reality of spiritual forces is ignored or denied. In such a situation, health, which it is the object of healing to restore, is inadequately defined, and healing ceases to be complete and comprehensive in its scope and practice. The Church in its healing ministry must, however, insist on the wholeness of the human being in all aspects of that being, and not least in the spiritual aspect, and seek to recover the spiritual dimension of human life of which former generations of western society were very much aware.

## 2. The rise in the status of medicine

In the Hellenistic world, medicine did not enjoy a very high status. Amongst the Greeks the influence of Hippocrates had already waned, and with a few outstanding exceptions medicine was practised on the basis of theories and *theriac*. The latter was a panacea originally prescribed by Galen and made up of about seventy ingredients all compounded together in treacle. According to the elder Pliny, the Romans had got on well without doctors (but not without medicines) for six hundred years.[3] However, with the fall and destruction of Corinth in 146 BC, the Roman power over Greece became supreme and Greek physicians began to migrate to Rome although they were not held in very high repute there. The practice of medicine was beneath the dignity of a Roman citizen and was left to slaves and foreigners. Its pharmacopoeia of effective drugs was small, its instruments few and crude, and the basis of its practice was often mere empiricism and superstition.

In contrast, medicine today enjoys a very high status in western society. Its practice is no longer based on empiricism and superstition but on an advanced knowledge of the structure and function of the human body, the origin and processes of disease and of the external and internal factors which influence the course of diseases. The great advances in surgical technology and the discovery of potent drugs have combined to give modern medicine a prestige and a status higher than it has ever known. The physician is now a prominent and trusted member of modern society and tends to be credited with a surprising omnicompetence. It is true, of course, that it is now being recognised that much healing occurs in the world for which orthodox medicine is not responsible. There is even a view which regards modern medicine as no more effective in the control and treatment of disease than primitive medicine was, and dismisses its claims as myth.[4] However, the majority of people still believe in its effectiveness, and modern medicine continues to enjoy great prestige within the communities of the western world.

## 3. The emergence of the medical profession

A well-organised medical profession exists in most countries today, which has established professional corporations to protect its rights and privileges, and to control entry into its ranks and monitor the practice of its art. This appears to be no new phenomenon in the history of the world, although the degree and effectiveness of professional organisation has varied from time to time and from country to country.

In New Testament times, the Romans left the practice of medicine to slaves and Greeks who were certainly not organised into a medical profession. We know that there were physicians in Palestine who treated the sick. Jesus confirmed this by his comment that those who were healthy did not need a physician, but those who were sick (Mark 2.17). The Talmud advised scholars not to live in a town where there was no physician, but no indications survive of how many towns did have a physician.[5] Physicians were held in high regard in Jewish society as early as the second century BC as we can see from Ben Sirach's advice to patients in Ecclesiasticus 38.1-15. According to Muntner some kind of medical guild existed in Rabbinic times which had for its insignia the *harut*, which is the branch of a palm tree or a balsam bush.[6] However, we know little about such a guild and it certainly cannot be compared with a modern medical profession.

Today, then, in most countries an organised medical profession exists, whose practice is controlled by law and professional self-regulation. This means that if the Church wishes to become involved in the practice of medical healing today it must do so in accordance with the rules and regulations governing the practice of medicine which have been drawn up by the representatives of the medical profession and embodied in the laws of the state.

## 4. The establishment of national health services

The fourth feature of the modern situation which affects the practice of the healing ministry of the Church is the establishment in western countries of national health services. These services have been established as part of the provision of the Welfare State of personal and social care for its citizens.[7]

The concept of the Welfare State arose out of the Christian teaching about the nature and destiny of human beings and the Christian concern for one's neighbour. The Christian view of the human being gave human personality a status, worth and dignity independent of the state and superior to the state, which it should be the function of the state to recognise and preserve. After the Reformation the state began to assume responsibility for the welfare of its citizens and to provide services which in former times had been provided by the Church. These services included those required for the care and cure of the sick.

Today, therefore, there exists in Great Britain a comprehensive national health service which provides facilities for the prevention, diagnosis and treatment of disease and disability. In other words, it is a service which seeks to promote health and practise healing. This means that any service provided by the Church as part of its ministry of healing must take account of those services which are already provided by the state in a national health service.

## 5. The uncertainty of the Church about healing

One result of these changes in society and in medicine has been an increasing uncertainty on the part of the Church about the nature of its healing ministry and its place in the practice of healing. Also, factors within the Church have increased this uncertainty as when the truth and historicity of the accounts of the healing miracles of Jesus in the gospels have been questioned and the authenticity of the words of Jesus recorded there, doubted.

## 6. Recent trends in healing

In addition to these changes there are more recent trends in society which also form part of the context in which the Church is called to exercise its ministry of healing. These include an increasing disenchantment of patients with the services of orthodox medicine shown by the popularity of what is variously called 'alternative medicine', 'complementary medicine' and 'non-conventional therapy'.[8] Another recent feature is the rise of 'consumerism' with the increasing recognition of patient autonomy or the right of patients to decide about the management of their particular illness or disability.

## THE PRACTICE OF HEALING BY THE CHURCH TODAY

If it is accepted that the modern Church has the authority and power to heal the sick in the name of Jesus Christ, and is called to do so in a situation which is very different from that of apostolic times, the next questions which arise concern the practice of healing by the Church today.

## Where is the healing ministry of the Church to be practised?

In the gospels, the healing ministry of Jesus was practised in the community at large wherever the sick were brought to him, or wherever he found those whom he healed. In the Acts, healing was carried out equally in the community at large and within the newly-established Christian community. In the epistles, however, the healing ministry of the Church is confined within the Christian community. The gift of healing, like the other gifts of the Spirit, is to be used within the Christian community for the common good of that community (1 Corinthians 12.7, 28). If Christian believers fall ill they are to call for the elders of the congregation to come and heal them (James 5.14). Also members of the congregation are to pray for the sick amongst them that they may be healed (James 5.16). In other words, the congregation plays a vital part in the healing ministry of the Church.[9]

However, there is more to be said than this when we consider the Church's healing ministry in the modern situation. As well as the congregation's practice of healing in which the Church acts corporately to practise what is essentially non-medical healing, there is also the individual practice of healing by Christians trained in the art and science of medical healing and in the work of the various health care professions. As members of the Church they are practising a healing ministry in the community at large in the course of their daily work. They are the Church scattered in the community at large and their work of healing is part of the Church's ministry of healing even though it is exercised in secular situations and institutions. They do not, however, practise in isolation for in their daily work they are upheld and supported by prayer and in other practical ways by the Church gathered as a community in worship and witness.

The ministry of healing of the Church is, therefore, to be practised within the Christian community by the corporate concern and activity of the elders and members of the congregation, and in the secular world at large by the activity and witness of its members engaged in their work as members of the health care professions. There are thus two aspects of the Church in its practice of healing. There is the Church gathered for worship, praise and prayer through which healing may be found. There is also the Church scattered as its members practise healing in their daily work and witness in the community.[10]

## Who practises the healing ministry of the Church?

In the epistles three groups of people were expected to practise healing:

1. Those who had been given the gift of healing by the Holy Spirit (1 Corinthians 12.9).

2. The elders of the Church who were called for by the sick (James 5.14).

3. The ordinary members of the Church who by confession to each other and by prayer for each other could produce healing (James 5.16).

The emphasis in all these references is not on the individual but on the Church as a community. Those who are given the gift of healing are placed by God in the Church to manifest and use their gift for the common good (1 Corinthians 12.7,28). The elders and Church members are spoken of by James in the plural which suggests that the authority to heal is not vested in them as individuals but in the Church as a corporate body which they represent in their ministry of healing. There is no mention of any special training of the members of these three groups. It is implied that they are able to heal by virtue of belonging to the Church and because of their function in it. Their healing is non-medical in character and does not depend on any medical training or skill.

In the modern Church there is no difficulty about the recognition of the elders and the ordinary members of the Church of whom James speaks, but there is controversy about those who may possess the gift of healing. When we discussed what the epistles had to say about healing, we took the view that the gift of healing was neither natural nor supernatural, but shared the characteristics of both spheres. It was given by God to certain individuals as a natural endowment which was then supernaturally enhanced by the Holy Spirit once they became Christians.

Healing is possible in some cases on the basis of this natural endowment. Only in this way can we explain how healing results from the activity of the traditional healers of Africa and elsewhere, or how exorcism results from the practice of non-Christian exorcists such as Jesus himself recognised in Matthew 7.22 and Luke 11.19. This natural endowment includes such characteristics as sympathy or the ability to enter into another person's situation and difficulties, patience or the facility to listen to their story, wisdom to know how to advise them on what to do in their particular case, and confidence to encourage them to expect recovery and healing.

In the modern situation it is also possible to combine the gift of healing with training in the art and practice of medicine, whether it consists of a natural endowment alone or a natural endowment supernaturally enhanced. Some members of the three groups in the Christian community which we have already mentioned may therefore be medically qualified or trained in some branch of health care. By virtue of their medical training and the professional recognition of their qualifications, they are able to practise medical healing and so bring medical practice into the healing ministry of the Church. It is not always clearly taught or realised that, as Bittlinger points out, there is no *Christian* activity that is independent of the Holy Spirit.

In practical terms this means, for example, that for the Christian doctor his total activity is charismatic activity. A prescription or an inoculation are only different ways of laying on of hands. Both are done prayerfully and in fellowship with Jesus. Because he knows that God is the one who heals, he will use his medical skill in utter dependence upon God.[11]

Those who are most conscious of combining medical practice with a gift of healing are the Christian professional health care workers who serve in a hospital or community health care scheme provided by the Church as part of its healing ministry. In situations in which other agencies provide a comprehensive health care service, the committed Christian staff who work within this service may not be so conscious of forming a part of the healing ministry of the Church. Nevertheless, they are exercising the Church's ministry of healing and fulfilling their own Christian vocation, even though they work within a secular health care service. By staffing the public or private health care services provided by other agencies and by bringing into those services a deeper and more comprehensive conception of health and healing than can be provided on a purely secular basis, the members of the Church are sharing in the ministry of healing of the Church and enriching the services in which they serve.

## How is the healing ministry of the Church to be practised?

The same methods of healing are available to the Church today as Jesus and the apostles used in the New Testament. These methods are four in number: prayer, word, touch and means.

1. **Prayer**. The basic method by which the Church practises its healing ministry today is by prayer. Prayer is the foundation of all Christian healing, whether medical or non-medical. It may be all that is required in any particular situation, or it may be combined with the use of the other methods whether medical or non-medical. This paramount importance of prayer in healing was pointed out by Jesus after his cure of the epileptic boy. Mark records how that after the boy had been healed, the disciples asked Jesus why they had not been able to cast out the demon which was the cause of the boy's epilepsy, and he answered simply, 'This kind cannot be driven out by anything but prayer' (Mark 9.29). Prayer for the sick may be offered in their presence as in Acts 9.40 and 28.8, or in their absence as in the case of the centurion's servant (Mark 7.24-30) or the Syrophoenician girl (Luke 7.1-10) where in both cases, Jesus healed them at a distance. Individual members of the Church join in its healing ministry as they pray for the sick privately or corporately in special meetings of intercession for the sick at which the sick are not usually present, but may be named. Prayer also forms an essential part of services which may be held for the sick, often with the sick persons present.

2. **Word**. In their sanatorium at Bad Boll, the Blumhardts practised healing in the context of worship and the proclamation of the Word of God.[12] They found that the words of Jesus in the gospel and the accounts of his healing miracles could still bring healing to men and women in the modern world as they were read and expounded in private study or public worship.

The use of a word of command is still the means of casting out demons as it was with Jesus in the gospels. In the case of the epileptic boy, although Jesus said that the kind of demon which possessed him could be driven out only by prayer (Mark 9.29), it was by a word of command that he expelled the demon (v.25). Every form of service which has been prepared for Christian exorcism suggests a form of words to be addressed to the demon for it is by prayer and the word of authority from Jesus Christ that demons are still cast out today.

3. **Touch**. The laying on of hands or the touching of a sick person was a method of healing used by Jesus and the apostles; consequently we have the

example of their practice to guide us in the modern practice of healing by the Church. Touch is a means of conveying sympathy to a person, but it is more than this when it is done in the name of Jesus Christ. It was never used in the casting out of demons, and so has no place in Christian exorcism. It may be used combined with prayer or accompanied by other methods of healing. In the New Testament it was often combined with a word as in the case of the bent woman in Luke 13.13.

It is not always stated where Jesus or the apostles applied their hands when they touched the sick. Sometimes it was to the affected part of the body as when Jesus touched the eyes of the blind men in Matthew 9.29 to restore their sight, or when he touched the injured ear of Malchus in Luke 22.51. At other times we are simply told that Jesus laid his hands on the sick person without any precise indication of where on their body he did so, as for example in the healing of the man with advanced leprosy in Matthew 8.3. In modern practice, hands are commonly laid on the head or shoulders of the sick person, but they may also be laid on the part of the body which is diseased, where this is known.

4. **Means.** There are several instances in the Bible where medical means are used. The most unequivocal example in the Old Testament is where the prophet Isaiah prescribes a fig poultice for King Hezekiah's boil in 2 Kings 20.7 and Isaiah 38.21. In the New Testament we find Jesus using saliva as part of the treatment in three of his healing miracles, once in the case of the deaf and dumb man in Mark 7.33, and twice in the case of blind persons in Mark 8.23 and John 9.6. Also in the gospels there is mention of the disciples anointing the sick with olive oil and healing them in Mark 6.13. Anointing the sick with olive oil as part of the healing procedure is mentioned also in James 5.14 and we suggested in our discussion of this verse in Chapter Twenty-one that it is probable that we should understand the use of olive oil there as medicinal rather than ritual. A final possible reference to the use of means in the treatment of sickness in the New Testament is in 1 Timothy 5.23 where Paul prescribes a little wine for Timothy's recurrent dyspepsia.

The Church today is able to practise a healing ministry using the same methods as Jesus did during his earthly ministry. Prayer still forms the basis of its ministry of healing, but a far greater variety of means is available now than was available then. More is known of the identity, activity and efficacy of medicines and of the nature and effectiveness of medical and surgical procedures than was known in New Testament times. This knowledge also is at the disposal of those who practise healing and may be used along with the other recognised methods of healing as part of the healing ministry of the Church by those who are suitably qualified and skilled to use it. This ministry includes all methods of healing, both physical and spiritual, medical and non-medical, for all true healing comes from God.

# NOTES AND REFERENCES
## Key to Abbreviations

| | |
|---|---|
| AB | *Anchor Bible* (Philadelphia: Doubleday & Co.). |
| BAG | Walter Bauer, *A Greek-English Lexicon of the New Testament*, translated and edited by W.F. Arndt & F.W. Gingrich (Chicago: University of Chicago Press, 1979), second edition. |
| BDB | Francis Brown, S.R. Driver & C.A. Briggs, *A Hebrew and English Lexicon of the Old Testament* (Oxford: Clarendon Press, 1957). |
| Bennett | Risdon Bennett, *The Diseases of the Bible* (London: The Religious Tract Society, 1887). |
| Brown | M.L. Brown, *Israel's Divine Healer* (Grand Rapids: Zondervan Publishing House/Carlisle: Paternoster Press, 1995). |
| BSDA | Don Brothwell & A.T. Sandison (eds.), *Diseases in Antiquity* (Springfield, Illinois: Charles C. Thomas, 1967). |
| CBSC | *Cambridge Bible for Schools & Colleges* (Cambridge University Press). |
| CGT | *Cambridge Greek Testament for Schools & Colleges* (Cambridge Univ. Press). |
| Cranfield, Mark | C.E.B. Cranfield, *The Cambridge Greek Testament Commentary on the Gospel according to Saint Mark* (Cambridge University Press, 1959) |
| Danby | *The Mishnah*, translated by Herbert Danby (London: Oxford University Press, 1933). |
| DNTT | *The New International Dictionary of New Testament Theology*, edited by Colin Brown (Exeter: Paternoster Press/Grand Rapids: Zondervan Publishing House, 1975-1978). |
| DSB | William Barclay, *Daily Study Bible* (Edinburgh: St Andrew Press, 1975-1976), revised edition. |
| EBC | *Expositor's Bible Commentary*, edited by F.E. Gaebelein (Grand Rapids: Zondervan Publishing House, 1976-1992). |
| Edersheim | Alfred Edersheim, *The Life and Times of Jesus the Messiah* (London: Longmans, Green & Co., 1906/Grand Rapids: William B. Eerdmans Publishing Co., reprint). |
| EGT | *The Expositor's Greek Testament* (London: Hodder & Stoughton/Grand Rapids: William B. Eerdmans Publishing Co., 1901-1910). |
| EQ | *Evangelical Quarterly*. |
| ET | English Translation. |
| ExpT | *Expository Times*. |
| Fergusson | Andrew Fergusson (ed.), *Health: The Strength to be Human* (London: Inter-Varsity Press, 1993). |
| Galen | Claudius Galen, *Opera Omnia*, edited by C.G. Kühn (Leipzig: Charles Cnoblochius, 1821-1833). |
| Guthrie | Douglas Guthrie, *A History of Medicine* (London: Nelson, 1945). |
| HDB | *Hastings' Dictionary of the Bible* (Edinburgh: T. & T. Clark/New York: Charles Scribner's Sons, 1898-1909). |
| Hobart | W.K. Hobart, *The Medical Language of St Luke* (Dublin: Hodges, Figgis & Co., 1992). |
| ICC | *International Critical Commentary* (Edinburgh: T. & T. Clark/ New York: Charles Scribner's Sons). |

IDB          *Interpreter's Dictionary of the Bible* (Nashville: Abingdon Press, 1962).
ISBE         *International Standard Bible Encyclopedia* (Grand Rapids: William B. Eerdmans Publishing Co., 1979-1988).
Knox         R.A. Knox, *A New Testament Commentary for English Readers* (London: Burns Oates & Washbourne, 1953-1956).
LCL          The Loeb Classical Library edition (London: William Heinemann/ Cambridge, Massachusetts: Harvard University Press).
LNL          J.P. Louw & E.A. Nida, *Greek-English Lexicon of the New Testament based on Semantic Domains*, (New York: United Bible Societies, 1988).
Loos         H. van der Loos, *The Miracles of Jesus* (Leiden: E.J. Brill, 1965).
Marshall,    I.H. Marshall, *The New International Greek Testament Commentary on the*
Luke         *Gospel of Luke* (Exeter: Paternoster Press, 1978).
Metzger      B.M. Metzger, *A Textual Commentary on the Greek New Testament* (London & New York: United Bible Societies, 1971).
Micklem      E.R. Micklem, *Miracles and the New Psychology* (Oxford: Oxford University Press, 1922).
Milligan     George Milligan, *Selections from the Greek Papyri* (Cambridge: Cambridge University Press, 1927).
MM           J.H. Moulton & George Milligan, *The Vocabulary of the Greek Testament* (London: Hodder & Stoughton, 1949).
NCB          *The New Century Bible* (London: Marshall, Morgan & Scott).
NICNT        *The New International Commentary on the New Testament* (Grand Rapids: William B. Eerdmans Publishing Co.).
NICOT        *The New International Commentary on the Old Testament* (Grand Rapids: William B. Eerdmans Publishing Co.).
NIGTC        *The New International Greek Testament Commentary* (Exeter: Paternoster Press).
Palmer       Bernard Palmer (ed.), *Medicine and the Bible* (Exeter: Paternoster Press, 1986).
Preuss       Julius Preuss, *Biblical and Talmudic Medicine*. Translated from the German and edited by Fred Rosner (New York: Sanhedrin Press, 1978).
SB           H.L. Strack & Paul Billerbeck, *Kommmentar zum Neuen Testament aus Talmud und Midrasch* (Munich: C.H. Beckshe Publ. House, 1956), third edn.
Short        A.R. Short, *The Bible and Modern Medicine* (London: Paternoster Press, 1953).
SJT          *The Scottish Journal of Theology*.
Taylor,      Vincent Taylor, *The Gospel according to St Mark: The Greek Text* (London:
Mark         Macmillan/New York: St Martin's Press, 1957).
TDNT         *Theological Dictionary of the New Testament*, edited by Gerhard Kittel & Gerhard Friedrich (Grand Rapids: Wm. B. Eerdmans Publishing Co.).
TDOT         *Theological Dictionary of the Old Testament*, edited by G.J. Botterweck & Helmer Ringgren (Grand Rapids: Wm. B. Eerdmans Publishing Co.).
TNTC         *Tyndale New Testament Commentaries* (Leicester: Inter-Varsity Press/Grand Rapids: William B. Eerdmans Publishing Co.).
TOTC         *Tyndale Old Testament Commentaries* (Leicester: Inter-Varsity Press).
TWOT         *Theological Wordbook of the Old Testament*, edited by R.L. Harris, G.L. Archer Jr. & B.K. Waltke (Chicago: Moody Press, 1980).
Weather-     L.D. Weatherhead, *Psychology, Religion and Healing* (London: Hodder &
head         Stoughton, 1952), second edition.
WHO          World Health Organisation.

# Chapter References

## Introduction: Healing in Medicine and Theology

1. Lewis Carroll, *Alice through the Looking Glass* (London: Dent/New York: E.P.Dutton, 1929), Everyman edition, p.159.
2. Brian Inglis, *Fringe Medicine* (London: Faber & Faber, 1964), p.212.
3. Andrew Stanway, *Alternative Medicine* (Harmondsworth: Penguin Books, 1982), p.135.
4. British Medical Association, *Complementary Medicine: New Approaches to Good Practice* (London: BMA, 1993), p.x.
5. E.J. Cassells, *The Healer's Art* (Harmondsworth: Penguin, 1978), p.14.
6. Karl Barth, *Church Dogmatics* (Edinburgh: T. & T. Clark, 1961), vol. 3, part 4, pp.369-371.
7. Paul Tillich, 'The Meaning of Health', *Perspectives in Biology & Medicine*, vol. 5 (1961), pp.92-100. See also his *Systematic Theology* (London: Nisbet, 1968), vol. 3, chapter 30, pp.293-300, 'The Healing Power of the Spiritual Presence'.
8. Jürgen Moltmann, *God in Creation* (London: SCM Press, 1985), pp.270-275, 'Life in Health and Sickness'. See also his book, *The Spirit of Life* (London: SCM Press, 1992), pp.188-192, 'The Healing of the Sick'.
9. See Chapter Twenty-three of this present book for an account of the work of Pastor Blumhardt.
10. Rudolf Bultmann, *Kerygma und Mythus* (Hamburg: Herbert Reich, 1948), p.150. Quoted in Barth, *op.cit.*, p.370.
11. W.N.Clarke, *An Outline of Christian Theology* (Edinburgh: T. & T. Clark, 1899/New York: Charles Scribner's Sons, 1898), sixth edition, p.184. It is difficult to see how a dismissive remark such as this can be justified theologically when God created human life only in the form of bodily life; when a human body was the medium of the Incarnation; and the human body will be the subject of renewal at the resurrection.See Dietrich Bonhoeffer, *Ethics* (London: Collins/Fontana, 1964), pp.155-158.
12. The Church of England, *The Church's Ministry of Healing. The Report of the Archbishops' Commission* (London: Church Information Office, 1958), p.12.
13. Guthrie, p.146.
14. Adolf Harnack, *Luke the Physician* (London: Williams & Norgate/New York: G. P.Putnam's Sons, 1907), p.3, n.2. Harnack suggests that just as the phrase 'the beloved son' in 2 Timothy 1.2 means 'my beloved son', so the similar phrase 'the beloved physician' in Colossians 4.14 means that Luke is described by Paul as 'my beloved physician'. See also Chapter Thirteen (p.163) of this present book for Harnack's suggestion that Luke practised medicine on Malta (Harnack, *op.cit.*, pp.15-16).
15. A.A. Hodge, *Popular Lectures on Theological Themes* (Philadelphia: Presbyterian Board of Publication, 1887), pp.107-116.
16. Guthrie, p.30.
17. See the discussion of these terms in the *Report of the Church of England Commission* (ref. 12 above), pp.12-14.

## Part One: The Biblical Understanding of Health

1. Quoted by D.S. Cairns, *The Faith that Rebels* (London: SCM Press, 1933), fifth edition, p.56.
2. Augustine, *Quaestiones in Exodum*, 73. See also his *De Catechizandis Rudibus*, 4.66-68.

## Chapter One: The Concept of Health in the Old Testament

1. The word 'health' occurs in the Old Testament fifteen times in the AV, six times in the RSV, five times in the NRSV and ten times in the NIV.
2. W.D. Stacey, *The Pauline View of Man* (London: Macmillan/ New York: St Martin's Press Inc., 1956), p.94. It is interesting to note that the Greek word *soma*, which is the common word for the body in the New Testament first appeared in Homer where it denoted a dead human or animal body. It was only in the fifth century BC that it came to mean the whole human body whether alive or dead (See Eduard Schweizer, TDNT (1971), vol. 7, pp.1025-1026, s.v. *soma*).
3. H W. Wolff, *Anthropology of the Old Testament* (London: SCM Press/Philadelphia: Fortress Press, 1974), p.28.
4. A.R. Johnson, *The Vitality of the Individual in the Thought of Ancient Israel* (Cardiff: University of Wales Press, 1949), p.7.
5. Walter Eichrodt, *Theology of the Old Testament* (London: SCM Press, 1967), vol. 2, p.131.
6. John Murray, *Collected Writings* (Edinburgh: Banner of Truth Trust, 1977), vol. 2, p.21.
7. John Wilkinson, 'The Body in the Old Testament', EQ, vol. 63 (1991) pp.195-210.
8. G.L. Carr, TWOT, vol. 2, p.931, s.v. *shalom*.
9. BDB, p.1022, s.v. *shalom*.
10. Johannes Pedersen, *Israel: Its Life and Culture* (London: Oxford University Press, 1926), vol. I-II, p.311.
11. Gerhard von Rad, TDNT (1964), vol. 2, p.402, s.v. *eirene*.
12. Johannes Pedersen, *op.cit.*, p.313, See also BDB, p.1022, s.v. *shalom*.
13. G.J. Wenham, *TCOT on Numbers* (1981), p.90. Cp. Johannes Pedersen, *op.cit.*, p.313: *Shalom* 'comprises all that the Israelite understands by "good"'. Pedersen quotes Lamentations 3.17, Jeremiah 8.15 and 14.19.
14. The bones, 'in the language of Hebrew poetry, denote the whole physical organism of the living man, as being the fundamental part of it. Hence they are the seat of health (Proverbs 16.24), or of pain, as in Psalm 6.2. In some passages, "the bones" come to be identified with the man himself, as a living agent. Cp. Psalm 35.10'. A.F. Kirkpatrick, *CBSC on the Psalms* (1901), p.26.
15. G.L. Carr, *op.cit.*, p.931, s.v. *shalom*.
16. WHO Basic Documents: Constitution (Geneva: WHO, 1948), p.1.
17. N.H. Snaith, *The Distinctive Ideas of the Old Testament* (London: Epworth Press, 1944), pp.72-73. Snaith rejects the alternative etymology of the root which suggests that its original meaning was 'hardness' not 'straightness' (See John Skinner, HDB, vol. 4, p.274).
18. A.B. Davidson, *The Theology of the Old Testament* (Edinburgh: T. & T. Clark/New York: Charles Scribner's Sons, 1904), p.130.
19. See Walter Eichrodt, *op.cit.*, vol. 1, p.240.

20. Gerhard von Rad, *Old Testament Theology* (Edinburgh: Oliver & Boyd, 1962), vol. 1, p.370.

21. K.L. Vaux, *Health and Medicine in the Reformed Tradition* (New York: Crossroad, 1984), p.108.

22. Edmond Jacobs, *Theology of the Old Testament* (London: Hodder & Stoughton, 1958), p.179.

23. C.G.K. Gillespie, *The Sanitary Code of the Pentateuch* (London: Religious Tract Society, 1894). See also A.S. Darling, 'The Levitical Code: Hygiene or Holiness', in Palmer, pp.85-99, and G.J. Wenham, 'The Theology of Unclean Food', EQ, vol. 53 (1981), pp.6-15. A good description of the 'Hygiene Conditions in Ancient Israel (Iron Age)' is given by Edward Neufeld in *The Biblical Archaeologist*, vol. 34 (1971), pp.42-66.

24. Klaus Seybold, TDOT (1980), vol. 4, pp.399-409, s.v. *choli*.

25. Karl Barth, *Church Dogmatics* (Edinburgh: T. & T. Clark, 1961), vol. 3, part 4, p.357.

26. Jürgen Moltmann, *God in Creation* (London: SCM Press, 1985), p.273.

27. David Atkinson, 'Towards a Theology of Health', in Fergusson, p.33.

28. Brown, p.82.

29. G.J. Wenham, *NICOT on Leviticus* (1970), p.18. See also the comments on holiness on pp.18-25, 155-156 & 264-265.

30. J.A.T. Robinson, *The Body: A Study in Pauline Theology* (London: SCM Press, 1952), pp.15-16.

31. For a discussion of the relationship between holiness and cleanness see Wenham, *op.cit.*, pp.18-25 and Mary Douglas, *Purity and Danger* (London: Routledge & Kegan Paul, 1966). Douglas writes as a social anthropologist.

32. David Atkinson, *op.cit.*, p.30.

33. See the Report of the Thirty-seventh World Health Assembly, 7th to 17th May 1984, published in the *WHO Chronicle*, vol. 38 (1984), p.174.

34. See the consensus statement on the meaning of health drawn up by a group of health care professionals and theologians in June 1989 and reproduced in Fergusson, pp.9-10.

## Chapter Two: The Concept of Health in the New Testament

1. See e.g. Homer, *Iliad* 2.797 (LCL vol. 1, p.109).

2. C.L. Mitton, IDB (1962), vol. 3, p.700, art. 'Peace in the New Testament'.

3. R.C. Trench, *Synonyms of the New Testament* (London: Kegan Paul, Trench, Trübner & Co., 1901), new edition, pp.86-90.

4. William Barclay, *DSB on the Gospel of John* (1975), vol. 1, pp.136-137.

5. Milligan, p.91, n.13.

6. Charles Bigg, *ICC on the Epistles of St Peter & St Jude* (1901), p.102.

7. C.E.B. Cranfield, *ICC on the Epistle to the Romans* (1975), vol. 1, p.88.

8. Westminster Confession (1647), chapter I, section vii.

9. William Barclay, *More New Testament Words* (London: SCM Press, 1958), p.28.

10. Ambrose, *Exposition of the Gospel of Luke*, 5.49. The word *beatitudo* appears to have been coined by Cicero (*De Natura Deorum* 1.34: LCL p.93), but was not accepted in classical Latin literature and later found a congenial home in the Christian Church. See R.C. Trench, *On the Study of Words* (London: Kegan Paul, Trench, Trübner & Co., 1851), eighteenth edition, p.210.

11. Aristotle, *The Nicomachean Ethics* 1.10,14 (LCL p.55).

12. H.W. Robinson, *The Christian Doctrine of Man* (Edinburgh: T. & T. Clark, 1911), p.108.

13. Gerhard Delling, TDNT (1972), vol. 8, pp.75-77, s.v. *telos*.

## Part Two: Disease and Healing in the Old Testament

## Chapter Three: Epidemic Disease in the Old Testament

1. Klaus Seybold, TDOT (1980), vol. 4, p.300, s.v. *chalah*.

2. Klaus Seybold and U.B.Mueller, Sickness and Healing (Nashville: Abingdon Press, 1981), pp.23-24. In post-Biblical Hebrew literature the term *nega* is used exclusively of skin disease as it is in Leviticus 13.1-46.

3. BDB, p.184, s.v. *deber*. The Mishnah defines a pestilence as follows: 'If, in a city that can count three hundred men of war, three dead go forth in three days, one after the other, this is deemed a pestilence; but less than this is not deemed a pestilence', *Taanith* 3.4 (Danby, p.198).

4. S.B. Blakely, 'The Medicine of the Old Testament', *Medical Record*, vol. 87 (1915), p.936 (June 5th).

5. Herbert Loewe in Hastings' *Encyclopaedia of Religion & Ethics* (Edinburgh: T. & T. Clark/New York: Charles Scribner's Sons, 1911), vol. 4, p.756, art. 'Disease and Medicine (Jewish)'. The text at the head of this section comes from Deuteronomy 28.21.

6. R.K. Harrison, *TOTC on Leviticus* (1980), p.232.

7. Max Sussman in *The Anchor Bible Dictionary* (New York: Doubleday, 1992), vol. 6, p.8, art. 'Sickness and Disease'. See Preuss, pp.164-167 for discussion of meaning of *yeraqon*.

8. Alexander Macalister, HDB, vol. 3, p.324, art. 'Medicine'.

9. John Wilkinson, 'The Philistine Epidemic of 1 Samuel 5 & 6', ExpT vol. 88 (1976-77), p.138.

10. P.C. Craigie, *NICOT on Deuteronomy* (1976), p.344.

11. G.B. Gray, *ICC on Numbers* (1903), p.118. The verb *karat* in the Niphal means 'to cut off or to fail'. Only in this passage is it translated 'to chew' (v.33). Its use here is best understood to refer not to the biting off or chewing of the meat by the teeth, but to the failure of the meat supply. The onset of the disease thus occurred not before the meat had been chewed, but before the supply of the meat had run out as suggested by the GNB translation.

12. Preuss, p.559.

13. Charles Creighton, *Encyclopaedia Biblica* (London: A & C Black, 1914), one-volume edition, col. 3391, art. 'Quail'.

14. Edmond Sergent, 'Les cailles empoisonneuses dans la Bible et en Algérie de nos jours', *Arch. Inst. Pasteur d'Algérie*, vol. 19 (1942) no. 2, pp.161-192 (June).

15. Theodore Ouzounellis, 'Some Notes on Quail Poisoning', *Journal of the American Medical Association*, vol. 211 (1970) pp.1186-1187 (February 16th).

16. Bennett, p.59.

17. D.J. Wiseman, 'Medicine in the Old Testament World' in Palmer, p.24. Wiseman suggests that the correct number of those who died in the plague may have been fourteen and not fourteen thousand. Cp. Reference 22 below.

18. Bennett, p.60.

19. E.L. Curtis & A.A. Madsen, *ICC on the Books of Chronicles* (1910), p.416.

20. John Wilkinson, art. cit., p.141.

21. Otto Neustatter, 'Where did the identification of the Philistine Plague (1 Samuel 5 & 6) as bubonic plague originate?' *Bulletin of the History of Medicine*, vol. 11 (1942), pp.36-47.

22. D.J. Wiseman, *TOTC on 1 and 2 Kings* (1993), p.284. Wiseman suggests that the figure 185,000 of 2 Kings 19.35 could be interpreted as 185 'officers' (see 2 Chronicles 32.21).

23. Herodotus 2.141 (LCL vol. 1, pp.447-449). Herodotus appears to describe the same incident as 2 Kings 19.35.

24. The adjective translated 'fiery' is derived from the Hebrew verb *saraph* which means 'to burn' and which has been explained as a reference to the burning sensation at the time of the bite or the inflammation which followed it (so G.B. Gray, *ICC on Numbers* (1903), p.277). The LXX translated the word as 'deadly' (*thanatountas*) and it has been suggested that the Hebrew word simply means 'poisonous' in this context. See D.J. Wiseman, *Tyndale Bulletin*, vol. 23 (1972), pp.108-110.

25. The Mishnah suggested that the reason why Moses was instructed to mount the serpent on a standard-bearing pole was to direct the thoughts of the people to heaven where God lived who was their true healer (*Rosh ha-Shanah* 3.8: Danby, p.192).

26. Noth suggested that the snake was the representative or symbol of a healing god and Moses invited the people to worship this mounted symbol in order to be released from the effects of their snakebites. See Martin Noth, *Numbers: A Commentary* (London: SCM Press, 1968), p.158. This suggestion finds no support in the text.

27. Bennett, pp.133-138. This suggestion was originally made by Thomas Bartholin (1616-1680), an anatomist of Copenhagen, according to Preuss, p.197. Amongst modern authors this suggestion is favoured by R.J. Wolff in ISBE (1988), vol. 4, pp.1209-1210.

28. G.S. Cansdale, *Animals of Bible Lands* (Exeter: Paternoster Press, 1970), pp.205-207. See also R.K. Harrison, *Numbers: An Exegetical Commentary* (Grand Rapids: Baker Book House, 1992), p.376.

29. T.E. Lawrence, *Revolt in the Desert* (London: Jonathan Cape/New York: G.H. Doran, 1927), p.93.

## Chapter Four: Systemic Disease in the Old Testament

1. R.K. Harrison, ISBE (1979), vol. 1, p.955, art. 'Disease'. See also Short, p.63.

2. Preuss, p.307.

3. Babylonian Talmud, *Sanhedrin* 48b and *Sotah* 10a. See Preuss, p.168 and Fred Rosner, *Medicine in the Bible and Talmud* (New York: Ktav Publishing House, 1977), pp.59-60.

4. D.J. Wiseman, *TOTC on 1-2 Kings* (1993), p.157 and in Palmer, pp.33-34.

5. D.J. Wiseman, *op.cit.*, p.146 and in Palmer, p.28.

6. Edward Davies, 'Raynaud Phenomenon in Moses', *Advances in Microcirculation*, vol. 10 (1982), pp.110-111.

7. Preuss, p.183.

8. E.L. Curtis & A.A. Madsen, *ICC on the Books of Chronicles* (1910), pp.417-418. See also C.F. Keil & Franz Delitzsch, *Biblical Commentary on the Books of Chronicles* (Edinburgh: T. & T. Clark, 1857/Grand Rapids: Wm. B. Eerdmans Publishing Co., 1976 reprint), p.400.

9. R.E. McGrew, *Encyclopedia of Medical History* (London: Macmillan, 1985), p.273, art. 'Poliomyelitis'. This stela is now in the Carlsberg Glyptotek in Copenhagen.

10. Short, pp.62-63.

11. J.B. Hardie, 'Medicine and the Biblical World', *Canadian Medical Association Journal*, vol. 94 (1966), p.34 (January 1st). See also Rabbi Manna in the Jerusalem Talmud, *Yebamoth* 15.14d and Preuss, p.169.

12. Bennett, p.104.

13. Short, pp.61-62.

14. Preuss, p.169.

15. *Ibidem*, p.299.

16. *Ibidem*.

17. A.T. Sandison, 'Diseases of the Eyes' in BSDA, p.459. See also the same author's article, 'The Eye in the Egyptian Mummy', *Medical History*, vol. 1 (1957), p.336-339.

18. A.T. Sandison, 'Diseases of the Skin' in BSDA, pp.451-455. A photograph of the head of Rameses V showing the rash resembling smallpox is reproduced on p.453. See also G.E. Smith, *The Royal Mummies* (Cairo: Egyptian Museum, 1912).

19. Short, p.54.

20. John Wilkinson, 'The Book of Job', *Proceedings of the Royal College of Physicians of Edinburgh*, vol. 25 (1995), pp.516-517.

21. G.R. Driver, quoted by S.G. Browne in Palmer, p.104.

22. J.F.A. Sawyer, 'A note on the etymology of *sara'at*', *Vetus Testamentum*, vol. 26 (1976), pp.243-244.

23. G.R. Driver, HDB, one-volume edition (Edinburgh: T. & T. Clark/New York: Charles Scribner's Sons, 1963), second edition, p.575.

24. E. V. Hulse, 'The Nature of Biblical "Leprosy" and the Use of Alternative Medical Terms in Modern Translations of the Bible', *Palestine Exploration Quarterly*, vol. 107 (1975), pp.87-105.

25. Brown, p.94.

26. G.R. Driver, *op.cit.*, p.577.

27. John Wilkinson, 'Leprosy and Leviticus: The Problem of Description and Identification', SJT, vol. 30 (1977), pp.165-166.

28. This may possibly be a reference to an infirmary or a health care institution according to Klaus Seyboldt & U.B. Mueller, *Sickness and Healing* (Nashville: Abingdon, 1981), p.21. If it is, this is the only mention of such an institution in the Old Testament and appears to be for the use of the king alone.

29. John Wilkinson, 'The Book of Job', *Proceedings of the Royal College of Physicians of Edinburgh*, vol. 25 (1995), pp.516-517.

30. George Campbell, personal communication.

31. C.F. Keil & F.J. Delitzsch, *Biblical Commentary on the Old Testament: The Pentateuch* (Edinburgh: T. & T. Clark, 1878/Grand Rapids: William B. Eerdmans Publishing Co., 1976 reprint), vol. 1, p.487. For the suggestion of pemphigus see Sussman Muntner, *Encyclopaedia Judaica* (Jerusalem: Keter Publishing House, 1971), vol. 11, p.1179, art. 'Medicine'.

32. Preuss, p.342 and Arturo Castiglioni, 'The Contribution of Jews to Medicine' in Louis Finkelstein (ed.), *The Jews: Their Role in Civilisation* (New York: Shocken Books, 1971), fourth edition, p.192.

33. Short, p.55.

34. BDB, p.142, s.v. *basar*.

35. Preuss, p.354.

36. C. Dennie, *A History of Syphilis* (Springfield, Illinois: Charles C. Thomas, 1962).

37. B. Baker & G. Armelagos, 'The origin and antiquity of syphilis', *Current Anthropology*, vol. 29 (1988), pp.703-738.

38. C.F. Keil & F.J. Delitzsch, *Biblical Commentary on the Books of Samuel* (Edinburgh: T. & T. Clark, 1866/Grand Rapids: William B. Eerdmans Publishing Co., 1976 reprint), p.221.

39. J.V. Kinnier-Wilson, 'Mental Diseases of Ancient Mesopotamia' in BSDA, p.731.

40. J.V. Kinnier-Wilson, *Assyriological Studies* (Chicago: Chicago University Press, 1965), no. 16, p.289.

41. Klaus Seyboldt & U.B. Mueller, *op.cit.*, p.35.

42. R.K. Harrison, *Introduction to the Old Testament* (Grand Rapids: William B. Eerdmans Publishing Co., 1969/London: Tyndale Press, 1970), pp.1114-1117, where the author describes a case of boanthropy which he personally observed in a British mental institution in 1946.

## Chapter Five: Healing in the Old Testament

1. Brown, p.25.

2. Preuss, p.14.

3. Brown, pp.25-28.

4. BDB, p.73, s.v. *arak*.

5. BDB, p.74, s.v. *aruka*.

6. Karl Barth, *Church Dogmatics* (Edinburgh: T. & T. Clark, (1961), vol. 3, part 4, p.369.

7. Sussman Munter, 'Medicine in Ancient Israel', in Fred Rosner, *Medicine in the Bible and Talmud* (New York: Ktav Publishing House, 1977), p.9.

8. Helen Spurrell, *Translation of the Old Testament Scriptures from the Original Hebrew* (London: 1885), in loc. cit.

9. T.J. Meek in *The Complete Bible: An American Translation* (Chicago: University of Chicago Press, 1939), p.65.

10. Brown, p.31.

11. *Ibidem*, p.74.

12. *Ibidem*, p.78.

13. Robert Dickinson, *God Does Heal Today* (Carlisle: Paternoster Press, 1995), p.44. Another case in which God healed directly was that of the paralysed hand of King Jeroboam which he healed in response to the prayer of the unnamed man of God from Judah (1 Kings 13.6).

14. Sussman Muntner, *Encyclopaedia Judaica* (Jerusalem: Keter Publishing House, 1971), vol. 11, p.1179, art. 'Medicine'.

15. Babylonian Talmud, *Sanhedrin* 17b.

16. Mishnah, *Shekalim* 5.1-2 (Danby, p.157, n.8). Preuss (p.14) points out that this officer is not called a physician and was probably a priest who knew which wines were beneficial for intestinal complaints as the Jerusalem Talmud suggests in *Shekalim* 5.48d.

17. Preuss, p.24 and Brown, p.46. See also Fred Rosner, *Modern Medicine and Jewish Ethics* (New York: Yeshiva University Press, 1985), pp.9-11 and Immanuel Jakobovits, *Jewish Medical Ethics* (New York: Bloch, 1959), p.3.

18. Fred Rosner, *op.cit.*, p.11. See also Moses Maimonides, *Mishneh Torah, Hilchot Rotze'ach* 1.14.

19. Brown, pp.48-53. An alternative explanation for Asa's denunciation is that the physicians he sought to consult were in fact pagan, or at least magical or idolatrous practitioners. However, there is no evidence of this in the context, which does provide some evidence of the character of Asa.

20. Alexander Macalister, HDB, vol. 3, p.321, art. 'Medicine'.

21. D.J. Wiseman, 'Medicine in the Old Testament World' in Palmer, p.42.

22. Gustav Dalman, *Sacred Sites and Ways* (London: SPCK, 1935), pp.81-82.

23. D.J. Wiseman, *TOTC on 1 and 2 Kings* (1993), p.197.

24. *Ibidem*, p.204.

## Part Three: Healing in the Gospels

1. Adolf Harnack, *The Mission and Expansion of the Christianity in the First Three Centuries* (London: Williams & Norgate, 1908) ET by James Moffatt, vol. 1, p.101.

2. Ignatius, *Ephesians 7.2* (LCL vol. 1, p.181).

3. Clement Alex., *Paedagogus* I: 1.1; 2.6; 6.36; 8.64 and 12.10.

4. *Ibidem*, 2.6.

5. Origen, *Contra Celsum* 2.67, end.

6. Origen, *Homily on Leviticus*, 8.1.

7. Eusebius, *Ecclesiastical History* 10.4,11 (LCL vol. 2, p.405).

## Chapter Six: The Records of Healing

1. S.L. Davies, *Jesus the Healer* (London: SCM Press/New York: Continuum Publishing Co., 1995), p.10.
2. M.L. & T.A.L. Davies, *The Bible: Medicine and Myth* (Cambridge: Silent Press, 1991), pp.206-217.
3. F.W. Beare, *The Earliest Records of Jesus* (Oxford: Blackwell, 1962), p.176.
4. Rudolf Bultmann, *The History of the Synoptic Tradition* (Oxford: Blackwell, 1968), p.213.
5. J.A. Fitzmyer suggests the term 'demon-sickness' for those cases in which demon possession expresses itself in physical symptoms and signs (*AB on the Gospel of Luke [1981]*, vol. 1, p.545).
6. C. J. Singer & Abraham Wasserstein in *The Oxford Classical Dictionary*, edited by N.G.L. Hammond & H.H. Scullard (Oxford: Clarendon Press, 1970), second edition, p.660, art. 'Medicine'.
7. For usage of the word in Hippocrates see Hobart, p.2.
8. W.M. Alexander, *Demonic possession in the New Testament* (Edinburgh: T. & T. Clark, 1902), pp.67-68.
9. Micklem, p.53.
10. W.M. Alexander, *op.cit.*, p.88.
11. S.V. McCasland, *By the Finger of God. Demon Possession and Exorcism in the Early Church in the Light of Modern Views of Mental Illness* (New York: Macmillan, 1951).
12. A.C.P. Sims, 'Demon Possession: Medical Perspective in a Western Culture', in Palmer, pp.165-189. See also M.G. Barker, 'Possession and the Occult - A Psychiatrist's View', *Churchman*, vol. 94 (1980), pp.246-253.
13. In Matthew 17.15 the most probable reading is the rarer phrase *kakos paschei*, 'he feels bad' and not *kakos echei* 'he has bad' as in the *Textus Receptus*. See Metzger, p.43.
14. MM, p.430, s.v. *nosos*.

## Chapter Seven: The Words for Healing

1. C.J. Hemer, 'Medicine in the New Testament World' in Palmer, p.53.
2. Plato, *Euthyphro* 13B (LCL p.49).
3. The Rabbinic parallel is 'Physician, heal your limp' (Jerusalem Talmud, *Bereshith Rabba* 23.15c. Cp. SB, vol. 2, p.156). Many other similar sayings exist in ancient literature (For examples see Alfred Plummer, *ICC on the Gospel of St Luke* [1901], p.126). There is an echo of this proverb in the taunt addressed to Jesus on the cross by the Jewish rulers in Luke 23.35.
4. Homer, *Iliad* 5.899 (LCL vol. 1, p.261) and *Odyssey* 9.520 & 525 (LCL vol. 1, p.343). See also C.J. Hemer, *art. cit.* in Palmer, p.43.
5. Hobart, p.9.
6. A.H. McNeile, *The Gospel according to St Matthew* (London: Macmillan, 1915), p.420.
7. F.V. Filson, *A Commentary on the Gospel according to St Matthew* (London: Black, 1960), p.296.
8. Werner Foerster, TDNT (1971), vol. 7, p.990, s.v. *sozo*.
9. E.M.B. Green, *The Meaning of Salvation* (London: Hodder & Stoughton, 1965), p.218.
10. Jerome, *Commentary on Matthew* on 12.13. See Edgar Hennecke, *New Testament Apocrypha* (London: Lutterworth Press, 1965), vol. 1, p.148.
11. The other healing which took place in two stages was that of the man born blind in John 9.1-7.
12. LNL, vol. 1, section 23.137, p.269, s.v. *katharizo*.

13. For a fuller discussion of the use of *katharizo* see John Wilkinson, 'The Mission Charge to the Twelve and Modern Medical Missions', SJT, vol. 27 (1974), p.316.

14. The following clause, 'and had spent all her living upon physicians' included in the text of the AV, but put in the margin of subsequent versions, is not present in some early manuscripts. Metzger (p.145) says the evidence for its omission is 'well-nigh compelling' while Marshall notes that 'a clear-cut decision is impossible'. See Marshall, Luke, p.344.

15. Hobart, pp.16-17.

16. LNL, vol. 1, section 76.1, p.680, s.v. *dunamis*.

17. Otfried Hofius, DNTT (1976), vol. 2, p.627, s.v. *semeion*. In the usage of the Hellenistic papyri, the word *semeion* means 'a seal or an outward distinguishing mark' (MM p.572).

18. C.K. Barrett, *The Gospel according to St John* (London: SPCK, 1978), second edn., p.75.

19. W.L. Lane, *NICNT on the Gospel of Mark* (1974), pp.276-277.

20. Our modern use of the word 'miracle' for the healing acts of Jesus overemphasises the aspect of wonder. This word is derived from the Latin *miraculum* which means 'a thing which causes wonder', and significantly is not used in the Latin versions of the New Testament.

21. F.F. Bruce, *The Acts of the Apostles: Greek Text* (Grand Rapids: William B. Eerdmans Publishing Co., 1990), third edition, p.410.

22. BAG, p.169, s.v. *daimonion*. The derivation of the word 'demon' is uncertain. It may be derived from the Greek verb meaning 'to divide or tear apart' so that it originally meant 'corpse-eater'. On the other hand it may reflect the belief that these supernatural agents assigned the destinies of human beings. In the New Testament it means 'supernatural evil beings'.

23. See the discussion of this phrase in Chapter Eleven, pp.139-140.

## Chapter Eight: The Approach to Healing

1. C.K. Barrett, *The Gospel according to St John* (London: SPCK, 1978), second edition p.353. This is also the view of Leon Morris, *The Gospel according to John* (London: Marshall, Morgan & Scott, 1972), p.477.

2. C.H. Dodd, *The Apostolic Preaching and its Developments* (London: Hodder and Stoughton, 1936), pp.3-5. For a recent assessment of Dodd's thesis see G. P.Hugenberger, ISBE (1986), vol. 3, pp.941-2, art. 'Preach'.

3. Joseph Klausner, *Jesus of Nazareth* (London: Macmillan, 1925), p.266.

4. References to Rabbis raising the dead are given in SB, vol. 1, pp.523-524 and 560.

5. Loos, pp.142-150.

6. Alan Richardson, *The Miracle Stories of the Gospel* (London: SCM Press, 1941), p.32.

7. J.B. Lightfoot, *The Epistle to the Philippians* (London: Macmillan, 1908), fourth edition, p.86. See also MM, p.584 and BAG, p.762, s.v. *splanchnizomai*.

8. Mishnah, *Kelim* 1.1 (Danby, p.604).

9. Taylor, Mark, p.187.

10. Metzger, p.76.

11. John Wilkinson, 'Leprosy and Leviticus: The Problem of Description and Identification', SJT, vol. 30 (1977), pp.153-169 and also 'Leprosy and Leviticus: A Problem of Semantics and Translation', SJT, vol. 31 (1978), pp.153-166.

12. Vincent Taylor, *The Names of Jesus* (London: Macmillan, 1953), pp.38-51.

13. *Ibidem*, p.24.

14. *Ibidem*, p.14.

15. Taylor, Mark, p.194. See also David Hill, *NCB on the Gospel of Matthew* (1972), p.170.

16. Weatherhead, pp.49-50.

17. H.G. Liddell & Robert Scott, *A Greek-English Lexicon* (Oxford: Clarendon Press, 1940), ninth edition, p.444, s.v. *doxa*. In Hebrew the word *Shekinah* means 'the presence' (of God). For this see R.A. Stewart, *Rabbinic Theology* (Edinburgh: Oliver & Boyd, 1961), pp.39-42.

18. For a discussion of the Christological significance of the *semeia* see Rudolf Schnackenburg, *The Gospel according to St John* (London: Burns & Oates, 1968), vol. 1, pp.512-525.

19. Marshall, Luke, p.181.

20. Emil Schürer, *The History of the Jewish People in the Age of Jesus Christ* (Edinburgh: T. & T. Clark, 1979), revised edition, vol. 2, p.425. The passage which Jesus read was the *Haftarah* for the tenth month of Tishri which is the Day of Atonement (*Yom ha-Kippurim*), the most sacred day of the Jewish year. However, it is doubtful if the specific lessons for the synagogue services had been laid down by the time of the New Testament.

21. John Wilkinson, 'Physical Healing and the Atonement', EQ, vol. 63 (1991), pp.149-167.

## Chapter Nine: The Methods of Healing

1. Micklem, p.105.

2. Babylonian Talmud, *Erubin* 41b and *Shabbath* 33a. See SB, vol. 2, p.203.

3. Micklem, p.126.

4. R.C. Trench, *Synonyms of the New Testament* (London: Kegan Paul, Trench, Trübner & Co. 1901), new edition, pp.55-57. See also J.B. Lightfoot, *The Epistles to the Colossians and Philemon* (London: Macmillan, 1886), eighth edition, p.201.

5. This reference is in the Genesis Apocryphon (1Q-ap Gen. col. 20, lines 28-29. See Geza Vermes, *The Dead Sea Scrolls in English* (Harmondsworth: Penguin Books, 1991), fourth edition, p.294. However several significant differences between Abraham's laying his hands on Pharoah and the practice of Jesus have been pointed out. See R.H. Grundry, *Mark: A Commentary on His Apology for the Cross* (Grand Rapids: William B. Eerdmans Publishing Co., 1993), p.90.

6. Weatherhead, p.54.

7. Mishnah, *Zabiim* 5.6 (Danby, p.772). See also SB, vol. 1, p.520.

8. Loos, p.515, n.1.

9. Cranfield, Mark, p.185. See also W.L. Lane, *NINTC on the Gospel according to Mark* (1974), pp.192-193.

10. D.W. Burdick, *The Wycliffe Bible Commentary* (London: Oliphants, 1963), p.998.

11. *Beel-zebul* is the Greek form of the name of the Canaanite God Baal-zebub whom King Ahaziah wished to consult after his accident (1 Kings 1.2, 6 and 16). The name means 'the Lord of the Flies' (so LXX), 'the Lord Prince' (J.A. Montgomery & H.S. Gehman, *ICC on Kings* (1951), p.349) or 'the Lord of the House' (D.E. Aune, ISBE (1979), vol. 1, p.447, art. 'Beelzebul').

12. Heinrich Schlier, TDNT (1964), vol. 2, p.20, s.v. *daktulos*.

13. Galen, vol. 7, p.275.

14. Edward Langton, *Essentials of Demonology* (London: Epworth Press, 1949), p.151. See also Leon Morris, *TNTC on the Gospel according to St Luke* (1974), p.110.

15. Taylor, Mark, p.275.

16. Leon Morris, *op.cit.*, p.115.

17. F.W. Farrar, *CBSC on the Gospel according to St Luke* (1880), p.116.

18. J.A. Wharton, IDB (1962), vol. 4, p.437, art. 'Spit'.

19. Taylor, Mark, p.354.

20. *Ibidem*, p.355.

21. H.B. Swete, *The Gospel according to St Mark* (London: Macmillan, 1927), p.161.

22. Cranfield, *Mark*, p.252.

23. The rare word *mogilalos* is used in v.32 to describe the man's speech difficulty. According to BAG (p.525) the ancient Greek versions of the Old Testament understood the word to mean 'mute' or 'incapable of speech' as in Isaiah 35.6 LXX, but it may also mean 'having an impediment of speech'. As we have suggested, such an impediment could be due to 'tongue-tie', a condition in which a congenitally short frenulum binds the tongue down to the floor of the mouth more closely than is normally the case. The result is that the movement of the tongue is unduly restricted, thus making speech difficult. That this was the situation here is suggested by the reference to 'the bond (*desmos*) of his tongue' which was released when Jesus healed him (Mark 7.35 RV). See A.S.Weatherhead, 'The Healing of One Deaf and Dumb', ExpT, vol. 23 (1911-12), p.381.

24. William Barclay, *DSB on Mark* (1975), p.190.

25. Pliny, *Natural History* 28.7 (LCL vol. 8, p.27).

26. Tacitus, *Histories* 4.81 (LCL vol. 2, p.159-161) and Suetonius, *Vespasian* 7.8 (LCL vol. 2, p.299).

27. Galen, *Peri Phusikon Dunameon* (On the Natural Faculties) 3.7 (LCL p.251).

28. See references in C.K. Barrett, *The Gospel according to St John* (London: SPCK, 1978), second edition, p.358 and also in SB, vol, 2, p.530. Loos (p.309), however, says that 'in Judaism spittle was regarded as highly medicinal' and to support this statement refers to SB, vol. 2, pp.15-17.

29. W.E. Addis & Thomas Arnold, *A Catholic Dictionary* (London: Virtue, 1952), p.63, art. 'Baptism'.

30. R.C. Trench, *Notes on the Miracles of our Lord* (London: Kegan Paul, Trench, Trübner & Co., 1900), sixteenth edition, p.371.

31. J.H. Bernard, *ICC on the Gospel according to St John* (1928), vol. 1, p.clxxx.

32. *The Oxford English Dictionary* (Oxford: Clarendon Press, 1971), compact edition, vol. 2, p.3252, s.v. telepathy.

33. J.B. Rhine, *The Reach of the Mind* (Harmondsworth: Penguin Books, 1954).

34. R.C. Trench, *op.cit.*, p.245.

35. Weatherhead, p.75.

36. Eusebius, *Ecclesiastical History* 6.8,2 (LCL vol. 2, p.29). See also Jean Danielou, *Origen* (London & New York: Sheed & Ward, 1955), p.13.

37. J.R.W. Stott, *Christian Counter-culture* (Leicester: Inter-Varsity Press, 1978), p.89.

## Chapter Ten: The Case of the Epileptic Boy

1. Charles Creighton, *Encyclopaedia Biblica* (London: A. & C. Black, 1914), one-volume edition, col. 2833, art. 'Lunatic'.

2. H.G. Liddell & Robert Scott, *A Greek-English Lexicon* (Oxford: Clarendon Press, 1940), ninth edition, p.1590, s.v. *selenazo*.

3. For Calvin's view see John Calvin, *A Harmony of the Gospels Matthew, Mark and Luke* (Edinburgh: St Andrew Press, 1972), vol. 2, p.207.

4. Eusebius, *Ecclesiastical History* 3.39,15 (LCL vol. 1, p.297).

5. Rudolf Bultmann, *The History of the Synoptic Tradition* (Oxford: Blackwell, 1968), p.225.

6. Taylor, *Mark*, p.396.

7. F.W. Beare, *The Earliest Records of Jesus* (Oxford: Blackwell, 1962), p.144. Cp. J.P. Meier, *A Marginal Jew: Rethinking the Historical Jesus* (New York: Doubleday, 1994), vol. 2, p.653, where the author calls the story 'rambling, not to say incoherent'.

8. In the New Testament the word *pais* may be used of an infant (Matthew 2.16), a growing child (Matthew 17.18 and 21.15), the twelve-year old Jesus (Luke 2.43), and the young man (*neanias*) Eutychus (Acts 20.9,12). Albrecht Oepke describes him as a growing boy in TDNT (1967), vol. 5, p.637, s.v. *pais*.

9. Hippocrates, *Peri Hebdomadon* (Concerning the Seventh Day), edited by W.H. Roscher (Paderborn: 1913), 5. The seventh day was regarded by Greek physicians as the critical day in many diseases. This was a view which persisted in modern medicine in relation to acute lobar pneumonia before the advent of treatment by the sulphonamide group of drugs and the antibiotics.

10. A.M. Hunter, *Torch Bible Commentary on the Gospel according to St Mark* (London: SCM Press, 1949), p.94.

11. R.K. Harrison, IDB (1962), vol. 2, p.123, art. 'Epilepsy'. See also W.M. Alexander, *Demonic Possession in the New Testament* (Edinburgh: T. & T. Clark, 1902). Alexander suggests that this boy suffered from 'epileptic idiocy' and may have displayed 'the instability of temper and tendency to violence common to epileptic idiots', but there is no evidence of this in the narrative.

12. Galen, vol. 8, p.194. See Owsei Temkins, *The Falling Sickness* (Baltimore: Johns Hopkins University Press, 1972), p.37.

13. BAG, p.550, s.v. *xeraino*.

14. Cranfield, Mark, p.301.

15. Taylor, Mark, p.398.

16. A.B. Bruce, *EGT on the Gospel of Mark* (1901), vol. 1, p.402.

17. Loos, p.401.

18. Hippocrates, *Peri Hieres Nosou* (On the Sacred Disease), LCL vol. 2, pp.139-183. Plato suggested that epilepsy was called the sacred disease because it affects what he called 'the sacred substance', i.e., the brain. See Plato, *Timaeus* 85. A-B (LCL p.231).

19. Hippocrates, *op.cit.*, 10 (LCL vol. 2, pp.159-163). See Owsei Temkins, *op.cit.*, pp.4 and 52-53.

20. John Chadwick and W.N. Mann, *The Medical Works of Hippocrates* (Oxford: Blackwell, 1950), p.185.

21. Henry Hayman in his article on 'Medicine' in the second volume of Smith's *Dictionary of the Bible* (London: John Murray, 1863; pp.299-300) suggested that Luke was trained in the medical tradition of Aretaeus the Cappadocian. This is unlikely for two reasons. Firstly, Aretaeus was a close disciple of Hippocrates and does not represent a separate tradition, although he differed from him in accepting demon possession as the cause of epilepsy. Secondly, Aretaeus is now believed to have lived in the second century AD and not in the first century as previously thought. See Guthrie, pp.70-72.

22. Hippocrates, *op.cit.*, 13.20 (LCL vol. 2, p.167).

23. Celsus, *De Medicina* (On Medicine) 3.23 (LCL vol. 1, p.332, n.b.).

24. Celsus, *op.cit.*, 2.8,11 (the aura) and 3.23,1-3 (the fit). See LCL vol. 1, pp.137 & 333-335 respectively.

## Chapter Eleven: The Case of the Bent Woman

1. Marshall, Luke, p.558. Marshall prefers the interpretation of complete spinal immobility on the grounds that this stresses the severity of her complaint.

2. Weatherhead, p.50.

3. H.J. Ryle, 'The Neurotic Theory of the Miracles of Healing', *The Hibbert Journal*, vol. 5 (1907), pp.572-586.

4. See, for example, R.K. Harrison, IDB (1962), vol. 1, p.852, art. 'Disease'.

5. Hippocrates, *Peri Arthron* (On Joints) 41 (LCL vol. 3, pp.279-283).

6. A.J.E. Cave, 'The Evidence for the Existence of Tuberculosis in Ancient Egypt', *British Journal of Tuberculosis*, vol. 33 (1939), p.142.

7. Joseph Zias, 'Death and Disease in Ancient Israel', *Biblical Archaeologist*, vol. 54 (1951), p.152.

8. M.A. Ruffer, 'Arthritis deformans and Spondylitis in Ancient Egypt', *Journal of Pathology and Bacteriology*, vol. 22 (1918), pp.152-196. See also BSDA, pp.357-360.

9. Hippocrates, *loc. cit.*

10. D.G. Spencer, R.D. Sturrock and W.W. Buchanan, 'Ankylosing Spondylitis: Yesterday and Today', *Medical History*, vol. 24 (1980), pp.60-69.

11. Joseph Zias, *art. cit.*, p.153.

12. Alexander Macalister, HDB, vol. 3, p.328, art. 'Medicine'.

13. The English versions which understand this case to be one of demon possession include the TCNT (1904), the Jerusalem Bible (1966), Barclay (1968), the NEB (1970), the GNB (1976) and the REB (1989).

14. Knox, vol. 1, p.161.

## Chapter Twelve: The Case of the Man Born Blind

1. John Wilkinson, 'A Study of Healing in the Gospel according to John', SJT, vol. 20 (1967), pp.442-461.

2. Donald Guthrie, *New Testament Introduction* (Leicester: Inter-Varsity Press, 1990), fourth edition, p.314.

3. William Barclay, *The Gospels and Acts* (London: SCM Press, 1976), vol. 2, p.176.

4. The only use of the word demon (*daimonion*) in John is where Jesus is accused of having a demon (John 7.20; 8.48, 49 and 10.20).

5. R.E. Brown, *AB on the Gospel according to John* (1966), vol. 1, p.376.

6. *Ibidem*, p.377.

7. Joachim Jeremias, *Jerusalem in the Time of Jesus* (Philadelphia: Fortress Press, 1969), p.118.

8. *Ibidem.*

9. Mishnah, *Shabbath* 1.1 (Danby, p.100). Edersheim suggests that he came to sit at the gate of the Temple every day in order to keep himself in the public eye, but on the Sabbath he did not solicit alms (Edersheim, vol. 2, p.178).

10. Edersheim, vol. 2, pp.178-179. See the Midrash, *Bereshith Rabba* 34 and the Babylonian Talmud, *Sanhedrin* 91b. See also SB, vol. 2, pp.528-529.

11. John Wilkinson, 'The Book of Job', *Proceedings of the Royal College of Physicians of Edinburgh*, vol. 25 (1995), pp.512-517.

12. Joachim Jeremias, *op.cit.*, pp.246-267.

13. Flavius Josephus, *Antiquities of the Jews* 17.42 (LCL vol. 8, p.393). See also 13.373 and 379 (LCL vol. 7, pp.413 & 417 respectively).

14. Mishnah, *Yoma* 8.6 (Danby, p.172).

15. Mishnah, *Shabbath* 7.2 (Danby, p.108)

16. Babylonian Talmud, *Abodah Zara* 28b.

17. Jerusalem Talmud, *Shabbath* 14d & 17f.

18. Edersheim, vol. 2, p.182.

19. The clause at the end of John 9.3 can be interpreted in at least three ways. The first way is to regard it as a **purpose** clause, beginning with the words 'in order that' and meaning that the purpose of his being born blind was to demonstrate the power of God. We have rejected this meaning as inappropriate on ethical grounds. The second way is to regard the clause as a **result** clause, beginning with the words 'with the result that'. This

means that the healing of the man's blindness was not the purpose of his being born blind, but its result or consequence. The third way is to interpret the clause as an imperatival or **command** clause and translate the verse as: 'Neither this man nor his parents sinned. Let the works of God be displayed in him', i.e., let us proceed with his healing and so display God's power. This third way has not found favour with commentators, especially in view of the comparable thought in John 11.4 concerning the sickness of Lazarus. See D.A. Carson, *The Gospel according to John* (Leicester: Inter-Varsity Press, 1991), p.362 and C.F.D. Moule, *An Idiom Book of New Testament Greek* (Cambridge: Cambridge University Press, 1959), second edition, pp.144-145.

20. Knox, vol. 1, p.234.

21. There is some textual uncertainty about whether Jesus said 'we' or 'I'. The better manuscripts give 'we' as the more probable reading. See Metzger, p.227.

22. Charles Creighton, *Encyclopaedia Biblica* (London: A. & C. Black, 1914), one-volume edition, col. 1456, art. 'Eye, Diseases of the'.

23. The English word 'cataract' is used to describe the lens of the eye when it has become opaque. The name is derived from the Greek word for a portcullis in an obvious reference to the effect of the now opaque lens, which cuts off the entry of light from the outside.

24. Weatherhead, p.49.

25. John Calvin, *The Gospel according to St John* (Edinburgh: St Andrew Press, 1972), vol. 1, p.241.

## Part Four: Healing in the Apostolic Church

### Chapter Thirteen: The Records of Healing in the Acts

1. A.B. Bruce, *The Training of the Twelve* (Edinburgh: T. & T. Clark, 1888), pp.96-97.

2. F.F. Bruce's verdict on these verses which form the long ending of the Gospel of Mark is 'that while we cannot regard them as an integral part of the Gospel to which they are now attached, no Christian need have any hesitation in reading them as Holy Scripture'. See F.F. Bruce, 'The End of the Second Gospel', EQ, vol. 17 (1945), p.181. A full discussion of the problem of the ending of Mark will be found in *The New Testament in the Original Greek*, edited by B.F. Westcott & F.J.A. Hort (London: Macmillan, 1882), vol. 2, pp.28-51. These authors conclude that the long ending of the gospel 'is doubtless founded on some tradition of the apostolic age' (p.51). See also Metzger, pp.122-126.

3. A sixth century source places this event at the second milestone from Damascus according to C.K. Barrett, *ICC on the Acts of the Apostles* (1994), vol. 1, p.449.

4. J.G. Mackenzie, *Psychology, Psychotherapy and Evangelicalism* (London: George Allen & Unwin, 1940), p.104.

5. C.G. Jung, 'The Psychological Foundation of Belief in Spirits' in *The Proceedings of the Society for Psychical Research* for May 1920, quoted by R.H. Thouless, *Introduction to the Psychology of Religion* (Cambridge: Cambridge University Press, 1936), second edition, p.190.

6. R.K. Harrison, IDB (1962), vol. 1, p.449, art. 'Blindness'.

7. Stewart Duke-Elder, *Diseases of the Eye* (London: J. & A. Churchill Ltd., 1964), fourteenth edition, p.330.

8. We assume that Luke was using the Greek measurement of time by which the day began at dawn rather than at sunset according to Jewish custom. Verse eleven appears to imply the Greek method rather than the Jewish.

9. F.F. Bruce, *NICNT on Acts*, revised edition (1988), p.385. Bruce quotes Martial, *Epigrams* 1.117,7 (LCL vol. 1, p.103) where Martial says that he lived up three flights of stairs in a tenement block in Rome.

10. D.M. Beck, IDB (1962), vol. 2, p.181, art. 'Eutychus'. Cp. the restorations to life in 1 Kings 17. 21 (by Elijah) and 2 Kings 4.34 (by Elisha).

11. F.F. Bruce, *op.cit.*, p.499, n.17.

12. A convenient summary of what the third gospel reveals about the interests and personality of Luke is given in William Barclay, *The Gospels and the Acts* (London: SCM Press, 1976), vol. 1, pp.216-221.

13. Mishnah, *Middoth* 2.3 (Danby, p.592). The Nicanor Gate of the Temple lay between the Court of the Gentiles and the Court of the Women and is probably identical with the gate of Corinthian bronze described by Josephus as the most beautiful of the gates of the Temple (*The Jewish War* 5.201: LCL vol. 3, p.261).

14. W.M. Ramsay, *St Paul the Traveller and Roman Citizen* (London: Hodder & Stoughton, 1902), sixth edition, p.116. See also Metzger, p.422.

15. Hobart, p.6. See also Ernst Haenchen, *The Acts of the Apostles: A Commentary* (Oxford: Blackwell, 1971), p.302.

16. This phrase in Acts 9.33 could also mean 'from the age of eight years' but more probably means 'for eight years'. See F.F. Bruce, *The Acts of the Apostles: The Greek Text* (Grand Rapids: William B. Eerdmans Publishing Co., 1990), third edition, p.247.

17. The 'we' sections of the Acts are as follows: 16.10-17; 20.5-21.18 and 27.1-28.16 (F.F. Bruce, *op.cit.*, p.3).

18. Plutarch calls such fortune-tellers, 'ventriloquists' (*engastrimantes*), in his book *The Failure of the Oracles*, 9.414E. They uttered words not only apparently, but really, beyond their own control. The name means literally 'those who prophesy by a spirit in the belly'.

19. Adolf Harnack, *Luke the Physician* (London: Williams & Norgate, 1906), pp.15-16. See also W.M. Ramsay, *Luke the Physician and Other Studies* (London: Hodder & Stoughton, 1908), p.16. MM give examples of the medical use of *therapeuo* in the papyri (p.289, s.v. *therapeuo*).

20. F.J.F. Jackson and Kirsopp Lake, *The Beginnings of Christianity* (London: Macmillan, 1933), part 1, vol. 4, p.343. This view is shared by Ernst Haenchen, *op.cit.*, p.715.

21. This can be seen by comparing Luke 9.2 with Matthew 10.8; Luke 9.11 with Matthew 14.14, and Luke 9.18 with Matthew 9.24.

22. Hobart, p.35.

23. *Ibidem*, p.47.

24. Metzger, p.330.

25. Hobart, p.23.

26. *Ibidem*, p.193.

27. Metzger, pp.308-309.

## Chapter Fourteen: The Practice of Healing in the Acts

1. Luke appears to have been with Paul at this time because this account occurs in the 'we' section, Acts 16.11-18.

2. Metzger, p.112.

3. F.F. Bruce, *The Acts of the Apostles: The Greek Text* (Grand Rapids: William B. Eerdmans Publishing Co., 1990), third edition, p.361. See also E.D. Burton, *Syntax of Moods and Tenses in New Testament Greek* (Edinburgh: T. & T. Clark, 1898), third edition, p.9, para. 13.

4. An example of an adjuration which might be used in exorcism was found in an Egyptian papyrus which read, 'I adjure you by the god of the Hebrews'. See Adolf Deissmann, *Light from the Ancient East* (London: Hodder & Stoughton, 1927), revised edition, p.260.

5. Friedrich Blass & Albert Debrunner, *A Greek Grammar of the New Testament* (Chicago: University of Chicago Press, 1961), translated by R.W. Funk, p.167, para. 320.

6. I.H. Marshall, *TNTC on the Acts of the Apostles* (1980), pp.178-179. See also C.K. Barrett, *ICC on Acts* (1994), vol. 1, p.481.

7. F.F. Bruce, *op.cit.*, p.247. Ernst Haenchen regards the suggestion that the verb here means 'to prepare to eat' as 'misconceived'. See his *Commentary on the Acts of the Apostles* (Oxford: Blackwell, 1971), p.338, n.9.

8. Metzger, p.423.

9. F.F. Bruce, *op.cit.*, p.321.

10. I.H. Marshall, *op.cit.*, p.179. Marshall quotes 1 Kings 17.19 and 2 Kings 4.10 & 21 where the bodies of those who were subsequently restored to life were placed in an upper room. This would, of course, provide privacy.

11. Ernst Haenchen, *op.cit.*, p.51, decides against interpreting the phrase as a Semiticism and understands it to refer to an actual use of the hands. See also F.F. Bruce, *op.cit.*, p.410.

12. I.H. Marshall, *op.cit.*, p.326.

13. Metzger, p.330.

14. W.M. Ramsay, *St Paul the Traveller and Roman Citizen* (London: Hodder & Stoughton, 1902), sixth edition, p.115.

15. The NIV translates the phrase 'by the hands of' simply as 'through' and so misses the point of what we believe Luke is saying, namely that there were two kinds of healing practised in Ephesus, the one direct and the other indirect. See R.N. Longenecker, *EBC on Acts* (1981), p.496.

16. See Ernst Haenchen, *op.cit.*, pp.561-563.

17. See e.g. Acts 5.12 and 8.6-7.

## Chapter Fifteen: Healing in the Epistles

1. 1 Timothy 1.10; 6.3; 2 Timothy 1.13; 4.3; Titus 1.9, 13 and 2.1-2. See the note on 1 Timothy 1.10 in J.N.D. Kelly, *A Commentary on the Pastoral Epistles* (London: A. & C. Black, 1963), p.50.

2. C.E.B. Cranfield, *ICC on the Epistle to the Romans* (1975), vol. 1, p.88, comment on Romans 1.16b. Note however that in Philippians 1.19 the word appears also to be used for physical deliverance from prison.

3. Milligan, p.91, n.13.

4. MM, p.446.

5. The essential unity of the three parts or aspects of the human person is emphasised in this verse by the fact that the verb ('be kept') and the adjective ('whole') are both in the singular, although they refer to all three parts together. See Leon Morris, *TNTC on the Epistles of Paul to the Thessalonians* (1956), p.107.

6. J.A.T. Robinson, *The Body: A Study in Pauline Theology* (London: SCM Press, 1952), p.9.

7. W.D. Stacey, *The Pauline View of Man* (London: Macmillan, 1956), p.182. Rudolf Bultmann provides a long discussion of the meaning of the word *soma* in Paul's epistles, but decides that the understanding of this word is 'fraught with difficulty'. See his *Theology of the New Testament* (London: SCM Press, 1952), vol. 1, pp.192-203.

8. J. Armitage Robinson, *St Paul's Epistle to the Ephesians* (London: Macmillan, 1904), second edition, p.103.

9. J.B. Lightfoot, *St Paul's Epistles to the Colossians and to Philemon* (London: Macmillan, 1886), eighth edition, p.197.

10. The description of a group of people with common interests and activities as a 'body' is not infrequent in the classical authors. See e.g. Livy, *Roman History* 2.32 (LCL vol. 1, pp.323-325).

11. The word *splanchna* is used literally only once in the New Testament in Acts 1.18, where the death of Judas Iscariot was accompanied by the rupture of his abdominal wall and the herniation of his intestines (*splanchna*).

12. The AV translation of 1 Timothy 4.8 was, 'Bodily exercise profiteth little, but godliness is profitable unto all things'. Phillips renders this verse, 'Bodily fitness has a limited value, but spiritual fitness is of unlimited value'.

13. The AV adds the words 'and in your spirit, which are God's' but these are regarded as a later gloss. See Metzger, p.553.

14. Plato, *Phaedrus* 250C (LCL p.485).

15. Plato, *Cratylus* 400B-C (LCL p.63). See W.K.C. Guthrie, *Orpheus and Greek Religion* (London: Methuen, 1957), second edition, pp.156-157.

16. Oscar Cullmann, *Immortality of the Soul or Resurrection of the Dead? The Witness of the New Testament* (London: Epworth Press, 1958).

17. Cyril of Alexandria, *Commentary on St John's Gospel*, Book 12.1 on John 20.28. Cyril quotes and then comments on Luke 24.36-43. His dates are usually given as AD 376-444.

18. See J.A. Schep, *The Nature of the Resurrection Body* (Grand Rapids: William B. Eerdmans Publishing Co., 1964).

19. In 1 Corinthians 12.1 Paul uses the simple adjective *pneumatikon* (spiritual) without any noun. The gender of the adjective may be either masculine or neuter. If it is masculine we should translate it 'spiritual persons', while if it is neuter it would mean 'spiritual things'. In this context it is usually taken to be neuter and translated 'spiritual gifts'. See C.K. Barrett, *First Epistle to the Corinthians* (London: A. & C. Black, 1971), second edition, p.278. Barrett suggests that little difference in sense is involved for 'spiritual persons are those who have spiritual gifts'.

20. J.R.W. Stott, *Baptism and Fullness* (Leicester: Inter-Varsity Press, 1975), second edition, p.87.

21. F.F. Bruce, *NCB on 1 & 2 Corinthians* (1971), p.118.

22. Arnold Bittlinger, *Gifts and Graces* (Grand Rapids: William B. Eerdmans Publishing Co./London: Hodder & Stoughton, 1967), pp.25-26.

23. Wilhelm Hollenweger, quoted by Bittlinger, *op.cit.*, p.72.

24. Arnold Bittlinger, *Gifts and Ministries* (Grand Rapids: William B. Eerdmans Publishing Co., 1973/London: Hodder & Stoughton, 1974), pp.17-20.

25. *Ibidem*, p.20.

26. J.R.W. Stott, *op.cit.*, pp.90-94.

27. Alexander Robertson & Alfred Plummer, *ICC on the First Epistle to the Corinthians* (1914), p.266.

28. John Calvin, *The First Epistle to the Corinthians* (Edinburgh: Oliver & Boyd, 1960), p.262.

29. C.K. Barrett, *The First Epistle to the Corinthians* (London: Black, 1971), second edition, p.275.

30. G.G. Findlay, *EGT on First Corinthians* (1901), vol. 2, p.883.

31. John Calvin, *op.cit.*, p.254.

32. J.B. Lightfoot, *Saint Paul's Epistle to the Philippians* (London: Macmillan, 1908), second edition, p.122.

33. BAG, p.562, s.v. *oinos*. Unfermented grape juice was called *oinos neos* (new wine) which was newly expressed and in which fermentation had not properly begun. As fermentation progressed it could be expected to burst old wine skins (Mark 2.2). Cp. LNL, vol. 1, p.77, sections 6. 197 and 198.

34. See 2 Maccabees 15.39 and the Mishnah, *Berakoth* 7.5 (Danby, p.8). See also B.L. Bandstra, ISBE (1988), vol. 4, p.1070, art. 'Wine'.

35. A.E. Brooke, *ICC on The Johannine Epistles* (1912), p.182. See the numerous examples of letters from the Egyptian papyri given in A.S. Hunt & C.C. Edgar, *Select Papyri* (LCL vol. 1, pp.269-395).

## Chapter Sixteen: The Thorn in the Flesh: Its Occurrence

1. The Oxford English Dictionary (Oxford: Clarendon Press, 1971), compact edition, vol. 1, p.558, s.v. corinthianise. The verb was first noted in English in 1810 as 'corinthize'.
2. The translation 'thorn in the flesh' occurs first in the AV. Earlier English versions had rendered the phrase as 'unquietness of my flesh' (Tyndale, 1526), 'warning given unto my flesh' (Coverdale, 1535) and 'prick in the flesh' (Genevan version, 1560). See Alfred Plummer, *ICC on the Second Epistle of Paul to the Corinthians* (1915), p.348.
3. Alfred Plummer, *ibidem*.
4. Homer, *Iliad* 18.177 (LCL vol. 1, p.301)
5. Homer, *Odyssey* 7.45 (LCL vol. 1, p.235) and Herodotus 9.97 (LCL vol. 4, p.273).
6. Euripides, *Iphigenia in Taurica* 1430 (LCL p.405) and *Electra* 898 (LCL p.81).
7. Amongst the papyri found in Egypt last century was a letter from an anxious mother to an absent son. She had heard that he had a sore foot owing to a splinter and was able to walk only slowly. In a note on this papyrus, Milligan says that this letter shows 'that in the vernacular *skolops* had come to mean "splinter" or "thorn" rather than "stake"'. See Milligan, p.105, n.9. See also MM, p.578.
8. See e.g. 'a stabbing pain' (Phillips, 1972), 'a sharp physical pain' (NEB, 1976), and 'a painful physical ailment' (GNB, 1979).
9. There are similar lists in Romans 8.35; 1 Corinthians 4.9-13; 2 Corinthians 4.8-18; 6.4-5 and 12.10.
10. E.D. Burton, *ICC on the Epistle to the Galatians* (1921), pp.492-493. See also William Barclay, *Flesh and Spirit* (London: SCM Press, 1962), pp.176-22.
11. V.P. Furnish, *AB on Second Corinthians* (1984), p.529. See also Friedrich Blass & Albert Debrunner, *A Greek Grammar of the New Testament* (Chicago: University of Chicago Press, 1961), translated by R.W. Funk, pp.101 & 107, sections 188 & 199 respectively.
12. V.P.Furnish, *op.cit.*, p.524.
13. Furnish suggests the translation, 'that he should constantly abuse me', *op.cit.*, p.529.
14. James Denney, *The Expositor's Bible on Second Corinthians* (London: Hodder & Stoughton, 1903), p.353.
15. William Barclay, *DSB on the Letters to the Corinthians* (1975), p.192. Nevertheless, this experience of Paul in Asia has been understood by some commentators as one of a severe physical illness. See e.g. Henry Alford, *The Greek Testament* (London: Rivingtons, 1871), sixth edition, vol. 2, p.630 and also E.B. Allo, *Saint Paul: Seconde Épître aux Corinthiens* (Paris: Gabalda, 1956), second edition, p.317, n.1.
16. W.M. Alexander, 'St Paul's Infirmity', ExpT, vol. 15, (1903-1904), p.546 and E.B. Allo, *op. cit.*, p.12.
17. See Friederich Fenner, 'Die Krankheit im Neuen Testament', *Untersuchungen zum Neuen Testament*, vol. 18 (1930), pp.30-40. Cp. K.L. Schmidt, TDNT (1966), vol. 3, p.819, n.10, s.v. *kolaphizo*.
18. Rudolf Bultmann, *Theology of the New Testament* (London: SCM Press, 1952), vol. 1, p.351.
19. W.M. Ramsay, *The Bearing of Recent Discovery on the Trustworthiness of the New Testament* (London: Hodder & Stoughton, 1914), pp.90-95.
20. James Denney, *op.cit.*, p.168.

## Chapter Seventeen: The Thorn in the Flesh: Its Identity (I)

1. Adolf Deissmann, *Paul: A study in Social and Religious History* (London: Hodder & Stoughton, 1926), second edition, p.60, n.5.

2. Soren Kierkegaard, *Edifying Discourses* (Minneapolis: Augsburg Press, 1946), vol. 4, 'The Thorn in the Flesh', p.52.

3. E.M. Merrins, 'St Paul's Thorn in the Flesh', *Bibliotheca Sacra*, vol. 64 (1907), p.661.

4. Edgar Hennecke, *New Testament Apocrypha* (London: Lutterworth Press, 1965), vol. 2, p.354. See also M.R. James, *Apocryphal New Testament* (Oxford: Clarendon Press, 1924) p.273, and F.W. Farrar, *The Life and Work of St Paul* (London: Cassell, 1885), p.758.

5. Alfred Plummer, *ICC on the Second Epistle of St Paul to the Corinthians* (1915), p.283 provides other references.

6. A.P. Stanley, *The Epistles of St Paul to the Corinthians* (London: John Murray, 1876), fourth edition, p.547.

7. J.B. Lightfoot, *St Paul's Epistle to the Galatians* (London: Macmillan, 1902), tenth edition, p.186.

8. John Chrysostom, *Homilies on Second Corinthians* (Oxford: Parker, 1848), Homily 26, p.293. For a modern exposition of this view see T.Y. Mullins, 'Paul's Thorn in the Flesh', *Journal of Biblical Literature*, vol. 36 (1957), pp.299-303.

9. Knox, vol. 2, p.204.

10. R.V.G. Tasker, *TNTC on Second Corinthians* (1958), p.176.

11. Weatherhead, p.143.

12. P.H. Menoud, *Studia Paulina* (Haarlem: Böhn, 1953), p.170.

13. Metzger, p.596.

14. John Calvin, *The Second Epistle of Paul the Apostle to the Corinthians* (Edinburgh: Oliver & Boyd, 1964), p.159.

15. John Calvin, *The Epistles of Paul the Apostle to the Galatians, Ephesians, Philippians and Colossians* (Edinburgh: Oliver & Boyd, 1965), p.79.

16. William Estius, *In omnes Pauli Epistolas Commentaria* (Douay, 1614), comment on 2 Corinthians 12.7.

17. Cornelius à Lapide, *Commentaria in omnes divi Pauli Epistolas* (Paris, 1638). ET of volume on Second Corinthians and Galatians by W.F. Cobb (Edinburgh: Grant, 1908), pp.185-190.

18. J.B. Lightfoot, *op.cit.*, p.188, n.3.

19. *Ibidem*, p.188, text.

20. J.L. Robertson (ed.), *The Poetical Works of Robert Burns* (Oxford: Oxford University Press, 1904), p.88, lines 55-60.

21. J.J. Lias, *CBSC on the Second Epistle to the Corinthians* (1882), pp.17-21.

22. V.A. Holmes-Gore, 'The Thorn in the Flesh', *Theology*, vol. 32 (1936), pp.111-112.

23. Martin Luther, *Commentary on St Paul's Epistle to the Galatians* (London: William Tegg, 1854), ET by E. Middleton, pp.332-334. See also J.B. Lightfoot, *op.cit.*, p.189, n.1.

24. J.J. O'Rourke in R.E. Brown, J.A. Fitzmyer & R.F. Murphy (eds.), *The Jerome Biblical Commentary* (London: Geoffrey Chapman, 1969), vol. 2, p.289.

25. Alfred Plummer, *CGT on the Second Epistle of Paul the Apostle to the Corinthians* (1912): pp.239-245, Appendix C, 'S. Paul's Thorn for the Flesh'.

## Chapter Eighteen: The Thorn in the Flesh: Its Identity (II)

1. BAG, p.275, s.v. *sarx*.

2. P.E. Hughes, *Paul's Second Epistle to the Corinthians* (London: Marshall, Morgan & Scott, 1962), p.448.

3. R.V.G. Tasker, *TNTC on The Second Epistle of Paul to the Corinthians* (1958), p.175.

4. K. Lowther Clarke, *New Testament Problems* (London: SPCK, 1929), chapter 16, 'Was St Paul a Stammerer?', pp.136-140.

5. C.K. Barrett, *A Commentary on the Second Epistle to the Corinthians* (London: A. & C. Black, 1973), p.315. See also E.A. Mangan, 'Was Saint Paul an Invalid?', *Catholic Biblical Quarterly*, vol. 5 (1943), pp.68-72.

6. M.L. Knapp, 'Paul the Deaf', *The Biblical World*, vol. 47 (1916), pp.311-317.

7. Marcus Dods, HDB, vol. 2, p.94, art. 'Epistle to the Galatians'.

8. Nigel Turner, *Grammatical Insights into the New Testament* (Edinburgh: T. & T. Clark, 1965), p.94.

9. Tertullian, *De Pudicitia* (On Modesty), 13 in Alexander Roberts & James Donaldson (eds.), Ante-Nicene Christian Library, *The Works of Tertullian* (Edinburgh: T. & T. Clark, 1870), vol. 3, p.88.

10. Alfred Plummer, *CGT on the Second Epistle to the Corinthians* (1912), p.239.

11. *Ibidem*, p.241.

12. Galen, vol. 12, p.592.

13. E.A. Johnson, 'St Paul's Infirmity', ExpT, vol. 39 (1927-1928), pp.428-429.

14. H. Gobel, H. Isler & H.P. Hasenfratz, 'Headache Classification: Was St Paul's thorn in the flesh migraine?', *Cephalalgia*, vol. 15 (1995), pp.180-181.

15. W.M. Ramsay, *The Teaching of Paul in Terms of the Present Day* (London: Hodder & Stoughton, 1913), chapter 48, 'The Theory that Paul was an Epileptic', pp.306-328.

16. J.B. Lightfoot, *St Paul's Epistle to the Galatians* (London: Macmillan, 1902), tenth edition, p.191.

17. Plautus, *De Captivi* (The Captives) 3.4,550 (LCL vol. 1, p.515).

18. Pliny, *Natural History* 28.7 (LCL vol. 8, p.27): 'We spit on epileptics (*comitiales morbos*) in a fit, that is, we throw back infection. In a similar way we ward off the witchcraft and bad luck which follows meeting a person lame in the right leg'.

19. Heinrich Schlier, TDNT (1964), vol. 2, p.448, s.v. *ekptuo*.

20. Owsei Temkins, *The Falling Sickness* (Baltimore: Johns Hopkins Press, 1971), second edition revised, p.380.

21. E.B. Allo, *Saint Paul, Seconde Épître aux Corinthiens* (Paris: Gabalda, 1956), p.317, n.1.

22. *Ibidem*, p.316.

23. A. Hisey & J.S.P. Beck, 'St Paul's "Thorn in the Flesh": A Paragnosis', *Journal of the Bible & Religion*, vol. 29 (1961), pp.125-129.

24. Thomas Lewin, *The Life and Epistles of St Paul* (London: Bell, 1851), vol. 1, pp.213-219.

25. F.W. Farrar, *The Life and Work of St. Paul* (London: Cassell, 1885): pp.710-715, Excursus X, 'St Paul's "Stake in the Flesh"'.

26. F.W. Farrar, *op.cit.*, p.714.

27. Short, p.69. Short writes that if trachoma 'was not Paul's thorn in the flesh, it is vain to seek other explanations'.

28. J.B. Lightfoot, *op.cit.*, p.191, n.1.

29. W.M. Ramsay, *St Paul the Traveller and Roman Citizen* (London: Hodder & Stoughton, 1902), sixth edition, pp.39-39.

30. Leprosy as a possible diagnosis is maintained by H.J. Schoeps, *Paul* (London: Lutterworth Press, 1961), p.81, n.1.

31. John Chrysostom, *Homilies on Second Corinthians* (Oxford: Parker, 1848), Homily 26, p.293.

32. W.M. Alexander, 'St Paul's Infirmity', ExpT, vol. 15 (1903-1904), pp.469-473 and 545-548.

33. W.M. Ramsay, *The Church in the Roman Empire before AD 170* (London: Hodder & Stoughton, 1893), second edition, p.63.

34. The details of Ramsay's suggestion assume the truth of the South Galatian theory of Paul's travels in Asia Minor. According to this theory Paul visited Galatia during his first missionary journey, and the cities he visited were all situated in the southern part of the Roman province of Galatia for which Perga in Pamphylia was the natural port of entry. See W.M. Ramsay, *St Paul, The Traveller and the Roman Citizen* (London: Hodder & Stoughton, 1902), sixth edition, pp.94-97.

35. Guthrie, p.358.

36. W.H.S. Jones, 'The Prevalence of Malaria in Ancient Greece', BSDA, pp.170-176. For more detail see the same author's book, *Malaria: A Neglected Factor in the History of Greece and Rome* (London: Macmillan, 1907).

37. W.M. Ramsay, 'The Greek of the Early Church and Pagan Ritual', ExpT, vol. 10 (1898-1899), p.110.

38. See the classical description of the case of a patient suffering from an attack of malaria given by Hippocrates in his *Epidemics I*, case 1 (LCL vol. 1, p.187). Ramsay quotes the inscription on an execration tablet found in Rome which reads: 'May he suffer fevers, chill, torments, pallors, sweatings, heats by day and by night'. See W.M. Ramsay, *A Historical Commentary on St Paul's Epistle to the Galatians* (London: Hodder & Stoughton, 1899), p.423. This is an excellent concise clinical summary of the symptoms of malaria.

39. V.P. Furnish, *AB on Second Corinthians* (1984), p.524.

40. W.M. Ramsay, *St Paul, the Traveller and the Roman Citizen* (London: Hodder & Stoughton, 1902), sixth edition, p.97.

41. On the South Galatian theory of Paul's travels in Asia Minor, his first visit to Galatia would be dated about AD 47, while according to the North Galatian theory the visit would have been paid about AD 52. If Paul had experienced the visions and revelations about AD 42, as we have suggested above, this would leave a gap of five to ten years respectively before the onset of the thorn in the flesh.

42. J.B. Lightfoot, *op.cit.*, p.190.

43. The dates of the silent period of Paul's life are variously estimated. For those given in the text (namely, AD 35-46), see F.F. Bruce, *Paul: Apostle of the Free Spirit* (Exeter: Paternoster Press, 1980), revised edition, pp.127 and 475.

## Chapter Nineteen: The Thorn in the Flesh: Its Significance

1. An alternative explanation is that 'this is a conventional use of the passive voice to avoid mentioning the divine name' (V.P. Furnish, *AB on Second Corinthians* (1984), p.528). This certainly was a Jewish custom (and still is), but it seems unlikely that Paul would observe it after he became a Christian. He certainly does not observe it elsewhere in his epistles where he uses the name of God quite freely and in the active voice.

2. In the same way we should understand the other two 'theological passives' where Paul speaks of the man in Christ being 'caught up' (vv. 2 and 4), as meaning that he was caught up by God.

3. Karl Barth, *Church Dogmatics* (Edinburgh: T. & T. Clark, 1956), vol. I, part 2, p.332.

4. John Chrysostom, *Homilies on Second Corinthians* (Oxford: Parker, 1848), 26, p.294.

5. C.K. Barrett, *The Second Epistle to the Corinthians* (London: A. & C. Black, 1973), p.316.

6. James Denney, *Expositor's Bible on the Second Epistle to the Corinthians* (London: Hodder & Stoughton, 1903), p.354.

7. This word 'paradise' was first used in Greek by Xenophon to denote the royal gardens or parks which the Greek mercenaries came across in the course of their expedition in support of Cyrus the Younger, the pretender to the Persian throne after the death of his father Darius II in 405 BC. It was a local loan-word from Persian. See Xenophon, *Anabasis* 1.2,7 and 2.4,14 (LCL pp.13 and 141 respectively).

8. William Barclay, *DSB on Corinthians* (1975), p.257. See Esther 1.5.

9. This is the translation of 2 Corinthians 12.9 by E.H. Peterson in *The Message: The New Testament in Contemporary English* (Colorado Springs: NavPress Publishing Group, 1993), p.385.

10. H.H. Rowley, *The Faith of Israel* (London: SCM Press, 1956), p.114-116. See also Brown, p.211.


## Chapter Twenty: Healing in the Epistle of James (I)

1. Alfred Wikenhauser, *New Testament Introduction* (Dublin: Herder & Herder, 1958), p.482. See also J.H. Moulton & W.F. Howard, *A Grammar of New Testament Greek* (Edinburgh: T. & T. Clark, 1929), vol. 2, p.27.

2. Donald Guthrie, *New Testament Introduction* (Leicester: Inter-Varsity Press, 1990), fourth revised edition, pp.723-747.

3. Flavius Josephus, *Antiquities of the Jews* 20.200 (LCL vol. 9, p.497).

4. A.M. Hunter, *Introducing the New Testament* (London: SCM Press, 1957), second edition, p.167.

5. Martin Luther, *Introduction to the German New Testament* (Wittenberg: September 1522) in the American edition of Luther's Works (Philadelphia: Fortress Press, 1932), vol. 6, pp.439-444. This comment was omitted in the Introduction to the first edition of the complete German Bible published in 1534. The phrase used by Luther was based on 1 Corinthians 3.12 where Paul describes the materials which the Christian may use to build on the foundation of Jesus Christ, of which straw is the least durable.

6. Martin Luther, *Table Talk* (Weimar: Verlag H.B. Nachfolger, 1921), vol. 5, p.382, no. 5,854.

7. A.M. Hunter, *op.cit.*, p.165.

8. Martin Luther, *Preface to St James and St Jude* (1522) in the American edition of Luther's Works, edited by E.T. Bachmann (Philadelphia: Concordia Publishing House, 1960), vol. 35, p.397. See also his Table Talk comment No. 5,443 (1542) in vol. 54 (1967) of the American edition, where he says somewhat less dramatically that 'there is no order or method in the epistle' (p.425).

9. John Calvin, *Commentary on the Epistle of James* (Edinburgh: St Andrew Press, 1972), p.259.

10. W.O.E. Oesterley, *EGT on The General Epistle of St James* (1910), vol. 4, p.407.

11. Knox, vol. 3, p.111. R.P. Martin gives a list of the correspondences between the epistle and the Sermon on the Mount in his *Word Biblical Commentary on James* (Waco, Texas: Word Books, 1988), pp.lxxv-lxxvi.

12. P.B.R. Forbes, 'The Structure of the Epistle of James', EQ, pp.147-153. See also F.O. Francis, 'The Form and Function of the Opening and Closing Paragraphs of James and 1 John', *Zeitschrift für die Ntl. Wissenschaft*, vol. 61 (1970), pp.110-126.

13. Nigel Turner in J.H. Moulton & W.F. Howard, *op.cit.*, vol. 4 (1976), p.116.

14. Alfred Plummer, *Expositor's Bible on St James & St Jude* (London: Hodder & Stoughton, 1891), p.323.

15. R.A. Knox, *The Holy Bible: A Translation from the Latin Vulgate* (London: Burns & Oates, 1961), *in loc. cit.*

16. Adolf Harnack, *The Mission and the Expansion of Christianity* (London: Williams & Norgate, 1908), vol. 1, p.121. In additional support of this statement Harnack quotes 1 Corinthians 12.26.

17. Nigel Turner, *op.cit.*, vol. 3 (1963), pp.79-81. The aorist participle here has been called the 'quite regular "contemporaneous aorist" which is used to express not precedence in time to the main verb but completeness of the process of anointing' according to James Adamson, *NICNT on The Epistle of James* (1976), p.197. See also J.H. Ropes, *ICC on The Epistle of St. James* (1916), p.305.

18. J.B. Mayor, *The Epistle of St James* (London: Macmillan, 1913), third edition, pp.177-179.

19. James Adamson, *op.cit.*, pp.205-210, Excursus I: 'The Prayer of a Righteous Man'.

20. Joachim Jeremias, TDNT (1964), vol. 2, pp.928-938, s.v. Elias.

21. See C.L. Mitton, *The Epistle of James* (London: Marshall, Morgan & Scott, 1966), pp.207-208.

21. See C.L. Mitton, *The Epistle of James* (London: Marshall, Morgan & Scott, 1966), pp.207-208.

22. Peter Davids, *NIGTC on the Epistle of James* (1982), p.192.

23. Hippocrates, *The Oath*, lines 16 and 25 (LCL vol. 1, p.299).

24. F.J. Wright, 'Healing: An Interpretation of James 5.13-20', *Journal of the Christian Medical Fellowship*, vol. 37 (1991), p.20, where it is suggested that this word may be linked with the word 'camel', the beast of burden and work.

25. R.V.G. Tasker, *TNTC on the General Epistle of James* (1956), p.133.

26. BAG, p.402, s.v. *kamno*.

27. Martin Dibelius, *Hermeneia Commentary on the Epistle of St James* (Philadelphia: Fortress Press, 1976), revised edition by Heinrich Greeven, p.252. E.C. Blackman takes a similar view in his *Torch Commentary on James* (London: SCM Press, 1957), p.153. Sophie Laws comments on this view that James was giving instructions on how to perform an exorcism as follows: 'This is an unwarranted elaboration of the picture. James clearly knows enough of exorcist language (cf. 2.19 & 4.7) to have given his instructions in those terms if he had wished to do so.' See her *Commentary on the Epistle of James* (London: A. & C. Black, 1980), p.228.

28. H.H. Rowley, *The Faith of Israel* (London: SCM Press, 1956), p.114. See also Brown, p.211.

29. J.B. Mayor, *op.cit.*, p.174.

30. The REB returns to the more usual translation of 'the elders of the Church'.

31. Martin Dibelius, *Hermeneia Commentary on the Epistle of James* (Philadelphia: Fortress Press, 1976), revised edition by Heinrich Greeven, p.252.

32. J.A. Bengel, *Gnomon Novi Testamenti* (Berlin: Gustavus Schlawitz, 1855), reprint of third edition (1773), p.624. It is interesting to find that Polycarp (AD 69-153) writing to the Philippian Church does not include healing amongst the duties of the elders. See *Polycarp to the Philippians* 6.1 (LCL, *The Apostolic Fathers*, vol. 1, p.291).

## Chapter Twenty-one: Healing in the Epistle of James (II)

1. R.C. Trench, *Synonyms of the New Testament* (London: Kegan Paul, Trench, Trübner & Co., 1901), new edition, p.129. See also BAG, p.25, s.v. *aleipho* & p.887, s.v. *chrio* and MM, pp.25 & 693 under the same words. There is a similar distinction in the Old Testament in the usage of the Hebrew verbs *mashach* (meaning 'to consecrate' and equivalent to *chrio*) and *suk* (meaning 'to pour' and equivalent to *aleipho*). The name Messiah ('The Anointed One') is derived from the former Hebrew verb.

2. E.H. Sugden, *Abingdon Bible Commentary* (London: Epworth Press/Nashville: Abingdon Press, 1929), p.1337. See D.W. Burdick, *EBC* (1981), vol. 12, p.204: 'It is evident, then, that James is prescribing prayer and medicine'. See also the discussion by B.B. Warfield in his book, *Miracles: Yesterday and Today, True and False* (Grand Rapids: William B. Eerdmans Publishing Co., 1965), pp.171-173.

3. Pliny, *Natural History* 15.5 (LCL vol. 4, p.301).

4. Flavius Josephus, *Antiquities of the Jews* 17.172 (LCL vol. 8, p.451) and *The Jewish War* 1.657 (LCL vol. 2, p.313).

5. Mishnah, *Shabbath* 14.4 (Danby, p.113).

6. Jerusalem Talmud, *Maasar Sheni* 53.3. For references to the medicinal use of oil in Jewish society see SB, vol. 1, pp.426-427 (on Matthew 6.17); vol. 2, pp.11-12 (on Mark 6.13) and vol. 3, p.203 (on James 5.14). Other references to its use in the ancient world generally will be found in Peter Davids, *NIGTC on the Epistle of James* (1982), p.193.

7. Celsus, *De Medicina* (On Medicine) 2.14,4 (LCL vol. 1, p.177).

8. W.M. Abbott (ed.), *The Documents of Vatican II* (London: Geoffrey Chapman, 1967), p.161.

9. Robert Dickinson, *God Does Heal Today* (Carlisle: Paternoster Press, 1995), pp.83-86.

10. John Calvin, *Commentary on the Epistle of James* (Edinburgh: St Andrew Press, 1972), p.314. See also his *Institutes of the Christian Religion*, 4.19,20.

11. G.S. Shogren, 'Will God Heal Us? A Re-examination of James 5.14-16a', EQ, vol. 61 (1989), pp.105. It should be noted that there is a vital difference between Calvin's view and Shogren's. For Calvin the symbolic use of oil was only temporary for he believed that the power to heal was withdrawn from the Church after the apostolic period; Shogren believes that the Church still possesses it.

12. J.A. Motyer in J.D. Douglas (ed.), *New Bible Dictionary* (Leicester: Inter-Varsity Press, 1982), second edition, p.50, art. 'Anointing'.

13. Jesus did, of course, recognise the medical use of olive oil in the treatment of wounds as illustrated in his parable of the Good Samaritan (Luke 10.34).

14. Michael Zohary, *Plants of the Bible* (Cambridge: Cambridge University Press, 1982), p.56.

15. Heinrich Schlier, TDNT (1964), vol. 1, p.231, s.v. *aleipho*.

16. Marshall, Luke, pp.475-476.

17. The omission of anointing with oil in exorcism may also be explained by the fact that anointing would involve touching the person of the possessed, and healing by touch is also never used in exorcism procedure.

18. H.B. Swete, *The Gospel according to St Mark* (London: Macmillan, 1927), third edition, p.119.

19. F.W. Puller, *The Anointing of the Sick in Scripture and Tradition* (London: SPCK, 1904), p.72.

20. Innocent, *Epistle 25 to Bishop Decentius*. See Puller, *op.cit.*, pp.53-57. The epistle is dated March 19th, AD 416.

21. For the relevant references see J.B. Mayor, *op.cit.*, p.171.

22. Peter Lombard, *Book of Sentences* (1158), 4.23,1-3. See J.P. Migne (ed.), *Patrologia Latina* (Paris: Migne, 1854), vol. 192, division '*De Sacramento Unctionis Extremae*', pp.899-900. The name 'extreme (or last) unction' has two possible derivations. The first is from its administration to persons who are *in extremis* immediately prior to death. The second is from its being the third or last so-called sacramental unction which can be administered to a person in life, the other two being those administered at baptism and at confirmation according to Roman Catholic practice.

23. Sophie Laws, *Commentary on the Epistle of James* (London: A. & C. Black, 1980), pp.227-228.

24. Babylonian Talmud, *Abodah Zara* 27b and Tosefta, *Hullin* 2.22. See Ethelbert Stauffer, *Jesus and His Story* (London: SCM Press, 1960), p.20.

25. James Adamson, *op.cit.*, p.198.

26. Morris Maddocks, *The Christian Healing Ministry* (London: SPCK, 1995), third edition, p.117. The phrase 'to pray over (*proseuchomai epi*)' means simply that the elders should concentrate their prayer on the sick person and their sickness.

27. B.I. Riecke, *AB on the Epistle of James* (1982), second edition, p.59.

28. Sophie Laws, *op.cit.*, p.227.

## Part Five: Healing in the Modern Church

### Chapter Twenty-two: The Healing Commission to the Disciples

1. T.W. Manson, *The Sayings of Jesus* (London: SCM Press, 1949), p.73.

2. Manson points out that the distinction between these two words is important. *Exousia* signifies 'official right', while *dunamis* means 'personal force'. This is brought out by the modern comment that 'what was wrong with the Church in so many instances was that the men who possessed the *exousia* had not the *dunamis* and that the men who possessed the *dunamis* had not the *exousia*. Luke provides that the Twelve Apostles shall have both'. See T.W. Manson in *The Mission and Message of Jesus*, edited by H.D.A. Major, T.W. Manson & C.J. Wright (London: Ivor Nicholson & Watson, 1937), p.84. The comment is attributed to E.W. Benson, a former Archbishop of Canterbury.

3. Vincent Taylor, *The Life and Ministry of Jesus* (London: Macmillan, 1961), p.107. See also the extended note in Cranfield, *Mark*, pp.201-203.

4. Metzger, p.27.

5. Barclay, *DSB on the Gospel of Matthew* (1975), vol. 1, p.365. See also John Fenton, 'Raise the dead', ExpT, vol. 80 (1968-1969), pp.50-51.

6. Mishnah, *Berakoth* 9.5 (Danby, p.10). The Babylonian Talmud in *Berakoth* 54a and *Yebamoth* 6b interprets this regulation as prohibiting the use of the Temple area as a thoroughfare or for any purpose other than the worship and service of God.

7. H.B. Swete, *The Gospel according to St Mark* (London: Macmillan, 1927), third edition, p.119.

8. F.W. Farrar, *CBSC on the Gospel according to St Luke* (1880), p.182.

9. Vincent Taylor, *op.cit.*, p.111. Taylor, however, makes no reference to this suggested failure of the Mission of the Twelve in his commentary on Mark (Taylor, *Mark*, pp.302-306).

10. J.A. Fitzmyer, *AB on the Gospel of Luke* (1985), vol. 2, p.843.

11. Marshall, Luke, pp.412-414.

12. Alfred Plummer, *ICC on the Gospel according to St Luke* (1901), p.270.

13. Eusebius, *Ecclesiastical History* 1.12,1 (LCL vol. 1, p.83).

14. D.A. Carson, on the Gospel of Matthew in *EBC* (1984), vol. 8, p.241. The inclusion of the Twelve in the membership of the Seventy could be implied by Luke 22.35, but this is not certain (See Marshall, Luke, p.824).

15. The word used of the Seventy in Luke 10.1 is *heteros* which means 'different in number' (BAG, p.315, s.v. *heteros*). This distinguishes them from the Twelve described in the previous chapter as being sent on a mission (vv 1-6) and then later accompanying Jesus on his journey to Jerusalem (vv. 54-57).

16. E.E. Ellis, *NCB on the Gospel of Luke* (1966), p.155.

17. Henry Cowan in *Dictionary of Christ and the Gospels*, edited by James Hastings (Edinburgh: T. & T. Clark, 1906), vol. 2, p.618, art. 'Seventy'.

18. John Calvin, *A Harmony of the Gospels Matthew, Mark & Luke* (Edinburgh: St Andrew Press, 1972), vol. 2, p.18.

19. Moffatt, *in loc.*

20. P.L. Garlick, *Man's Search for Health* (London: The Highway Press, 1952), pp.226-234.

21. J.C. Peddie, *The Forgotten Talent: God's Ministry of Healing* (London: Oldbourne, 1961), pp.15-16.

22. John Richards, *But Deliver Us from Evil: An Introduction to the Demonic in Pastoral Care* (London: Darton, Longman & Todd, 1974).

23. S.G. Browne, *Leprosy in the Bible* (London: Christian Medical Fellowship, 1974), second edition, pp.21-22.

24. John Wilkinson, 'Leprosy: The problem of description and identification', SJT, vol. 30 (1977), pp.153-169.

25. R.K. Harrison, IDB (1962), vol. 3, p.112, art. 'Leprosy'.

26. Marshall, Luke, p.824.

27. D.A. Carson, *op.cit.*, pp.241-2.

28. The Mission of the Seventy appears to have been confined to the towns and places of Peraea, the region beyond the Jordan between the Rivers Jabbok and Arnon. See Plummer, *op.cit.*, p.270 and also Norval Geldenhuys, *Commentary on the Gospel of Luke* (London: Marshall, Morgan & Scott, 1950), p.303.

29. W.F. Arndt, *The Gospel according to St Luke* (St Louis: Concordia Publishing House, 1956), p.284.

## Chapter Twenty-three: From the Commission to the Ministry

1. A.J. Gordon, *The Ministry of Healing; or Miracles of Cure in all Ages* (London: Hodder & Stoughton, 1882). The first official Church use of the phrase which we have been able to trace is in the *Report of the World Missionary Conference* held in Edinburgh in 1910 (Edinburgh: Oliphant, Anderson & Ferrier, 1910), vol. 1, p.317.

2. In this chapter we have used the term 'non-medical healing' which also is not satisfactory, because it is a negative term and because it obscures the fact that the ministry of healing of the Church also includes medical healing.

3. P.L. Garlick, *The Wholeness of Man: A Study in the History of Healing* (London: The Highway Press, 1943) and *Man's Search for Health* (London: The Highway Press, 1952).

4. M.T. Kelsey, *Healing and Christianity in Ancient Thought and Modern Times* (London: SCM Press, 1973).

5. Evelyn Frost, *Christian Healing: A Consideration of the Place of Spiritual Healing in the Church of Today in the Light of the Doctrine and Practice of the Ante-Nicene Church* (London: A.R. Mowbray & Co. Ltd., 1940).

6. M.T. Kelsey, *op.cit.*, pp.210-211. See also F.H. Garrison, *An Introduction to the History of Medicine* (Philadelphia: Saunders, 1929), fourth edition, pp.168-169.

7. Origen, *Contra Celsum* 1.46-47; 2.33 and 3.24. For the references in Basil, Gregory and Chrysostom, see Kelsey, *op.cit.*, pp.171-177.

8. Kelsey, *op.cit.*, pp.184-189 (Augustine) and pp.213-220 (Aquinas).

9. V.L. von Seckendorf, *Historical Commentary on Lutheranism and the Reformation* (Leipzig: 1688-1692), vol. 3, p.133. This account is quoted by Gordon, *op.cit.*, pp.111-112.

10. M.T. Kelsey, *op.cit.*, p.233.

11. John Calvin, *Institutes of the Christian Religion*, 4.18. See also John Wilkinson, 'The Medical History of John Calvin', *Proceedings of the Royal College of Physicians of Edinburgh*, vol. 22 (1992), pp.368-383.

12. M.T. Kelsey, *op.cit.*, p.234.

13. *Ibidem*, p.235, where full references to *Wesley's Journal* are given.

14. P.L. Garlick, *Man's Search for Health* (London: The Highway Press, 1952), pp.205-207.

15. Charles Cullis, *Dorothea Trüdel or The Prayer of Faith* (Boston: Willard Tract Repository/London: Morgan & Chase, 1872).

16. Percy Dearmer, *Body and Soul: An Enquiry into the Effects of Religion upon Health, with a Description of Christian Works of Healing from the New Testament to the Present Day* (London: Pitman, 1909), pp.378-379.

17. *Ibidem*, p.77. See also Friedrich Zündel, *Johann Christoph Blumhardt* (Zürich: Hohr, 1880), p.432.

18. W.E. Boardman, *Faith Work under Dr Cullis in Boston* (Boston: Willard Tract Repository, 1874).

19. D.G. Reid (ed.), *Dictionary of Christianity in America* (Downers Grove, Illinois: InterVarsity Press, 1990), p.543, art. 'Holiness Movement' (H.E. Raser). See also the *New Encyclopaedia Britannica* (Chicago: Encyclopaedia Britannica Inc., 1988), fifteenth edition, vol. 6, pp.2 & 6-7, art. 'Holiness movement'.

20. A.B. Simpson, *The Gospel of Healing* (London: Morgan & Scott, 1915). See also D.G. Reid, *op.cit.*, p.424, art. 'Faith Healing' (W.E. Warner).

21. Mrs W.E. Boardman, *The Life and Labors of the Rev. W.E. Boardman* (Boston: Willard Tract Repository, 1887).

22. J. du Plessis, *The Life of Andrew Murray* (London: Marshall Brothers, 1919), pp.337-352.

23. J.L. Graf (ed.), *Healing: The Three Great Classics on Divine Healing* (Camphill, Pennsylvania: Christian Publications, 1992).

24. J.G. Melton, *The Encyclopedia of American Religions* (Wilmington, North Carolina: McGrath Publishing Co., 1978), vol. 2, p.245.

25. R.V. Bingham, *The Bible and the Body* (Toronto: Evangelical Publishers, 1952), fourth edition, p.21.

26. W.J. Hollenweger, *The Pentecostals* (London: SCM Press, 1972), pp.116-118.

27. D.G. Reid, *op.cit.*, p.886, art. 'Pentecostal Movement' (R.G. Robins).

28. W.J. Hollenweger, *op.cit.*, p.118. See also D.G. Reid, *op.cit.*, p.865, art. 'Charles Fox Parham' (P.T. Thigpen).

29. Churches' Council for Health and Healing, *Guilds and Fellowships of Healing* (London: CCHH, 1967). See also A.W. Jones (ed.), *Resources for Christian Healing Ministry* (London: CCHH, 1996).

30. See D.G. Reid, *op.cit.*, p.425, art. 'Faith Healing' (W.E. Warner).

31. P.G. Garlick, *Man's Search for Health* (London: The Highway Press, 1952), pp.223-225.

32. John Wilkinson, *The Coogate Doctors: The History of the Edinburgh Medical Missionary Society* (Edinburgh: EMMS, 1991), pp.12-20.

33. John Wilkinson, *Making Men Whole: The Theology of Medical Missions* (London: The Christian Medical Fellowship, 1990).

34. S.G. Browne, Frank Davey and W.A.R. Thomson (eds.), *Heralds of Health: The Saga of Christian Medical Initiatives* (London: Christian Medical Fellowship, 1985).

35. The author of this present book was a participant in both these consultations.

36. *The Healing Church: The Report of the First Tübingen Consultation on the Healing Ministry of the Church* (Geneva: World Council of Churches, 1965), pp.34-35.

37. *Health: Medical-Theological Perspectives: The Report of the Second Tübingen Consultation* (Geneva: World Council of Churches, 1967).

38. J.C. McGilvray, *The Quest for Health and Wholeness* (Tübingen: German Institute for Medical Missions, 1981), pp.41-52.

39. Christoph Benn (ed.), *The Vision and the Future: 25 Years of CMC* (Geneva: World Council of Churches, 1995).

Chapter Twenty-four: The Healing Ministry of the Church Today

1. Jürgen Moltmann, however, regards the healing of the sick as still 'an essential part of the Church's apostolate' today. He gives no reason other than the fact that Jesus charged his disciples to heal the sick in Matthew 10.8. See his book, *The Spirit of Life: A Universal Affirmation* (London: SCM Press, 1992), p.189.

2. For an analysis of the features of the contemporary situation in relation to medical ethics see John Wilkinson, *Christian Ethics in Health Care* (Edinburgh: Handsel Press, 1988), pp.138-147.

3. Pliny, *Natural History* 29.5 (LCL vol. 8, p.191).

4. See Ivan Illich, *Medical Nemesis: The Expropriation of Health* (London: Calder & Boyars, 1975). See also Ian Kennedy, *The Unmasking of Medicine* (London: George Allen & Unwin, 1981 - the Reith Lectures of 1980).

5. Babylonian Talmud, *Sanhedrin* 17b.

6. Sussman Muntner in the *Encyclopaedia Judaica* (Jerusalem: Keter, 1971), vol. 11, p.1182, art. 'Medicine'.

7. The term 'Welfare State' appears to have been first used in print by William Temple in his book, *Citizen and Churchman* (London: Eyre & Spottiswoode, 1941), p.35. Its first inclusion in a dictionary was in the addenda to the Shorter Oxford English Dictionary in 1956.

8. See British Medical Association, *Complementary Medicine: New Approaches to Good Practice* (London: BMA, 1993) and also Robina Coker, *Alternative Medicine: Helpful or Harmful?* (Crowborough: Monarch Publications, 1995).

9. John Wilkinson, 'Healing and the Congregation' in *The Healing Church: The Report of the First Tübingen Consultation on the Healing Ministry of the Church* (Geneva: World Council of Churches, 1965), pp.29-32. See also 'The Task of the Congregation in Relation to Health' in *Health: Medical-Theological Perspectives: The Report of the Second Tübingen Consultation* (Geneva: World Council of Churches, 1967), pp.35-60.

10. Michael Wilson, *The Church is Healing* (London: SCM Press, 1996), Chapters 2 & 3.

11. Arnold Bittlinger, *Gifts and Graces* (London: Hodder & Stoughton, 1967), p.72.

12. Percy Dearmer, *Body and Soul: An Enquiry into the Effects of Religion upon Health, with a Description of Christian Works of Healing from the New Testament to the Present Day* (London: Pitman, 1909), p.376.

# SELECT BIBLIOGRAPHY

The modern literature on the subject of health and healing is enormous, and this bibliography consists of only a selection of the books and other publications which are available. Those listed here were used in the preparation and revision of the studies which compose the present volume, or appear to make a significant contribution to some aspect of health and healing in Biblical and Christian thought and practice.

## MEDICINE AND THE BIBLE

1. Risdon Bennett, *Diseases of the Bible* (London: Religious Tract Society, 1887).
2. D.M. Blair, *A Doctor looks at the Bible* (London: Inter-Varsity Fellowship, 1936).
3. Don Brothwell & A.T. Sandison (eds.), *Diseases in Antiquity: A Survey of the Diseases, Injuries and Surgery of Early Populations* (Springfield, Illinois: Charles C. Thomas, 1967). See Chapter 16: 'Diseases in the Bible and the Talmud' by Max Sussman, pp. 209-221.
4. R.B. Greenblatt, *Search the Scriptures: Modern Medicine and Biblical Personages* (Philadelphia: J.B. Lippincott Company, 1968), second enlarged edition. Reprinted in 1985 by Chancellor Press, Carnforth, Lancashire, England.
5. J.R. Gwilt, 'Biblical Ills and Remedies', *Journal of the Royal Society of Medicine*, vol. 49 (1986), pp.738-743.
6. E.W.G. Masterman, *Hygiene and Disease in Palestine in Modern and in Biblical Times* (London: Palestine Exploration Fund, 1920).
7. Bernard Palmer (ed.), *Medicine and the Bible* (Carlisle: Paternoster Press, 1986).
8. A.R. Short, *The Bible and Modern Medicine: A Survey of Health and Healing in the Old and New Testaments* (London: Paternoster Press, 1953).
9. C.R. Smith, *The Physician Examines the Bible* (New York: The Philosophical Library, 1950).

## HISTORICAL STUDIES

1. S.G. Browne, Frank Davey & W.A.R. Thomson (eds.), *Heralds of Health: The Saga of Christian Medical Initiatives* (London: Christian Medical Fellowship, 1985).
2. G.G. Dawson, *Healing: Pagan and Christian* (London: SPCK, 1935).
3. Percy Dearmer, *Body and Soul: An Enquiry into the Effects of Religion upon Health, with a Description of Christian Works of Healing from the New Testament to the Present Day* (London: Pitman, 1909).

4. Evelyn Frost, *Christian Healing: A Consideration of the Place of Spiritual Healing in the Church of Today in the Light of the Doctrine and Practice of the Ante-Nicene Church* (London: A.R. Mowbray, 1949), second edition.

5. P.L. Garlick, *The Wholeness of Man: A Study in the History of Healing* (London: The Highway Press, 1943).

6. P.L. Garlick, *Health and Healing: A Christian Interpretation* (London: The Cargate Press, 1948).

7. P.L. Garlick, *Man's Search for Health: A Study in the Inter-relation of Religion and Medicine* (London: The Highway Press, 1952).

8. A.J. Gordon, *The Ministry of Healing, or Miracles of Cure in all Ages* (London: Hodder & Stoughton, 1882).

9. M.T. Kelsey, *Healing and Christianity in Ancient Thought and Modern Times* (London: SCM Press 1973).

10. W.J. Shiels (ed.), *The Church and Healing: Vol. XIX of Studies in Church History* (Oxford: Blackwell, 1982).

11. B.B. Warfield, *Miracles: Yesterday and Today, True and False* (Grand Rapids: William B. Eerdmans Publishing Co., 1965). This book was originally published by Charles Scribner's Sons in 1918 with the title, *Counterfeit Miracles*. Warfield devotes a whole chapter (pp. 157-196) to a review of Gordon's book (No. 8 above).

## DISEASE AND HEALING IN THE OLD TESTAMENT

1. C.J. Brim, *Medicine in the Bible: The Pentateuch* (New York: Froben, 1936).

2. M.L. Brown, *Israel's Divine Healer* (Carlisle: Paternoster Press/Grand Rapids: Zondervan Publishing House, 1995).

3. C.G.K. Gillespie, *The Sanitary Code of the Pentateuch* (London: Religious Tract Society, 1894).

4. Julius Preuss, *Biblical and Talmudic Medicine* (New York: Sanhedrin Press, 1978). Translated and edited by Fred Rosner from the original German edition of 1911.

5. Alexander Rattray, *Divine Hygiene: Sanitary Science and Sanitarians of the Sacred Scriptures and the Mosaic Code* (London: James Nisbet & Co., 1903).

6. Fred Rosner, *Medicine in the Bible and Talmud* (New York: Ktav Publishing House, 1977).

7. John Wilkinson, 'The Body in the Old Testament', *Evangelical Quarterly*, vol. 63 (1991), pp. 195-210.

## HEALING IN THE GOSPELS

1. William Barclay, *And He had Compassion on Them: A Handbook on the Miracles of the Bible* (Edinburgh: St Andrew Press, 1955).

2. D.S. Cairns, *The Faith that Rebels: A Re-examination of the Miracles of Jesus* (London: SCM Press, 1933), fifth edition.

3. Michael Harper, *The Healings of Jesus* (London: Hodder & Stoughton, 1986).

4. C.S. Lewis, *Miracles: A Preliminary Study* (London: Geoffrey Bles, 1947).
5. H. van der Loos, *The Miracles of Jesus* (Leiden: E.J.Brill, 1965).
6. M.A.H. Melinsky, *Healing Miracles: An Examination from History and Experience of the Place of Miracle in Christian Thought and Medical Practice* (London: Mowbrays, 1958).
7. Alan Richardson, *The Miracle Stories of the Gospels* (London: SCM Press, 1941).
8. R.C. Trench, *Notes on the Miracles of Our Lord* (London: Kegan Paul, Trench & Trübner, 1900).

## DEMON POSSESSION AND EXORCISM

1. W.M. Alexander, *Demonic Possession in the New Testament: Its Relations Historical, Medical and Theological* (Edinburgh: T. & T. Clark, 1902).
2. Graham Dow, 'The case for the existence of demons', *Churchman*, vol. 94 (1980), pp. 199-208.
3. Michael Green, *I Believe in Satan's Downfall* (London: Hodder & Stoughton, 1981).
4. Edward Langton, *Essentials of Demonology: A Study of Jewish and Christian Doctrine: Its Origin and Development* (London: Epworth Press, 1949).
5. F.S. Leahy, *Satan Cast Out: A Study in Biblical Demonology* (Edinburgh: Banner of Truth Trust, 1975).
6. S.V. McCasland, *By the Finger of God: Demon Possession and Exorcism in the Light of Modern Views of Mental Illness* (New York: Macmillan, 1951).
7. J.W. Montgomery (ed.), *Demon Possession: A Medical, Historical, Anthropological and Theological Symposium* (Minneapolis: Bethany Fellowship, 1976).
8. J.L. Nevius, *Demon Possession and Allied Themes* (New York: Fleming H. Revell Co., 1893).
9. Robert Petitpierre (ed.), *Exorcism: The Exeter Report* (London: SPCK, 1972).
10. John Richards, *But Deliver Us from Evil: An Introduction to the Demonic Dimension in Pastoral Care* (London: Darton, Longman & Todd, 1974).
11. John Richards, *Exorcism, Deliverance and Healing: Some Pastoral Guidelines* (Nottingham: Grove Books, 1976).
12. J.S. Stewart, 'On a neglected emphasis in New Testament Theology', *Scottish Journal of Theology*, vol. 4 (1951), pp. 292-301 (September).
13. G.H. Twelftree, *Christ Triumphant: Exorcism Then and Now* (London: Hodder & Stoughton, 1985).
14. M.F. Unger, *Biblical Demonology* (Wheaton, Illinois: Scripture Press, 1952).

## HEALING IN THE EPISTLES

1. Arnold Bittlinger, *Gifts and Graces: A Commentary on 1 Corinthians 12-14* (London: Hodder & Stoughton/Grand Rapids: William B. Eerdmans Publishing Co., 1967).
2. Arnold Bittlinger, *Gifts and Ministries* (London: Hodder & Stoughton/Grand Rapids: William B. Eerdmans Publishing Co., 1974).

3. Donald Bridge & David Phypers, *Spiritual Gifts and the Church* (London: Inter-Varsity Press, 1973).

4. R.P. Martin, *The Spirit and the Congregation: Studies in 1 Corinthians 12-15* (Grand Rapids: William B. Eerdmans Publishing Co., 1984).

5. F.W. Puller, *The Anointing of the Sick in Scripture and Tradition* (London: SPCK, 1904).

6. J.A.T. Robinson, *The Body: A Study in Pauline Theology*. Studies in Biblical Theology, No. 5 (London: SCM Press, 1957).

7. W.D. Stacey, *The Pauline View of Man* (London: Macmillan, 1956).

8. Max Turner, *The Holy Spirit and Spiritual Gifts: Then and Now* (Carlisle: Paternoster Press, 1996).

9. Ernest White, *Saint Paul: The Man and his Mind. A Psychological Assessment* (London: Marshall, Morgan & Scott, 1958).

## THE CHRISTIAN MINISTRY OF HEALING

1. Howard Booth, *Healing is Wholeness: A Resource Book to encourage Healing Ministry Initiatives in the Local Church* (London: The Methodist Church & the Churches' Council for Health & Healing, 1987).

2. D.F. Allen, L.P. Bird & R.L. Herrmann (eds.), *Whole-Person Medicine: An International Symposium* (Downers Grove, Illinois: InterVarsity Press, 1980).

3. W.H. Boggs, *Faith Healing and the Christian Faith* (Richmond, Virginia: John Knox Press/London: Elek Books, 1957).

4. Michael Botting, *Christian Healing in the Parish* (Nottingham: Grove Books, 1977).

5. John Crowlesmith (ed.), *Religion and Healing: Essays by Members of the Methodist Society for Medical and Pastoral Psychology* (London: Epworth Press, 1962).

6. Robert Dickinson, *God Does Heal Today* (Carlisle: Paternoster Press, 1995).

7. Denis Duncan, *Health and Healing: A Ministry to Wholeness* (Edinburgh: St Andrew Press, 1988).

8. Evelyn Frost, *Christ and Wholeness: An Approach to Christian Healing* (Cambridge: James Clarke, 1985)

9. H.W. Frost, *Miraculous Healing* (London: Marshall, Morgan & Scott, 1951).

10. J.L. Graf (ed.), *Healing: The Three Great Classics on Divine Healing* (Camphill, Pennsylvania: Christian Publications, 1992). This volume contains the full text of the books on Christian healing as originally written by Andrew Murray (1884), A.J. Gordon (1882) and A.B. Simpson (1915).

11. C.W. Gusmer, *The Ministry of Healing in the Church of England: An Ecumenical-Liturgical Study* (London: SPCK, 1974).

12. Harry Hutchison, *The Church and Spiritual Healing* (London: Rider, 1955).

13. International Review of Mission, 'The Healing Ministry', vol. 57 (1968), pp. 151-216 (April).

14. International Review of Mission, 'Health and Healing in Mission', vol. 83 (1994), pp. 223-311 (April).

15. A.W. Jones (ed.), *Resources for Christian Healing Ministry* (London: The Churches' Council for Health and Healing, 1996).

16. Ernest Lucas (ed.), *Christian Healing: What Can We Believe?* (London: Lynx Communications, SPCK, 1997)

17. Morris Maddocks, *The Christian Healing Ministry* (London: SPCK, 1995), third edition.

18. Francis MacNutt, *Healing* (Notre Dame, Indiana: Ave Maria Press, 1974).

19. Francis MacNutt, *The Power to Heal* (Notre Dame, Indiana: Ave Maria Press, 1977).

20. Bernard Martin, *The Healing Ministry in the Church* (London: Lutterworth Press, 1960).

21. J.C. Peddie, *The Forgotten Talent: God's Ministry of Healing* (London: Olbourne, 1961).

22. C.G. Scorer, *Healing: Biblical, Medical and Pastoral* (London: Christian Medical Fellowship, 1979).

23. John Richards, *The Question of Healing Services* (London: Darton, Longman & Todd, 1989).

24. Max Warren, *I Believe in the Great Commission* (London: Hodder & Stoughton, 1976).

25. James Watt (ed.), *What is Wrong with Christian Healing?* (London: The Churches' Council for Health and Healing, 1993).

26. John Wilkinson, *Healing and the Church* (Edinburgh: The Handsel Press, 1984).

27. Michael Wilson, *The Church is Healing* (London: SCM Press, 1966).

28. B.E. Woods, *The Healing Ministry* (London: Rider & Company, 1961).

## THE THEOLOGY OF HEALING

1. J.P. Baker, *Salvation and Wholeness: The Biblical Perspectives of Healing* (London: Fountain Trust. 1973).

2. Karl Barth, *Church Dogmatics* (Edinburgh: T. & T. Clark, 1961), vol. 3, 'The Doctrine of Creation', part 4, pp. 356-374.

3. David Dale, *In His Hands: Towards a Theology of Healing* (London: Darton, Longman and Todd, 1989).

4. D.R.P. Foot, *Divine Healing in the Scriptures* (Worthing: H.E. Walter Ltd, 1967).

5. John Goldingay, 'Theology and Healing', *Churchman*, vol. 92 (1978), pp.23-33.

6. Dorothea Hoch, *Healing and Salvation* (London: SCM Press, 1958).

7. G.W. Kirby (ed.), *The Question of Healing* (London: Victory Press, 1967).

8. R.A. Lambourne, *Community, Church and Healing: A Study of some of the corporate aspects of the Church's Ministry to the Sick* (London: Darton, Longman & Todd, 1963).

9. Jürgen Moltmann, *God in Creation* (London: SCM Press, 1985), pp. 270-275.

10. Jürgen Moltmann, *The Spirit of Life: A Universal Affirmation* (London: SCM Press, 1992), pp. 188-193.

11. E.R. Morgan, *The Ordeal of Wonder: Thoughts on Healing* (London: Oxford University Press, 1964).

12. M.H. Scharlemann, *Healing and Redemption: Toward a Theology of Human Wholeness for Doctors, Nurses, Missionaries and Pastors* (Missouri & London : Concordia Publishing House, 1965).

13. M.G. Sheldon, *Health, Healing and Medicine* (Edinburgh: The Handsel Press, 1987).

14. T.A. Smail, *The Quest for a Theology of Healing* (London: Churches' Council for Health and Healing, 1993).

15. T.A. Smail, Andrew Walker & Nigel Wright, *Charismatic Renewal: The Search for a Theology* (London: SPCK, 1995).

16. Paul Tillich, *Systematic Theology* (London: Nisbet, 1968), vol. 3, pp. 293-300.

17. Paul Tillich, 'The Meaning of Health', *Perspectives in Biology & Medicine*, vol. 5 (1961), pp. 92-100. This article was reprinted in S.E. Lammers & Allen Verhey (eds.), *On Moral Medicine: Theological Perspectives in Medical Ethics* (Grand Rapids: William B. Eerdmans Publishing Co., 1987), pp. 161-165.

18. Paul Tournier, *A Doctor's Case Book in the Light of the Bible* (London: SCM Press, 1954).

19. John Wilkinson, 'The Theological Basis of Medicine', *Scottish Journal of Theology*, vol. 8 (1955), pp. 142-154.

20. John Wilkinson, 'Healing in Semantics, Creation and Redemption', *Scottish Bulletin of Evangelical Theology*, vol. 5 (1986), pp. 17-37 (Spring).

21. John Wilkinson, 'Healing and Salvation: Some Theological Considerations', *Journal of the Christian Medical Association of India*, vol. 3 (1988), pp. 14-20.

22. John Wilkinson, *Making Men Whole: The Theology of Medical Missions* (London: Christian Medical Fellowship, 1990).

23. John Wilkinson, 'Physical Healing and the Atonement', *Evangelical Quarterly*, vol. 63 (1991), pp. 149-167.

## CHRISTIAN HEALING IN CONTROVERSY

1. R.V. Bingham, *The Bible and the Body: Healing in the Scriptures* (London: Marshall, Morgan and Scott, 1921).

2. Donald Bridge, *Signs and Wonders Today* (Leicester: Inter- Varsity Press, 1985).

3. R.F.R. Gardner, *Healing Miracles: A Doctor Investigates* (London: Darton, Longman & Todd, 1986).

4. John Goldingay, *Signs, Wonders and Healing* (Leicester: Inter-Varsity Press, 1987).

5. John Gunstone, *Signs and Wonders: The Wimber Phenomenon* (London: Darton, Longman & Todd, 1989).

6. Philip Jensen & Andrew Payne, *John Wimber: Friend or Foe?* (London: St Matthias Press, 1990).

7. David Lewis, *Healing: Fiction, Fantasy or Fact?* (London: Hodder & Stoughton, 1989).

8. Dan McConnell, *The Promise of Health and Wealth: A Historical and Biblical Analysis of the Modern Faith Movement* (London: Hodder & Stoughton, 1990).

9. T.J. McCrossan, *Bodily Healing and the Atonement* (Tulsa, Oklahoma: Faith Library, 1982). Originally published in 1930.

10. A.W. Pink, *Divine Healing. Is it Scriptural?* (Welwyn: Evangelical Press, 1952).

11. John Wimber, *Power Healing* (London: Hodder & Stoughton, 1986).

12. John Wimber with Kevin Springer, *Practical Healing* (London: Hodder & Stoughton, 1987).


## REPORTS ON HEALTH AND HEALING

1. British Medical Association, *Divine Healing and Co-operation between Doctors and Clergy* (London: BMA, 1956).

2. Christian Medical Commission, *Healing and Wholeness: The Churches' Role in Health* (Geneva: World Council of Churches, 1990).

3. Church of England, *The Church's Ministry of Healing: The Report of the Archbishops' Commission* (London: The Church Information Office, 1958).

4. Church of Scotland, *Spiritual Healing: The Report of the Church of Scotland Commission* (Edinburgh: St Andrew Press, 1958).

5. David Dale (ed.), *Whole Person Medicine: A Christian Perspective. The Report of a Joint Working Party to the Churches' Council for Health and Healing and the Royal College of General Practitioners* (London: CCHH, 1989).

6. Vincent Edmunds & C.G. Scorer (eds.), *Some Thoughts on Faith Healing: The Report of a Medical Study Group* (London: Christian Medical Fellowship, 1979), third edition.

7. J.C. McGilvray (ed.), *Health: Medical-Theological Perspectives. The Report of the Second Tübingen Consultation 1967* (Geneva: World Council of Churches, 1967).

8. Presbyterian Church (USA), *The Relation of Christian Faith to Health* (Philadelphia: Office of the General Assembly of the PCUSA, 1960).

9. Presbyterian Church of England, *The Ministry of Healing in the Church: A Handbook of Principles and Practice* (London: Independent Press, 1963).

10. Synod of South Australia, *The Healing Ministry* (Adelaide: Uniting Church in Australia, 1983).

11. United Church of Canada, *Sickness and Health* (Toronto: Board of Evangelism & Social Service, 1967).

12. United Lutheran Church in America, *Anointing and Healing* (New York: Lutheran Board of Publication, 1962).

13. John Wilkinson (ed.), *Health and Healing: The Report of the Makumira Consultation in Tanzania* (Arusha: Evangelical Lutheran Church of Tanzania, 1967).

14. John Wilkinson (ed.), *Health is Wholeness: The Report of the Limuru Consultation in Kenya* (Nairobi: Protestant Churches' Medical Association, 1970).

15. World Council of Churches, *The Healing Church: The Report of the First Tübingen Consultation 1964* (Geneva: WCC, 1965).

# INDEX OF SUBJECTS

# INDEX OF AUTHORS

This index includes only the names of authors who are mentioned in the text of the book. The names of the numerous other authors and sources which were consulted in its preparation are given in the section of Notes and References.

# INDEX OF HEBREW AND GREEK WORDS

# INDEX OF MAIN SCRIPTURE REFERENCES

## I. REFERENCES TO VERSES

### OLD TESTAMENT

# APOCRYPHA

# NEW TESTAMENT

# II. REFERENCES TO INCIDENTS OF DISEASE AND HEALING

## OLD TESTAMENT

## NEW TESTAMENT

**The Gospels**